Nationals Abroad

It is a fundamental term of the social contract that people trade allegiance for protection. In the nineteenth century, as millions of people made their way around the world, they entangled the world in a web of allegiance that had enormous political consequences. Nationality was increasingly difficult to define. Just who was a national in a world where millions lived well beyond the borders of their sovereign state? As the nineteenth century gave way to the twentieth, jurists and policymakers began to think of ways to cut the web of obligation that had enabled world politics. They proposed to modernize international law to include subjects other than the state. Many of these experiments failed. But, by the mid-twentieth century, an international legal system predicated upon absolute universality and operated by intergovernmental organizations came to the fore. Under this system, individuals gradually became subjects of international law outside of their personal citizenship, culminating with the establishment of international courts of human rights after the Second World War.

Christopher A. Casey received his BA, MA, Ph.D., and JD at the University of California, Berkeley.

Human Rights in History

Edited by

Stefan-Ludwig Hoffmann, University of California, Berkeley
Samuel Moyn, Yale University, Connecticut

This series showcases new scholarship exploring the backgrounds of human rights today. With an open-ended chronology and international perspective, the series seeks works attentive to the surprises and contingencies in the historical origins and legacies of human rights ideals and interventions. Books in the series will focus not only on the intellectual antecedents and foundations of human rights, but also on the incorporation of the concept by movements, nation-states, international governance, and transnational law.

A full list of titles in the series can be found at
www.cambridge.org/human-rights-history

Nationals Abroad

Globalization, Individual Rights, and the Making of Modern International Law

Christopher A. Casey

CAMBRIDGE
UNIVERSITY PRESS

CAMBRIDGE
UNIVERSITY PRESS

University Printing House, Cambridge CB2 8BS, United Kingdom

One Liberty Plaza, 20th Floor, New York, NY 10006, USA

477 Williamstown Road, Port Melbourne, VIC 3207, Australia

314–321, 3rd Floor, Plot 3, Splendor Forum, Jasola District Centre, New Delhi – 110025, India

79 Anson Road, #06-04/06, Singapore 079906

Cambridge University Press is part of the University of Cambridge.

It furthers the University's mission by disseminating knowledge in the pursuit of education, learning, and research at the highest international levels of excellence.

www.cambridge.org
Information on this title: www.cambridge.org/9781108489454
DOI: 10.1017/9781108784047

First published 2020

A catalogue record for this publication is available from the British Library.

Library of Congress Cataloging-in-Publication Data
Names: Casey, Christopher A, 1984- author.
Title: Nationals abroad / Christopher A Casey, University of California, Berkeley.
Description: Cambridge, United Kingdom ; New York, NY, USA : Cambridge University Press, 2020. | Series: Human rights in history | Based on author's thesis (doctoral - University of California Berkeley, 2017). | Includes bibliographical references and index.
Identifiers: LCCN 2019054965 | ISBN 9781108489454 (hardback) | ISBN 9781108746557 (ebook)
Subjects: LCSH: International law. | Citizenship. | Diplomatic protection. | Aliens. | Persons (International law)
Classification: LCC KZ3410 .C37 2020 | DDC 341.4/8--dc23
LC record available at https://lccn.loc.gov/2019054965

ISBN 978-1-108-48945-4 Hardback

For my parents, sister, and grandfather

Men of no importance, born in an obscure rank, go to sea; they go to places which they have never seen before; where they can neither be known to the men among whom they have arrived, nor always find people to vouch for them. But still, owing to this confidence in the mere fact of their citizenship, they think that they shall be safe. . . . Take away this hope, take away this protection from Roman citizens, establish the fact that there is no assistance to be found in the words "I am a Roman citizen;" that a praetor, or any other officer, may with impunity order any punishment he pleases to be inflicted on a man who says that he is a Roman citizen . . . and at one blow, by admitting that defense, you cut off from the Roman citizens all the provinces, all the kingdoms, all free cities, and indeed the whole world, which has hitherto been open most especially to our countrymen.

Marcus Tullius Cicero, *In Verrem*, 70 BCE

Contents

Acknowledgments

I always like to stay through the credits of movies. I probably do it, in part, for the closure and because my parents always stay. But when my friends tug (literally or metaphorically) at my shirtsleeve to go, my need for closure or my long-held habits seem like weak justifications to demand an extra five minutes of their patience. Instead, I tell them that my desire to stay is about politics. Credits, which recognize many (although certainly not all) of those who contributed to creating a film, make it one of the more democratic media. As with movies, so it should be with books.

I want to thank the innumerable people I have never met – papermakers, machinists, mechanics, drivers, loggers, recyclers (hopefully), printers, chemists, and others – but without whom the physical production of this book would not be possible.

As this is my first book, I must also acknowledge those who supported the education that led up to this point. As such, I need to thank, first and foremost, the people of the State of California for generously funding much of the research that went into this book and my entire education, from the first grade through JD and PhD studies, with their taxes. I can't claim to be worthy of their generosity, but I hope they'll see fit to expand the support of state public education in the coming decades. I also must acknowledge the more than fifty public primary and secondary school teachers I had at Mt. Diablo Elementary School, Diablo View Middle School, and Clayton Valley High School, to whom I owe a debt of gratitude. But special thanks are due to Mr. Hanson, Mr. Kepner, Mrs. Kepner, Mr. Penovich, Mrs. Rodriguez, Mrs. Steen, Mr. Turnbull, Ms. Whitmore, Mr. Wilson, and Mr. Wright. I also need to thank the faculty, staff, and graduate student instructors at numerous public undergraduate institutions, including Los Medanos College, Diablo Valley College, and the University of California, Berkeley, who provided guidance during my undergraduate years. Special thanks are due to Ken Alexander, Peggy Anderson, Kate Boisvert, Leah Flanagan, Bill Fracisco, John Gillis, David Hobbs, JoAnn Hobbs, Judy Myers, Kim Shelton, Diana Stover, and David Wetzel.

Thanks to the people of the State of California (as mentioned before), the University of California (UC) (through the Graduate Division, the Department of History, the School of Law, the Institute for International Studies, the Institute for European Studies, the UC Press, the Center for British Studies, Brian DeLay, Tom Laqueur, and Daniel Sargent), New York University's School of Law, the Foreign Language and Area Studies program, the people of the United States, and my parents. All generously funded the research and writing of this book (or housed or employed me during it) in one way or another.

I also need to thank the diligent stewards of the books and documents at the heart of this book – the archivists and librarians. Thanks to the librarians at the Peace Palace Library, the British Library, the Library of Congress, the Bibliothèque nationale de France, the library of the Graduate Institute of Geneva, the Clayton Public Library, the Berkeley Public Library, and the United Nations Library. Special thanks to what Charles Franklin Doe called "the heart of the university and the center of its most serious work" – the UC Library and, particularly, the infinitely patient interlibrary loan staff. Extra-special thanks to the staff of the incredible Berkeley Law Library and to Marci Hoffman, who's easily the best international law librarian this side of The Hague. Thanks to the archivists at the United Kingdom's National Archives; France's Archives nationales; the Archives de Ministère des Affaires ètrangères in Nantes and La Corneuve; the National Archives and Records Administration in College Park, MD, and Washington, DC; the Peace Palace Archives; the International Law Association Archives; the International Chamber of Commerce Archives; the United Nations Archives; the BNP Paribas Archives; and the Lloyds Bank Archives. But special thanks must be made to the two finest archivists that I've ever had the pleasure of encountering – Jacques Oberson and Lee Robertson of the League of Nations Archive in Geneva. The two of them made conducting much of the research for this project a genuine pleasure.

The majority of the research and writing of this book was done while I was at Berkeley. David Lieberman, Daniel Sargent, and James Vernon advised me during much of the research and the writing of this book, and I owe a substantial debt of gratitude to them. I'd like to thank Daniel for his patience and for having enough faith to give me time and space to create a project that was a reflection of my interests (and for helping me to find funding whenever I was in need of it). James taught me as an undergraduate and a graduate student, and I'd like to thank him for his incomparable diligence, his dedication to all of his many students, and for being a constant source of support. I'd like to thank David for introducing me to legal history and being my link between disciplines.

Although they were not official advisors, Peggy Anderson, Richard Buxbaum, Tom Laqueur, and Katerina Linos, all might as well have been. Tom was unfailingly generous and kind to me these many years and provided advice on all manner of things. Buxbaum gave me my first advice on archives, carefully read and critiqued most of the chapters in this book, and taught me the ins and outs of international business transactions. Katerina also did more than her fair share of reading what became this book and has also been a helpful mentor in navigating the space between law and history. Peggy taught me as both an undergraduate and a graduate student. I admire her dedication to her craft and her students. Many of the themes in this book were drawn from the several courses that I took from her.

I also wish to thank the many other Berkeley faculty and staff, in both history and law, who provided advice and inspiration over the past eight years, especially Bob Bering, Andrew Bradt, Marianne Bartholomew-Couts, John Connelly, Brian DeLay, David Henkin, Marci Hoffman, Patricia Hurley, Erin Leigh Inama, Mabel Lee, Hilja New, Mark Peterson, Caitlin Rosenthal, Carla Shapreau, and David Wetzel.

While the writing of this book started at Berkeley, I mostly finished it while I was a Samuel I. Golieb Fellow at New York University's School of Law. While in New York, Richard Epstein, David Golove, Dan Hulsebosch, Judge Gary Katzmann, Benedict Kingsbury, Karin Loevy, Bill Nelson, Judge Al Rosenblatt, and the members of the Legal History Colloquium all provided invaluable feedback and mentorship. I'd also like to thank my co-Golieb, Christian Bursett (who suffered through reading this entire manuscript with care) as well as past-Golieb, Ben Brady, and future-Golieb, Noah Rosenblum, for their friendship and insights into all things both legalish and historical. Nathan Wright provided emotional support, friendship, literal warmth in the form of space heaters, and endless interesting conversation during my first departure of indefinite length from my beloved California Republic to the East Coast.

Bathsheba Desmuth, Eric Johnson, Danny Kelly, Erica Lee, Sam Robinson, Jason Rozumalski, Andres Schwarzenberg, and Sam Wetherell, as well as the members of Berkeley's Legal History Workshop and New York University School of Law's Legal History Colloquium all read one or more of these chapters with care and provided much-appreciated feedback, as did the generous and kind anonymous reviewers selected by Cambridge University Press.

I owe the initial spark for this book to my students at Berkeley. In the fall of 2011, I had the pleasure to teach Tom Laqueur's course on the history and practice of human rights. My students in that course were energetic, perspicacious, curious, and everything else that a teacher could hope for. Their questions while discussing statelessness one early Thursday morning led directly to my initial thoughts for the project that culminated in this book.

Still many others contributed to this book through their intellectual engagement, emotional support, and friendship. It would be impossible to name them all or even begin to acknowledge the extent of their contributions, but I want to give special thanks to Ari Edmundson, Sophie Fitzmaurice, Anthony Gregory, Katie Harper, J.T. Jamieson, Eric Johnson, Joey Kellner, Danny Kelly, Andrew Kornbluth, Ivana Mirkovic, Jason Morton, John Olmsted, Giuliana Perrone, Nova Robinson, Sam Robinson, Andres Schwarzenberg, Brenden Shanahan, Julia Shatz, Melissa Turoff, Julia Wambach, Sam Wetherell, Timothy Wright, and anyone who ever ate lunch in the parking circle behind Dwinelle Hall.

I'd like to thank Christopher Jantzen and Sean Rizzotti, my two oldest friends, have been a constant source of support. My time and travels with each of them provided a lot of the inspiration for this book. I'd also like to thank William Campbell, Drew Salzborn, and Ryan Burger for their decades of friendship.

During the writing of this book, Jason Rozumalski was one of the best friends, as well as the best adventure and archive companion, that someone could want. Our banter about history, law, life, literature, and everything else has made me a better scholar and person.

I also need to thank Erica Lee, whose beautiful mind polished my every idea, whose warmth and care thawed my every cold despair, whose grace and poise inspired my every day, and whose brilliance always lights my every way.

I'd also like to thank my entire extended family, but particularly my Grandfather, Alfred Seifert. He was endlessly supportive of my studies, loving, devoted, and inspirational. He was, for a time, quasi-stateless and helping him manoeuvre through several state bureaucracies to make him, once again, a man with a country, helped inspire some of this book. He is missed every day.

Finally, I'd like to thank my parents and sister (Robert Casey, Cynthia McGrath, and Sara Casey). The three of them created a safe, happy, and nurturing home. They filled it with love and books and movies. They did the most to make this book possible. To them, I owe everything.

This was a long project, and the list of names above should make it clear that I didn't build it, but, nevertheless, all faults are my own.

Abbreviations

AJIL	*American Journal of International Law*
ASIL	American Society of International Law
BITs	bilateral investment treaties
GATT	General Agreement on Tariffs and Trade
ICC	International Chamber of Commerce
ICJ	International Court of Justice
ICSID	International Centre for Settlement of Investment Disputes
IIL	Institute of International Law (Institute de Droit International)
ILA	International Law Association
ILC	International Law Commission
ILO	International Labour Organization
IMF	International Monetary Fund
ITO	International Trade Organization
LN	The League of Nations
LN Doc.	League of Nations Document (published)
LNA	League of Nations Archives
LNOJ	*League of Nations Official Journal*
LNTS	League of Nations Treaty Series
NAFTA	North American Free Trade Agreement
NARA	National Archives and Records Administration
PCA	Permanent Court of Arbitration
PCIJ	Permanent Court of International Justice
UKNA	The National Archives of the United Kingdom
UN	The United Nations
UN Doc.	United Nations Document (published)
UNTS	United Nations Treaty Series

Introduction

> The only way to erect such a common power, as may be able to defend them from the invasion of foreigners, and the injuries of one another, and thereby to secure them in such sort as that by their own industry and by the fruits of the earth they may nourish themselves and live contentedly, is to confer all their power and strength upon one man, or upon one assembly of men, that may reduce all their wills, by plurality of voices, unto one will.
>
> Thomas Hobbes, *Leviathan*, 1651

People move. That might seem to be a rather self-evident statement with which to begin, but it's the central fact of this book. We are creatures capable of traveling substantial distances at a rapid pace. And it is fair to say that our ability to walk (and run) extraordinarily long distances is one of our defining traits as a species, along with our technological augmentations of that ability.[1] Despite its obviousness, this fact is often obscured from the central narratives of international politics and the development of international law.

States, at least in the modern era, tend not to move (at least not much). Borders are adjusted, or some states disappear. But if they do reappear they seldom move to entirely new geographic positions.[2] It wasn't always true that states, state-like formations, or political communities didn't move. The nomadic empires of the steppes of Asia moved a great deal. Also, it wasn't always true that states were defined by reference to geographically defined spaces. Sovereignty over physical space has often been relational and relative and conceived of as rights to seasonal migration routes, sea lanes, or, more often, the spaces inhabited by kith and kin wherever they happened to be.[3] Nor has the territory of the state and its law always been homologous and coterminous. Overlapping, mobile, and nonterritorial jurisdictions were common in Europe through the eighteenth century.[4] Even more common was law that attached to a person regardless of where on the planet she roamed (a kind of law that still exists). But, at some point in the nineteenth century, defined territory became an essential element of the definition of a legitimate state or sovereign political community in international law.

According to the most widely adopted legal description in the nineteenth and twentieth centuries, a state has four elements: a population, a territory, a government, and the capacity to enter into relations with other states.[5] That description, while not explicitly hierarchical, has an implicit order. People are more essential than territory.[6] Territory is more essential than a government. A government is more essential than the capacity to enter into international relations.[7] It's the first two elements with which this book is concerned, specifically with the tension between people, who move, and territory, which doesn't.

The title of this book, *Nationals Abroad*, highlights this problem of incongruence in the modern era. To be abroad requires one to be beyond the spatial boundary of one's political community. The French, Spanish, and German equivalents of the word abroad – *À l'étranger*, *en el extranjero*, and *ausland* – are more literal renderings of the same idea and have the same requirements. And, as would be expected in a global age, the use of all four words increased dramatically in the nineteenth century.[8] To be outside of the literal and metaphorical walls of one's village, town, city, or state – to be outside of one's own political community in the European context – was certainly not a new phenomenon.[9] But it was one that became far more prevalent in the nineteenth century. With the collapse of European empire in the Americas, dozens of new republics lined the Atlantic's western shores. The American subjects of the kings of England, France, and Spain gained new political identities as citizens of Virginia, Haiti, and Mexico. Migration across the Atlantic from Europe now almost always entailed leaving one's political community and entering another – going abroad. Changes in the relative cost of transportation led to massive levels of migration both within Europe and without. By the latter half of the nineteenth century, a significant proportion of the European population began to spend significant amounts of time outside the political community of its birth. It was also a time of intense trade and investment. While international commerce had never been entirely restricted, the mercantilist impulses of the seventeenth and eighteenth centuries ensured that international investment and international trade – that is, investment or trade between different legal systems, in different jurisdictions, subject to different sovereigns – were relatively rare.[10] However, by the second half of the nineteenth century, it was common. Goods, money, and corporations, like their livelier human counterparts, found themselves increasingly abroad.

At least one of the central purposes of the state, or so its proponents have claimed, is to provide security for the lives, liberty, and property of its residents.[11] Sovereigns robe their subjects in their protection and demand allegiance in exchange. That protection often came in the form of a literal or metaphorical wall – of stone, of wood and canvas, of men, of steel – enclosing a country, town, village, or keep. Protection was usually territorially limited. But protection was also needed at times when subjects ventured beyond their sovereign's realms and walls. When a subject was abroad, protection came in the form of a threat. The sovereign declared to others, "this man is mine; harm him and you insult me; insult me and you will answer for it."[12] Just how far that threat could legally travel was a subject of debate. But, by the eighteenth century, it was well accepted among legal theorists and sovereigns that "[w]hoever uses a citizen ill, indirectly offends the state, which is bound to protect this citizen; and the sovereign of the latter should avenge his wrongs, punish the aggressor, and, if possible, oblige him to make full reparation; since otherwise the citizen would not obtain the great end of the civil association, which is safety."[13] War, it seemed, could be carried out to protect subjects (or nationals) abroad.

But just who were those subjects? Who were those nationals whom a sovereign had a right (and perhaps a duty) to protect while abroad? While the relationship between communities and their constituent parts has, perhaps, never been simple to define, in the nineteenth century, it became nearly impossible.

The legitimacy of European and American states was increasingly defined by direct reference to people.[14] Democratization and nationalism altered the locus of sovereignty in Europe away from the literal and metaphorical person of the monarch and toward "the people" (however that collective noun might be defined) or, even more problematically, toward "the nation."[15] New technologies of rail, road, steam, and electricity along with new practices of mass conscription, newspaper consumption, industrial manufacturing, travel, and schooling formed diverse peoples into nations and bound them to powerful political centers – Paris, Berlin, London, Rome.[16]

The infrastructural and administrative logics of the new regime produced a historical irony in which states that increasingly based their legitimacy on representing a people also became increasingly territorial in their definition and governance. According to Charles Maier, the premise of this territorial age was that "a nation's 'identity space' was coterminous with its 'decision space.'"[17] Governance turned inward, and "[t]erritory

[was] envisaged not just as an acquisition or as a security buffer but as a decisive means of power and rule."[18]

Law, one of the primary instruments of governance, increasingly became defined territorially, and many of the vestiges of personal and feudal law supposedly faded away. As a leading scholar noted near the start of the twentieth century,

> The history of the legal relation between the state and individuals, its own citizens and aliens, is largely a history of the transition from the system of personal laws to the territoriality of law, accompanied both by a growing control of a central power over the individuals within its jurisdiction and by the appearance of certain characteristics, territorial independence and sovereignty, as essential qualifications for admission of a state into the society of states.[19]

That is, law increasingly went from something that applied *to* the French or *to* the Italians to being something that applied *in* France or *in* Italy.[20] This became all the more true as democracy accelerated the pace of lawmaking and the growth of centralized administration.[21]

But the idea of a homologous and coterminous "identity space" and "decision space" (a term for which we might substitute jurisdiction) is precisely the premise that was challenged by human mobility in an increasingly global age. Nationalism, as Ernest Gellner succinctly defined it, is a "political principle that holds that the political and the national unit should be congruent."[22] Yet, the technologies and practices that formed peoples into nations rarely stopped at the frontier. The age of national rail was quickly the age of international rail. The technologies that built nations were the same technologies that challenged the spatial coherence of nations. Steam helped to forge a unified Italy, but it also helped to send millions of Italians abroad. Print capitalism may have helped make Bavarians and Prussians feel German, but it also enabled millions of ethnic Germans living abroad to read daily news from the Fatherland.[23] Were Germans who had lived outside Germany for years, or even decades, entitled to Germany's protection? Was a state's right to protect its nationals limited only to temporary sojourners? Or did it apply to its emigrants everywhere?

In the nineteenth century, then, political units were increasingly defined by reference to territory and legitimated by reference to people or nations. It was an age that idealized the nation-state. Yet, it was an age when nation and state – when people and territory – were increasingly incongruent. Dealing with that incongruence has been the central problem of international politics during the past 200 years and, as such, the central problem of international law.

Could a state make a claim to protect a national thousands of miles away in space and several generations away in time? Just what were the limits of the relationship between a sovereign and her protected subjects? While protection abroad might have made sense for merchants and ministers (who were limited in number), what about for the millions of others who found themselves far from home in the nineteenth century? Nineteenth-century legislators, jurists, and political theorists may have idealized territorial sovereignty, but they couldn't escape the reality that millions of people were living outside the territory of their sovereign.

The relationship between states and persons was in flux. The assumption that states would serve as champions of individuals as they invested, traded, and resided abroad – far beyond their sovereign's walls – began to change at the turn of the twentieth century. The causes and consequences of that change is the subject of this book. This book tells the story of how the tension between mobile people and immobile states created "modern" international law; that is, an international law that attempted to include among its subjects more than just states and provides some limited avenues for individual human beings to make claims for the protection of their person or property themselves, rather than relying upon their sovereign to do it for them.

Now, a brief aside to define two terms around which this books revolves.

The first and most important term to define for our story is nationality. Nationality, like citizenship, denotes a relationship between a polity, usually a state, and a person.[24] The primary difference between citizenship and nationality is that the former denotes a political relationship between a citizen and her state, one in which the citizen is invested with rights. The latter denotes a relationship between a national and her state, one in which there is no implied set of rights, merely an explicit claim of "belonging" to the state. Citizenship is an internal status, nationality external. To use an extreme example, American Indians in the nineteenth century were American nationals, but they certainly weren't citizens. Such uses are historically specific, and their origins are discussed at length in Chapter 2. But for the most part, this book will hew close to that use for clarity. "Nationality" and "subjecthood" and their related nouns "national" and "subject" will be used to denote individual human persons and, occasionally, juridical persons, who are claimed as belonging to a sovereign state.

The other important term, which will be discussed at great length in Chapter 1, is "diplomatic protection." Diplomatic protection is the term used to describe the international legal process through which nationals are protected abroad. It does not, contrary to its awkward phrasing, involve the protection of diplomats or the immunity of diplomats. It is the term that is used to describe the cloaking of a person (either real or juridical) in the protection of their sovereign state.

This book argues that changing ideas about political belonging and state legitimacy fundamentally altered what nationality meant in international law and politics. The right of a state to send a gunboat to protect its nationals and their property abroad became untenable when millions of a state's nationals lived or owned property abroad. And the duties of states toward foreigners became difficult when no sovereign would claim them—when they became stateless. As such, individuals gradually became subjects (of a sort) of international law because of the inability of the international system to reconcile two essential elements of the state – population and territory – in an age of nationalism, democratization, mass migration, global trade, and foreign investment.

In doing so, this book finds the protection of property and investments, in addition to traditional humanitarian concerns, at the center of the effort to give international rights to individuals and to establish international courts and tribunals to vindicate those rights. Capitalists and merchants used the language and institutional aims most associated with human rights movements to protect their property and investments abroad.

This book, to be clear, is *not* about human rights (not entirely). Rather, it is about the emergence of a set of international legal theories and practices that focus on protecting individuals rather than just regulating relationships between states – such protection has often been expressed in the language of law and could be described as individual international rights.[25] If this description sounds like human rights, that's because much (although certainly not all) of the human rights regime, as it has emerged in the past half-century, has been expressed in a juridical mode and in the terms of international law. The idealized central institutions of the proponents of human rights are often international courts – the European Court of Human Rights, the International Criminal Court, the Inter-American Court of Human Rights. And the documentary basis of human rights are often international declarations and treaties – the Universal Declaration of Human Rights, the International Covenant on Civil and Political Rights, the European Convention on Human Rights.

I chose to avoid the use of "human rights" to escape its connotations. In the past two decades, historians have turned the history of human rights into a cottage industry, churning out tome after tome on the phenomenon.[26] Whether critical, celebratory, or hagiographic, these books and articles explore human rights as a program for protecting the classically oppressed – minorities, dissidents, women. The primary spin-off subject, the history of humanitarianism, has been concerned with why we care for those who are distant, for those who are close, and for those who are different. But again, they explore the phenomenon of care for the classically oppressed – slaves, colonial subjects, refugees. The substantive human rights at the heart of recent scholarship have been those that traditionally fell under the Lockean categories of "life" and "liberty" – freedom of religion, freedom from arbitrary arrest or detainment, freedom of speech, freedom from torture.[27] Absent from most of the narratives has been the Lockean category of "property."[28] When property is discussed, it is almost always in the context of the failure of international social and economic justice rather than the successful internationalization of private property and investment protection.[29]

The Universal Declaration of Human Rights provides, "No one shall be held in slavery,"[30] "No one shall be subjected to torture,"[31] and "All are equal before the law,"[32] among other celebrated rights. The declaration even includes the explicit and familiar statement "Everyone has the right to life, liberty and . . . "[33] but chooses to finish that invocation of Locke and Thomas Jefferson with "security of person" rather than "property" or "the pursuit of happiness." Nevertheless, property is not absent. Article 17 declares, "No one shall be arbitrarily deprived of his property."[34] Freedom from torture, equal protection under the law, and the right to life and liberty are discussed by historians of human rights ad nauseam – the same cannot be said for the right to private property. And the Universal Declaration's liberal intellectual predecessors likewise included property rights. Fedor Martens, one of the leading international legal minds of the late nineteenth century, included the rights to property and to contract in his enumeration of the "international rights of man."[35] The 1929 Declaration of the International Rights of Man produced by the prestigious Institute of International Law and one of the direct inspirations of the Universal Declaration, likewise declared in its first article that all individuals had "an equal right to life, liberty, and property."[36] Yet historians have been obsessed with the trajectories of life and liberty.

In part, this has been because of the isolation of scholars in both history and law who work on human rights from historians and lawyers working on trade, investment, or the trendy "history of capitalism."[37] But it also owes much to the development of human rights as a field of historical inquiry. First, academic historians rarely write celebrations, beatifications, and hagiographies (at least explicitly) on people and institutions focused on the maintenance of property rights. Rights like freedom of speech, religion, and conscience are generally beloved within the academy. The rights to private property or to the enforcement of a contract debt, in contrast, generate significantly less sympathy. Moreover, mainstream human rights activists have rarely placed much emphasis on the right to property in the past fifty years and have said very little on the subject. The result is that many of the historical analyses of human rights that have been crafted in the past decade have focused on life and liberty, and ignored property.[38]

Second, those critical of histories of human rights have cast themselves as naysayers, concerned with countering Panglossian and Pollyannaish narratives of the origins of the current human rights moment. For example, Samuel Moyn observed, "when people imagine global justice, most often they picture a courtroom."[39] In reviewing two recent works[40] on the origins of international criminal courts, Moyn argued "it is obvious that strong and wealthy nations are never going to legally mandate their own loss of superiority and money . . . ."[41] The reason to study their past, he continued, was "not just to register their heroic possibilities but also to acknowledge their humbling limitations."[42] That's fair. The International Criminal Court has a mixed record, and the United States has refused to submit itself to its jurisdiction. But Moyn's comments demonstrate the limitations of the field itself. Scholars of human rights have cultivated narratives about the emergence of the international protection of life and liberty; their critics have usually met them on that plain. Critics of the histories themselves point to the lack of precision in the deployment of the term.[43] Critics of human rights themselves – usually working in a postcolonial tradition – have focused on cultural imperialism, racism, and other contradictions they see as inherent in a universalist and individualist project.

When we shift our gaze down from the sacred rights of life and liberty and toward the more profane right of property, the picture looks different. If, as Moyn noted, global justice looks like a courtroom, then plenty of strong and wealthy nations have legally mandated their own loss of superiority and money in trade and investment courts and arbitral tribunals. Through contract, states all over the world, including the ever-protective-of-its-sovereignty United States, have given power to international tribunals to adjudicate disputes between themselves and individual investors. Many states have likewise agreed to allow others to execute those contractual awards, should they be unwilling to comply, by seizing their assets. Today, traders' and investors' utopian visions of global justice and international rights are much closer to reality than the visions of those seeking justice for the tortured, arrested, or censored. Commerce, today, is increasingly sovereign.

How and why did we end up with international investment and trade courts? How did we end up with a system, known increasingly as investor-state dispute settlement (ISDS), which permits individual human beings to bring sovereign states before private tribunals who render decisions that are enforceable around the world? These are some of the questions this book answers. As Moyn and Stefan-Ludwig Hoffmann have both argued, human rights sat alongside other rights regimes that were at times more pervasive and more salient. Internationalism, international socialism, anticolonial nationalism, economic liberalism, human rights, and other "utopias" existed alongside one another, and the partisans of each paradise often found themselves in conflict with each other (as the unevenly ratified International Covenant on Civil and Political Rights and International Covenant on Economic, Social and Cultural Rights illustrate).[44] International rights, as one of the utopias, has also come in different flavors, like international minority rights, international labor rights, and others.[45] This book, in part, explores different conceptions of international rights as they emerged in the interwar period to better understand the relationship between the modern individualistic rights regime and other international rights regimes – minority rights, refugee rights, national rights, and others. In doing so, it exposes the role that international business organizations and their interests played in the creation of international rights regimes, of which the part of human rights has become the most visible, but hardly the most significant, instantiation.[46] Many of these international committees and treaties used international law and international courts as the instruments of their realization. Including international courts and international rights, in all their guises, in this story reveals the interrelated origins of the modern global investment regime, minority rights, human rights, and others. After all, wealthy foreign investors and Chechens alleging violations of human rights share the desire to hale the Russian government before an international court. While the rights claims of the investor and the torture victim are different, they rely upon similar institutions and similar ideas about the place of the individual in the international order. Those similarities have often been overlooked and should be investigated further.

I also chose to focus on the place of the individual in international law because this book takes as its primary legal subject the rights of foreigners under international law. Human rights connotes a regime whose law applies to everyone, regardless of their nationality. Human rights ideally will protect the French from the French government or the Germans from the German government. In contrast, the rights and law discussed in this book apply only (although there are exceptions) to foreigners – migrants, refugees, the stateless, foreign investors, foreign traders, foreign corporations. These are the rights that protect Italians living in the United States from the U.S. government, and the rights that protect Canadian investors from the Californian government. The rights of aliens and the rights of states to protect nationals abroad are the legal topics at the heart of this project.

Geographically, this book centers on the Atlantic and is Eurocentric for much of its analysis. International law was but one system of European rule in the mid-nineteenth century – the others being formal empire, which Europeans exercised in much of Africa and South Asia, and explicit extraterritorial jurisdiction, which they exercised in North African, Ottoman, Chinese, and Japanese territories. International law applied between states recognized by Europe as belonging to what they termed "international society" – a single, coherent, legal space including all of Europe, and by 1850, most of the North and South American mainlands. In the twentieth century, as formal empire gave way, international society expanded. International law, in sum, replaced formal empire as the means of overcoming legal difference. And so the geographic scope of this book expands – to a degree – with the geographic scope of international law. It tracks changes to the law that accompanied the collapse of empires in the early nineteenth century as well as in the interwar and postwar periods.[47]

The narrative of this book is broken up into three parts (divided here with three *Mises-en-scène* that introduce various actors, institutions, and legal principles). The first part begins in the latter half of the nineteenth century and ends with the First World War. The second covers the interwar period, and the third section covers the period following the Second World War.

The first part of this book (Chapters 1 and 2) details the development, rules, context, and complications in a system of legal protection based upon the right of states to protect their nationals abroad. Chapter 1 details the origin and development of the system in the first age of globalization. States could and did intervene on behalf of their nationals. But just who were those nationals? Who was a state entitled to claim as its national or subject? Chapter 2 excavates the problem created when millions of people moved from one country, one continent, or one hemisphere, to another. States had every right to define their nationals, but what did that mean for human beings born thousands of miles beyond the territory of the state that laid claim upon them? When a woman married a foreigner, what did that mean for her separate legal identity and her claim to the protection of her native land? A system that was predicated upon a reciprocal and mutually exclusive relationship between nationals and their state was increasingly unstable when legal identities were in flux in an age of migration.

The second part of the book (Chapters 3, 4, and 5) looks at alternative conceptions of sovereignty and international rights from the 1850s to the 1930s. Chapter 3 looks at the attempt to put the nation, rather than the state, at the center of international law and its expression in the form of minority protection regimes. Chapter 4 explores the interwar refugee crisis and both practical and theoretical developments to put the individual at the center of international law. Chapter 5 traces the efforts to remedy the problems faced by merchants and investors, primarily to create an individual right for a merchant or investor to bring complaints against sovereign states. In all cases, nationality continued to complicate the international order.

The third part of the book (Chapter 6) looks at the emergence of individual international rights as the primary alternative conception of international order and the one that was least reliant on nationality as a fundamental category.

***

In the nineteenth century, the Atlantic world entangled itself in a web of legal obligations. The states of Western Europe saw their nationals sail and steam across the Atlantic to newly independent states. They also saw their nationals invest heavily in Eastern Europe, the Americas, and elsewhere. Whereas in the eighteenth century it was exceptional to wander beyond the protective walls of the state; in the nineteenth century, it was common to find oneself a stranger in the keeping of another sovereign. At first the conflicts were easily handled through diplomatic channels, through ad hoc international arbitrations convened whenever a serious dispute arose. States asserted their right to protect the life, liberty, and property of their nationals abroad. During the late nineteenth century, however, the relationship between states and their nationals was also in flux. Nationalism challenged traditional legal identities and increasingly enabled states to lay claim to peoples who had never lived within the territorial boundaries of the state, but who, through kinship, were part of the national community the state claimed to represent.

Entangled in knots of obligation, the international legal system began to try and untie itself in the decades after the First World War. Scholars, lawyers, activists, humanitarians, and diplomats proposed fundamental alterations to the international legal order, most of which were predicated on freeing individuals from their reliance upon their states or their nations to defend their rights. In this, business interests and international humanitarians found common cause but not common outcomes. This book tells that story.

Part I

Mise-en-scène

The International Legal World, 1850–1914

Nations or states are bodies politic, societies of men united together for the purpose of promoting their mutual safety and advantage by the joint efforts of their combined strength. . . . *The law of nations is the science which teaches the rights subsisting between nations or states, and the obligations correspondent to those rights.*[1]

Emer de Vattel, 1768

The second half of the long nineteenth century (particularly the years between 1870 and 1914) was the golden age of international law that has since been forgotten.[2] Although Hugo Grotius and Emer de Vattel (two of the more famous expositors on the subject of international law) wrote in the seventeenth and eighteenth centuries, respectively, their texts were as much works of philosophy, in both its political and natural guises, as they were works of law.

It was in the nineteenth century that both the international law textbook and the legal treatise came onto the market en masse.[3] These tomes certainly flirted with political philosophy. But they had a more practical bent than Grotius or Vattel. Instead of referencing scripture or the classics as support for their propositions, as had been the style of the seventeenth- and eighteenth-century publicists, nineteenth-century writers referenced the historical (usually recent) practice of states.[4] Some of these texts were written by scholars, others by diplomatic officials or legal advisors, and many by people who bridged both the fields of academia and diplomacy. The books were used in university courses and referenced by statesmen and their legal advisors to answer international legal questions.

Academics and practitioners penned and published thousands of articles on international law in law reviews and periodical journals over the course of the nineteenth century. These same groups established their own specialist journals and reviews dedicated to international law in both its private and public manifestations. The *Revue de droit international et de législation comparé* was founded in 1869, the *Journal du droit international privé* in 1874, the *Revue générale de droit international public* in 1894, the *Journal of Comparative Legislation and International Law* in 1896, the *Revue de droit international privé et droit pénal international* in 1905, and the *American Journal of International Law* in 1907.

In part, these tomes on public international law are evidence of the expansion of bureaucracy and the creation of a "meritocratic" civil service designed around specialization and expertise.[5] The rise of the international lawyer within the European Atlantic world was intimately tied to the rise of experts and proto-technocracy in the late nineteenth century. As foreign ministries became staffed with professionals, whence those professionals came was an open question and law was one answer commonly given. Beginning in the last quarter of the nineteenth century, lawyers were increasingly consulted with regard to international issues.[6] Legal advisors increasingly could be found inside foreign ministries. The Law Officers of the Crown, in Great Britain, the Solicitor at the U.S. Department of State, the Ottoman Office of Legal Counsel,[7] and many others were established in the latter half of the nineteenth century to provide legal expertise to increasingly bureaucratized governments. The result was that diplomacy gradually adopted a legal language to both compliment and occlude its more traditional political one.

The late nineteenth century was also the heyday of the peace movement. Hundreds of organizations located on both sides of the Atlantic mobilized to replace armed conflict with arbitration by international jurists.[8] The world got a sense of what that looked like when, in 1871–1872, the United States and Great Britain, two countries that had been rattling their sabres following Britain's breach of neutrality during the American Civil War, used what was by then the somewhat frequent practice of resolving their differences by arbitration.[9] Representatives of the two powers met in Geneva and argued their case before a commission composed of jurists and diplomats from Britain and the United States, as well as tie-breaking members from Italy, Switzerland, and Brazil.[10] The commission famously awarded, and Britain paid, the enormous sum of 15,500,000 USD to the United States.[11] Indeed, the success of the Alabama Claims commission would usher in an age of expanded international arbitration in the late nineteenth century, culminating with the 1899 and 1907 Hague Peace Conferences. Between 1900 and 1908, 75 treaties requiring mandatory arbitration of disputes were signed, more than 35 of which had a Great Power as a party.[12]

Following the disaster of the Franco–Prussian War in 1870 and the success of the Alabama Claims, two major organizations were founded that will appear frequently in this book.[13] The first, the Institute of

International Law (*Institut de Droit International*), became one of the preeminent societies dedicated to the research of international law. Comprised of the world's preeminent jurists, the organization met annually to discuss the state of international law and to propose standards and codes for adoption. As the foremost body of scholars dealing with international law issues, they were consulted frequently in arbitral proceedings.[14] The second, the International Law Association, was founded initially by peace activists and was "to consist of Jurists, Economists, Legislators, Politicians and others taking an interest in the question of the reform and Codification of Public and Private International Law, the Settlement of Disputes by Arbitration, and the assimilation of the laws, practice and procedure of the Nations in reference to such laws."[15]

Peace societies, foreign offices, university chairs and curricula, textbooks, journals, and academic and professional conferences all began to coalesce into a proper field of expertise. And as expertise is wont to do, it began to insinuate itself into the language of governance in the latter half of the nineteenth century – the age of arbitration, an age of diplomatic intervention, and an age that increasingly draped its politics in the purple velvet of the law. So, as people began to do what they are wont to do, move, law was the language in which disputes over just who belonged to whom were worked out.

1 The Walls of Gilgamesh

> This is the wall of Uruk, which no city on Earth can equal. See how its ramparts gleam like copper in the sun. Climb the stone staircase, more ancient than the mind can imagine, . . . walk on the wall of Uruk, follow its course around the city, inspect its mighty foundations, examine its brickwork, how masterfully it is built, observe the land it encloses: the palm trees, the gardens, the orchards, the glorious palaces and temples, the shops and marketplaces, the houses, the public squares.
>
> The Epic of Gilgamesh, ca. 2100 BCE[1]

As the bells tolled noon on Easter Sunday in 1847, thousands of worshippers filed out of their churches and into the sun-soaked squares of Athens.[2] On a typical Easter Sunday, the Orthodox Christians of the city would have gathered together in their neighborhoods to celebrate the end of Lent. Many would have excitedly crowded around effigies of Judas Iscariot that had been ceremoniously hanged two days prior on Good Friday in imitation of his suicide. Then, with a touch of somber ceremony, they would have set those effigies aflame and reveled in the symbolic immolation of the Betrayer of Christ. But the Easter Sunday of 1847 was not typical. During that year, the Greek government was buckling under the weight of its accumulated debt, and on that Sunday, it was hosting Baron Charles de Rothschild, a prominent Jewish banker from whom the government hoped to receive substantial financial assistance. Wary of offending their financial savior, the Greek government banned the ceremonial burning of Judas, colloquially referred to as "the burning of the Jew."[3]

Enraged by their government's decision to ban the tradition, two or three hundred angry Greeks rushed to the home of David "Don" Pacifico, a noted leader of the local Jewish community. The torrential mob "battered" down his door with "large pieces of stone" and flooded into his house. They smashed his "windows, doors, tables, chairs, and every other article of furniture." They looted his jewels and money. They shredded his personal papers, some of which were records concerning investments and substantial amounts of money owed to Pacifico. They beat his wife and children. Pacifico begged the local police to intervene. But his appeals were in vain; the Greek authorities did nothing but watch the violence surge through the house. When the crushing flood of the mob ebbed, Pacifico surveyed the destruction in despair.[4]

Had Pacifico been a Greek national, there would have been little he could have done and this story might have ended here, just another unremarkable strand in the already thick tapestry of European anti-Semitism. But Pacifico was not a Greek national. In 1784, Pacifico had been born to Portuguese–Jewish parents on a large rock jutting out of the Iberian Peninsula and into the Mediterranean Sea. That rock, known as Gibraltar, was ruled then (as it is now) by the British Crown. By mere accident of birth, Pacifico was a British subject.[5]

Since his birth, Pacifico had spent little time in Britain. In fact, he had spent much of his career in service to the Portuguese government. Yet, in 1847, the "alienation of allegiance" – that is the renunciation of one's nationality (known today as expatriation) – was unknown, unrecognized, or illegal in most of Europe, especially in Britain. This meant that despite having served as an agent for the Portuguese government, despite having lived in Athens for more than a decade, and despite having spent little time in the British Isles, Pacifico was, and would forever be, a British subject. So, Pacifico dispatched a letter to Edmund Lyons, the British Minister in Athens, and begged for help. Lyons forwarded the complaint to the Greek government as well as to the British foreign secretary, John Henry Temple, better known as Lord Palmerston.

Over the next year, Lyons, with Palmerston's explicit support, pressed the Greek government to compensate Pacifico for the damage and the violence wrought upon him, his property, and his family by the Easter Day mob.[6] The Greek government angrily retorted:

> Mr. Pacifico persists in managing his claims through the channel of Her Majesty's legation instead of through the competent [local] tribunals . . . By renouncing the nationality of the country that he represented here as Consul General . . . under the pretext of having been born in Gibraltar, by hiding behind British protection, when the nature of his complaint obliged him to appeal to the justice of the country in which he had lived for so long and where the acts of which he complains occurred, by following this irregular route [in seeking justice], Mr. Pacifico has left no doubt that even he considers that his claims are either baseless or very exaggerated.[7]

Despite persistent appeals by the British government, the Greek government refused to compensate Britain for Pacifico's claims. Palmerston issued an ultimatum. The Greek government did not budge. In response, Palmerston ordered a naval squadron to blockade Piraeus, the port of

Athens, until the Greek government agreed to allow Pacifico's claims to be settled by an international tribunal. The Greek government angrily retorted: "The Russian and French governments were furious with the blockade."[8] The sabers of Europe were rattling in their sheathes.[9]

In the debates that followed in Parliament, critics attacked Pacifico. They questioned both the legitimacy of his status as a British subject and the propriety of his claims.[10] With more than a hint of anti-semitism in their rhetoric, many Members and Lords of Parliament took note of the dramatic variance between Pacifico's monetary resources and his purported material wealth.[11] William Gladstone, for example, to illustrate the implausibility of Pacifico's claim, sardonically observed that other than "having his house crammed full of fine furniture, fine clothes and fine jewels, Monsieur Pacifico was in all other respects a pauper."[12] Most importantly, critics chastised Pacifico for deviating from international norms by not first seeking redress in the Greek courts, a violation of the custom under international law that one first "exhaust" local remedies before seeking international redress. Under international law, they argued, it was a well established principle that one needed to work his or her way through the local legal system before appealing to his or her government.[13]

Yet, Pacifico had many champions at Westminster. Alexander Cockburn,[14] for example, responded to the argument that Pacifico should have first sought justice in Greek tribunals by naming cases of justices who had been dismissed from their posts for rendering judgments against the Greek government. John Roebuck, likewise, excoriated the Greek authorities:

> The very day on which the outrage took place, a complaint was made to the Government. Now, in those countries there is a public prosecutor. It was the business of the Government to investigate that matter. They did investigate it, and they declared that it did take place in the broad day on the Easter Sunday. People were known to be there by name; the whole of Athens knew it; and yet they declared that they could not find the criminals. Now, was not that a denial of justice?

Roebuck then pointed to another, competing principle of international law, arguing, "If you have reason to believe that what you deem justice cannot be thus done, by all the rules of what is called international law, you have a right to make an appeal to the Government at home."[15] Lord Palmerston, moreover, continued to stand by Pacifico.

Following the House of Lords condemnation of his decision to blockade Piraeus, Palmerston took to the floor and delivered a nearly four-and-a-half-hour speech in which he vigorously defended Pacifico.

Palmerston's adversaries were themselves in awe, with William Gladstone describing the speech as a "marvel for physical strength, for memory and for lucid and precise exposition of his policy as a whole."[16] Palmerston concluded his speech at 2:20 in the morning by thunderously exclaiming:

I therefore fearlessly challenge the verdict which this House, as representing a political, a commercial, a constitutional country, is to give on the question now brought before it; whether the principles on which the foreign policy of Her Majesty's Government has been conducted, and the sense of duty which has led us to think ourselves bound to afford protection to our fellow subjects abroad, are proper and fitting guides for those who are charged with the Government of England; and whether, as the Roman, in days of old, held himself free from indignity, when he could say *civis Romanus sum* [I am a Roman citizen]; so also a British subject, in whatever land he may be, shall feel confident that the watchful eye and the strong arm of England, will protect him against injustice and wrong.[17]

Finally, on July 18, 1850 the British and Greek governments concluded a treaty that established an arbitral commission. The commission consisted of one Greek and one British representative as well as an umpire appointed by the government of France. The Greek government deposited 150,000 drachmas to guarantee the execution of any award rendered by the tribunal with the balance to be returned to Greece.[18] The tribunal sat, heard evidence, and awarded the British government a sum of 150 British Pounds, quite short of Pacifico's original claim, which had run in excess of 21,000 British Pounds. A check was sent by the British government to Pacifico on August 1, 1851, and the matter was deemed closed.[19]

Civis Romanus Sum and Informal Empire in an Age of Globalization

The story of Don Pacifico and Palmerston's exclamation of "*civis Romanus sum*" is illustrative of many of the geopolitical tensions that would play out over the last half of the nineteenth century and reshape the relationship between states and individuals under international law. During that "first age of globalization," a tremendous volume of people, ideas, goods, and capital sped around the globe creating what Eric Hobsbawm described as a "World Unified."[20] Between 1869 and 1870, railways spanning the United States and India as well as the canal at Suez were all completed. Phileas Fogg would embark upon all three to complete his fictional trip around the world in less than eighty days; as would Nellie Bly to complete her non-fictional circumnavigation in less than seventy-two.[21]

It was an age of migration. Pacifico may have been a peculiar official whose migration pattern was relatively uncommon in the 1840s, but millions of Europeans would have equally complex trajectories over the next half century. Europeans migrated within Europe. Italians headed north; Poles and Germans headed west. Europeans emigrated from Europe. Between 1820 and 1920 more than 60 million of them embarked on ships bound for the Western Hemisphere. Although mass migrations had occurred in previous eras, the latter half of the nineteenth century was the first time in which transoceanic migration was not almost entirely permanent. Between 1890 and 1914, nearly one-third of those who migrated to countries in the Western Hemisphere returned to Europe. In some countries nearly half of all immigrants returned to their country of origin. Many others travelled back to the lands whence they came for visits or business. Depending on the group and the time, rates of return could climb as high as 80 percent.[22] As a pair of economists recently put it, the level of migration in the nineteenth century was "staggering by modern standards."[23] And migration could also mean travel. In record numbers, the haute bourgeois of the late nineteenth century made temporary transatlantic trips or transcontinental sojourns; a theme that at times seems inescapable in late nineteenth-century literature (particularly American).[24]

It was an age of communication. News could make its way around the globe in a single day. As Henry Pratt Judson remarked in 1893, "To-day the world is bound together by steam and telegraph.... We know every day what happened in the preceding 24 hours in all parts of the globe. Our Minnesota millers guide their business by crop reports from Odessa; our bankers are in intimate communication with the financial centres of Europe."[25] Nor were the powers of steam and copper wire limited to the realms of news and finance; painters, musicians, writers, architects, scientists, poets, philosophers, and academics freely traveled and cheaply communicated their ideas, creating what Peter Gay described as a "free international commerce of ideas."[26]

It was an age of trade. Commodities and finished goods crisscrossed the globe on water and rail in unprecedented quantities and at unprecedented speeds. Between 1830 and 1870, the value of foreign trade for every national of Britain, France, Germany, Austria, and Scandinavia increased by a factor of four to five. For every Dutchman, it increased by a factor of three. For every American, it increased by a factor of two. By 1913, more than 15 percent of the GDP of Britain, the Netherlands, Norway, Belgium, Finland, and Switzerland was from the export of finished products alone. The cost of shipping commodities declined dramatically. Transit rates per ton of coal fell from 16 shillings per ton in

1780 to less than 3 by 1910. The volume of trade was so great and the cost of shipping so low that distance and time were nearly "eradicated" as a factor in the price of commodities.[27] In fact, the trade-to-GDP ratios of the 1890s were remarkably similar to the 1990s.[28]

It was an age of international investment. Between 1885 and 1889, nearly 50 percent of domestic savings in Britain was invested abroad. Moreover, the annual foreign investments by British subjects exceeded domestic capital formation by 1870. In Germany, the figure was 20 percent. In France, it was more than 10 percent. By 1913, more than 33 percent of all British wealth was invested overseas. These investments often represented an extraordinary proportion of the capital in the receiving countries. In 1913, for example, foreigners owned nearly half of Argentina's stock market.[29] Indeed, the capital flows throughout the Atlantic world were greater in the period from 1870 to 1913 than they were in the early 1990s.[30]

In short, it was an age of globalization. These extraordinary levels of migration, communication, trade, and investment produced a new age of anonymity. The mercantilism of the eighteenth century had created global markets and protected traders by keeping migration, trade, and investment within a single legal system. Migrants were protected by their own legal system. An Englishman found the King's justice nearly as readily in Boston as in London. A contract between a merchant in Paris and his counterpart in Quebec City was covered by a single legal system. Similarly, business interests were often protected by their own customs. Yet the mercantilism of the eighteenth century was giving way to the free trade of the nineteenth century as the Atlantic revolutions destroyed the empires that had sustained it. In previous eras, when migration and trade spanned legal systems, migrants, traders, and investors relied upon a combination of family, ethnic, and religious connections along with trade organizations and investment associations.[31] But, as transactions and migrations increased in frequency, distance, and volume, anonymity became a more intractable problem. To whom could immigrants turn when they found themselves the victims of arbitrary violence? To whom could merchants turn when a partner residing far across the sea in another country broke a contract? To whom could investors turn when individual or even sovereign debtors defaulted on their obligations? European states faced an existential crisis: how could they continue to protect their populations as they moved beyond the state's protective boundaries, beyond where the writ of their law ran?

States crafted three methods of eliding legal difference and eradicating the frictions of long-distance life created by the problems set out above. The first, formal empire, effectively eradicated legal difference by replacing the law of the conquered territory with that of the metropole.[32] The second, extraterritoriality, was infamously imposed by the countries of Europe and, later, the United States, upon China, Japan, the Ottoman Empire, and Tunisia. Extraterritorial privilege eradicated legal difference by permitting foreigners to be governed by the law of their distant sovereign.[33] These two methods both involved the formal imposition of law upon territories that Europeans considered to be outside of international society and not entitled to sovereign equality. They were overtly imperial methods that could not be applied within international society as it was conceived of in the nineteenth century – that is within the world of formal states that made up the Western Hemisphere and Europe. The third method, and the subject of this chapter, turned to international law and made reference to the "responsibility of states," "standards of civilization," and "international comity" to protect aliens in states not susceptible to overt imperialism. It was the legal basis of a kind of covert imperialism and of "informal empire."[34] It was this third method that was at the center of the Don Pacifico affair. It was this method that compelled Lord Palmerston to exclaim "*civis Romanus sum*" in the early hours of the morning.

This informal empire, and the international law through which it operated, was increasingly a transatlantic phenomenon. Europe and the Western Hemisphere together formed a conceptually coherent juridical space. As the territories of the Western Hemisphere transitioned to independence in the late eighteenth and early nineteenth centuries, many of the legal structures of the old empires remained. Domestically, the states of the Western Hemisphere retained many of their colonial legal traditions and institutions. The young United States retained the Common Law. The states of Latin America adopted civil codes of the kind sweeping across the European continent. Internationally, the states of the Western Hemisphere engaged in the same terms, using the same language, and following the same procedures. The states of the New World were theoretically sovereign and equal to the states of the Old World.[35] Although some scholars thought of the Western Hemisphere as having its own public law, and an international law distinct from Europe, they were a small minority.[36] It was taken for granted that the states of the Western Hemisphere were part of the community of states and subject to an international law that was at the very least transatlantic, if not universal.[37] Indeed, it was the project of many non-European jurists to appropriate international law for their own purposes, and by the early twentieth century, international lawyers in the Atlantic world formed a coherent, transnational profession, that both articulated and critiqued an increasingly global legal regime.[38]

The phrase *civis Romanus sum* was on the lips of many notables and statesmen in that transatlantic world in second half of the nineteenth century. Philip Lindsley, the former president of Princeton University, gave a speech shortly before the Don Pacifico affair in which he insisted, "to be a Roman citizen . . . was not only a passport, honorary and credential, the wide world over, but a talisman of defense and security. [It] was the eloquent and effective plea, which caused the unrighteous judge to tremble, which opened prison doors, which arrested the executioner's arm, and which procured for the doomed and otherwise helpless victim, a fair hearing and impartial trial." He went on to assert his hope that "I am an American citizen" would soon "prove not less potent or availing, when uttered by the humblest of our countrymen, in the wildest and remotest regions of the globe."[39] A member of the Canadian Senate alluded to the Palmerstonian exclamation in 1888, arguing, "Our ships float in every sea and are found in every corner of the globe, and they are protected: how? By the power and prestige of England. Our flag – the flag of the Empire – secures us everywhere from insult and injustice more fully than did the proud boast of the Roman of old, 'I am a Roman citizen'."[40] In Italy, Francesco Crispi, a compatriot of Giuseppe Mazzini and Giuseppe Garibaldi and an architect of Italian unification, also expressed to a cheering crowd his sincere wish that the citizens of Italy would soon be able to exclaim "*civis Romanus sum*" and be taken seriously.[41] Similarly, Kaiser Wilhelm II in a speech given at a reconstructed Roman fort in Saalburg in 1900, expressed his hope that soon "one could shout, with the same pride that one once said '*civis Romanus sum*,' 'I am a German citizen.'"[42] Nor was the refrain limited to Europe and North America. Enrique Tocornal in an address to the Chilean Chamber of Deputies chastised the Chilean minister of foreign relations for believing that Chileans who had left Chile were not entitled to protection and "should suffer the consequences they face [when abroad]." Tocornal lamented that Chileans, unlike the Romans, could not "say the words *civis Romanus sum*" and demanded that Chile protect its subjects against unjust imprisonment or state-sanctioned murder wherever they were.[43]

The phrase itself was later used to define the age retrospectively. André Siegfried, a noted French academic, when nostalgically describing the ease that a European could navigate during the years before the World War I, argued that the phrase "*civis Romanus sum*" was the only passport one needed. So much did he associate the phrase with the nineteenth-century world that he included it in almost all his descriptions of age.[44]

Yet the phrase was not without its critics. Joseph Story, one of the most influential jurists of the nineteenth century, once opined that the exclamation "*civis Romanus sum*" was "founded not on any legal principle, but upon the fact that his barbarian countryman had overrun the world with their arms, reduced all laws to silence, and annihilated the independence of foreign legislatures."[45] Similarly, in his opposition to Lord Palmerston's famous exhortation, William Gladstone rhetorically asked, "What then, Sir was a Roman citizen?" before answering, "He was a member of a privileged caste; he belonged to a conquering race, to a nation that held all others bound down by the strong arm of power. For him there was to be an exceptional system of law; for him principles were to be asserted, and by him rights were to be enjoyed, that were denied the rest of the world."[46] Several years after the Pacifico affair, *Fraser's Magazine* made light of the imperial exclamation and observed that "a courteous man has a better chance [of traveling peacefully] than one who goes about crying *civis Romanus sum*!"[47]

Civis Romanus sum was an interesting melange of pride and law. The idea behind the Latin declaration *civis Romanus sum* and its progeny – I am a British citizen, *Je suis un citoyen français*, I am an American citizen, *Soy chileno, Ich bin deutscher* – was that many statesmen in the nineteenth century shared the aspiration that their nationality would both command respect and provide protection beyond their borders in an age when many of their nationals traveled or resided far beyond the protective laws of the state. The phrase was selected, no doubt, because it conjured up powerful and meaningful images from deep within the psyche of European statesmen. The governing classes of the nineteenth-century Atlantic world were often nursed on Greek, reared in Latin, and bathed in scripture. Cicero's exclamation of "*civis Romanus sum*" in his prosecution of Gaius Verres would have been exceedingly familiar as both a patriotic phrase and as a cry for protection,[48] as would have St. Paul's mobilization of his Roman citizenship during his arrest.[49]

The phrase originated as an imperial exclamation, yet it was deployed in a modern state-centric order. The debate over the appropriateness of the phrase was tied up with broader discussions over empire and sovereignty. The juridical norm behind the exclamation assumed that the complaint was being levied against a full member of the international community – a sovereign equal. Yet it allowed for intervention diplomatically and even militarily if the complaint went unanswered. The juridical norm was used throughout Europe and the Americas, not merely as a way of obscuring predations by the strong against the weak (although that was certainly common) but also between two theoretical peers.

Indeed, the principle was used to protect Italians in the United States as well as in Argentina; it was used to protect Americans in Austria as well as in Mexico; it was used to protect Englishmen in Belgium as well as in Peru.[50] The juridical instrument of informal empire was, at the same time, the juridical instrument that adapted the state order to an age of globalization.

States and Territory

States are inveterate wall builders. The construction of barriers, both physical and legal, is the oldest function of state-like entities. *The Epic of Gilgamesh* begins with a simple boast, "This is the wall of Uruk, which no city on Earth can equal." The narrator invites us to walk the wall and to "find the cornerstone and under it the copper box that is marked with his name. Unlock it. Open the lid. Take out the tablet of lapis lazuli. Read how Gilgamesh suffered all and accomplished all."[51] The deeds of the king, the lawgiver, are contained beneath the cornerstone of the wall he restored. Walls demarcated both spaces of law and contained the law itself. The oldest renderings of the Greek word for law (*nomos*), the Greek and Latin words for city (*polis*, *urbs*), and the English word town all connoted rings, fences, enclosures, and walls.[52] Ancient Mesopotamians inscribed property deeds, decrees, and treaties on large nails of sculpted clay and physically embedded them into the walls of homes and cities – building physical walls out of laws.[53] As Hannah Arendt observed, "The law (*nomos*) of the city-state was neither the content of political action . . . nor was it a catalogue of prohibitions . . . . It was quite literally a wall."[54] Indeed, it was the very cost of building increasingly elaborate walls (either literal ones of stone or metaphorical ones of wood and canvas) that was generative of the modern fiscal apparatuses of the European state.[55] In the eighteenth and nineteenth centuries, the walls of European cities fell, and along with the walls, fell local law, local guilds, and many local social services. Centralizing states, in turn, drafted new national laws, established national guilds, offered new national social services, and erected new walls at their frontiers as each state turned itself "into a fortified city writ large."[56]

While states built their walls, scholars still disagreed over just what a state was. States in modern Europe often defined themselves by reference to the people who constituted them. In the seventeenth century, the Dutch jurist and "father" of international law, Hugo Grotius, defined the state as "a compleat Body of free Persons, associated together to enjoy peaceably their Rights, and for their common Benefit."[57]

Thomas Hobbes, likewise, defined his *Leviathan* as, "One Person, of whose Acts a great Multitude, by mutuall Covenants one with another, have made themselves every one the Author, to the end he may use the strength and means of them all, as he shall think expedient, for their Peace and Common Defence."[58] In the eighteenth century, Vattel, following in the tradition of Grotius, defined the state as a society "of men united together for the purpose of promoting their mutual safety and advantage by the joint efforts of their combined strength."[59] In the early nineteenth century, John Bouvier defined the state as "a self-sufficient body of persons united together in one community for the defense of their rights, and to do right and justice to foreigners."[60] None of the definitions explicitly reference territory. Indeed, late medieval and early modern legal thought rarely contained any limits upon the theoretical territorial scope of the state, preferring instead to demarcate spatial limits by reference to the limits of actual power.[61]

In contrast, the nineteenth century has been described as an age of territoriality – as an age when states, to use one popular definition, attempted "to influence, affect, or control objects, peoples and relationships by delimiting and asserting control over a geographic area."[62] In international jurisprudence and sociology, explicit references to territory begin to appear in definitions of the state. Robert Phillimore, writing in 1854, defined the state as "a people permanently occupying a fixed *territory*, bound together by common laws, habits, and customs into one body politic, exercising, through the medium of an organized Government, independent sovereignty and control over all persons and things within its *boundaries*, capable of making war and peace, and of entering into all International relations with the other communities of the globe."[63] Max Weber, a prominent German sociologist writing at the turn of the twentieth century, defined a state as "a human community that (successfully) claims the monopoly of the legitimate use of physical force within a given *territory*."[64] Most jurisprudence in the nineteenth century placed explicitly territorial limitations on jurisdiction. No longer was the law's reach defined by an explicit reference to power – defined by "where the King's writs could ride" – but instead jurisdiction was increasingly defined territorially.[65]

Yet territoriality sat uneasily with the centrifugal forces of the age. As people, goods, and money spun out to the four corners of the world, it seemed less like an age of territoriality than an age of extraterritoriality. And social theorists took note. Weber, for example, immediately followed his definition (the last word of which was territory) with the emphatic request that the reader "note that 'territory' is one of the characteristics of the state;" a request that implies that territory was not necessarily as self-evident a characteristic of the state as many nineteenth-century jurists and twenty-first-century historians would have us believe.[66] Indeed, some writers explicitly rejected any territorial qualification in the definition of the state. Robert Lansing, a prominent American international lawyer and President Wilson's Secretary of State, observed that making territory a requisite part of the definition would "deprive a large number of independent communities of a name to which they appear to be entitled by the completeness of their political organization and the influence which they have exerted upon the world's history."[67] The point is, in short, the centrality of territory to statehood was hardly a settled matter.

States built new walls and fortifications at their frontiers.[68] States mapped and delimited their frontiers.[69] Yet, just as territorial boundaries were becoming more clearly defined, nationals were quickly traveling far beyond them. And many self-identified foreigners were becoming trapped within them. Both Joseph Story and Friedrich Savigny, the two most important scholars of private international law in the nineteenth century, acknowledged the primacy of territoriality with regard to jurisdiction. Yet both were also reluctant to adopt such strict territoriality in a system of private international law. Savigny, for example, noted, "The more multifarious and active the intercourse between different nations, the more will men be persuaded that it is not expedient to adhere to such a stringent rule...."[70] While states were theoretically justified, according to Story and Savigny, in being strictly territorial, it was a difficult principle to put into practice owing to the mobility of the age. Writing in 1832, Joseph Story captured the essence of the legal conundrum territoriality created, writing, "The laws of no nation can justly extend beyond its own territories...," before qualifying his statement, "except so far as regards its own citizens."[71]

Diplomatic Protection

Between the late eighteenth and the mid-nineteenth century, a new international regime emerged to deal with the twisted relationship between the boundaries of the state and the place of its people. The purpose of that new regime was to protect the people and property involved in long-distance migration, trade, and investment.[72] Long-distance interactions in the eighteenth century often occurred within a unified imperial framework; legal expectations were set by reference to domestic laws. But as a new state-centric international order in Europe and the Americas emerged between 1776 and 1840, reference could no longer be made to domestic law with regard to the protection of individuals and their property. International law was increasingly the law at the center of international interactions.

International law at the end of the eighteenth century was defined as the rules and customs governing conduct between sovereigns, leaving no room for individuals to stand as subjects.[73] If a sovereign injured an individual, that individual theoretically had no recourse beyond the courts of the very sovereign who had rendered the injustice. However, as the Don Pacifico affair demonstrated, that theoretical limitation on the scope of international law had a significant and important loophole.

Under international law, states were obligated not to harm one another without just cause. Through the construction of a legal fiction, specifically that an injury done to a subject could be equated to an injury to the sovereign itself, harm to individuals could become the subject of international complaints. The foundations of this legal fiction rested upon two ancient social norms. First, that a host owes his guests hospitality. Second, that a sovereign owes its subjects protection.[74]

The first social norm is that a host owes his duly admitted guests hospitality and, reciprocally, that guests owe their host temporary obedience. It's doubtlessly an ancient norm with widespread adherence in many civilizations and cultures.[75] In the Old Testament, God commanded Moses, "If a stranger sojourn with thee in your land, ye shall not vex him." Moreover, God elaborated, "The stranger that dwelleth with you shall be unto you as one born among you, and thou shalt love him as thyself, for ye were strangers in the land of Egypt."[76] The command given to Moses wound its way through European jurisprudence and became firmly ensconced in the work of natural law theorists and international jurisprudence.[77] At the state level, that norm has traditionally meant that a sovereign was obligated to protect foreigners traveling through, or living in, his territory. What this means in modern practice is that states are expected to provide foreigners (at a minimum) the same protection of the laws that they do for their own nationals.[78] This standard is rendered in international legal jargon as "national treatment."[79]

The second social norm, that a sovereign owed its subjects protection, was at the heart of the European conception of the reciprocal obligations that bound subjects and sovereigns to each other.[80] As Blackstone observed, "Allegiance is the tie, or *ligamen*, which binds the subject to the king, in return for that protection which the king affords the subject."[81] Protection was foundational to the relationship. The contract between a sovereign and subject was only as good as the literal and metaphorical walls it provided.[82] Conceptually, that protection was marked through the metaphorical absorption of the subject by the sovereign. In the act of homage, to cite a ceremonial rather than a textual manifestation of this principle, two men would stand face to face. One would place his hands together. The other would grasp those hands between his own symbolizing the relationship in which the former offered his labor in exchange for the protection of the latter. The latter became "the man" of the former.[83] Hugo Grotius made that point himself, arguing, "Our main and chiefest Care should be, for those who are under our Direction and Management, whether in a Family or in a State. For they are, as it were, a Part of him who governs."[84]

The combination of these two social norms – that a sovereign owes strangers temporary hospitality in exchange for temporary allegiance and that a sovereign owes its subjects permanent protection for permanent allegiance – created the principle in international law that concerned itself most with the protection of human beings in times of peace. The sovereign subsumed the subject, and any harm by another sovereign against that subject was transitively a harm on the sovereign. It was this idea that enabled Grotius to justify the principle that "war may be justly undertaken by a Prince for the Interest of his Subjects." Grotius cited Cicero, noting, "[The Romans] often commenced a War if but one of their Merchants and Mariners had been ill dealt with."[85] As one anthropologist observed of an analogous practice (albeit in a culture far removed from feudal Europe in time and space), "Protection is personal, unqualified, explicit, and conceived of as the dressing of one man in the reputation of another. . . . But the essential transaction is that a man who counts 'stands up and says' . . . to those to whom he counts: 'this man is mine; harm him and you insult me; insult me and you will answer for it.'"[86]

Swiss jurist Emer de Vattel is credited with first fully articulating this modern legal principle, which became widely known as "diplomatic protection," by the end of the nineteenth century.[87] Writing in his *The Law of Nations*, Vattel noted that states had a responsibility to ensure the safety of foreigners legally admitted onto their territory. In what became the oft-cited formulation of the principle, Vattel wrote, "Whoever uses a citizen ill, indirectly offends the state, which is bound to protect this citizen; and the sovereign of the latter should avenge his wrongs, punish the aggressor, and, if possible, oblige him to make full reparation; since otherwise the citizen would not obtain the great end of the civil association, which is safety."[88] Moreover, Vattel continued, a sovereign who allows his subjects to "injure a foreign nation either in its body or its members, [does] no less injury to that nation than if he injured it himself."[89] One specific way in which a sovereign could "[use] a citizen ill," was to deny that citizen justice by (1) refusing him access to courts, (2) unduly delaying his access to courts, or (3) by rendering "an evidently unjust and partial decision."[90] Vattel had brought the metaphor of the body politic into the international realm by creating a transitive association between the subject and the sovereign. To harm a subject was to harm the body politic, harming the body politic harmed the sovereign, harming a sovereign was a breach of an international duty.

Writing in the middle of the eighteenth century, Vattel was perhaps the most popular international jurist of the next century.[91] He was read widely and was part of the legal libraries of many diplomats and politicians as well as political and legal thinkers. During the debate over American independence, Vattel's tome was "continually in the hands of the members of... [the Continental] congress."[92] George Washington, during his first presidency, checked out Vattel's tome from the New York Society Library in 1789 and never returned it.[93] His influence on international law in Europe in the nineteenth century was also unmatched.[94] Alfred Chrétien, a member of the Institute of International Law, noted in 1893 that Vattel had been "translated into nearly every language," and by the turn of the nineteenth century, was "the ordinary breviary of all the chancelleries." Chretian continued his praise by noting, "Today, Vattel is cited and consulted more often than ... Grotius himself."[95]

Vattel's popularity ensured that his formulation of the principles of diplomatic protection, the responsibility of states, and denial of justice became the standard in the late eighteenth and nineteenth centuries and persists to this day. In the late eighteenth century, echoes of Vattel's formulation of "diplomatic protection" and "state responsibility" are visible even in *The Federalist Papers*, in which Alexander Hamilton opined that a federal judiciary should have jurisdiction over cases involving foreigners because "an unjust sentence against a foreigner" would be "an aggression upon his sovereign" if left unredressed.[96] A half century later, during the debates over the Don Pacifico affair, Members and Lords of Parliament hurled quotations from Vattel back and forth across the aisle, referring to him as "a very high authority."[97] The Marquess of Lansdown, in favor of intervening on Pacifico's behalf, stated, "If the noble Lord looks to what Vattel and other writers on the law of nations say, he will find that a denial by delay is as bad as a disallowance of justice altogether."[98] The Earl of Aberdeen, who opposed intervening on behalf of Pacifico, retorted, "Vattel says, with reference to persons living in a foreign country, that 'The prince, therefore, ought not to interfere in the causes of his subjects in foreign countries, and to grant them his protection, excepting in cases where justice is refused, or palpable and evident injustice done, or rules and forms openly violated'."[99] No other international jurist was cited.

Writing in 1914, Albert de Lapradelle remarked that Vattel's formulation of the denial of justice had been so influential "that it can no longer be considered without referring to him."[100]

In 1924, the Permanent Court of International Justice (PCIJ), the League of Nation's judicial organ, reaffirmed Vattel's specific formulation of the principle when it held, "By taking up the case of one of its subjects and resorting to diplomatic action or international judicial proceedings on his behalf, a State is in reality asserting its own right – its right to ensure, in the person of its subjects, respect for the rules of international law."[101] Scholars, even now, still refer to the transitive association between an injury done to a subject and sovereign as the "Vattelian fiction."[102]

Mechanisms of Enforcement

But legal norms and rules on their own do little good without a process for resolving a violation. Vattel's transitive association was merely an intellectual trick that enabled the real harms inflicted on real human beings to be brought into the abstract realm of international law from which they were often absent. In Grotius and Vattel's formulations, a harm done to a subject violated the norm of international law, which holds that states should not harm each other without just cause. Prior to the nineteenth century, if an offending sovereign failed to make amends for damage done to a subject, international law prescribed that the victim's sovereign issue a letter of reprisal authorizing the victim to seize the assets of the offending sovereign or its subjects up to the value of the damage. Physical violence and even war were possible resolutions.[103]

Vattel, however, offered a broader array of options for resolving such impasses. As Vattel noted, again in his widely read *Law of Nations*, public international arbitration was "a very reasonable mode... for the decision of every dispute which does not directly interest the safety of the nation."[104] "Arbitration," simply defined, is the use of an arbitrator to decide a dispute. As a form of dispute resolution, arbitration is deployed in all manner of circumstances in both domestic and international contexts. Public international arbitration, as its name suggests, is a method by which international disputes are settled by reference to either one or more arbitrators. The parties themselves select the arbitrators with a neutral judge or umpire selected either by agreement or by reference to a neutral third party. The parties agree by treaty to abide by the decision. "Mixed commissions," or "claims commissions," refer to a subset of public international arbitration designed to handle a specifically agreed upon class of disputes, almost exclusively involving the claims of individual subjects.[105] As the eighteenth century drew to a close, international arbitration and mixed commissions were about to undergo a renaissance of sorts.

In 1776, several of Britain's North American colonies declared their independence. The armed conflict lasted until 1783, but disputes over boundaries and wartime debts continued well into the 1790s. To resolve these continuing sources of conflict, Britain and the United States (perhaps still with Vattel "continually in the hands of the members of... congress") agreed to establish commissions charged with resolving the disputes. The most successful, and perhaps most important, part of the Jay Treaty's arbitration provisions were not those that dealt with the establishment of the boundary between Canada and the United States, but rather the provisions establishing a claims tribunal to settle complaints of individual American nationals. The claims tribunal met in London over a period of eight years and awarded American claimants more than 11 million USD. As one legal scholar argued, "This was the notable success of the Jay Treaty."[106] While recently historians have downplayed the importance of the Jay Treaty as the start of the modern era of international arbitration, the treaty's real importance was its deployment of mixed commissions as a method for dealing with the gradual collapse of formal empire and the birth of a new state-centric order.[107]

That same ideological motivation was applied to Europe twenty years later as the Great Powers convened in Vienna to rebuild Europe after decades of revolutionary conflict. The final treaty was extensive, consisting of 121 articles. Among the many innovations of the Congress of Vienna was the decision that "all the arrangements made by the Congress would be included in a single general treaty."[108] Having all the major participants sign the treaty in its entirety legitimated the collective decision making of the Congress, "effectively creating a new system of public law for Europe."[109] That public law was a dramatic repudiation of both universal monarchy, international dynastic politics, as well as the solidification of an order of states within Europe. Part of that new "public law" included huge numbers of arbitral agreements, which were woven into the treaty along with the establishment of more than a dozen claims commissions. These commissions were not charged with merely distributing reparations for physical damage caused in the course of the conflict – as had been common in previous conflicts.[110] Instead, many commissions were charged with determining the level of compensation due to foreign nationals for the loss of their investments. The convention dealing with the claims of British subjects, for example, established a claims commission – composed of two British and two French commissioners – to fix the amount of compensation distributed to British subjects who had possessed a number of different financial instruments that had been seized or repudiated by the French Government: stock, life annuities, or loans. The convention included detailed legalistic provisions on everything from the standards of evidence, the calculation of interest, and protocols for tie breaking. Likewise, the convention provided for the restitution of both movable and immovable property expropriated by France during the French Revolution.[111]

The Jay Treaty and the work of the Congress of Vienna bespoke a new emphasis on remedying damage done to either individual subjects or their property while in a foreign state. Mercantilism crumbled alongside the Atlantic empires. The new "public law" of Europe eschewed dynastic politics, shifting alliances, claims of universal monarchy, and territorial expansion within Europe in favor of maintaining a stable order of territorial monarchical states.[112] Simply put, Europe and the Americas had begun their transformation from continents of empires to continents of states. The old imperial methods of reducing legal friction through formal empire or dynastic politics could no longer apply to commerce and migration within Europe and between Europe and the Western Hemisphere. The Vattelian fiction and international arbitration together constituted a new regime to manage the cries of Pacificos throughout the Atlantic world.[113] The use of diplomatic protection and arbitration remained limited in the decades after 1815. After all, there was still only one independent state in the Western Hemisphere. But as the Spanish Empire in the Western Hemisphere eroded, and as international migration, trade, and investment rapidly expanded from the 1840s onward, the new regime was at the ready.

Diplomatic Protection in an Age of Globalization

Cicero began his famous description of the import of Roman citizenship by observing: "Men . . . go to sea; they go to places which they have never seen before; where they can neither know or be known to the men among whom they have arrived."[114] For Cicero, the object of concern was the man at sea. As they coasted from port to port, sailors and merchants were marooned, left behind, injured, became ill, or suffered abuse. Often isolated in urban environments and alienated from communities of support and protection, sailors and merchants were the first members of the modern world. The sailor was the quintessential object of protection abroad. And the consulate was the agency of that protection.

Consulates and embassies are institutions with which the reader may be familiar and may even treat as synonymous. But they are distinctive. Embassies are institutions of high diplomacy. Ambassadors and their embassies represent the political interests of the state abroad. Consuls and consulates, in contrast, are charged with protecting the everyday interests of nationals abroad. Consulates are the places you go if you lose your passport, if you have trouble with the local authorities, if you – for whatever reason – find yourself in some sort of dire need while abroad. The consulate, above all, is an institution that will ferry you back home should all else fail.[115]

The consulate is not a recent invention. Having existed in some form since antiquity, the modern institution began to emerge sometime in the Middle Ages as a way of protecting merchants and sailors in port cities throughout the North and Mediterranean Seas.[116] By the eighteenth century, the role of the consulate was increasingly formalized. When nationals abroad got into disputes with each other, consuls were charged with resolving those disputes. When nationals abroad needed to send letters home, consuls acted as postmen. When nationals abroad found themselves in conflict with locals, consuls acted as advocates for their nationals with local authorities. When nationals abroad found themselves the victim of injustices, consuls represented their interests and, if need be, forwarded their complaints up the administrative apparatus. Those nationals in the eighteenth century were, more often than not, sailors or merchants.[117]

By the late eighteenth century, the state increasingly intervened to protect sailors from the predations of foreign states and to guard their health and welfare from the travails of an unmoored life. When sailors were arrested or forced to serve upon a foreign vessel, it was to the consul they turned. But increasingly when sailors found themselves destitute and marooned, it was to the consul they turned.[118] In one famous tale of seamanship, Richard Henry Dana, Jr. recalled the ordeal of a fellow sailor with elephantine feet who found himself without clothes and without shoes during a frosty January in London. The shoeless sailor reported to the American consul, who provided him with a new set of clothes and found a cobbler to craft a pair of uncommonly large shoes for the sailor's uncommonly large feet.[119] Protection, however, extended to more than just shoes. Consulates ensured that sailors and merchants were provided for or returned home should they fall destitute while abroad. Furthermore, regulations in various countries provided for the care of seamen should they fall ill. Indeed within a few years of the ratification of the Constitution of the United States, that government levied a tax on all seamen's wages in order to pay "for the temporary relief and maintenance of sick or disabled seamen."[120] In addition to creating an account to pay for sick sailors, the bill also provided for the establishment of hospitals throughout the United States and abroad. The practice was even better developed in Europe. Nearly every country with a maritime presence made similar provisions to comply with the well-established principle of international law that discouraged states from throwing the burden of maintaining their destitute and sick subjects onto other governments. This principle, it should be noted, was not restricted to sailors.[121]

Palmerston's exclamation of "*civis Romanus sum*" bombastically heralded a new era for the international protection of people. The expansion of global trade, migration, investment, and the collapse of the Atlantic empires had made many more people into metaphorical sailors, plying the world's seas and marooned in foreign lands. As a result, consuls became increasingly concerned with the welfare of many more nationals. Writing in the middle of the nineteenth century, one consul described his role at its most basic as "the protector of his countrymen." But, a good consul, in his estimation, would do much more than simply protect his fellow nationals. A good consul "will see that they travel, or live in a foreign country, with the same security and peace, and that they are treated with all that respect and allowed to enjoy all that liberty, which the most favored of its own subjects enjoy."[122]

Indeed, by the late nineteenth century, political leaders were explicitly trying to formalize the protections offered to sailors abroad to the general public. President Ulysses S. Grant, for example, exhorted Congress to extend the protections that were offered to sailors to the general population:

> Congress from the beginning of the Government has wisely made provision for the relief of distressed seamen in foreign countries. No similar provision, however, has hitherto been made for the relief of citizens in distress abroad other than seamen. It is understood to be customary with other governments to authorize consuls to extend such relief to their citizens or subjects in certain cases. A similar authority and an appropriation to carry it into effect are recommended in the case of citizens of the United States destitute or sick under such circumstances. It is well known that such citizens resort to foreign countries in great numbers. Though most of them are able to bear the expenses incident to locomotion, there are some who, through accident or otherwise, become penniless, and have no friends at home able to succor them. Persons in this situation must either perish, cast themselves upon the charity of foreigners, or be relieved at the private charge of our own officers, who usually, even with the most benevolent dispositions, have nothing to spare for such purposes.[123]

Grant's exhortation failed to convince Congress to extend the social protections provided to sailors abroad to the general population. But it did not lessen the fact that more nationals were going abroad and falling upon hard times while far from traditional networks of support. Also, it was part of a larger transatlantic debate over the extent and nature of a state's responsibilities to its nationals abroad. Was it merely protection from the depredation and abuse of a foreign government or its officials? Or was it protection from illness and destitution?[124]

The transatlantic legal world of the late nineteenth century was one in which states could demand compensation for injuries to the physical person or physical property of their nationals through some sort of intentional wrong and provide for nationals abroad who had fallen on difficult times. The emphasis in both cases was on mobile human beings and their movable property. The purpose was to ensure that people could live and work without risk of discrimination, without the risk of lawlessness, and with the security of mind that, should something terrible happen, they had someone to whom they could turn in their time of need. While there were controversial aspects of international claims, they fit into a fairly conventional mode of protection.

But Palmerston's famous peroration was twinned with a subtler announcement related to international investment. In 1848, Palmerston issued a circular arguing that it was within Britain's discretion to protect bondholders from foreign defaults. "There can be no doubt whatever of the perfect right which the government of every country possesses to take up . . . any well-founded complaint which any of its subjects may proffer against the government of another country." Extending the logic from the individual abroad to an entire class, Palmerston argued that the state's right to intervene was not diminished simply because, "instead of there being one individual claiming a comparatively small sum, there are a great number of individuals to whom a very large amount is due."[125] But Palmerston had another point in his circular. This "perfect right" of the state to take up the complaint of one of its nationals was entirely discretionary. In Vattel's formulation, a sovereign was under a kind of obligation to avenge the wrong inflicted upon a national. Yet, in Palmerston's formulation, it was "simply a question of discretion" whether the claim of a national would become the subject of diplomatic intervention. If a few "imprudent men" lost their money on a bad investment, the government would consider it a teachable moment for investors – a bulwark against the moral hazard of having Britain's "strong arm" guarantee money loaned to poor governments at usurious rates. But should the investment become too big to fail, Palmerston warned, the British government was entirely within its rights to insist upon payment, and the "time may come when the British nation will not see with tranquility the sum of 150 millions due to British subjects, and the interest, not paid." And, as Palmerston ominously reminded the House of Commons, Britain certainly had the "means of enforcing the rights of British subjects."[126]

Palmerston's dual declarations served as a convenient marker and exposition of the logic of the new regime. British subjects would be protected from the failure of foreign states to adequately secure their territory, to prevent civil disturbance, and from the abuse of police power. But more than just the traditional protection of corporeal realm of people and property, diplomatic protection was moving further into the incorporeal realm of contracts and debts. British bondholders would be protected from the failure of foreign states to pay their bills. Britons who stayed at home could be sure that their money would be safe when it was sent abroad.

While the protection of merchants and travelers had always been one of the chief duties of consulates, after 1850 the general protection of nationals and their interests abroad increasingly became a central concern of foreign ministries themselves. The best illustration of the new orientation of foreign ministries is in the quantity and type of paperwork that piled up in their sparsely staffed offices. Beginning mid-century, foreign ministries were buried under an avalanche of correspondence relating to the protection of nationals abroad. The British Foreign Office, for example, saw its total number of dispatches double from 51,000 in 1849 to 102,000 in 1869.[127] In response, the Foreign Office peppered the Law Officers of the Crown with questions related to passports, nationality, naturalization, and protection.[128] In France, the picture was similar. With the increase in the number of French nationals living abroad came an expansion in the number of consuls and the scope of their duties; by the last decade of the nineteenth century, the directorate of Consulate and Trade Affairs was responsible for more than 70 percent of the correspondence flowing through the entire Ministry of Foreign Affairs.[129] The U.S. Department of State, unique among the world's major foreign ministries, kept a unified indexical record of all outstanding claims on behalf of individuals made either by or against the United States between 1900 and 1936. Requiring two archival staff members to lift, the record itself is a colossal, leather-and-wood-bound ledger containing more than 1,100 pages stacked more than 10 inches high. Each page – more than two feet in width – was capable of recording up to fifteen outstanding claims.[130] The size and weight bespeak the burden that foreign claims placed upon the State Department. Similarly, until the Office of the Legal Advisor replaced it, the U.S. Department of State relied upon the Solicitor, an advisor from the Department of Justice to weigh in on legal matters. In a report on the Solicitor's duties in 1911, the Department of State noted, "Owing to the almost continual increase of foreign enterprise, the number of claims and complaints lodged by American citizens (who have gone and are going to foreign countries in large numbers, and who have invested in such countries enormous amounts of capital) has become very great and is increasing."[131] The claims, which those citizens would file in the event of a problem, the same report noted, could run in excess of 2,000 pages.[132] The result was that by far the largest category of work undertaken by the chief legal advisor to the U.S. Department of State involved the protection of nationals and their investments abroad.[133]

The increased flow of paper through the foreign ministries cannot merely be attributed to the burgeoning of state bureaucracies. The French Foreign Ministry, the U.S. State Department, and the British Foreign Office had neither a comparable increase in staff nor a comparable increase in other activities.[134] Instead, the ocean of paper documents the increase in global migration, trade, and investment and demonstrates the heightened potential for conflicts in an age of global mobility. Each one of these complaints had the potential to lead to armed conflict.[135]

In 1868, Emperor Theodore of Ethiopia imprisoned several British nationals to use as hostages in negotiations for British support. News of the imprisonment circulated widely within the British press, as did letters from the hostages themselves. Public pressure mounted. In response, the British government launched a massive rescue operation. Thousands of troops were dispatched. Miles of railway tracks were laid. Miles of roads were paved. The capital of Abyssinia was sacked, and the hostages were freed.

Indeed, much (and perhaps most) of the rationales for military action in the nineteenth century could be traced to the protection of nationals and their property abroad. Between 1830 and 1900, the United States (the only major power to keep unified statistical use of force records) employed military force abroad more than seventy-five times. Nearly sixty of those instances were premised upon the protection of American nationals or property abroad or reprisals for uncompensated damages.[136] Britain, according to one scholar's count, employed military force in Latin America at least forty times between 1815 and 1914, of which twenty-six interventions were premised on the protection of British nationals and their property.[137] The Blockade of Athens, the Bombardment of Greytown, the Boer War, the Opium Wars, the British Occupation of Egypt, the Mexican–American War, the Third Anglo-Ashanti War, the Venezuelan Blockade, the American siege of Veracruz, the French invasion of Mexico, and the U.S. invasion of Cuba, just to name some of the many examples, were all justified with reference to the right to protect nationals and their property abroad. As President McKinley put it before the U.S. invasion of Cuba, "We owe it to our citizens in Cuba to afford them . . . protection."[138] On the other side, Enrique Enríquez, a delegate to Mexico's Constitutional Convention in 1917, thought that the property claims of foreign nationals caused most of Mexico's international conflicts.[139]

Likewise, the vast majority of international arbitrations between 1794 and 1945 were the result of disputes involving individuals. As mentioned, the Jay Treaty and even the treaties arising out of the Congress of Vienna were heavily concerned with compensating individuals harmed by a foreign state. But the trend accelerated in line with trade and commerce in the middle of nineteenth century. There were more than 200 uses of arbitration to deal with disputes involving individual issues between 1845 and 1914.[140] In 1899, the Peace Conference held at The Hague called for the establishment of a Permanent Court of Arbitration to supplement the ad hoc tribunals that had been common in the nineteenth century. Between 1902 and 1914, the fledgling court heard fourteen cases. Of those fourteen cases, nine involved complaints of injured nationals.[141]

Similarly, between 1845 and 1945, excluding the numerous tribunals established after the First World War, there were more than sixty mixed claims commissions established as part of arbitral agreements. Many of these tribunals dealt with hundreds or thousands of individual claims. The 1923 claims commission between Mexico and the United States, for example, heard 3,617 cases.[142] Such was the caseload of each commission that by the end of the nineteenth century the vast majority of written decisions of an international character involved individuals – not high affairs of state. Owing to the vast storehouse of case law that emerged out of these tribunals, a prominent international jurist argued, "The international law governing the responsibility of states for injuries to aliens [became] one of the most highly developed branches of [international] law."[143] But even outside of the elaborate claims commissions, which were established to remedy large numbers of disputes between two or more states, many tribunals were set up, like that established during the Pacifico affair, to hear individual conflicts that arose between states over wrongs done to their subjects. In short, the claims of individuals or groups of individuals were tied to the explosion in the use of arbitration in the second half of the nineteenth century.[144]

Treatises and legal research reflected this new emphasis on individuals. Prior to the second half of the nineteenth century, treatment of the protection of nationals abroad or the responsibility of states was constrained to small sections of consular manuals or included only as a part of a more general treatise on international law. By the 1890s, the first legal treatises exclusively on the subject began to appear en masse (or at least as en masse as can be in the world of legal publishing). Edmond Pittard, the future Swiss delegate to the League of Nations, authored the first as his dissertation.[145] Several works followed,[146] with Anzilotti's *Teoria generalla della responnsabilita dello stato nel diritto internazionale* being the most influential owing to the author's prominent position within the Institute of International Law.[147] This turn-of-the-century academic interest in the subject culminated with the publication of Edwin Borchard's *The Diplomatic Protection of Nationals Abroad* in 1915.[148] At more than 1,000 pages, it is still the longest treatment of the subject.

These works on diplomatic protection and state responsibility were accompanied by the release of several massive compendia containing all the decisions of international arbitral tribunals convened since the Jay Treaty.[149] Many of the cases contained within these compendia involved sovereign bond defaults or the repudiation of concessions granted to foreigners and fit in with a narrative of informal economic imperialism. Many of the cases, however, involved the protection of individual civil rights – protection from arrest, destruction of property, prolonged detainment. The complaint of a British whaler improperly arrested and detained by the Dutch received attention, and he was awarded compensation.[150] The complaint by a British trade unionist of improper arrest and expulsion by Belgium received ample attention, with the case arbitrated by an expert from the Institute of International Law.[151] Cases like these were common and handled systematically by foreign ministries. As Elihu Root, the American Secretary of State from 1905 to 1909 and an internationally renowned scholar of international law, noted in an address to the American Society of International Law:

> The diplomatic history of this country presents a long and painful series of outrages on foreigners by mob violence.... [D]efenseless Chinamen were mobbed at Denver in 1880, and at Rock Springs, Wyoming, in 1885; Italians were lynched in New Orleans in 1891, and again at Rouse, Colorado, in 1895; and Mexicans were lynched at Yreka, California, in 1895; and Italians at Tallulah, Louisiana, in 1899, and again at Erwin, Mississippi, in 1901. Our Government was practically defenseless against claims for indemnity because of our failure to extend over these aliens the same protection that we extend over our own citizens, and the final result of long diplomatic correspondence in each case was the payment of indemnity for the real reason that we had not performed our international duty.[152]

All of this is indicative of an extensive regime of protection that had built up over the course of the nineteenth century. Disputes between states involving the improper arrest, detention, imprisonment, expulsion, personal injury, or even death as a result of negligence of state authorities were resolved by reference to a clear, collectively agreed upon procedure throughout much of the Atlantic world.[153] The process was not invented anew with each and every dispute. An injured national would file a complaint with his or her consulate. The consulate would, if the complaint were valid, forward it on to the bureaucrats of the foreign ministry. Lawyers – like the Law Officers of the Crown, the Solicitor at the U.S. Department of State, or the Ottoman Office of Legal Counsel – would offer a legal opinion. If a resolution was not readily available, arbitration might be had, either in a single hearing or through the use of a standing mixed commission. Cases were quietly adjudicated, and money was distributed. Disputes involving sovereign default and expropriation were resolved by reference to the same procedure.[154] The protection of migrants and sojourners and the protection of merchants and investors involved the same institutions, the same procedures, and the same set of practices. The exercise of the sovereign authority to avenge an injury to a national had been regularized and turned into a legal process that mediated competing claims over human beings. It also effectively created an international realm of legal protection. As long as someone had nationality, they could enjoy the rights and protections of international law. Nationality, as one German put it, was a necessary condition of *völkerrechtliche Indigenat*, more clumsily expressed in English as international legal indigenousness, or put another way, a necessary condition of belonging to the international community.[155]

Writing in 1915, Borchard described the principle of diplomatic protection as it then existed:

> The bond of citizenship implies that the state watches over its citizens abroad, and reserves the right to interpose actively in their behalf in an appropriate case. Too severe an assertion of territorial control over them by the state of residence will be met by the emergence of the protective right of the national state.... The principles of territorial jurisdiction and personal sovereignty are mutually corrective forces. An excessive application of the territorial principle is limited by the custom which grants foreign states certain rights over their citizens abroad, sometimes merely the application of foreign law by the local courts, sometimes, in acknowledgement of the principle of protection, a certain amount of jurisdiction.[156]

While it was assumed the system worked, near the turn of the twentieth century, there were those who hoped that the diffusion of legal principles around the world would reduce the need for such intervention. In 1910, one legal scholar observed, "One of the notable results of increasing civilization has been the ever-growing recognition of the rights of the stranger. The more completely such rights are recognized and vindicated by internal authorities and tribunals, the less occasion there is for result to external diplomatic pressure, and the less danger there is of international friction."[157]

The Problem with Diplomatic Protection

This system, however, was not without controversy. States under this regime had become legal advocates, mutually enforcing standards of state behavior and expectations. Yet that advocacy was discretionary. Some of the earliest treatise writers on the subject of diplomatic protection as a procedure or on the responsibility of states as a set of legal norms noticed the potential for trouble. Edmond Pittard, the author of the first treatise dedicated to the subject, took note of the potential pitfalls:

> The protection of nationals abroad is a dangerous weapon in the hand of states... it frequently happens that protection is only a pretext and that the true object of the intervention reveals itself only after the intervening state has made a serious attack on the rights of another state. Oppression hides itself under protection.[158]

Similar critiques, especially with regard to the European application of the principle in Latin America, appeared in writings on diplomatic law.[159]

But it was the work of Carlos Calvo that came to most famously embody the critique. Calvo was the most prominent Latin American jurist of the nineteenth century and the only founding member of both the Institute of International Law and the International Law Association who had not been from Europe or the United States. For a while, he, therefore, was the only representative of the legal perspectives of Latin America in these influential organization.

The states of Latin America had been the target of an overwhelming number of complaints.[160] The privilege of being a part of international society meant that the Latin American states could not be formally integrated into European empires. Their sovereignty was to be, at least formally, respected. Furthermore, because the legal systems of Latin America were essentially the same as the legal systems of Europe, the claim of "backwardness" that had served as a rationale for European and American extraterritorial jurisdiction over their nationals in the Ottoman Empire, Japan, and China, was inapplicable. Instead, states made reference to the "Standards of Civilization;" that is, the standards of protection for the personal safety and personal property that was required by all members of the international society of which Latin American formed a part.[161] As Borchard put it:

[States] are admitted into the international legal community on condition that they... manifest their power to exercise jurisdiction effectively and... to assure foreigners within it of a minimum of rights.... In countries which habitually maintain effective government, the protective function of the national government of a resident alien is usually limited to calling the attention of the local government to the performance of its international duty. The right, however, is always reserved, and in the case of less stable and well-ordered governments frequently exercised, of taking more effective measures to secure their citizens abroad a measure of fair treatment conforming to the international standard of justice.[162]

The endemic political and civil unrest and the resulting judicial irregularities in Latin America provided plenty of pretext for those looking to extricate commercial claims from Latin American courts and place them in the international legal sphere where they would be judged using European standards of property rights, protection, and contractual supremacy.

Calvo, in his treatise on international law, increasingly critiqued the system of diplomatic protection, arbitration, and military intervention. The first object of his critique was with the standards that were used to determine when a state's treatment of a foreigner rose to the level of a breach of international duty. In determining when they could justly levy a complaint on behalf of a national, Europeans made reference to the "Standards of Civilization," as the threshold for determining when diplomatic protection was warranted.[163] These standards for civil and property rights were set with reference to European practices. Calvo, in his opposition, articulated a standard that established the level at "national treatment;" that is, a foreigner should expect standards of policing that were neither better nor worse than what a national could expect. If that treatment fell below the national level, the foreigner was obligated to first go to the local courts to seek justice for the harm. Under Calvo's scheme, only when (1) a foreigner's treatment by the state fell below that of nationals and (2) he had exhausted local remedies and (3) in exhausting those local remedies suffered a denial of justice was there a breach of an international duty that warranted the mobilization of diplomatic protection.[164]

***

One of the most persistent criticisms levied against Don Pacifico was that he was not *really* British. He had spent much of his life in service to a foreign crown and had lived in foreign lands. It was this difficulty, not the "Standards of Civilization" or the procedure, but the determination of *nationality* that would befuddle international jurists and fundamentally alter international law. The Vattelian fiction was premised on the idea that the injured national was a member of the body politic, or as Grotius put it, that the national was a "part of Him who governs."[165] Vattel likewise argued that it was an international wrong to "injure a foreign nation either in its body or its members."[166] This relationship was based on the correlation of allegiance and protection that bound a sovereign to his subjects. It was this link that made the regime function in theory. It was this link that aided in the management of a global age. It was this link that transfigured the protective walls of the state into the personal armor of its nationals. But it was also this link that a global age began to strain.

2 Making Nations, Breaking Nationality

> The United States, when they receive a man to citizenship, require of him a renunciation of all other allegiance. They would as soon tolerate a man with two wives as a man with two countries; as soon bear with polygamy as that state of double allegiance which common sense so repudiates that it has not even coined a world to express it. A slave cannot have two masters; nor a freeman two lieges.
>
> George Bancroft, 1849.[1]

On January 21, 1847, Alexander Herzen alighted from his sledge and plunged his feet with a crunch into the white snow.[2] He stood in Chërnaya Gryaz, a small town on the Russo-Prussian frontier. Behind him, marking the domain of the Romanovs, stood a milestone marked with a double-headed eagle. Before him was a checkpoint, the last in Russia. A "little old soldier in a clumsy shako covered with oilskin, carrying a rifle" checked Herzen's documents and, finding everything in order, lifted the barrier to let the sledge pass. Herzen bid a tearful farewell to the friends who had accompanied him to the border. The sledge glided onward, and Herzen, at last, passed out of the domain of the Romanovs. Before him now stood a milestone marked with the single-headed eagle of the Hohenzollerns. As he looked at it he thought to himself, "That's a good thing: one head less."[3]

At last Herzen had left Russia with his family. For two long years, Herzen, a romantic Russian intellectual and aspiring revolutionary, had pleaded in vain for permission to leave the Russian Empire.[4] Following the intervention of some influential friends, he was finally granted a passport, the key to getting that "little old soldier" in Chërnaya Gryaz to raise the gate and let him depart the domains of the Romanovs. The passport, a relatively anomalous document at the time in much of Western Europe, was required for exiting Russia, and Herzen's was valid for only six months.

While in Europe, Herzen became passionately involved in the revolutionary romance that was gripping the continent. As one of the only major Russian intellectuals in the West, he became the default representative of revolutionary Russian thought.[5] And he used his liberty abroad to support the ideas of revolutionary intellectuals in Russia. Writing to his friends back in Moscow, Herzen declared, "Here I am your uncensored voice, your free press, your chance representative."[6] Unsurprisingly, the Tsar was unhappy. Over the next several years, Herzen became the target of the Tsar's persecutions. In 1849, the Russian government attempted to deprive him of his property *in absentia* by refusing to transfer his money abroad – a predicament that took the significant influence of the Rothschild banking house to resolve. In September of the next year, the Tsar demanded that Herzen return to Russia. The would-be revolutionary curtly rebuffed the order, and by December, the Tsar had exiled Herzen and deprived him of all his remaining property in Russia.[7] Herzen was no longer legally a Russian. But he wasn't anything else either. Herzen was effectively stateless.

But in contrast to the horror that statelessness would represent in the twentieth century, the problem of being without a state in the nineteenth century was more of a temporary irritation than an existential crisis. To obtain the protection of another state and to find his way "out of the category of people without a passport," Herzen, like many other Europeans in that liberal century, shopped for a new legal nationality. Indeed, he could have gone almost anywhere.[8] But Herzen, having had quite enough of monarchs, did not want to be a "subject," a desire that severely limited his options within monarch-infested Europe. Herzen pondered. He considered America – that land of republican liberty – but was turned off by an observation made by Giuseppe Garibaldi, the Italian nationalist, that America was "a land for forgetting one's own."[9] Herzen, who was both a romantic nationalist and a dedicated reformer, had no intention of forgetting his own and had every intention of triumphantly returning to Russia to aid in forging a new future for the Russian people.[10] Herzen settled on neutral Switzerland. Reflecting later upon his choice, Herzen declared, "Except for Swiss naturalization, I would not have accepted citizenship in any European country, not even England."[11] So, in the summer of 1851, he made his way to Châtel, a small town in the foothills of the Alps, where he took up lodgings. After a short residence and, perhaps most importantly, the deposit of 25,000 francs in a local bank,[12] Herzen became a citizen of Friebourg and a Swiss national.[13]

During a banquet held in the otherwise sleepy town of Châtel to honor the conferral of his Swiss nationality, Herzen made a speech in which he thanked his fellow citizens for welcoming him. But, he declared, he had not left his "native land to seek another."[14] Indeed, Herzen had absolutely no intention of remaining in Switzerland permanently. Nor did he think of naturalization as marking an end to his Russian identity or potentially preventing his return to Russian to aid in its reform. "Naturalisation... is no hindrance at all to a career at home," wrote Herzen with characteristic humility, "I have two illustrious examples before my eyes: Louis Bonaparte... and Alexander Nikolayevich..., both became emperors after their naturalization. I am not going so far as that."[15] For Herzen, as it was for many others in a globalizing world, nationality was a legal tool as much as it was an identity.

In an era of mass movement and relatively liberal processes of naturalization, dual nationality became increasingly common. Herzen, like many others, benefited from the relatively unrestrictive naturalization regimes of the nineteenth century. It did not take much for Herzen to become a Swiss national, he only needed to convince the small village of Châtel to adopt him as a resident, which he was able to do through the offer of a small monetary contribution;[16] however, it would take a far more significant deposit in the Bank of Friebourg to grease the stickier Cantonal wheels.[17] Throughout Europe, small states made naturalization easy. In San Marino, like in Friebourg, nationality could be painlessly purchased by those with means. Nationality could be found even more easily in the Western Hemisphere where states were actively competing for immigrants and thus made naturalizing relatively easy.[18]

In the late nineteenth century, naturalization was easy in the Western Hemisphere. But, in contrast to the twentieth century, naturalization was in no way required to live a relatively full life in most places. Herzen wanted to naturalize precisely because he had been exiled and had no effective nationality. But for many migrants, naturalization was of little concern so long as they retained the nationality of their place of birth. At the end of the nineteenth century, there were fewer *domestic* social or economic privileges associated with being a citizen, subject, or national of a state than today. In many of the countries of the Atlantic world, aliens could often own real property, sometimes vote in elections, and sue and be sued in courts of law.[19] Also, aliens were not excluded from expansive statewide welfare programs because these programs didn't exist. The "Standards of Civilization" required that all states both respect and protect the person and property of duly admitted aliens.[20] At a minimum, international law required that aliens be granted the same protection of person and property that a state accorded to its own nationals, a rule that even the most vocal critics of those international standards acknowledged.[21] Indeed, aliens had more protection. If foreigners felt that they had been denied justice in domestic courts of law, they had a further remedy – they could run to their nearest consul and ask for intervention and protection, a privilege that their naturalized and native neighbors certainly did not have.

That aliens had this recourse was one of the biggest geopolitical problems facing the Atlantic world. Millions of migrants left their homes and settled elsewhere over the course of the nineteenth century. Millions would naturalize and obtain two, three, or even more nationalities. But millions would choose not to, living out their days as foreigners. Every problem that one of these millions of human beings found themselves in had the potential of escalating into an international conflict. And, indeed, many occasionally did. What has gone without substantial comment was that *nearly* every trans-hemispheric conflict in the nineteenth century (that was not explicitly an independence movement) involved the protection of nationals abroad. Whether protecting a national was the central motivating reason for an intervention is certainly debatable. And it probably goes without saying that in many[22] cases, the protection of a national was a pretext for some other political or economic ambition.[23] And one does not often have to search far to find an unsavory answer to the question: why protect *this* national? But that doesn't change the fact that the language of protection, like the language of human rights in the late twentieth century, provided *a legitimate* pretext for intervention – perhaps *the* legitimate pretext for intervention.[24]

At the root of this problem was the bond of allegiance that tied a person to his or her state. How did that bond form? What happened to that bond when a person lived far beyond the boundaries of his or her state? In a world of migration, trade, and international investment, how would that bond be defined? This chapter is about that bond of allegiance and how it was reconceptualized in an age of globalization. In it I make three arguments. First, that the collapse of the mercantilist empires in the late eighteenth and early nineteenth centuries created a crisis of allegiance in which bonds were multiplied and stretched, entangling international politics. Second, that both people and corporations instrumentalized their nationality as a way to obtain a kind of insurance in a volatile world. Third, several states and the international law community recognized this instrumentalization and attempted to curb it only to run into irreconcilable hemispheric disputes over how to define nationality. This irreconcilable hemispheric dispute effectively destroyed nationality as a form of viable protection in a globalized world and would lead to the proliferation of international legal regimes in the twentieth century.

Nationality's Many Meanings

There are many words in the English language that denote the link between a person and a sovereign: subjecthood, allegiance, citizenship, and nationality are some that might spring to your mind. Yet there's no English word that denotes the link between people and their sovereign in its purest sense. Subjecthood and allegiance connote subjugation and feudal obligation. Citizenship denotes a link that carries with it the right to participate in the political community. Nationality can denote a link to a sovereign people, to a nation.[25] Other European languages have a similar problem. The French *citoyenité* and *nationalité* share denotations and connotations with their English cognates, as does the Spanish *ciudadano* and *nacionalidad*. There are some exceptions. The German *staatsangehörigkeit*, loosely translated as the quality of belonging to a state, is perhaps the closest to a neutral term that I could find in the languages of Western Europe.[26]

Part of the reason for this linguistic confusion is the double character of any relationship between a state and its subjects. There is an internal identity – the relationship of a subject to his or her state from the perspective of the state. But there is also an external identity – the relationship of a subject to his or her state from the perspective of other states or sovereigns. As Edwin Borchard put it, citizenship in domestic law and nationality in international law are "not necessarily coextensive terms."[27] Few languages or writers have been attentive to that distinction, and no term survives long before its inevitable muddling. Paul Weiss, one of the preeminent modern scholars of the subject, notes this problem as well, arguing, "Conceptually and linguistically, [nationality and citizenship] emphasize two different aspects of the same notion.... 'Nationality' stresses the international, 'citizenship' the national, municipal aspect."[28] While Weiss is correct in that today nationality can denote the simple link between a person and his or her sovereign, that denotation, free of the conceptual baggage of its etymological relation, "nation," is true only in the field of international jurisprudence and only in the second half of the twentieth century, when the nation-state became normalized.

That "nationality" and "national" would end up being the words used in French and English – the languages of international law in the twentieth century – to describe the relationship between a human being and his or her sovereign was not a foregone conclusion. "Nationality" is a word of French origin, and in the nineteenth century, it was a word of relatively recent origin. George Cogordon, the preeminent French scholar on nationality, noted in 1876 that "this word... is of recent origin in our language," before he cited the word's first appearance in the 1835

Dictionnaire de l'Académie Française.[29] The word had been in use before the dictionary entry and entered the English lexicon with its legal denotation in the mid-eighteenth century, but it was used rarely until the mid-nineteenth century.[30] Its French counterpart first appeared in a dictionary in 1735[31] but did not take on a legal flavor until the first decade of the nineteenth century.[32] "National" is of an even more recent vintage than "nationality." As late as 1924, it was possible for a legal scholar to note, "There is no word at all that describes membership of a nation. Diplomatic documents sometimes speak of 'nationals'; but the term is not in general use, and in any case it only refers to membership of a body politic without any reference to its character."[33] Likewise, Ernest Mason Satow, author of the breviary of modern diplomatic practitioners, opined, "We sometimes find [the French term national] simply adopted as an English word, but surely it is not desirable to introduce neologisms into our own language which are understood only by the initiated."[34]

When Vattel and other eighteenth- and nineteenth-century jurists described the link between a subject and his or her sovereign, it was often (although not nearly always) done in the language of allegiance and subjecthood, not in the contemporary language of nationality.[35] In an age of social contract theory, rather than a single word denoting the link, the correlative and logically circular relationship between allegiance and protection was instead often described.[36] Sovereigns were sovereign because they protected their subjects. Subjects were subjects because they were under the protection of a sovereign.[37]

For most of the eighteenth century, the children of Europe and the Americas[38] were born as subjects.[39] They emerged into the world swaddled in the protection of their sovereign, to whom they owed a debt of allegiance in exchange.[40] That debt, in the words of William Blackstone, "[could not] be forfeited, cancelled, or altered, by any change of time, place, or circumstance."[41] One could not throw off his allegiance at will, nor could one easily pledge allegiance to another sovereign. Allegiance was *nearly* immutable so long as a sovereign provided protection.[42]

In a mercantilist age this state of affairs did not pose much of a problem. The state of the sixteenth and seventeenth centuries had identified its power and vitality with the numerical maintenance of its human, monetary, and physical resources. To deter migration, state authorities operated restrictive regimes upon the bodies and minds of their subjects by closely regulating the freedom of exit and forbidding the voluntary alienation of allegiance or expatriation. All over Europe, from Sweden to Italy, from Spain to Russia, state authorities attempted to prevent emigration. They required passports to exit. They colluded with religious authorities to emphasize the sinfulness of emigration. They published propaganda detailing the dangers of the Atlantic passage. They imposed legal sanctions that often included the loss of economic and political rights upon those who dared to leave. They threatened imprisonment upon return. And the political theorists of the age – Grotius, Pufendorf, Wolff (and to a lesser extend Blackstone and Vattel) – aided states in providing *some* intellectual justification for the restrictions. The walls of the state could imprison as well as repel.[43]

To deter foreign trade, state authorities operated restrictive regimes upon the shipment of goods and the exploitation of natural resources. Shortly after establishing a new lucrative sea route to Asia, the Portuguese established the *Casa de India* (India House) to control access to the trade. Within 10 years of Columbus' return from the West Indies, the Spanish had established a similar institution, the *Casa de la Contratación* (House of Trade), to control trade with Spain's burgeoning empire in the New World. Britain played that game as well with its Navigation Acts, which strictly limited trade with the American Colonies.[44]

People and goods crisscrossed the Atlantic, but did so within empires. The British primarily traded with, and migrated to, British Colonies. The Spanish primarily traded with, and migrated to, Spanish Colonies. The French primarily traded with, and migrated to, French Colonies.[45] Being "abroad" in the sense of being outside the domains of one's sovereign was a rare occurrence. But even in an age of global trade and transatlantic settlement, when subjects moved beyond the frontiers of their sovereign, it was usually clear to whom they owed allegiance. Language and custom set apart the subjects of one monarch from those of another. Even on ships – perhaps the most cosmopolitan of spaces in the eighteenth century – sailors were readily identifiable based upon accents, language, and behavior.[46] There was no need for identification papers when a single utterance betrayed one's place of origin. There was, to borrow another historian's phrase, a "common sense of nationality."[47] Legal identity was stable and dual allegiance was almost nonexistent. A person had one – and only one – allegiance from the perspective of international law and that allegiance was readily identifiable in the Atlantic world.[48] But that all began to change at the end of the eighteenth century with the fracturing of the Atlantic empires.

Although allegiance was practically inalienable, it was a well-accepted principle that a sovereign could punish disobedient subjects by placing them outside of its protection. This was the sovereign's prerogative. And there are innumerable examples of sovereigns banishing, exiling, and refusing to protect subjects outside of the realm.[49] Traditionally, there was no way for subjects to alienate their allegiance.[50] Although, for practical reasons, living outside the sovereign's realm for long enough was recognized as a kind of de facto renunciation.[51]

But, by the middle of the eighteenth century, following on the work of John Locke and others, theorists of the social contract began to argue that subjects owed sovereigns allegiance only insofar as they provided protection and that should sovereigns fail to provide protection, subjects would no longer owe them allegiance.[52] Emer de Vattel, whom readers might remember from the first chapter, was the most widely read international legal theorist among the prominent agitators in colonial North America. He argued that a person had an "absolute right to renounce his country and abandon it entirely."[53] That right, Vattel continued, was "founded on reasons derived from the very nature of the social compact."[54] For Vattel, perpetual allegiance was an absurdity. If a sovereign failed to uphold its end of the social bargain, there was no reason why its subjects should still be required to fulfill their end. As Vattel put it, "For if one of the contracting parties does not observe his engagements, the other is no longer bound to fulfil [sic] his; for the contract is reciprocal between the society and its members."[55]

The Declaration of Independence and the war that followed severed the reciprocal bonds of allegiance and protection between the English King and more than two million of his subjects in the North American colonies – proving, at least in practice, that allegiance was not perpetual.[56] In the lead up to their rebellion, the British colonists in North America echoed Locke, Vattel, and others and articulated the principle that a failure to provide protection was a rationale for declaring independence.[57] George III helped in making the intellectual case for separation when he gave his royal assent to the Prohibitory Acts, which placed the colonies outside the protection of the Crown.[58] That action enabled the former colonies, when declaring themselves to be "free and independent States," to argue that the King had "abdicated government here by declaring us out of his protection."[59] The subsequent state constitutions made similar arguments. New Jersey declared in its constitution, "Allegiance and protection are, in the nature of things, reciprocal ties, each equally depending upon the other, and liable to be dissolved by the other's being refused or withdrawn."[60] North Carolina, likewise, argued, "Allegiance and protection are, in their nature, reciprocal, and the one should of right be refused when the other is withdrawn."[61]

The British government did not agree. The dispute was arbitrated via arms and at Yorktown the world turned upside down when the judgment came down in favor of the Americans.

The Challenge of the Americas

With the recognition of the United States as thirteen independent sovereigns, the cultural and political boundaries of the Atlantic empires crumbled. The King's English was now spoken in fourteen states instead of one empire. Whereas the Atlantic had been surrounded by monarchs, it was now bounded in the west by thirteen young republics. The tradition of perpetual allegiance had no power over the legislatures of the thirteen former colonies that had rebelled against their sovereign lord. For many colonial intellectuals, the reciprocal relationship between sovereign and subject was contractual. Thomas Jefferson, for example, held that "the right of expatriation to be inherent in every man by the laws of nature."[62] Jefferson's views made their way into the laws of the Commonwealth of Virginia.[63] And the expatriation revolution did not end there. Over the next several decades, influential intellectuals would take up the issue. The French Philosopher Antoine Louis Claude, for example, argued in 1817, "Expatriation should always be permitted."[64] Law and practice, in some respects, followed theory. Beginning in 1776, each of the newly independent states of the United States began to declare expatriation, the renunciation of allegiance, a right.[65] Likewise, the French Civil Code of 1804 provided four avenues for expatriation and the loss of "the quality of being a Frenchmen." Among these avenues was "naturalization in a foreign country."[66] Napoleon carried that code and its provisions across Europe over the next eleven years.

Despite these declarations, codes, and theoretical exclamations, expatriation was far from a universally recognized right. While many of the United States and many of their officials had declared expatriation a right, *the* United States did not provide a clear statutory path to renounce allegiance until near the end of the following century.[67] Britain, likewise, remained a stubborn adherent to the doctrine of perpetual allegiance until late into the nineteenth century. Expatriation's legal status in the Atlantic world was uncertain. Once one was in a reciprocal relationship with a sovereign, one was still often in it for life.

Yet naturalization became exceedingly easy in the Western Hemisphere. The mercantilist empires in North America had all severely limited emigration from and immigration to their colonies, and there were little or no naturalization opportunities. Britain's policy on naturalization and migration had been one of the many grievances cited by the United States in the Declaration of Independence. "[The King] has endeavoured," the Declaration read, "to prevent the population of these States; for that purpose obstructing the Laws for Naturalization of Foreigners; refusing to pass others to encourage their migrations hither."

While the British colonists cited the policy as one of their grievances, the restrictions on immigration imposed by the British were no harsher than those Spain imposed on its American colonies. In Spanish America, the immigration of foreigners (non-Spanish subjects) was forbidden in general (although there were some rare exceptions).[68] France too prevented migration to its North American colonies. Britain, France, Spain, several German states, and even Switzerland (to an extent) all followed the same mercantilist logic. But that mercantilist age was coming to a close.[69]

With independence, the United States implemented an exceedingly easy naturalization policy.[70] With the first Naturalization Act, "any alien, being a free white person" could become a citizen after having been a resident just two years.[71] The requirement was raised to five years in 1795.[72] But even those relatively lax requirements were easily dispensed with. Prior to the twentieth century, naturalization was carried out by judges, not by a central administration, and obtaining a certificate of naturalization required little more than the applicant to declare under oath that he had resided in the United States for at least five years.[73] There was no real bureaucracy to verify such claims, and by the twentieth century, officials frequently complained of fraud.[74] Even so, that was all that was required to become a *citizen*. But what about a *national* entitled to protection abroad? Here, the United States was again exceedingly lax. The 1795 Naturalization Act required applicants to take an oath before a judge declaring their intent to naturalize.[75] As part of that oath, the act required that they "renounce forever all allegiance and fidelity to any foreign prince, potentate, state or sovereignty."[76] While it did not provide *citizenship*, the mere declaration of the intent to become a citizen was enough to warrant protection abroad by US consuls – or, to use modern technical parlance, the mere declaration was enough to become an American *national*.[77]

As the states of Latin America, one by one, gained their independence, they too adopted laws to make naturalization easy for those who came to their shores.[78] The governing elites of Latin America, in an attempt to encourage immigration, crafted policies that often included free passage for Europeans willing to settle or work on plantations.[79]

Moreover, what Aristide Zolberg has called the "exit revolution" was in full swing in the mid-nineteenth century as more and more states ended mercantilist restrictions on *emigration*, albeit without the right of expatriation.[80] The German states took an increasingly pro-emigration stand following the revolutions of 1848. Spain liberalized its emigration in 1853. Italy freely allowed emigration from its inception in the 1860s.[81]

With relatively easy naturalization and increasingly lax policies on emigration, the number of human beings in the Atlantic world with two (or more) allegiances began to grow. For nearly a century after independence, the United States and Great Britain would fall into disputes again and again over the question of allegiance and of the mutual obligations of allegiance and protection.

But the problem affected more than just the United States and Britain.

Migration and Dual Allegiance

The nineteenth century was an age of migration. Millions of Europeans sailed and steamed for the Western Hemisphere, settling in the new republics that lined the western shore of the Atlantic. Between 1846 and 1940, 55 to 58 million people from Europe, along with another 2.5 million from India, China, Japan, and Africa, emigrated to the Americas.[82] In the decade before the outbreak of World War I, more people made their way to the New World than in the entirety of the colonial period – a flow of humanity that, at this writing, is still unmatched as a percentage of the global population.[83] To put into relative perspective just how many foreign nationals were making their way to cities in the Western Hemisphere, in any given decade between 1865 and 1914 nearly half of the population of Buenos Aires and New York City was foreign born with upwards of 80 percent being either foreign born or the children of foreigners.[84]

Nineteenth century migration, moreover, was not merely transatlantic – similar numbers of people migrated around the Indian Ocean and Pacific Rims. Between 48 and 52 million people from India and southern China, along with another 4 million from Africa, Europe, the Middle East, and Asia emigrated to Southeast Asia.[85]

But it was an era of *migration*, not merely emigration. With long-distance oceanic fares dropping steadily, long-distance return migration was frequent, and even seasonal.[86] By 1900 it took less than a week to make the New York–Hamburg run, and fares ran between 20 and 30 USD, which would equate to a real price of 582 to 874 USD or a real value of 1,740 to 2,210 USD in 2015. It was an expensive purchase, but a price within reach of the average European worker.[87] Indeed, Alfred Stieglitz's iconic photograph of transatlantic migration, *The Steerage*, was taken aboard the ship *Kaiser Wilhelm II* as it was *returning* to Europe from New York.[88] To give a sense of scale to the level of return migration, between 1860 and 1910 the number of departures from Argentina to Italy was roughly 50 percent of the number of arrivals to Argentina from Italy. Between 1910 and 1920, the number of departures from Argentina was more than 100 percent the number of arrivals, meaning that more Italians were leaving Argentina to return to Italy than were arriving.[89] While there is no hard data on the motivations for the return, it is possible that the Italians flooding back to Italy in the 1910s were patriotically answering the call to mobilize for war (loyalties did, indeed, seem to span oceans). As people traversed the seas, the threads of allegiance that bound subjects to sovereigns unspooled and stretched from country to country and continent to continent. And as some of those migrants naturalized, the threads multiplied and snarled.

Making Nations in an Age of Migration

This age of migration was a strange time to be making nation-states. Yet it was an age of nation building. The railways, roadways, and seaways that linked city to town to country all quickly crossed frontiers and linked state to state. And upon those rails, roads, and seas the very communities whence the nation-state derived its legitimacy were scattered across the globe. Nationalist movements were taking hold across Europe just as the mass emigration across the Atlantic began.[90]

The relationship between nationalists and emigrants was ambiguous. Some interpreted the loss of tens of thousands of compatriots per year as a vital threat to the continued prosperity of the nation. Giuseppe Garibaldi, you might recall, had himself lamented to his friend Alexander Herzen that America was "a land for forgetting one's own."[91] Yet others saw an opportunity in emigration to strengthen a nation by spreading beyond its territory and to turn émigré peasants into Italians, Germans, Czechs, and Poles. Confronted with millions leaving their homelands, nationalists responded by trying to tighten and multiply the cultural, economic, and legal threads that bound people to their nation and state. Francesco Crispi, a compatriot of Mazzini and Garibaldi and a user of the phrase *civis Romanus sum*, wrote that emigrants "must be like arms which a country extends far away into foreign places to draw them into its orbit of labor and exchange relations; they must be like an enlargement of the boundaries of its actions and its economic power."[92]

One manifestation of this attempt to bind emigrants to their state was through state-directed colonialism. Undirected emigration might waste vital national resources and potentially dilute a nation's cultural and economic power through the assimilation of emigrants into their new societies. But, directed emigration presented an opportunity to establish little Germanys in Missouri, Little Czech enclaves in Ohio, or little Italys in Argentina. While modern states might have had territorial limits, nations did not.

For example, between 1820 and 1840, Germany saw its number of emigrants increase by an order of magnitude from 3,000 departures per year to more than 30,000. By 1850, the number of annual departures topped 80,000.[93] During the 1848 revolutions, mass emigration was taken up by the Frankfurt Parliament.[94] Legislation was passed to protect emigrants from abusive emigration agents and to establish and maintain consulates abroad where Germans abroad might seek assistance.[95] Individual German states, likewise, attempted to establish programs to group emigrants together, encourage emigrants to establish German communities abroad together, and maintain connections with those communities, so they might resist assimilation as well as provide valuable economic connections for Germany. In effect, these communities were attempting de facto "colonization" because geopolitical exigencies had denied them de jure colonies.[96] Bradley Naranch, in his essay, *Inventing the Auslandsdeutsch*, observes that in the decades following 1848, *auslandsdeutsche*, translated as "German abroad," increasingly replaced the older term *auswanderer*, translated as "one who wanders out." *Auslandsdeutsche* was a more capacious category that could include emigrants as well as peoples of German descent whose ancestors had left the homeland long ago. The term "[endorsed] a general incorruptibility and spiritual unity of the German people as an ethnically homogenous population" even as they wandered the globe.[97] It also mirrored an accelerating trend within the German states to define citizenship by reference to blood descent, or *jus sanguinis*, in order to maintain legal ties to the German diaspora.[98]

Many other European countries with mass emigrations followed Germany's lead.[99] Some states began to include their emigrants in their national census.[100] Others implemented blood descent citizenship laws to ensure that those born abroad were not lost to the motherland.[101] States also expanded nascent social welfare protections to ensure that emigrants were not swindled and doomed to a life of unregulated toil in the factories of New York or the plantations of Brazil.[102] And the expansion in the number of consulates and foreign cultural organizations continued apace.[103] In short, states were beginning to culturally and socially protect their nationals abroad. Those who emigrated were not *lost* to the nation, but became increasingly central to national projects, as were their children and grandchildren.[104]

Law and the Nation Abroad

Law, both public and private, reflected this concern with the nation abroad. In 1851, Pasquale Stanislao Mancini, Professor of Law at Turin, soon-to-be-foreign minister, and future member (and sometimes

President) of the Institute of International Law, delivered what has become his most famous work that laid out what became his life's primary intellectual project. The address, given at Turin as a prelude to his course on international and maritime law, was entitled *Nationality as the Foundation of the Law of Nations*.[105] The title, as only the titles of legal treatises can do, tightly (and blandly) describes the content of his talk and much of his subsequent intellectual output. Mancini was a liberal nationalist extraordinaire and served as the unofficial legal theorist of Italian nationalism. For Mancini, a nation was "a natural society of men whom the unity of territory, of origin, of customs and of language has shaped into a community of life and of social conscience."[106] And it was Mancini's argument that *nations*, not states, and certainly not individuals, were the basic unit of international law. Nations, he argued, were not just constructs, but an objective reality that had an existence beyond the subjective will of individuals.[107] For example, while he supported the use of plebiscites as *evidence* of nationality, he did not think that they should be definitive. A personal denial of nationality did not unmake an Italian, or a German, or a Czech, a belief that made Mancini a less-than-enthusiastic supporter of the liberal tenet of expatriation.[108] Mancini had, likewise, been a strong supporter of the modern Italian nationality law, based on *jus sanguinis*, and he heaped praise upon "the novel Code which has paid homage to this great principle by proclaiming Italian the person born in whichever place to an Italian father, namely to an Italian family."[109]

Mancini's theories, as applied to public international law, gained a substantial following among liberal nationalists. His doctrine, however, was the subject of substantial criticism and never became a foundational doctrine within the discipline of *public* international law (although, as we will see, the arguments voiced by Mancini were taken up again and again by national activists and were influential in shaping the politics of the interwar period).[110] However, his doctrine did become a central principle in continental *private* international law.

Private law generally refers to the law governing the relations between persons. Public law, in contrast, refers to the laws governing the relations between persons and the government.[111] Private law deals with questions like: What is a person's legal status? Can a person make a contract? What specific laws govern the formation of contracts, marriages, and wills? Private international law, which alternatively goes by the name "conflict of laws" in Anglo-American contexts, is the branch of law that deals with answering those questions when the controversy crosses borders.

To give an example of the type of problem with which private international law is concerned, you might imagine two people, one a French *éleveur de boeuf* (cattle farmer) and the other a seventeen-year-old

German *metzger* (sausage maker). The French *éleveur de boeuf* agrees to sell one steer, whom we'll call Ferdinand, to the *metzger*. In exchange, the *metzger* agrees to give the *éleveur de boeuf* 50 percent of the sausage made from poor Ferdinand. The two meet in Aachen, a small town on the Franco-German border, and sign the contract. Two weeks later, the *metzger* delivers only 25 percent of the sausage made from poor Ferdinand. Outraged, the *éleveur de boeuf* walks into a French *tribunal d'instance* (civil court) and sues the *metzger* for breach of contract. When looking at whether the contract is valid, the *tribunal d'instance* has to decide what law to apply. Should it use the French law for determining whether the contract is valid (after all it is a French court and in France)? Or the German (after all the contract was signed in Germany)? Was the seventeen-year-old German *metzger* old enough to make a contract? Under which law, France's or Germany's? And the questions go on and on.

Traditionally, reference was made either to the territory or to the domicile (habitual residence) of the parties. But, Mancini (and others, but Mancini was the most influential) argued that courts should use *nationality* instead of domicile. Echoing Montesquieu, Mancini believed that the different environments of the world produced distinctive physiologies, cultures, and behaviors that all in turn produced different national psychologies. Because of the variety of environments and thus the variety of national psychologies, it was "impossible to fix in a uniform manner the age of majority for all the peoples, for those placed under the equator and for the inhabitants of the glacial lands of the poles."[112] Hence, when determining the age of majority, for example, reference should be made to *nationality* rather than to territory or domicile. To return to our example, if German law said that the age of majority for our sausage maker was sixteen, then he was competent to sign the contract. If, however, the German law said the age of majority was eighteen, then he was incompetent,[113] the idea being that the German law was the best way of determining the competency of a German national. As Mancini put it:

> Climate, temperature, geographical situation, whether mountainous or maritime, the nature and fertility of the soil, the diversity of needs and of mores, determine in the land of each people . . . their legal system. They determine in a greater or lesser degree the precocity of physical and moral development, the organization of family relations, the preferred occupations, and the kinds of business and commercial relations which are the most frequent. For these reasons the status and capacity of persons in the private law of the different nations must differ in accordance with the difference in conditions. One cannot ignore that difference [in conditions] without offending nature, and without upending the effects with a striking injustice.[114]

In an age of migration, the adoption of this principle into private international law made sense as it, like the establishment of consulates, the enshrining of *jus sanguinis* in nationality codes, and the creation of cultural organizations to support emigrants, bound nationals abroad more tightly to their metropole. Advocates of the nationality principle in private international law hoped that German or Italian or Polish laws concerning marriage or the family would continue to govern the intimate lives of Germans, Italians, or Poles as they settled across borders and seas. Mancini's doctrine influenced the writings of jurists in Italy, Belgium, France, Germany, Spain, Poland, and even Japan, all of which adopted, to a greater or lesser degree, nationality as the foundation of their private international law.[115] By the turn of the twentieth century, the principle had achieved nearly European-wide recognition with The Hague Conventions on Private International Law.[116]

By increasingly enshrining *jus sanguinis* principles of nationality into their laws, European states were ensuring that more and more of their emigrants continued to be bound to their state, to their state's law and legal community, and to the legal traditions of their ethnic forebears. The American states, however, maintained principles of *jus soli* and domicile, privileging the legal traditions of their territorially proximate community. This, in effect, created an interhemispheric dispute between the states of emigration and the states of immigration that would play out in diplomatic dispatches well into the twentieth century.[117]

Breaking Nationality

Traditionally, nationality was part of what international jurists called the "reserved domain." Unlike many international legal terms, "reserved domain" is fairly self-descriptive. It refers to the set of powers that are immune from international regulation or dispute. The "reserved domain" is the set of issues that fall within the sovereign prerogatives of a state. And the power to define the population was certainly within the reserved domain in the nineteenth century.[118] However, having two competing principles for determining nationality posed a problem for the international system. Montes de Oca, a member of Argentina's Chamber of Deputies, aptly summed up the problem when he observed that the children of immigrants born in Argentina "would be Argentine by birth and at the same time, foreigners, which is to say that they would have prerogatives not available to the children of the Republic of Argentina."[119] Those "prerogatives" were the benefits that being a member of a state entailed, including the right to request protection from the state of one's nationality, and, in some instances, the right to have one's national law apply in private disputes. Argentinians could only hope to appeal to the highest court in the land should they find themselves arbitrarily arrested or forcibly deprived of their property. Argentinians could only rely upon the beneficence of the Argentinian government for compensation for a house burned down in a riot or for harm resulting from wrongful detainment. But, children of Italian or German or French or British parents could walk to the Italian or German or French or British consulate in Buenos Aires and demand that their *other* government come to their aid.[120]

As millions of people crisscrossed the Atlantic, they entangled the world in a web of competing legal obligations. From 1850 to 1914, an age sometimes defined by its territoriality,[121] there were millions and millions of people who were entitled to have foreign law apply to them and to be protected by more than one sovereign. But the great Atlantic migrations were not alone in wrapping the world in obligation.

Colonial Subjects and Nationality

Colonies, like the new republics on the western edge of the Atlantic basin, presented new problems for defining the relationship between people and their sovereigns. How increasing numbers of colonial subjects would fit into the domestic and international legal regimes of Europe and the Americas was, in the second half of the nineteenth century, ambiguous. In the settler colonies of the eighteenth century, the answer was clear – colonists were subjects of their respective monarchs. But in nonsettler colonies, the question became murkier. To whom could Indians working in East Africa turn to if they ran into legal trouble or if they were abused? Would Algerians be considered French nationals for the purposes of extraterritorial jurisdiction in the Ottoman Empire? Were Filipinos legally American nationals even if they were not American citizens?

These were precisely the questions consular officials asked in dispatches back to the foreign ministries of Britain, France, the United States, and elsewhere in the latter half of the nineteenth century. Were colonial subjects nationals from the standpoint of international law? By the end of the nineteenth century, in all cases, the answer was unequivocally yes. Foreign ministries, attorneys general, and international legal theorists with resounding (and surprising) clarity declared that indigenous colonial subjects were entitled to the same protections abroad as their metropolitan counterparts. Nor was this a purely theoretical distinction; states did, in fact, offer access to consular services and protection to their colonial subjects in whatever foreign land they found themselves.

In Britain, the concern centered around Indians. If anything can be said about Indians' legal status in the late nineteenth-century British Empire, it is that they were not citizens.[122] But they were subjects.[123] While much of the Indian migration was to other British colonies, Indian traders became central to trade in East Africa. Over the course of the latter half of the nineteenth century, hundreds (maybe even thousands) of Indian traders arrived in East Africa every year.[124] Following the partition of East Africa, it was increasingly common for Indian traders to find themselves in German-controlled East Africa, and the German government even named its East African currency the "Rupie."[125] The British government, facing questions about the legal status of their colonial subjects, was quite quick to conclude that because they were indisputably "British subjects," they were entitled to the same protection abroad and access to British consulates just as any Englishman would be.[126] There was even some dispute surrounding the status of Indians who inhabited the Protected States, which were technically outside of the annexed territory of British India but still under the management of the British government. Internally, these Indians were the subjects of their respective princes. Yet externally, those subjects of the Protected States were British subjects. As the legal advisor to the India Office put it, "subjects of Native States should, when found in foreign countries, enjoy the same measure of protection as is accorded to British subjects."[127] Nor was this a theoretical protection. When Indians ran into trouble abroad, they could and did turn to British consulates.[128] Even beyond India, Britain had a clear policy of providing protection abroad to all those who fell under its dominion.[129]

But it wasn't just Indian traders who were making their way to foreign ports. Indentured laborers, or "coolies," were sent around the world in the second half of the nineteenth century. Again, while they were often sent to British colonies, occasionally they wound up in French or Dutch territorial possessions. Like their wealthier counterparts, Coolie laborers were technically entitled to diplomatic protection. But it wasn't undue detainment, expropriation of property, or denials of justice that coolie laborers encountered. Instead, the British government was concerned about labor standards in colonies not directly under its control. Traditional diplomatic practice did not accord a state a right to intervene because of poor domestic labor standards. Instead, the British needed to devise alternative methods to protect indentured laborers from poor conditions abroad.[130] In 1889, for example, the India Office called for the creation of a "British protector of Indian immigrants," who would be "vested with very much larger powers of control and supervision . . . [including the] full power to visit and inspect all estates on which immigrants are employed."[131] With colonial subjects, Britain began to run up against the limits of traditional forms of diplomatic protection. What would international law have to say about labor standards? How could states, wary of races to the bottom, begin to ensure that their poor were not abused abroad?

In France, the concern centered around Algerians. Following their conquest of Algeria in 1830, the status within France of "indigenous" Algerians was an open question for decades. But the Sénatus-Consulte of July 14, 1865 declared, "The indigenous Muslim is French." An Algerian could serve in the army, the navy, and the civil service. They were, however, not French *citizens*. They were something lesser. Algerians could request to become French citizens (so long as they renounced their right to be governed under Muslim law), but few took advantage of that provision. Instead, a gradient of relationships between subjects and their state existed internally.[132] However, externally there were no real gradients of status. In a circular issued in 1869, the director of Consulates and Commercial Affairs made it abundantly clear that the Sénatus-Consulte had brought native Algerians under the protection of France.[133] "One of the consequences of . . . the Sénatus-Consulte of 1865 has been to give to [native Algerians], by tightening the links which bind them to France, more extensive rights than before to the protection of our diplomatic and consular agents."[134] He then instructed French consular officials, "native Algerians have the right, in all places and at all times, to the protection of the Government of the Emperor."[135] Nor, he continued, could that right be easily taken away by residence abroad.[136]

In the United States, the question was centered on Filipinos. Already by the late nineteenth century, Filipinos were a common sight on international shipping vessels throughout the South Pacific. Following the annexation of the Philippines in 1899, American consular officials had to answer new questions. In places as far afield and unexpected as landlocked Switzerland, consular officials found themselves writing to Washington to determine the international legal status of these far flung Filipinos.[137] While the determination of their legal status took several years to resolve domestically,[138] there was little question as to their status internationally.[139] Already by 1901, the attorney general had published an opinion saying that although Filipinos were not *citizens* of the United States, they were, "from an international standpoint, subjects of the United States, or, to use a term that has been suggested, 'nationals.'" The attorney general added, "In a general way our Government is responsible to them and for them."[140] Their status was further solidified by an act of Congress in 1902, which provided, "That all inhabitants of the Philippine Islands... shall be deemed and held to be citizens of the Philippine Islands and as such entitled to the protection of the United States, except such as shall have elected to preserve their allegiance to the Crown of Spain."[141]

Nor should this be all that surprising when placed in the context of an imperialism that was often predicated on effective governance. If the failure to meet international obligations was a valid pretext for the intervention by an imperial power, and if the legitimacy of a claim to territory rested on the reciprocal link between allegiance and protection, then any imperial power that wanted to maintain its grasp on a far-flung colony had to meet this most basic obligation, lest another imperial power challenge their claim. Even in cases where there was no direct annexation, as in the case of the British in Egypt or in the case of the Protected States of India, the responsibility of protecting the inhabitants of these informal colonies or protectorates was assumed by the colonial power.

The international jurists of the time also took note of this practice, and in many of the most influential tomes, it was held that the inhabitants of colonies were entitled to the protection of the metropolitan state while abroad – that is they were considered nationals.

There were no degrees of nationality under international law as there were with citizenship or subjecthood under domestic law. The international category was binary. One was either a national, or one was not. In the international realm there was a theoretical legal equality that was impossible domestically. A Frenchmen and an Algerian did not have the same rights in Marseille, but they did in Spain. An Englishman and a Bermudan did not have the same rights in London (or even in Mumbai), but they did in Florida. A Californian and a Filipino did not have the same rights in Arizona, but they did in Switzerland. Despite being unequal under the law domestically, colonial subjects were equal under the law internationally. States were still responsible for the actions of their nationals, and, moreover, they had a right to intervene on behalf of their colonial subjects wherever they traveled in the world.[142]

From the perspective of international law, then, some imperial powers had far more nationals residing outside of their metropolitan territory than within it. The sheer size of the French and British empires in 1907 placed them firmly in that category. India alone had more than seven times the population of the United Kingdom. And each Indian soul, theoretically, had the same right to protection when abroad as Don Pacifico had in Greece. What would happen when these subjects began to emigrate?

Juridical Persons and Nationality

Just as real persons[143] were flitting around the globe in ever greater numbers, so too were their fictional counterparts, and in doing so, those fictional counterparts haunted nineteenth-century international law. The juridical person, or corporation, unlike a real person, can be immortal. Despite the rampant deployment of corporeal metaphors when discussing this creature,[144] a corporation has no literal body, no literal soul, and no literal mind. But that immortal, incorporeal, soulless, and mindless wraith does have a nationality.

But what is that nationality? Panamanian shell companies, Cayman bank accounts, umbrella entities, and uroboric strings of subsidiaries certainly make contemporary corporate structures seem alien when compared with their national mid-twentieth century predecessors.[145] However, when compared with their nineteenth-century forebears, the modern corporation can seem downright parochial.[146] For all the ambiguities we still face, the law has (almost) settled on the question of corporate nationality. Today, a company is *usually* the national of the state in which it was incorporated or the state in which the corporate charter places its administrative seat.[147] Geoffrey Jones, in surveying the difference between multinationals of the twenty-first century and those of the nineteenth has argued, "In the early twenty-first century, ownership, location and geography still mattered enormously in international business. Indeed, in some respects they may matter more than in the past.... [Today] the nationality of a firm [is] rarely ambiguous, and usually a major influence on corporate strategy."[148]

In the nineteenth century, there was no clear answer. Although, there were several possible answers.[149] For one, a juridical person, better known as a corporation, is a legal fiction. It's an entity that exists because a state has decided that it's a useful fiction either for limiting liability and encouraging investment, for securing intergenerational transfers of wealth, or for supporting some other social value. As François Laurent, one of the premier nineteenth-century jurists, eloquently put it, "A man exists because of God, he exists because God called him to life, and he exists everywhere. A corporation exists because of the law."[150] Since a state had prescribed the incantations necessary to inspirit the wraith, it seemed only reasonable that the twain be bound. Or, in a less metaphorical mode, the nationality of a corporation should be decided by the place of incorporation.[151]

But others were more reluctant to ascribe nationality to an incorporeal being. At the turn of the twentieth century, it was generally assumed that corporations did not have nationality.[152] Instead, attention was paid to the corporeal investors and managers.[153] After all it was their interests that were at stake. "A corporation," wrote Edwin Borchard, "... is composed of human beings and has a real personality, which is a reality in every state."[154] But did that mean that a corporation shared its nationality with each and every one of its investors? Or even more indirectly, was a harm done to a corporation a harm done to its investors and by the transitive association between subject and sovereign a harm done to the state of the investors? Or did it share its nationality with those who were in "de facto control of its affairs?"[155]Or, perhaps, did it have the nationality of whatever country it had its primary operations?[156]

The nature of multinational enterprises in the nineteenth century, therefore, ensured that the ambiguity with regard to the nationality of the enterprise further entangled the world with threads of allegiance and protection. It was not uncommon to have enterprises that spanned continents and hemispheres with thousands of shareholders, each possibly possessing several nationalities and the potential to make an international claim.[157]

The Delagoa Railway dispute serves as a fine illustration of just how complex things could become. That tale begins with "Colonel" Edward McMurdo, an American by birth, who was a typical nineteenth-century tycoon. He began his career investing in mines, and by midlife, he had established operations in California, Colorado, North Carolina, Portugal, Honduras, and the Transvaal – a collection of locales representing every quarter of the globe. Following upon his successes in mining, McMurdo entered the railway industry.[158]

In 1883, the Portuguese government granted McMurdo a concession to build a railway in Mozambique from the port of Lourenço Marques to the Transvaal. McMurdo then sold that concession to the Lourenço Marques and Transvaal Railway Company (LMTR), a company he conjured under the laws of Portugal. In exchange, McMurdo took nearly all of LMTR's shares. He then made his way to London where, following the prescribed formalities, he summoned up the Delagoa Bay and East African Railway Company (D-BEAR) under the laws of England. McMurdo then assigned the shares he owned of LMTR to D-BEAR and proceeded to solicit investors in London. So, you have McMurdo, an American living in London, along with many other British investors who own shares in a British company that itself owns nothing more than shares in a Portuguese company that itself only owns a concession to build a railway in Mozambique.[159]

Construction commenced in 1884 and was delayed numerous times until 1889, when the Portuguese government canceled the concession.

Furious, McMurdo and D-BEAR's shareholders petitioned their government to come to their aid, and it was not long before the British and American governments stepped in on their behalf, claiming damages in excess of 599,816,198 GBP, a laughably large sum.[160] Portugal decided to arbitrate the matter. In establishing the arbitral tribunal, Portugal consented to the claim, so whether the British or American governments were even entitled to pursue the claims of injured shareholders remained an open question from the standpoint of international jurisprudence. At the conclusion of the proceedings, which lasted nine years, the tribunal awarded the British and American governments 15,314,000 French francs plus 5 percent interest.

The point of this somewhat long and convoluted story is to illustrate in detail just how expansive the threads of obligation and protection ran in the nineteenth-century business world. Technically, the revocation of the concession only directly injured LMTR, the holding company that McMurdo established in Portugal under Portuguese law. Yet the claims made by the United States and the United Kingdom were on behalf of shareholders and bondholders (in the United Kingdom's case the shareholders were even further removed, being shareholders in D-BEAR, which then held shares in LMTR). If injury to a shareholder or a bondholder could create an international injury to a state, there were few limits on how expansive an international intervention could grow. Because corporations had many (seemingly limitless and often ambiguous) nationalities, the number of states that might potentially be interested in any conflict proliferated.

Nor did the problem of corporate nationality get settled by the first quarter of the twentieth century. The major law associations struggled to devise a workable solution.[161] And as the numbers of claims began to proliferate with the onset of the Mexican and Russian revolutions, and the mass seizures of property that accompanied both of those events, the problems grew more complex with regard to corporate nationality, as an American report from 1918 wonderfully highlights:

> Large numbers of the claimants against foreign Governments are corporations, and it is very often a perplexing question to determine whether [they] are properly entitled to the diplomatic protection of this government. The claimant may be a corporation organized in the United States, but owned largely or principally by aliens, or it may be a foreign corporation whose stock is owned in the main by American citizens. Again, the ownership of stock by American citizens may be merely nominal and may have been arranged for the particular purpose of obtaining diplomatic protection for interests which substantially and equitably belong to aliens.[162]

Broken Nationality

Naturalization was easy, and colonial subjects were nationals. And, what precisely was the status of juridical persons was unclear. The effect was that by the 1870s, in most of the world, human beings and their immortal business counterparts had a nationality or could acquire one with relative ease from the standpoint of international law. Because nationality could be easily acquired, the number of people with multiple nationalities exploded. But more importantly, nationality became a tool for both fleeing obligation and obtaining protection.

The easy acquisition of nationality did, indeed, make escaping obligations easier. From the 1840s to the 1870s, the states of Europe and the states of the Americas were often in conflict over this issue because the states of Europe increasingly were concerned with the ability of their subjects to escape their obligations of taxation and military service – a fact that led to several diplomatic conflicts between states like Prussia and the United States. William Edward Hall, a prominent international jurist, when writing on nationality in 1890, argued that while it was entirely within the rights of a state to confer its nationality on whomever it pleased, it was "scarcely consistent with the comity which ought to exist between nations to render so easy the acquisition of a national character, which may be used against the mother state, as to make the state admitting the foreigner a sort of accomplice in an avoidance of him of obligations due to his original country."[163]

But beyond a means to escape the obligations to states, it was also a means of increasing the obligations of states. Specifically, it became a means to acquire added protection for travel, settlement, and business. After all, who would not want the "the watchful eye and the strong arm of England" protecting him from wrongs? People acquired new nationalities, binding themselves to more sovereigns. As those people traversed the oceans, they enmeshed the globe in a tangle of responsibility and obligation.

While binding themselves ever closer to nationals abroad could (and almost certainly did) serve state imperial interests throughout the nineteenth century, the tangled threads also dragged states unwillingly into diplomatic conflicts they had no wish to be a part of, particularly as more and more people began to instrumentalize state protection as a way of engaging in political activism, business, and financial speculation.

Already by the 1850s (perhaps spurred on by the Pacifico Affair), the potential for the abuse of protection had been noted. When proposals were floated within the British Home Office that would have further liberalized naturalization, significant attention was paid to the potential of abuse – particularly by merchants abroad. As one communication on the subject put it:

> In order, however, to prevent any abuse of this privilege and to preclude foreigners from becoming naturalized with no intention of permanently residing within the dominions of the British Crown, but merely for obtaining protection for their mercantile establishments abroad, Lord Clarendon proposes to restrict the validity of passports granted to naturalized aliens.[164]

The instrumentalization of protection in the colonies was also a problem, particularly as identities and legal status were often highly fluid (more so in the colonial entrepôts like Alexandria, Egypt).[165] The British Legation in Addis Ababa, Ethiopia, for example, wrote to the Foreign Office to complain in 1913 that there were many who were taking advantage of national protection. "There are many Armenians, Greeks and Levantines here who come from Egypt or the Sudan. When it suits them they are only too ready to claim Egyptian nationality and the protection of the legation, but they are equally prepared to claim Greek or Turkish nationality, when complaints are lodged against them before me, in order to evade justice."[166]

French officials, too, noted the potential for instrumental flexibility of identity (or abuse). The same circular that stated unequivocally, "native Algerians have the right, in all places and at all times, to the protection of the Government of the Emperor," also noted that with that status came new conditions designed to "prevent abuse." Indeed, the purpose of that circular was to prevent that abuse.[167] Passports, while not ubiquitous or necessary for the travel of most Frenchmen, became increasingly important for receiving the protection of French Consuls, with the circular noting that those who could not provide a passport should be refused protection unless the consular official was convinced the lack of a passport was due to "simple negligence." The granting of French nationality to millions of Algerians complicated the ready identification of French nationality based upon habits, language, and custom. Documentary evidence was increasingly important. But there were problems that better identification and record keeping could not solve. A mere four months after the circular had been issued to the consulates that native Algerians had a right to protection, consulates began to report abuse. According to French officials, Tunisians, Moroccans, and subjects of the Ottoman Empire would come to Algeria, naturalize, and leave, armed with the new confidence that the "strong arm" of France would be there to guarantee their property, their business, and their right to a trial that met the "standards of civilization" when they returned to their native lands.[168]

But it was not just poor colonial traders who were chafing state officials with their constant demands for protection and intervention. Large financial investors were creating plenty of foreign entanglements. In 1907, five years after the French navy had joined the German and British in blockading Venezuela to enforce the repayment of foreign debts, French Foreign Minister Stephen-Jean-Marie Pichon, speaking before the Chamber of Deputies in support of limitations on diplomatic protection, exclaimed, "We cannot risk the forces and engage the politics and the foreign relations of a country in all of the fortunate or unfortunate speculations of the great businessmen, the financiers and the bankers, who would allow themselves to be imprudently carried away."[169]

The Americans, likewise, found themselves involved in problems overseas. President Grant in his State of the Union complained of American nationals living in foreign countries "without any intention at any time to return" and who used their American citizenship "simply as a shield."[170] Five years later, Mr. Logan of the American Legation in Central America lamented:

> [There are] a large number of people floating through the Spanish-American Republics, claiming the protection of the American flag, a majority of whom, perhaps, are not entitled to the protection they demand. . . . Why should a person who practically has renounced all duty and allegiance to his country, who contributes nothing to its support in peace or war, and who escapes the obligations of all nationalities, become a charge upon his country, often involving it in expense, and sometimes in international difficulties? . . . [The United States should] declare the conditions under which involuntary or enforced expatriation shall occur.[171]

And nearly thirty years later, former Secretary of State Elihu Root complained:

> Natives of other countries . . . become naturalized here for the purpose of returning to their homes or seeking a residence in third countries with the benefit of American protection. Several years ago it was estimated that there were in Turkey seven or eight thousand natives of Turkey who had in one way and another secured naturalization in the United States and had gone home to live with the advantage over their friends and neighbors of being able to call upon the American embassy for assistance whenever they were not satisfied with the treatment they received from their own government. At the time of the troubles in Morocco . . . an examination of the list of American citizens in Morocco showed that one-half of the list consisted of natives of Morocco who had been naturalized in the United States and had left this country and gone back to Morocco within three months after obtaining their naturalization papers.[172]

An American consul-general in Morocco, likewise observed, "The lengths to which many natives – especially those who have some property, or who are 'wanted' by the Moorish Government, or who have powerful enemies – will go to secure protection [from European powers] is wonderful."[173]

Dual nationals, likewise, became the targets of scorn. In 1915, Theodore Roosevelt railed against the evils of dual nationality, asserting that "the hyphenated American is a danger to the country," and arguing, "we must decline to allow the principle of dual nationality in our life." Discrimination against immigrants was an evil, Roosevelt argued. But just as evil was to maintain affinity with a foreign country simply because of a "blood-connection."[174]

Between roughly the 1850s and the outbreak of World War I, the problem of the dual national had been increasingly on the minds of statesmen, lawyers, and the broader public. Friction between states over the legal status of individuals increased as the number of states in the Western Hemisphere proliferated and as the numbers of migrants from Europe to the Americas exploded in the latter half of the century. The War of 1812 between Britain and the United States had revolved around the issue of just who was a "British subject" and thus liable for impressment into Britain's naval forces.[175] The dispute was so intractable that it outlasted the war, becoming the "Banquo's ghost of Anglo-American relations" until 1870.[176]

But beginning in the 1850s, as emigrants from Europe began to flood into the Western Hemisphere, the problem was given new dimensions and new urgency. Under pressure, states had begun to seriously reconsider their laws on naturalization, nationality, citizenship, and allegiance in response to abuses and geopolitical strife.[177]

The United States, for example, chafing from the continual conflicts it had over the liability of both naturalized and native-born US citizens to foreign military service in Prussia and other European States, began to sign a series of treaties to deal with the conflicts in nationality laws.[178] These agreements became known as the "Bancroft Treaties" after George Bancroft, the historian and diplomat who negotiated the original instruments. Bancroft, as overtly attentive readers might remember, penned this chapter's epigraph in a letter to Lord Palmerston over the arrest of American citizens in Ireland.[179]

The British government established a commission in 1868 to answer such fundamental questions as "Who is a natural born subject?," "Who besides is, or can be, a British born subject?," "What is the legal status of a natural born British subject residing abroad?," and "What is the legal status of a Statute made British subject so residing?" Having spent three-quarters of the past century in disputes with the United States over the problem of dual nationality, the commission was increasingly aware of the problems that dual nationality presented.[180]

Writing to encourage reform, Alexander Cockburn argued, "It is obvious that the evil would be remedied if, by a law common to all nations, the rule as to nationality of origin were everywhere the same, and naturalization by a second country had the effect of superseding the allegiance due to that of birth."[181]

Yet, for all the treaties of the 1860s and 1870s, the problems were far from solved. André Weiss, one of France's preeminent jurists, noted in 1887 that the problem of nationality held a "great place in the preoccupations of jurists and statesmen." He noted, "The tide of emigration is mounting without cessation, feeding the rapid growth of the population in certain countries, and aided by the progress of a science, which has defeated nature and no longer knows distance." It was necessary, he argued, "to dispense with everywhere perpetual allegiance and to recognize the right to expatriation."[182]

There were moments when it seemed like the juridical, legislative, and foreign policy establishments could solve the problem. The British and German citizenship laws promulgated between 1870 and 1910 provided conditions under which the loss of nationality was automatic. In the British case, such a loss happened upon foreign naturalization. In the German, the loss occurred ten years after a person left Germany. The Americans, likewise, reformed their laws in 1907 so as to forcibly expatriate Americans who spent more than a few years abroad.[183] France provided for denaturalization in World War I and later made the policy permanent.[184] Moreover, the North German Confederation, Belgium, Norway, Sweden, Denmark, and Austria-Hungary all signed treaties with the United States in which naturalization and expatriation would be recognized following several years of residency. And the Institute of International Law and the International Law Association both took up the cause of reform in their own right.

Marriage, of course, also presented problems. What would happen if two persons of different nationalities married one another? Would each spouse retain his or her separate identity? Would each spouse be eligible for naturalization in the other spouses state of origin? Or would one spouse be subsumed into the person of the other? In an age straining to deal with the problems of nationality, marriage and children posed a special problem. If marriage under the law of a state permitted the retention of one's nationality and the easy adoption of another, then nationalities would proliferate. Similarly, if children were born with all the nationalities of both their parents (and potentially with that of the place where they entered the world), then nationalities would proliferate. And what of divorce?

As one would expect, the law, which was so good at further oppressing the already intimately oppressed, continued to do so. By the turn of the twentieth century, it was common for states to expatriate women who married foreign men. As they often took their husbands' names, so too did they often take their husbands' states. Many, but not all, European and American states held that a woman's nationality would follow that of her husband's. States could not agree to *jus sanguinis* or *jus soli*, but the global reach of patriarchy meant that the independent laws of most states limited the proliferation of plural nationality by ensuring that a woman had no nationality independent of her husband or, on occasion, no nationality at all.

While the practice of dependent nationality was more common than other principles of nationality, the forcible expatriation of women and the automatic conferral of nationality upon wives were uneven. Often women would lose their nationality upon marriage but not gain their husband's, rendering them effectively stateless.[185] While today we often think of the stateless person as a refugee cast out by their state in an act of violent dispossession, the statelessness problem was, in fact, one that affected first and foremost married women.[186]

But women's dependent nationality, while it potentially reduced the problem of plural nationality, did not always prevent the practices and problems that plural nationality created in terms of diplomatic protection. In Latin America, for instance, the attempts to limit the intervention of European powers to protect property manifested itself, in part, in attempts to limit foreign ownership of property. The Mexican Constitution of 1917, for example, explicitly barred foreign ownership of property unless they renounced their right to request diplomatic protection with respect to that property.[187] But that prohibition was one that women's dependent nationality might undermine. Foreign men, it was feared, could skirt the provision by marrying a Mexican woman who owned property. In that case, the Mexican woman would cease to be a Mexican national and the law of Mexico would assume that she had gained the nationality of her husband, thereby placing her property, in effect, under the protection of a foreign state.[188]

In general, but with women in particular, expatriation, instead of becoming increasingly a right, became instead an imposition. While reluctant to formally create the processes by which nationals might expatriate themselves, some states, by the early twentieth century, were increasingly using expatriation as a way to try to selectively cut themselves from the webs of obligation that had bound them up over the course of the nineteenth century.

The major international law institutions, scholars, and policy makers likewise, all took a crack at solving the problem. The Institute of International Law and the International Law Association drafted principles and resolutions and held several conferences on the subject. The ideal at the center of every effort was to make nationality mutually exclusive and universal. The Institute of International Law's "1895 Principles Relating to the Conflict of Laws in the Matter of Nationality" proclaimed as its first principle, "Nobody should be without nationality" and as its second principle, "Nobody can have simultaneously two nationalities."[189] The Institute followed up its principles with more specific resolutions, which it recommended the states adopt into their own domestic law. These model laws would eradicate the "scourge" of double-nationality by requiring the loss of one nationality whenever a person gained another. Similarly the plans would end statelessness by not permitting the revocation of a person's nationality until they had acquired another.[190]

But such reforms were generally abortive or short lived. A revision to the German citizenship law in 1913 not only repealed the automatic loss of German nationality, but ensured that Germans abroad were Germans for life. And so were their children. The same year, the Austrian legislature drafted a law that permitted emigrations only if "[the receiving country] guarantees the emigrants legal security, the preservation of his nationality and confession, and the undeniable right of the Austrian citizen to return home."[191] With the onset of European fascism, Italy and Germany both tried to tie their overseas populations (stretching back several generations) back to the Empire and Reich. Writing in 1931, Edwin Borchard lamented that other than a few "tactical" victories, voluntary expatriation had "practically become obsolescent," because "many countries have seen no reason to surrender their claims of indelible allegiance or to admit that citizenship can be abandoned without their consent."[192] And while states were busy strengthening bonds instead of severing them, expatriation was being used to forcibly remove from state protection undesirable domestic populations. France, Belgium, Italy, Egypt, Turkey, Austria, Germany, and Russia between 1915 and 1933 began to denaturalize persons who were, for example, not "worthy of Italian citizenship."[193] And women who married foreigners were, likewise, an undesirable population.

Over the first three decades of the twentieth century, then, links to populations abroad often multiplied and strengthened, while, simultaneously, pariahs were stripped of their nationality even when still residing in their place of birth. Indeed, by the first decade of the twentieth century, it was clear that nationality was going to be one of the knottiest legal problems of the age. Writing in 1907, Francis Taylor Piggott, frustratedly observed:

> It is extraordinary that so important a subject as nationality should still be in a state of confusion, that it should be still possible for a man not to know to what nation he belongs, that is should be still possible for a man to be claimed as subject by two, and perhaps two hostile, States. "Double-nationality" is still a possible state of existence, with its inevitable consequence, a two fold allegiance. And so also is "No-nationality," the state in which a man is cast adrift upon the world, and from which many curious consequences may flow.[194]

And, as in most things, the fretting was not limited to jurists – to minds categorizing and cataloging for the sake of an internal legal system. Prime ministers, statesmen, diplomats, and presidents all fretted as well.

Nationality and allegiance were broken concepts by the turn of the twentieth century. The constant transboundary movement of people bound the world up in a tangle of increasingly knotty obligations from which it was difficult to break free. With the outbreak of World War I, the problems only grew more complicated.

***

In 1847, Alexander Herzen had set out from Russia to Europe. In many ways he embodied the problem that nationality and mobility presented to the international system. On the one hand, he was willing to instrumentalize an international legal status to his own ends. He became a Swiss national without ever adopting a Swiss identity. He robed himself in the protection of the Swiss government while still feeling Russian to his core.

The Russian concept of "nationality," rendered as *narodnost* in Russian, had many meanings. As it was originally coined, it meant something along the lines of "that which belongs to the Russian state." But it could also mean "that which belongs to the Russian community or people." The latter connotation, according to Martin Malia, "tended to set the people apart from the government."[195] Herzen was "the most exuberant and imaginative messianic nationalist that Russia produced in the first half of the nineteenth century."[196] And for Herzen, to be Russian was not to be a loyal subject of the Tsar, but rather to be a part of the Russian people. Herzen took up the cause of nationalism, supporting the Polish insurrection of 1863 and the reorganization of the Russian Empire as a democratic federation of nations.[197] For Herzen and many others, nations rather than states were the fundamental unit of the international order. A person was a German, not a subject of the Kaiser. A person was a Frenchman, not a subject of the King of France. A person was a Czech, not a subject of the Emperor of Austria. This disassociation of politico-legal status from ethnic, cultural, or historical status was at the center of the tension over the protection of nationals abroad, nationality, and intervention, and it was a tension that would break the international legal system in 1914.

Part II

Mise-en-scène

The International Legal World, 1919–1939

> The initial wave of discouragement [with international law after World War I] was swiftly followed by that confidence in the future which has manifested itself in the movement for a complete revision of international law. Its regeneration, bringing up to date, renovation, recasting on democratic principles and development have been universally discussed.... Some recommend that international law be readapted to the new circumstances. Others urge that it must be changed, by substituting new principles for the old. The general conviction is, however, that international law has already entered, or is about to enter, on a new phase of its evolution.
>
> Nicolas Politis, 1928[1]

World War I did much to change the international legal order of the nineteenth century, although not in the ways one might suspect. Despite using 1919 as a temporal divide for this section, it's important to keep in mind that much remained the same. Foreign offices and the international law societies remained central in both the practical and theoretical realms of international law. Mixed commissions and international arbitration remained common tools for resolving interstate disputes. Following World War I and the Mexican Revolution, claims commissions were established that heard thousands of cases. The textbooks on international law that had existed before the war continued to be published with minor revisions. The preface to the first postwar edition of Lassa Oppenheim's popular textbook noted, "The war has involved changes in this volume; yet they are surely fewer than might have been expected."[2] As Oppenheim himself put it when discussing the League of Nations in a small volume he wrote shortly before his death, "You believe no doubt, because nearly everyone believes it, that the conception of a League of Nations is something quite new. Yet this is not the case."[3] A league of nations, he argued, had existed alongside international law since its foundation.[4] All that was new, according to Oppenheim, was that the international order's previously unwritten constitution had finally been written down.[5]

And Oppenheim was correct. It is wrong to see World War I as a hard boundary between an old and a new international *legal* order. The cataclysm of 1914–1918 did not in and of itself create a rupture in law as much as a rupture in the memory of that law. In doing so, the war created a new rhetorical space within the international realm. It did this in two different ways. First, it created new *physical* spaces for international politics. Second, it created a new *imaginative* space and served to rhetorically mark time.[6]

First, although Oppenheimer dismissed the League's novelty, what the establishment of the League did do was create new spaces, specifically physical and geographic fora, for making speeches and filing reports that a permanent and attentive press corps would carry around the world. It also created a space for international politics to be discussed. Geneva itself became a space for walking, talking, and politicking.[7] As Lord Robert Cecil observed in a speech at the opening of the first General Assembly of the League, "Publicity is the very lifeblood of the League of Nations"[8]

The treaties of peace also provided for the creation of the Permanent International Court of Justice (PCIJ), which began operation in 1921 and acted as the legal organ of the League. Unlike the Permanent Court of Arbitration (which was neither permanent, nor much of a court), the PCIJ was a sitting court with a full panel of justices. While precedent was not technically binding upon the new PCIJ,[9] the Court's existence provided the opportunity for the development of a body of international legal precedent, which might turn the abstract set of principles and practices that loosely constituted international law into a mature body of case law.

In short, the League and the PCIJ provided visible spaces to publicly debate and advocate the shape and direction of the international order. It provided buildings. It provided printing facilities. It provided a highly visible platform for discussing international law and politics.

The League and the PCIJ also *seemed* new to "nearly everyone."[10] Whether it was new, in fact, did not matter so much as the perception that the international order was in flux and that change was afoot and possible. Discussion of the international order was no longer limited to foreign ministries and ivied ivory towers. The world was watching the League, and thus people could speak about international politics to the world. One jurist observed, "People are commencing to discuss, to criticise, to contest many principles or rules hitherto considered intangible."[11]

The emergence of the League, the PCIJ, and a "new" political order created the opportunity for rhetorically crafting a "new" international law that stood in opposition to the "old" international law. But that required defining just what the "old" international law was. Often the "old" international law was presented as a troglodytic set of formalistic legal doctrines with a tired and anachronistic emphasis on the principles of sovereignty and a naive attempt to abolish politics.[12] Nicolas Politis, the Greek minister to the League of Nations, and a prominent member of the Institute of International Law, distilled his conception of prewar sovereignty into one damning paragraph:

> [The rights of states] while formerly absolute, subject only to the limits imposed by voluntary accords, . . . are now relative, having only that scope which is indispensable to fulfill the social purpose which brought them into being; in other words, while formerly they were founded on individualism, henceforth they are based on solidarity.[13]

This characterization of the "old" international law's obsession with sovereignty is not wholly accurate.[14] But, burning a straw man of the old law provided the intellectual space for a creative rebirth in the interwar period. While the immediate changes in international law were "surely fewer than might have been expected," the imagined potentials of a new age were often radical.

Among the most persistent reimaginings of international law was expanding just what could be a subject of international law. Since the seventeenth or eighteenth century (depending upon whom you ask), states had been the *demos* of international society and thus only states were subjects of international law.[15] But in the 1920s and 1930s, the prewar whispers and murmurs that nations, or peoples, or persons, or companies, or laborers should be subjects of international law became clamorous. After all, if the sovereignty of states was really on the table, just who or what might have the standing to challenge that sovereignty was an open question. Or put another way, if states were a little less sovereign, then who or what might be a little more sovereign?

If the eighteenth and nineteenth centuries were, as Jennifer Pitts argued, in part about deciding just what the boundaries of belonging to international society were in terms of polities, the twentieth was about deciding those boundaries in terms of subjects.[16] Would national minorities be protected by the new League of Nations? If so, how? Would minorities become subjects of international law? What about individuals? Would individuals have rights before international courts and tribunals? Even if minorities or individuals were not granted legal personhood before these international bodies, what would be the political or rhetorical effect of petitioning the new international bodies? How would the added visibility of these causes filtered through new eyes and ears in Geneva change the way in which governments and the broader global publics think about rights, privileges, and status in this new global order?

And it was a compelling subject. With the collapse of the European land empires, millions of people became stateless – and without protection in the international arena. Moreover, with the rise of the principle of self-determination, dozens of nations began to demand independence and recognition (and many indeed received it). The increased power of labor as a result of the war even enabled a tripartite vision of labor, business, and states as equal participants in the international order. States, it *seemed* to many, were on the verge of being dethroned as the sole sovereigns of the international order (not that they ever had been in practice or even in most theory, only in the memory).

In 1926, for example, Politis, who declared that the rights of states were "now relative," delivered a series of lectures at Columbia University, which were later compiled into a volume entitled *The New Aspects of International Law*. At the heart of those lectures was an assessment of the idea that individuals, rather than states, should be full subjects of international law.[17] "Looking upon the individual as the real object of all law, it proclaims the necessity of rendering international law democratic by placing individuals in the first rank of its subjects." Moreover, Politis observed, this reconstitution of the international order around individuals was "gradually gaining force and ground in all countries."[18]

In 1927, Edwin Borchard, the reigning expert on the protection of nationals abroad, a member of the Institute of International Law, and professor of International Law at the Yale Law School, invited Carl Brinkman, a German sociologist and economist from the Heidelberg University, to deliver Yale's annual lecture series on the "Responsibilities of Citizenship." Brinkman chose as his subject the "Recent Theories of Citizenship in its Relationship to Government." In his lecture, Brinkman identified multiple internationalisms spanning a "whole palette of colors." There was alongside the "Red International" of labor, he argued, "the Golden International of capital, the Black International of the Catholic Church, or even the Green International of peasants and farmers and the Blue or White International of monarchs and feudal aristocracies."[19] That is, there was a rich, expansive, and varied international civil society with many (often overlapping) interests. This society, moreover, could and did mobilize throughout the 1920s and 1930s to demand solutions to (their) international problems.[20]

This emergent international society ensured that throughout the 1920s, international law was in flux. Also, the question of who should be the subjects of international law and how international law should operate was a topic of intense global discussion among theorists, jurists, technocrats, policymakers, petitioners, and politicians.[21] Not all of this was new. Many of the stories that follow have their origins in the late nineteenth century.[22] But the intellectual, social, and political ferment of the 1920s created a somewhat more nurturing environment for ideas about international society and law to flourish.

The terms of debate, likewise, took on a more legal tenor. The professionalization of the diplomatic corps accelerated with the collapse of many of the European monarchies during World War I. Lawyers and other professionals flooded into the foreign ministries and brought with them their languages and biases.[23]

Law, as a collection of texts, is at its heart about the establishment of predictability – to be able to know, given a set of inputs, what a result will be. Law has difficulties in times of change. It often becomes more aspirational than descriptive (for in an age of rapid change, any printed description will surely be out of date by the time it reaches the hands of a legal practitioner, as will assumptions about the law's validity). International law, likewise, had difficulties with the geopolitical changes wrought between 1914 and 1945. National identities and diplomatic practices were in flux. The old system of dealing with the millions of human beings that lived outside the country of their birth was beginning to crumble.

The massive numbers of human beings and their corporate counterparts living abroad entangled politics by creating a situation that could potentially cause domestic dispute to erupt into international issues. Laurence Lafore (and the previous chapter) argued that Europe was beset with national imperfections before the onset of World War I. "Even the most 'mature' states, like Britain and France, had places like Ireland and Alsace that did not necessarily identify as part of the British of French nations.". These cancerous imperfections scarring the nationalist ideal were endemic in Eastern Europe, particularly in Austria-Hungary. And it was, therefore, no surprise that it was there that Europe was pulled into war. Claiming nationals and protecting nationals abroad had become politically toxic in an age of nationalism.[24]

The next three chapters are about how international law dealt with the problem of people living, working, trading, and investing beyond the borders of their state of nationality during this age of possibility. Each chapter looks at attempts to internationalize protection – that is to untangle the world from the Gordian knot of the legal and affective bonds that millions of people living abroad (either literally or metaphorically) had created. Chapter 3 looks at the plight of nations and minorities. Chapter 4 looks at the plight of individuals and refugees. Finally, Chapter 5 looks at the plight of businesses and investors. In nearly all cases, untangling the knot of nationality proved difficult.

3 Sovereign Nations

> The tide of war came in: and the temple of human rights crashed and fell on the shifting sands of nationality.
>
> R. S. Fraser, 1923[1]

On the afternoon of June 11, 1919, Edward F. Dunne, the former mayor of Chicago and governor of Illinois, and Frank P. Walsh, the former co-chairman of the U.S. National War Labor Board, made their way through the Sixteenth Arrondissement of Paris. They turned onto Place des États Unis and presented themselves at number 11 to speak with President Woodrow Wilson.

Dunne and Walsh had come to Paris to urge Wilson in their capacity as members of the American Commission on Irish Independence to support their organization's titular goal. Specifically, they hoped Wilson would (as the Senate had urged) grant an audience to Eamon de Valera (President of the revolutionary Irish Republic), Arthur Griffith, and Count George Noble Plunkett, all of whom had been selected by the people of Ireland to serve as delegates at the Peace Conference. The British had, of course, objected.

The two men greeted the President and began to make their case for Ireland. Walsh began by quoting the President extensively. For example, he read aloud the President's letter to the Pope: "Peace should rest upon the rights of peoples, not on the right of governments – the rights of peoples, great and small, weak or powerful; their equal right to freedom and security and self-government, and to participation, upon fair terms, in the economic opportunities of the world." Walsh said that he believed that Wilson had wanted peoples, not governments, and nations, not states, to be the bearers of rights in the international order.

Walsh summed up:

> Mr. President, when you uttered those words declaring that all nations had a right to self-determination; that it was an issue that had to be settled and once for all, and settled on the side of justice – those expressions I have read to you – you voiced the aspirations of countless millions of people that had been saying them to each other, and begging governments that oppressed them to recognize them.

When you, as the head of the post powerful nation in the world, uttered them, and they received the assent of the representatives of all the nations, it became a fact, Mr. President. These people are imbued with the principle. They may be killed trying to vindicate it, but they can no longer be kept in subjection by the action of diplomats, government officials, or even governments. They are free now.

After a few more exchanges, the President, no doubt with an air of regret, replied to Walsh, "When I gave utterance to those words, I said them without the knowledge that nationalities existed, which are coming to us day after day."

At the end of the conversation, Wilson pleaded: "I wish that you would bear in mind that I came here with very high hopes of carrying out the principles as they were laid down. I did not succeed in getting all I came after. I should say – I should say that there was a great deal – no, I will put it this way – there were a lot of things that I hoped for but did not get."[2]

Nationality in an Age of Nationalism

It had been called the "war to end all wars," and as statesmen from around the world steamed to Paris, peace activists hoped that international politics would be forever altered and that state sovereignty would be displaced from the center of the international order.

But, in the end, sovereignty endured and thrived. The reaffirmation of sovereignty within the League Covenant, the mandate system's affirmation of normative statehood, and the continued influence of positivism within international legal thought, both ensured that sovereignty became, like the Franco-German frontier, more firmly entrenched than before the war. But, that sovereignty remained at the core of international law did not mean that sovereignty, as a concept, was unchanged. The sovereignty of the interwar period had a new national tint, as the principle of "national self-determination" became the iron core of sovereign legitimacy. States remained sovereign, yet the League had, in principle, established an order of normative statehood for all nations (including colonial possessions). Moreover, "nationality" became, even more than before the war, a tool in political struggles. States attempted to ascribe nationality to people living well outside of their borders and, in doing so, make claims upon the right to intervene or, in the colonial realm, to annex. Within this context, it was impossible for the international legal category of nationality to remain separate from the inescapable gravity of "nation" as it was used in popular discourse.[3]

"Nationality" at the turn of the twentieth century had a precise meaning within international law. As most modern treatise writers made clear, a national was an individual subject of a state. Nationality, as a formal legal category, denoted that relationship.[4] As one jurist noted shortly after the First World War, "Nationality is the status of a person in relation to the tie binding such person to a particular sovereign nation." That tie was defined, as the jurist reminded his readers, by the municipal law of a state.[5] It was a simple political relationship from the standpoint of international law, denoting the exchange of protection and allegiance that formed the basis of membership in a political community. In the late eighteenth century, "subject" was commonly used to describe this correlative relationship. But "nationality" became the word of choice as a way to escape the connotations of "subject" in an age of "citizens."

"Nationality," however, had another meaning that had emerged over the course of the nineteenth century. "Nationality," in its sociological and more popular sense, denoted the relationship between a person and a *nation* rather than between a person and a sovereign state.[6] A nation was, at its simplest, a group of people. But whether that group was to be defined politically, institutionally, ethnographically, linguistically, historically, or even by reference to a moral conscience became the source of endless discussion in the nineteenth century.[7] "Nation" had so many meanings that it was rendered almost meaningless. It was a truly protean concept. Yet nation was also inescapable in an era described by contemporaries as the age of nationalism. Henry Morse Stephens,[8] in his Presidential address to the American Historical Association, for example, argued in 1916, "The belief in nationality has been in the nineteenth century as fundamental a doctrine as the belief in Christianity or in monarchy or democracy or aristocracy in previous ages."[9] The increasing connotative heft of "nation" had begun to weigh down the simple and light denotation of "nationality" within international jurisprudence. French, the language of international law, confounded the two meanings of "nationality," as did every other Romance language as well as Russian and English.[10] But the conflation was not merely the result of linguistic overlap.

Jurists often were conscious of the distinction between a *nation* and a *state*, particularly in the late nineteenth century. Pasquale Mancini famously argued in his inaugural address at Turin University that *nations* and not *states* were the legitimate subjects of international law.[11] Carlos Calvo, likewise, was careful to make the distinction in his treatise, noting, "[... the nation] indicates a relationship of birth, origin; it marks the community of race, generally characterized by the community of language, morals, customs, and often special aptitudes, or a particular genius."[12] Nevertheless, as Calvo himself lamented, the majority of authors (still taking their cues from Vattel) "confound the notions of the

State and the nation," defining "nation" politically and using the term synonymously with "state."[13]

While most authors still used the term politically, the potential for confusing it grew as jurists engaged in more and more discussions with sociologists and philosophers.[14] As jurists left their own epistemological communities, they had to contend with the definitions and programs of other fields of inquiry, like sociology, that were particularly bound up with the new connotations and denotations of the word "nation." By 1912, for instance, Lassa Oppenheim, the author of one of the more prominent treatises of the early twentieth century, had to warn his readers, "nationality as citizenship of a certain state must not be confounded with nationality as membership of a certain nation in the sense of a race," and reminded his readers that "although all Polish individuals are of Polish nationality *qua* race, they have been, since the partition of Poland... either of Russian, Austrian, or German nationality *qua* citizenship."[15]

Nations versus States

But it was politics that did the most to confound the categories. As the nineteenth century drew to a close, the logic of nationality destabilized world politics. As the reader might remember, already by mid-century, jurists and political philosophers had begun to reimagine the international order around the concept of the nation and to shift legal international personhood away from the state and toward the nation.[16] Nationalism, as the set of ideas became known, was, perhaps, the predominant ideology and language of international order in the nineteenth century.[17] One of its central progenitors, Giuseppe Mazzini (friend of Alexander Herzen), artfully expressed the nationalist creed when he declared that having thrown off the chains of monarchs, "each people will march forward in freedom toward the realization of that part of God's providence that has been set aside for their native land, and that appears inscribed in their traditions, their national language, and the shape of their territory."[18] People were sovereign in this model of the international order, not states, and as such nations (or at the very least nation-states), it was argued, should be at the center of international law.[19] The "alliance of the princes" was to give way to the "alliance of the peoples."[20] So what did that mean for borders? As French jurist George Cogordan put it, "Nationality is independent of the artificial divisions that wars and treaties have been able to trace upon the map of the world."[21]

John Emerich Edward Dalberg-Acton (better known as Lord Acton), a professor of history at Cambridge at the turn of the twentieth century, perhaps best summed up the principle of nationalism and its horrific potentialities:

> The greatest adversary of the rights of nationality is the modern theory of nationality. By making the state and the nation commensurate with each other in theory, it reduces practically to a subject condition all other nationalities that may be within the boundary. It cannot admit them to an equality with the ruling nation which constitutes the State, because the state would then cease to be national, which would be a contradiction of the principle of its existence. According, therefore, to the degree of humanity and civilisation in that dominant body which claims all the rights of the community, the inferior races are exterminated, or reduced to servitude, or outlawed, or put in a condition of dependence.[22]

By the late nineteenth and early twentieth centuries, it was increasingly clear that Acton's prognostications would prove correct. Irredentist[23] movements and ethno-nationalist activism had shifted geopolitics. In the age of nationalism, the politics of expansion and boundary claims were increasingly (although by no means exclusively) conducted by reference to people and their ethnolinguistic identities rather than to territory.[24] Battles were waged in schools, censuses, marriages, property ownership, the marketplace, and elsewhere to shape people into nationals and to lay claim over those of ambiguous or indifferent nationality.[25] Indeed, the language of primary education became one of the most contentious issues in Europe by the early twentieth century and lead to some of the more contentious cases in the new Permanent Court of International Justice (PCIJ).[26]

The First World War irreparably confounded the politico-legal and socio-linguistic categories. Nationalization efforts during the war in much of Europe created ethnic insiders and outsiders, particularly with regard to the economic sphere. Foreign investment and property ownership was suspect and enemy aliens and shareholders often found their property and businesses sequestered or seized as a matter of course.[27] But even ethnic minorities who were, nevertheless, nationals from the standpoint of international law or citizens from the standpoint of domestic law found themselves stripped of property as the boundaries of belonging shifted away from political allegiance and toward ethnolinguistic factors.[28] It was not only in the domestic sphere where the boundaries of belonging and the legal status of populations were in dispute. In order to gain allies and sow dissension among their enemies, the various belligerents stirred up nationalist sentiment by providing support and promising independence for ethnic minorities and colonial subjects as well as unification with for those peoples separated by "artificial" borders.[29]

It was two would-be peacemakers, Woodrow Wilson and Vladimir Lenin, who inflicted the real damage to the clarity of the politico-legal term. By raising the banner of "national self-determination," these two muddled international politics with national identity in their influential visions of postwar order.

In 1914, Lenin published his essay, "The Right of Nations to Self-Determination." He followed it two years later, in 1916, with his "The Socialist Revolution and the Right of Nations to Self-Determination."[30] While Lenin supported the right to *national* self-determination, he did so as a stepping stone toward socialist revolution. "Throughout the world," Lenin wrote, "the period of the final victory of capitalism over feudalism has been linked up with national movements."[31] The reason, he argued, was that unity in language was necessary for "genuinely free and extensive commerce on a scale commensurate with modern capitalism."[32] For Lenin, the source of irredentism and secessionist movements was economic struggle.[33] His idea of the merits and origin of agitation for national self-determination was very different from those of the anti-colonial and ethnolinguistic nationalists who would define the postwar attitudes toward the phrase. Yet, his advocacy for the principle was seized upon none-the-less.[34]

Wilson, in contrast, never uttered the phrase "national self-determination" before the end of the war. Instead, his program expressed the idea in principle and he was influenced by the writings of.[35] Taken together, six of his famous fourteen points articulated a program of redrawing the borders of Europe "along historically established lines of allegiance and nationality" and creating a League of Nations for the "purpose of affording mutual guarantees of political independence and territorial integrity . . . " for these newly redrawn states. These six points, which demanded that the boundaries of states be aligned with nations and guaranteed the sovereignty of those new states, affirmed the principle of sovereignty and gave it a national tint.[36] Wilson, a sometimes-instructor of international law and politics, and a sometimes-President of the United States, had come from an intellectual background in which he had, as many international jurists had done, used nation and state as virtual synonyms. Nations, for Wilson, were mutable and created through allegiance to a common and legitimate state. While there was certainly a historical component to a nation, so long as states were democratic, nations and states, he believed, had a natural tendency to come into congruence. Put another way, a nation was merely the population contained within a legitimate state.[37] Wilson himself had no idea that for much of Europe *nation* was just as much an ethnically as a historically or politically defined term. Indeed, by June of 1919, as the opening of this chapter indicated, Wilson acknowledged his own ignorance of the distinction.[38] Wilson's Secretary of State, Robert Lansing, had himself expressed his worry over the use of the phrase, writing in December of 1918, "When the President talks of self-determination what unit has he in mind? Does he mean a race, a territorial area, or a community? Without a definite unit which is practical, application of this principle is dangerous to peace and stability." Lansing ominously continued, "The phrase is simply loaded with dynamite."[39]

Amputating Empires and Crafting Nation-States at Versailles

Despite the variations in interpretation, "national" self-determination was the defining phrase of the postwar order and was responsible for many of the more contentious parts of the peace conference. The Big Four at the Paris Conference were intent on dismembering the former European land empires. In preparation for the surgery, ethnographers detailed the nationality of the peoples of Eastern Europe and the inhabitants voted in plebiscites to aid in determining the sites of amputation. But, despite such efforts, the uneven distribution of linguistic communities, the geopolitical realities involved in fixing borders, and the sometimes-confusing results of plebiscites ensured that the new boundaries were far from perfect.[40] Tens of millions of ethnic nationals now lived outside the boundaries of the new states crafted for their nation. Moreover, many of those ethnic nationals now lived in new states crafted for another nation.

Various proposals were floated at the peace conference to try and mitigate the situation and protect minorities who now lived in ethno-national states rather than in heterogenous empires. The original proposals had been sweeping, involving guarantees of enforcement by the League and access by minorities in the so-called "new states" to the proposed Permanent Court of International Justice (PCIJ). Instead, a series of minority treaties were put in place as a condition on the creation of the new states of Eastern Europe. These treaties required the general protection of a range of standard civil and political rights and charged the League Council with enforcing the guarantees.[41]

In addition to creating a guarantee for minorities, the treaties themselves attempted to express the liberal, juridical definition of national by requiring the new states to declare that everyone who had been (or whose parents had been) "habitually resident" in the territory of the new state regardless of their ethnic affiliation to be nationals.[42] Likewise, the treaties allowed individuals to opt for any nationality open to them.[43]

These treaties adopted, to sink into legal parlance, domicile, rather than nationality, as the model of belonging in these new states. To be Polish from the perspective of the international system was to have been habitually resident in the territory rather than to be ethnically or linguistically Polish.

Yet, the treaties, despite their best efforts, also contributed to the conflation of the legal and ethnic categories. Article 91 of the Treaty of Versailles, for example, declared, "Poles who are German nationals will have a . . . right to opt for Polish nationality . . . ."[44] In effect, treaty provisions like Article 91 linked membership within a political community to membership in an ethnic community. That is, "Poles" who were legal Germans could opt to fix that anomaly. As a clerk in novelist B. Traven's dark comedy on interwar nationality politics asked a sailor, "Did you, within the proper time given, declare before a German authority . . . that you wish to retain German citizenship after the Polish provinces according to the provisions of the Treaty of Versailles were returned to Poland?"[45]

More importantly, the treaties themselves revealed the horrific logic of the new national states. By their terms, the treaties encouraged any person opting for a nationality other than that of the state in which he or she resided to vacate the country. Article 91 guaranteed that for a period of twelve months after election, no export or import duties would be placed on moveable property and the ownership of immoveable property would be guaranteed, even to those who were now effectively foreign landholders.[46] The treaties did not mandate a transfer after electing a different nationality, but they did encourage it. Ideally, from the perspective of the states, there would be no permanent foreigners.

> I tell you, my good man, it sure will come to the point where the Poles, those stinking godless dirty pigs, will drive out of Poland all those Germans who have adopted of German citizenship. I assure you, Koslovski, we will do the same. The only way to deal with those bandits.[47]

By the time Traven had penned this dialogue in the early 1920s, organized and internationally sanctioned population exchanges were already happening in the Eastern Mediterranean between Greece and Turkey.[48] Disorganized exoduses were likewise happening across Europe.[49] Ethnic Germans poured out of former German territories and into Germany. Ethnic Magyars departed their homes in the newly-enlarged Romania and the newly-born Czechoslovakia and Yugoslavia and "returned" to the newly-independent Hungary.[50] By the late-1930s, facing millions of ethnic German speakers in the Sudetenland and an aggressive Germany, then-President Eduard Benes of Czechoslovakia wrote to Adolf Hitler to offer a swath of Czech territory in exchange for a compulsory population transfer of ethnic Germans out of the tiny republic.[51] Indeed, by 1948 it could be said that Traven's literary prediction had come true with respect to the Polish-German borderlands.[52] But even these mass movements could not undue the patchwork ethnolinguistic quilt of central and eastern Europe.

The Minority Problem

If clean dissections of the former empires were not possible, and if forced population exchanges were difficult, undesirable, or impossible in the case of nations without states, what then was to be done about the minority problem?

Despite the efforts of the surgeons at Paris and the diligent migrations of those souls who did not wish to live outside of their national states, the eight new states carved from the corpses of the Russian, German, and Austrian empires contained more than 25 million minorities, more than two-thirds of whom had national states nearby that were capable of pressing claims. Over the next twenty years, those minorities with strong states – namely Germans and Hungarians – constantly petitioned and lobbied the League for intervention with the backing of their compatriots abroad. In effect, strong states engaged in a type of virtual diplomatic protection of their ethnic nationals abroad. The ethnic Germans of Poland, by the operation of the minority treaty, were Polish nationals. Yet, like nationals abroad in other contexts, they made appeals to their compatriots abroad. Nationality had entangled Europe in a web of interest and intervention with horrific potentialities.

The minority regime represented a type of international supervision for the purpose of protecting the rights of minorities. But it was applied unevenly. The peace treaties had imposed the minority regime on the reconstituted states of Eastern Europe, but had done nothing for the minorities of the West. Reacting to pressure from the newly constituted states in Eastern Europe, by 1922 the Third Assembly of the League had passed a resolution *softly* extending the regime:

> The Assembly expresses the hope that the states which are not bound by any legal obligations to the League with respect to minorities will nevertheless observe in the treatment of their own racial, religious, or linguistic minorities at least as high a standard of justice and toleration as is required by any of the treaties and by the regular action of the Council.[53]

But, the resolution was not binding and over the next decade, a number of activists, as well as the representatives of the states subject to the minority regime, demanded the generalization of the system to all League members. In 1925, for example, the Lithuanian representative of the League Assembly requested that a special committee be established to draft a convention which would have the effect of generalizing the minority regime.[54] Yet, the members not already subject to the minority regime were loathe to place such restraints on themselves. The sole exception to this rule was – with more than a touch of historical irony – Germany, which continually expressed its willingness to bind itself to some sort of generalized minority regime.[55] The reasons for this were self-serving, of course. With millions of ethnic Germans living in the newborn states of Eastern Europe (the very states subject to the minority regime), Germany (for the most part) had been one of the most ardent defenders of the minority regime in order to ensure that the *Auslandsdeutsche* had "the chance to retain their independent existence ... " and to avoid "forcible assimilation" by the majorities in their countries of residence.[56]

German officials were able to make their argument because the Jewish population was not, in the estimation of German officials, legally a minority under international law as there was no Jewish state that could claim the Jews of Germany. As Friedrich von Keller, a German representative to the League argued:

> [T]he Jewish question has frequently been confused with the minority question. The Jewish question is a peculiar problem of race, and must not be connected with the general question of minorities. First and foremost, the Jews in Germany are neither a linguistic nor a national minority. They do not look upon themselves as such, and have never expressed any desire to be treated as a minority.[57]

The infamous events of 1933 highlighted just how unsatisfactory the selective imposition of the minority regime could be. In April, the Nazi controlled government of Germany promulgated its first anti-Jewish measures, which excluded non-Aryans and opponents of the Nazi regime from the civil service, law, and other select professions.[58] While the Jews in most of Germany were helpless to protest against the discriminatory measure, the same was not true for the Jews of Upper Silesia. The complicated economic, political, and ethnographic makeup of the region had caused the League Council to recommend, and Germany and Poland to sign, an agreement, which divided the region between the two states, provided for the application of minority guarantees, and created a claims tribunal to hear disputes.[59]

So, Jewish Leaders from Upper Silesia met and selected Franz Bernheim, a Jew from the region who had been dismissed from his post under the new laws, to serve as a complainant before the League. A petition was drawn up on Bernheim's behalf, submitted to the Minorities Section of the League and brought up for debate in the Council.[60] The condemnation was broad and vocal. Representatives from several League members denounced Germany's failure to live up to the principles of the 1922 resolution. Several representatives threatened, again, to raise the issue of the generalization of the minority regime in the Assembly. The Swedish representative, for example, declared, "The time is now drawing near for serious consideration of the possibility and means of converting [the principles of the 1922 resolution] into more far-reaching undertakings."[61] And the Polish representative submitted a draft resolution which requested that the League Council appoint a committee "to study the problem and submit a draft general Convention on the Protection of Minorities to the next session of the Assembly."[62] Germany, despite being the target of much of the criticism, reiterated that it was still in favor of generalizing the regime.[63] It looked for a moment as if nationalities would become, in fact, subjects of international law – that they would have a kind of international legal standing and a kind of international legal protection. It appeared as if the *demos* of the international order would finally include nations and not just states.

But the debate that followed the submission of the Bernheim petition laid bare the problems plaguing the system.[64] Nazi Germany could be one of the strongest proponents of the minority regime, decrying over and over again the mistreatment of minority German populations abroad. Yet, at the same time, Nazi Germany could adamantly refuse to permit any interference in its domestic policies toward its own nationals.[65] In discussing the minority treaties, the German representative gave an impassioned defense of the minority system and the principle of nationality at its heart:

> [T]he individual in these days feels himself bound to his ethnic nationality and to the culture with which he is associated by ties much more close than those of former times. We call this tendency the avowal of the link with the *Volkstum* – that is to say, the ethnic nationality. This avowal expresses the unity of feeling in all those who are bound by common blood or by a common language, and who enjoy the same civilisation and customs. The members of a nation or an ethnic group living in a foreign environment constitute, not a total number of individuals calculated mechanically, but, on the contrary, the members of an organic community, and it is thus that, at the bottom of their hearts, they view themselves. They also desire recognition as a group where their rights are concerned. The very fact that they belong to a nation means that the nation in question has a natural and moral right to consider that all its members – even those separated from the mother country by state frontiers – constitute a moral and cultural whole.[66]

A nation-state, according to the German representative, had a right to define its population, including those residing far outside of its borders. Likewise, a state had the right to intervene on behalf of those co-nationals abroad. With ethnic Germans littered throughout Eastern Europe, Czechoslovakia and Poland began to get nervous. Eduard Benes, Czechoslovakia's Foreign Minister and soon-to-be President noted before the League that his country had signed on to the famous 1922 resolution on minorities because it required both that "all countries should respect minorities" and reciprocally that "minorities should be loyal at all times to the State if they desired to enjoy the rights of protection." But, Benes urged his colleagues to take care "not to give the impression that a minority constituted a personality in law."[67]

The Mandate Problem

Nationality politics were not limited to the European sphere. Just as nationality of persons played a central role in gambits for legitimacy and territory in interwar Europe, so too would it overseas.

Wilson, as part of his effort to put an end to traditional colonialism, advocated for the erection of a new transitional system, which would place the former German and Ottoman colonies in Africa, the Middle East, and the Pacific under the stewardship of a state (like Britain or France), which would govern the former colony until the people of the territory reached a more advanced stage of political and economic development. The governance of these territories, known as "mandates," were to be supervised by the newly created Permanent Mandates Commission of the League of Nations. Neither colony, nor independent sovereign, these territories presented the League with a number of conundrums. As the Mandates Commission set to work, "the first tricky issue," in the words of Susan Pedersen, "was nationality."[68] As had been an issue for more than 50 years, the question of what national status colonial subjects should have continued to be complex. As during the late nineteenth century, sovereignty over territory and protection of the population were intertwined. But, since the control of a mandate was explicitly not an annexation, the complexities multiplied. The Versailles Treaty had explicitly stated, "The native inhabitants of the former German oversea possessions shall be entitled to the diplomatic protection of the Governments exercising authority over those territories."[69] But what this meant in practice was unclear.

The League Covenant established three classes of Mandate, "A," "B," and "C." Class A Mandates were those former colonies that were considered to "have reached a stage of development where their existence as independent nations can be provisionally recognized subject to the rendering of administrative advice and assistance by a Mandatory until such time as they are able to stand alone."[70] Class A Mandates were, in effect, states unto themselves and as such their inhabitants were entitled to the nationality of their nascent state. The inhabitants of Iraq, for example, were entitled to Iraqi nationality.[71] Iraqis abroad were protected by Iraqi consulates. In states where there were no Iraqi Consulates or delegations, Britain agreed to represent the interests of Iraqis based upon the Anglo-Iraqi Treaty of 1922 and their obligations under the general Mandatory provisions.[72] Similarly, Syrians and Lebanese were entitled to Syrian and Lebanese nationality. Protection abroad, as per the Mandate charter, however, fell to France when there were no Syrian or Lebanese consulates respectively. Hence, in 1927, France was held to be the valid representative of Syrians and Lebanese claimants against the Mexican government for losses incurred during the Mexican Civil War.[73]

The case was more complicated when it came to Class B and Class C Mandates. Class B Mandates were "less developed" than Class A Mandates. In Class B Mandates, the Mandatory Power was to assume a more direct administrative role, although one that was still short of formal annexation.[74] Class C Mandates were territories that "owing to the sparseness of their population, or their small size, or their remoteness from the centres of civilisation, or their geographical contiguity to the territory of the Mandatory, and other circumstances, can be best administered under the laws of the Mandatory as integral portions of its territory. . . ."[75] Or, put another way, Class C mandates were *almost* annexed territories. But what this meant with regard to nationality and protection was confused. If managing a Class C mandate was just short of annexation, then what was the legal status of the inhabitants? As German colonial territories, most of the inhabitants of the Class B and Class C mandates had been German nationals. Indeed, one member of the Mandates Commission conclusively stated, "Until the signature of the Treaty of Versailles, [the native] populations had possessed a definite national status, they were German subjects."[76]

But did the renunciation of German possessions mean that the inhabitants had likewise lost their German nationality? A sub-committee of the Mandates Commission was sure that "under international law there was no doubt that the German residents in that country were still German nationals."[77] But by "German residents," they meant the non-indiginous population. What about the indigenous population? Before Versailles they had "a well-defined nationality."[78] That is, they had been German nationals. But what about now? Some officials argued that it would be wrong to deprive the inhabitants of the mandated territories of "the advantages of a clearly defined national status."[79] The inhabitants of these mandates, one official argued, would soon "be carrying on trade and establishing businesses in neighboring colonies, and they would emigrate to distant parts of the world." It would, therefore, "be desirable that they should enjoy the benefits of international treaties and conventions, for the protection of their persons and property."[80] The former subjects in the German colonies had to be nationals of some sovereign. But if they weren't German nationals, what were they? The sub-committee openly thought about the problem. They couldn't be nationals of the "Allied and Associated Powers," they argued, since as a group of States the Powers had no common or collective national status.[81] They also couldn't be nationals of the League of Nations, which "not being a super-state, was not a State at all."[82] While it would be possible to create a new artificial nationality for the inhabitants, it was thought that it would be "cruel" to inflict upon the peoples of the mandated territories "an artificial nationality which the world would not acknowledge" and which consequently would provide no international protection.[83] Therefore, some officials argued, it followed logically that the inhabitants should be granted the nationality of the Mandatory Power.[84]

That, however, was not acceptable to many.[85] William E. Rappard, director of the Mandates Section of the League Secretariat, warned that granting the nationality of the Mandatory Power to the indigenous inhabitants could be interpreted by others as *de facto* annexation – precisely the type of activity the regime had hoped to limit.[86] A legal analysis written a few years later echoed Rappard's concern, noting, "The acquisition of the nationality of the Mandatory Power by the indigenous inhabitants of the mandate would, in effect, be a kind of implicit annexation of the territory and would do away with any of the utility of the mandate regime."[87] Geopolitics continued to be played out through nationality. Just as Germans, Czechs and Poles used the minority regime to extend their influence abroad through the legal identities ascribed to human beings, so too did would-be imperialists' attempts to make Samoans, Rwandans or South-West Africans into Brits, Belgians, and South Africans to solidify their claims.

Working from recommendations made by the Permanent Mandates Commission, the Council of the League of Nations passed a resolution that prohibited the mass naturalization of individuals within mandate territories and made clear that the "native inhabitants of the Mandated territory [were] not invested with the nationality of the Mandatory Power."[88] The resolution further requested that the Mandatory Powers come up with (using a degree of precision characteristic of international agreements) "some form of descriptive title which will specify their status under the Mandate."[89] The Mandatory Powers obliged, each coining their own legal descriptions of the indigenous populations. The British, for example, adopted the pithy "British protected persons, native of the Mandated territory of British Togoland, British Cameroons or Tanganyika."[90] But just what that meant from an international standpoint was somewhat unclear. And more concerning was just what the indigenous inhabitants thought. Empire could, perhaps, be played out in the minds of the indigenous inhabitants. In 1927, Rappard and the Permanent Mandates Commission noted with concern that the indigenous inhabitants of the Mandatory Powers did not seem to know that they weren't British, or Belgian and that the Mandatory Powers didn't seem to be doing much to correct that mistaken assumption.[91] In response, the League Council passed a resolution requesting that Mandatory Powers provide the Council with information with respect to any actions pertaining to nationality or protection.[92]

Even as late as 1937, fifteen years after the Permanent Mandates Commission had decided to investigate the problem, the national status of the indigenous inhabitants of the mandates was still unclear. Assessing the state of the legal question, James C. Hales, one of the preeminent experts of the subject, concluded:

> ... it can be said that the native inhabitants of the B and C territories have been given an administrative status, but not a national status, as they are not deemed as yet to be nations or communities, in the international sense of the word. One thing at least is certain, and that is that they have lost their former nationality, if they formerly had any.[93]

While not quite stateless (they were all, under Article 22 of the League Covenant, entitled to the diplomatic protection of the Mandatory Power), they did not quite have a state either. The continued ambiguity was, without a doubt, the result of continued aims to play geopolitics through the legal identities of those abroad. Imperialism would be played upon the claims to people – territory might come later.

Mandates were not the only colonial environment where claims upon people caused friction in the interwar world. One of the Permanent Court of International Justice's most significant cases in the first years of its existence concerned imperial impositions of nationality.

In the early 1920s, French officials were increasingly concerned by the numbers of non-French Europeans in its North African colonial possessions.[94] What would happen if the number of non-French immigrants were to outnumber the French?[95] In response, decrees were issued in both Tunis and Morocco which declared that all persons born in Morocco and Tunisia who themselves had at least one parent who had been born there would be considered a French national. The decree imposed all the duties of French nationality, including liability for French military service. France, to better secure its position in North Africa, was playing with the national identities of its colonial subjects.

The decree provoked outrage. Many residents who were technically British subjects were now subject to French military obligations. Many of them were "visited by the French military police, handcuffed, and forcibly taken to the French barracks, in order to compel their acceptance of these obligations."[96] The British government formally protested the decrees, arguing that France could not simply impose its nationality upon British subjects without their consent.[97] They demanded France arbitrate the issue.[98] When France refused, they submitted the dispute to the League Council.[99] The Council, unsure of what to do, asked the Permanent Court of International Justice for an advisory opinion.[100] The Court held unanimously that for France the question of nationality in Morocco and Tunis was not "solely a matter of domestic jurisdiction."[101] The web of treaties and agreements that had established France's protectorates over the territories, the Court reasoned, created an international interest that had to be taken into account.[102] It was the first, but would by no means be the last, time that an international court would challenge the sovereign prerogative to define a population.

Throughout the interwar period, then, the question of nationality, that is, of the boundaries of belonging and of the state's right to claim and to protect a population against international wrongs, was unresolved. Nationality, as a concept, was broken and its protean nature a threat to international stability.

The Failed Nationality Fix

In the years leading up to the First World War, the Institute of International Law and the International Law Association, along with numerous scholars and policy makers, had attempted to repair nationality and eradicate the "scourge" of double-nationality by requiring the loss of one nationality whenever a person gained another. Similarly the plans would end statelessness by not permitting the revocation of a person's nationality until they had acquired another.[103]

When drafting the Statute for the Permanent Court of International Justice, the Advisory Committee of Jurists was careful to think about the sources of law from which the court might draw. To clarify some of the outstanding disputes over legal doctrine, the Advisory Committee of Jurists recommended that the League convene a conference to continue the project of codifying public international law. That project had begun with the Hague conferences of 1899 and 1907 but had been interrupted by war. The Advisory Committee believed that continued codification would provide the new court with a valuable source of law to apply. To that end, the Fifth Assembly of the League of Nations convened a committee of experts to begin preparations for a conference on codification. The Assembly intended the scope of any conference to be modest and made clear that they did not want the committee to craft a complete code of international law. Yet, the instructions given to the committee of experts were somewhat paradoxical. The committee was to select the areas of international law where differences of opinion had rendered the law unstable or uncertain. As the chairman of the committee experts, Hjalmar Hammarskjold, put it, the conference should aim for "the removal of certain contradictions and ambiguities which have weighed heavily upon international life."[104] Yet, the committee was also charged with confining their activity to areas of law upon which agreement might be reached.

The committee of experts was composed of the many of the world's preeminent international legal minds – with professors from many of the world's preeminent academic institutions present. Yet, it was not a committee composed entirely of academics. There were former or future members of the Permanent Court of International Justice. There were former members of the Permanent Court of Arbitration. There were former and future justices of the highest judicial bodies of several countries. And there were senior members of foreign ministries.[105]

To ascertain what exactly the "contradictions and ambiguities" were that weighed upon international life, the committee surveyed its members. Although each member submitted lists of different lengths and complexity, several issues were included in most or all of them. The most prominent, by far, was nationality. Nationality in general, double-nationality, statelessness, and the nationality of corporations were not just on the lists of nearly every member of the committee, but were often the first topics listed.[106] As James Brown Scott noted with regard to nationality, "[t]he confusion was so great, so universal, and so embarrassing, not to say exasperating, that in the First Conference for the Codification of International law . . . 'nationality' is the first of the three subjects [. . . which have been] singled out for agreement."[107] The third subject, the Responsibility of States, was intimately tied up with the first, since it was the nationality of a party that allowed the Vattelian fiction, that transitive association between human beings and the abstract state to which they belonged, to work. It had also been the second most common topic listed in the survey. Yet, as the committee of experts met in the late 1920s to discuss the subject, it became clear that no solution would be forthcoming.

Preliminary discussions for the conference began in 1926 and from the start the outcome looked grim. James Leslie Brierly, a Professor of International Law at Oxford, served as the British representative at the conference. Despite being only 41, he spent much of the conference in a state of amused frustration and approached the conference with a cautious pessimism that was a stark contrast to his older pollyannaish colleagues.[108] But the confident members were quickly disabused of their optimism. Bernard Loder, for example, had spent the first meetings of the conference suggesting that even "sovereignty" itself was ripe for codification. But within a few days, he had fallen silent. Brierly provided a colorful vignette that aptly illustrated the impossibility of reaching a solution:

> It was amusing to hear my Argentine colleague, who had previously been unable to see the smallest difficulty in codifying such matters as the recognition of states, their responsibility, and so on, protesting in the name of all Latin America that never never would they admit that any other state could claim (jure sanguines) an interest anywhere in one who was (jure soli) an Argentinian. And my Italian colleague said exactly the opposite with almost equal fervour.[109]

It didn't get much better. By 1930, on the eve of the actual conference, James Brown Scott noted that there still was no agreement in sight on the dispute between principles of *jus sanguis* and *jus soli*. As he put it, "There are at present seventeen countries in Europe in which *jus sanguinis* is the sole test of nationality, but there is no American country which accepts that principle as the sole test of nationality."[110] The Harvard Law School, in the introduction to its extensive research on nationality produced for the conference, noted, "Nationality has no positive, immutable meaning. On the contrary its meaning and import have changed with the changing character of states.... Nationality always connotes, however, membership of some kind in the society of a State or nation."[111]

On March 13, 1930, after nearly four years of preparation, the Conference for the Progressive Codification of International Law convened in The Hague. The preliminary meetings had set the agenda and prepared the delegates for the points of contention. Yet, the fundamental disputes remained. The Chinese delegate cogently summed up the stakes of the nationality question. States of emigration favored *jus sanguinis*, states of immigration preferred *jus soli*. The problem faced by countries of immigration, he argued, was that if "the descendants for indefinite generations should maintain allegiance to the country from which their ancestors came, the countries [of immigration] could never develop a nationality of their own. Their population would be composed of a sort of crazy quilt of nationalities and various groups maintaining their allegiance to the country from which their ancestors came."[112] Little had changed since the late-nineteenth century when jurists and statesmen made identical observations.[113]

As Brierly might have predicted, not much ultimately came of the conference's work on nationality or the responsibility of states. Four conventions were drafted and signed regarding nationality, although none of them was particularly far-reaching or effective. And none dealt with the problem of conflicting standards for defining a national. The preamble to the Convention on the Conflict of Nationality Laws expressed the conviction of the parties that "it [was] in the general interest of the international community to secure that all its members should recognise that every person should have a nationality and should have one nationality only. . . ."[114] As M. R. Standaert, one of Belgium's delegates to the conference put it, ". . . no person can, to all intents and purposes, possess two nationalities simultaneously – in the same way that he cannot have two mothers. . . ."[115] The Convention recognized, "that the ideal towards which the efforts of humanity should be directed in this domain is the abolition of all cases both of statelessness and of double nationality."[116] Only a dozen of the 39 signatories of the Convention ultimately ratified it.

Manly O. Hudson, echoing the Chinese delegate, summed up the reasons for the failures. Some states, he noted, desired to "receive freely immigrants from abroad, to enable such immigrants to cast off all prior allegiance, and to integrate and consolidate their heterogeneous populations." But other states, he observed, desired "to hold the allegiance of their nationals to increase their man-power, to enlarge their prestige, and to extend their influence."[117]

***

In January 1919, near the start of the Paris Peace Conference, Wilson proposed that the "Contracting Powers [unite] in guaranteeing to each other political independence and territorial integrity." But he created an important caveat, writing "but it is understood . . . that such territorial readjustments, if any, as may in the future become necessary by reason of changes in present racial conditions and aspirations or present social and political relationships, pursuant to the principles of self-determination . . . may be effected if agreeable to those peoples." Wilson had misunderstood just what such a proposal would entail. Six months later he had already lamented and acknowledged his ignorance to Edward F. Dunne and Frank P. Walsh.[118]

Others had not been so ignorant. David Hunter Miller, a legal adviser to the American commission to the Paris peace conference, had warned that founding international order on the right to national self-determination would doom any peace. In his comments on Wilson's draft treaty proposal, Miller warned that allowing for territorial readjustments based on the principle of national self-determination would "compel every Power to engage in propaganda and will legalize irredentist agitation in at least all of Eastern Europe."[119] His prognostications proved apt.

In 1929, a year before the meeting of the Hague Codification Conference, a German representative to the Congress of European Nationalities proclaimed, "A glance at an ethnographic map shows that the Germans of Czechoslovakia are not an ethnic minority in the Czech region of settlement, but a part of the total population of the German people that has been cast out over the present national borders."[120] As Hudson had said, states were holding on to their nationals to "extend their influence." In an age of nationalism, it was simply impossible to come to an agreement about political and legal identity in international law. In 1937, Imre Ferenczi,[121] chief of the Migration Section of the International Labor Organization, lamented that the codification conference had "succeeded only in recommending certain principles."[122] That failure, he thought, would have tragic ramifications. As Ferenczi ominously noted, "The National Socialist's conception of the political solidarity between all 'conationals' of German blood increases international frictions and creates difficulties in accomplishing civic duties."[123]

Two years later came Munich.

4 Sovereign Persons

Above the nations is humanity.

Henry Morse Stephens, 1916[1]

Lieutenant I. S. K. Soboleff was in retreat. After months of fighting against Bolshevik forces, Soboleff's unit was weary, short on supplies, isolated, and retreating toward Chinese Turkestan. As a condition for admission into China, border officials forced the beleaguered soldiers to abandon their arms and ammunition and enter in small groups at regular intervals. Penniless, the lieutenant sold his possessions one by one as he and a few of his compatriots made their way across the stark reaches of Chinese Turkestan and the parched expanse of the Gobi desert struggling with thirst, battling with venomous creatures, and altogether unsure of what their future held.[2]

After a string of adventures (which included serving briefly in the Chinese army), our protagonist found his way to Shanghai. Garbed in a woman's coat with a fur collar, white trousers, and a pair of canvas shoes, Soboleff made his way, at last, to the local refugee bureau where he was given some money and clothes. Safe, at last, the lieutenant settled in with his 18,000 compatriots. He joined the Russian Young Men's Association and whiled his time away. He had no job prospects in Shanghai, yet he didn't have enough money to go back to Europe.[3]

One evening the lieutenant was dining at the Russian Officers' Society and pondering what to do with his future. The conversation at the table turned to Charles Lindbergh's recent aerial voyage across the Atlantic. Inspired, Soboleff declared that he too would set out on an adventure, money be damned.

"Set out where?" one of his fellow officers asked.

"Oh, all around the world," he replied. "We Russians of the old régime are scattered in every country of the earth; surely it would be a fine idea to go and look them up and bring them news of their countrymen – to help them to realise that, though exiled for the time, we are still a part of the great Russian nation, and may some day return to our own country. Why should I stick here in Shanghai, when the roads of the world are open to me?"[4]

He pieced together a small wreck of a bike from a hodgepodge of parts. The Dunlop Tyre Company outfitted his wreck with some tires. The wife of a friend gave him a new riding outfit. Everything seemed to be coming together, albeit haphazardly.

Finally, on November 7, 1928, Soboleff set out from Shanghai. Yet he soon discovered that "the roads of the world did not seem so open and free as [he] had assumed." The problem was not material (although he certainly did and would have many problems of that nature), but rather legal. The lieutenant had trouble getting visas and papers in order – for Soboleff, along with hundreds of thousands of other Russians, had been forcibly denaturalized by the Soviet regime, yet Soboleff had not naturalized anywhere else. Soboleff was stateless.[5]

Statelessness

Statelessness begins in the wilderness. The idea that people existed free from the bonds of allegiance to a city, state, or some other sovereign was not new to the twentieth century. Criminals, vagrants, and nomads were all described as being something akin to stateless, even if the word was not explicitly used. As the Greek tragedian Sophocles put it, "when [man] obeys the laws and honors justice, the city stands proud." But, he continued, when he breaks the laws, "he is like a person without a city, beyond human boundary, a horror, a pollution to be avoided."[6] In this formulation, a person became stateless by rejecting the *polis* and the laws that demarcated its boundaries. Philip Nolan, the protagonist of Edward Everett Hale's *The Man Without a Country*, and perhaps the most recognizable stateless figure of the nineteenth century, was stateless because he had both committed treason and, in the course of his trial, blasphemed his own country.[7] One became stateless either by choice (by rejecting the city) or by action (by breaking the city's laws). Yet all of these conceptions incorporate, implicitly or explicitly, exile from the world of states. Being stateless implied an existence in a state of nature – a life lived beyond the walls of a city or beyond the frontier of a state and in the wildernesses of the world. It was partially a territorial idea – traditionally in order to be stateless someone had to be physically removed from the world of states. Indeed, into the last decade of the nineteenth century, it was thought that it was legally impossible for someone to be stateless while in the territory of a state.[8] But it was primarily an idea about personal allegiance – to be stateless was to have no sovereign. In medieval Europe, the lordless man, the man without a sovereign, owed no allegiance and received in return no protection. He was an outlaw.[9] A stateless person was a person without a sovereign and, therefore, without protection or a personal legal status.

But the reach of sovereigns extended inexorably in the nineteenth century. Around the world frontier lines pushed rapidly outward, collided, and melded into borders. Every spot of land on Earth – with the sole exception of Antarctica – was incorporated into the state order in one form or another.[10] Staring at a map sometime in the 1890s, Joseph Conrad's Marlowe lamented that the map of the world "had ceased to be a blank space of delightful mystery."[11] In that same decade, Frederick Jackson Turner, an American historian, bemoaned that the frontier line had vanished; settlement had drowned it in the Pacific.[12] When Hale wrote *The Man Without a Country*, he sent his protagonist not to another land, not into the western wilderness, but to sea – an indication of the inconceivability, even by 1863, of being outside the boundaries of a state while on dry land.[13] Both Stefan Zweig and B. Traven, writing decades later, echoed Hale when writing about the stateless. Zweig and Traven's protagonists, unable to find homes on land, die at sea.[14] Nor was the reach of sovereigns increasing merely in scope; new technologies of observation and management increased the scale of surveillance.[15] The territory of states themselves became increasingly regulated as burgeoning bureaucracies counted, categorized, and scrutinized their populations.[16] Cities and the countryside melted together into a single legal space, and it became increasingly uncomfortable for those without documentation, known in German as *schriftenlos*, to live without some kind of relationship to a sovereign. To be stateless was to be permanently abroad and without protection.

The earliest example of "stateless" being used to denote a person – "[n]ot recognized as a citizen of any country [or] having no official nationality" – was recorded by the *Oxford English Dictionary* in 1890.[17] The French equivalent, *apatride*, is of an even more recent vintage, not being used regularly until the turn of the twentieth century.[18] Although French writers had long described people as being *sans nationalité*, it was often to denote historical nomads or traitors (like Hale's Philip Nolan), not as a way of describing a juridical status for those residing within the world of states.[19] The German *staatenlos* is also a relatively recent example, although *heimatlos* has an older pedigree.[20] Few international legal treatises addressed the subject of statelessness in detail until the latter half of the century. But even the few that did discuss the subject usually confined their discussion to private, rather than public, international law.[21]

Scholars of European private international law, which increasingly used nationality to determine an individuals personal legal status with regard to age of majority, marriage, inheritance rights, and eligibility to contract, were the first to spill significant amounts of ink recording the complications that occurred when an individual lost her nationality either because of immigration or marriage (and it was almost always a her).[22] However, being without nationality within private international law was not to be stateless within the international order, but merely to have your legal status, as it pertained to wills, estates, marriage, and capacity to enter into contracts, determined by the law of the land you were in rather than the law of your homeland – that is by reference to domicile rather than nationality. But, as one commentator put it, even these were "isolated comicalities."[23]

The rarity of statelessness as a problem makes sense because expatriation was not a widely recognized right until the middle of the nineteenth century. Without expatriation and without alienation of allegiance, how could anyone in a modern political regime ever become stateless? Expatriation and statelessness went hand in hand. Women were often the first expatriates, as expatriation via coverture was more widely accepted than expatriation by choice – a fact that was at the center of some of the most vocal calls for reforming nationality as an international legal concept.[24] But as expatriation became a widely accepted international norm and as expatriation was even increasingly imposed upon those residing abroad, statelessness became a more common problem. The reintroduction of passport controls and the increased inspection of documents made the problem acute.[25]

But, as the earliest commentators noted, statelessness was simply not compatible with a world of states. Alexander Porter Morse, an American consul and legal scholar, remarked in his *Treatise on Citizenship* in 1881 that expatriation as a principle must include naturalization, normatively arguing, "The 'man without a country' may be a familiar and entertaining figure to readers of American fiction; but he has no place in the policy of civilized European states."[26] He continued by observing that permitting expatriation without naturalization would soon "obliterate one of the [lines] separating civilization from barbarism."[27] The eminent Swiss jurist and founding member of the Institute of International Law, Johann Caspar Bluntschli, argued, "There is a common interest in the civilized world of states that there are no stateless people."[28] The reason for the common interest was, as Lassa Oppenheim opined in 1905, that "such individuals as do not possess any nationality enjoy no protection whatever . . . as far as the Law of Nations is concerned, apart from morality, there is no restriction upon a State to abstain from maltreating to any extent such stateless individuals."[29] Ludwig von Bar, a prominent German legal scholar, echoed Bluntschli's sentiments, opining, "The general interests of the international legal order imperatively demand that every one should belong to some particular State, and that no one should be without a home." For if human beings could be stateless, Bar presciently remarked, it would be possible that "an indigent person should be tossed like a football from one State to another, or should be exposed somewhere on a desert island."[30]

The end of World War I brought with it a massive increase in stateless persons. Over the course of the 1920s, a series of bureaucratic and legal innovations attempted to solve the problem of statelessness. One method was to internationalize the protection of minorities and to fix nationality as an international legal concept – to eliminate cases of dual nationality and statelessness by making expatriation contingent on naturalization. That effort failed as state parties at The Hague Codification Conference could not reach an agreement on the subject. Nationality as a prime determinant of legal status remained broken. Instead, a number of legal projects, both pragmatic and intellectual, attempted to escape the strictures of nationality and establish a new international order in which individuals did not need states to serve as conduits through which they might grasp justice at the international level – to create, in effect, sovereign individuals from the perspective of the international order.

The Refugee Crisis

The collapse of the Russian Empire and the onset of the Russian Revolution created a situation that no statesman had encountered within living (or even recent historical) memory. Russia was a Great Power. It was an empire that spanned Asia and Europe. It was an empire that encompassed more than 125 million souls, who spoke more than a dozen recognized languages and countless dialects.[31] It was an empire that contained within it what would become more than a dozen sovereign states by the end of the twentieth century. In the course of two years, the territory that had once been simply the Russian Empire had fractured into a half-dozen states. As a result of Russia's political collapse and descent into civil war, an unprecedented flood of humanity began flowing west.[32]

The Russian refugee crises was the largest of the interwar period. Various estimates made following the war placed the numbers of displaced Russians globally at between 750,000 and 2 million. The League of Nations estimated that there were nearly 1 million Russian refugees in Europe alone – with between 300,000 and 600,000 of those in Germany. But as the range of the estimates indicates, determining the exact number was a Sisyphean task. Counting a transient population was a difficult proposition by itself. But classifying those populations was a political nightmare.[33] Even if one could find a group of people who stayed still long enough to count (and not double or triple count), how to identify those people was a contentious question. The establishment of new nation-states in the former Russian Empire created all sorts of complications for classification. "Certain refugees might be considered as Poles, but do not possess this nationality," stated a 1921 League report on the subject, "whilst others, coming from territory which has not been allocated to Poland, nevertheless appear able to claim Polish protection."[34] The treaties that were signed establishing these new states allowed inhabitants to declare their nationality. But strict deadlines and sluggish bureaucracies ensured that many people failed to do so, a situation that rendered them effectively stateless when the adjustment period expired. The crisis was further compounded by the mass denationalization of Russians abroad by the new Soviet regime. The Soviet Decree of October 18, 1921 (December 15, 1921) deprived Russians of their status as nationals if they left Russia after November 7, 1917 without the authorization of the Soviet authorities or if they had lived abroad for more than five years without obtaining a passport from a Soviet consulate.[35] Russians living abroad and all of those who had fled the violence of the revolution and the formation of the new states of Eastern Europe were rendered stateless.

The lack of a clear legal status left hundreds of thousands of people in legal limbo. Without a legal status, one was unable to travel, unable to find work, and unable to turn to a sovereign for assistance. Solving that problem was at the top of many agenda. In 1920, Gustav Ador, the president of the International Committee of the Red Cross, sent a letter to the League asking the organization to set up a committee to address the refugee problem and to establish a high commissioner for refugees. The first item he thought needed to be addressed was "to define the legal status of the refugees."[36] Other organizations, including the Jewish Colonization Association under the leadership of the indefatigable Lucian Wolf, showered Geneva with letters relating the plight of Russians in general and Russian Jews in particular. Wolf's goal was to resettle many of the Jews in South America, a difficult prospect for a class of people without passports or identification papers.[37]

In response, the League brought together a committee of former lawyers and officials who had fled Russia. André Mandelstam, a member of the Institute of International Law and the former director of the Legal Department of the Russian Ministry for Foreign Affairs, led the Committee. After several days of discussion, Mandelstam authored a memorandum for the Legal Section of the League Secretariat. His report set the agenda for the upcoming conference on the Russian refugee problem, which was to be held in Paris that same month. In his report, Mandelstam noted that there were two legal questions the conference should address, "that of the *personal status* of the refugees, and that of the *organisation and of the protection of their rights*."[38]

The first legal question, regarding "personal status," was concerned with how private law would apply to the refugees. The civil law of Continental Europe, in contrast to the common law of the United States and the British Empire, used nationality rather than domicile to determine legal status for the purposes of private law. The validity of contracts, wills, marriages, and the age of majority all turned on a clearly definable nationality. What law would apply to a Russian refugee living in a continental country? Would a judge apply the new Soviet laws to Russian nationals abroad? As Mandelstam noted, Soviet law had abolished all rights to private property. If Soviet law were applied, he argued, "No Russian could be allowed in France, Italy or Germany, to possess property, to enter into contracts, to bequeath or succeed to property."[39] Many refugees had fled Soviet law, yet, owing to the nationality principle of civil law systems, Soviet law had the potential to follow them abroad. At the time Mandelstam wrote his report, however, France, Italy, and Germany had not recognized the new Soviet regime. It was unlikely, therefore, that courts would apply the law of an unrecognized sovereign. But that lack of recognition presented another problem – specifically that if there was no national law that could apply to the refugees, then the law of the domicile – that is the law of their state of residence – would govern. It is a testament to how firmly enshrined the principle of nationality had become in civil law jurisdictions that such a prospect seemed to present genuine concerns for the Russian jurists. Mandelstam worried that applying the law of the domicile would denationalize Russians who wished to remain Russian and to live under the laws of their (now former) nation. Why should Russian women need the oversight of their husbands when crafting a contract, Mandelstam wondered, just because they were in France? Why should divorce between Russians be more liberal when in France than when in Russia? The solution for Mandelstam was that courts should apply Russian law as it existed before the Revolution. That is to simply pretend as if the civil law of Tsarist Russia were still in effect.[40]

The second question, concerning the "protection of their rights," dealt directly with issues coming under the regime of diplomatic protection, which had been the general means of securing the protection of the person and property of nationals traveling or residing abroad. Despite some intellectual trends to the contrary, a state was still necessary for seeking any kind of international redress. The collapse of the Russian Empire created an unprecedented situation within modern Europe. A Great Power, with a massive number of subjects residing outside of its territorial boundaries, had no effective government and uncertain consular representation. Moreover, rampant anti-Bolshevism ensured that none of the Great Powers was going to quickly recognize the Soviet government. Hundreds of thousands of Russians had become effectively stateless from the standpoint of both public and private international law.

Hannah Arendt would take note of this conundrum decades later, writing, "The second loss which the rightless suffered was the loss of government protection, and this did not imply just the loss of legal status in their own, but in all countries. Treaties of reciprocity and international agreements have woven a web around the earth that makes it possible for the citizen of every country to take his legal status with him no matter where he goes.... Yet, whoever is no longer caught in it finds himself out of legality altogether."[41]

The Nansen Passport

In August of 1921, in accordance with a resolution passed by the League, an intergovernmental conference convened in Geneva to study the problems presented by the massive number of refugees. Representatives attended from Bulgaria, China, Czechoslovakia, Finland, France, Greece, Poland, Romania, the Kingdom of the Serbs, Croats and Slovenes, and Switzerland along with representatives from the International Labor Organization (ILO), the International Committee of the Red Cross (ICRC), the League of Red Cross Societies, and the International Union of the "Save the Children Fund."[42] The conference concluded with a resolution emphasizing the importance of creating an identity document or passport to enable the refugees to travel. The next day the League Assembly appointed Fridtjof Nansen as the first high commissioner for Russian refugees to put him to work developing a plan.

Nansen was "a tall conspicuous figure," with an "athletic frame," and a "lean melancholy face."[43] He had been a world famous arctic explorer, marine biologist, and oceanographer. He walked, according to one admirer, with a "long swift step and the air of untrammeled freedom."[44] So it seems both an unexpected and fitting twist of fate that Nansen, who had spent so much of his time wandering the unbounded Arctic and Antarctic and sailing on the open seas, would be charged with negotiating the eccentricities of the interwar border regime. He began his task by soliciting the opinions of the ILO regarding the "legal status of Russian refugees *as workers*."[45] The high commissioner was concerned that a simple identity certificate would not prove sufficient protection for refugees. This concern was shared by the Conference of Private Russian Organizations, which was worried that refugees would not be able to benefit from labor protection laws. Without a proper passport and the protection it represented, who would ensure that Russians did not become, in effect, undocumented slave laborers?[46] The Conference of Private Russian Organizations, like the Conference of Russian Legal Experts, argued that the Commissioner might simply permit the old Russian consulates to continue to function in states which already had them, and establish new ones in states that did not. The proposal would have created a phantom state with a foreign ministry in exile charged with issuing passports and overseeing the welfare of the denationalized Russians.[47] It was a proposal that Nansen, whose work required him to delicately engage with the Soviet government, was unwilling to support.

Nansen, in conversation with the ILO, seriously considered two different plans for issuing identity documents. The first plan was somewhat radical. Identity documents would be issued by the high commissioner's office under the authority of the League. The high commissioner would ensure that refugees were protected from abuse. The second plan was more modest and traditional. Instead of creating a new internationally issued document, the states in which the various refugees had found temporary relief would issue the documents themselves. Nansen, aware of the strict mandate under which the League operated, was concerned that League members would not support a plan establishing a status akin to international citizenship.[48] A pragmatist to his core, Nansen got behind the more conservative plan. At an intergovernmental conference held in July, a passport regime was adopted. States would issue the passports. There would not be an international identification certificate. Instead, France, or Germany, or Spain, or whatever country would issue a certificate to a refugee who fell within the program. But it was still a certificate issued by, and anchored to, a state. German versions were typeset in a characteristic Gothic typeface. French versions lacked the second language characteristic of the passports in other countries (France undoubtedly assuming that French alone was more than sufficient in an international context). Nansen passports were fundamentally state documents merely issued under an internationally organized program.

The program was intended to remedy a problem caused by nationality. Yet the program remained anchored to nationality. The passports were only available to Russian refugees. But it was unclear precisely what a "Russian refugee" was. Would Poles living in the newly reconstituted Poland qualify? What about Estonians living in France? Would they be available only to ethnic Russians? Would there be a separate category for Russian Jews?[49] It was not until 1923 that the Legal Section of the League agreed to define "Russian refugee," as "any refugee originating from territory which formerly belonged to Russia and has not become part of an internationally recognized state, and not possessing any nationality except his original Russian nationality."[50] The definition stuck to the old inclusive imperial definition of Russian nationality. There was no ethnic component. The definition also hewed toward the ideal of eliminating dual nationality from the international system. One could only be a "Russian refugee" if they had not yet become a national of another state.

Although the definition provided clarity in terms of determining who could qualify for special assistance, it was never wholly satisfactory to many of those who fell within it. For years after the creation of the passport, Jewish jurists and advocates floated the idea of whether a distinct status should be created for Jewish refugees.[51] Nor was it only Jews, the perennial pariahs of Europe, that chaffed under the political definition of "Russian." By 1930, the League had received dozens of written protests from Ukrainian organizations all over the world demanding that their status be listed in League reports and other official documents as "Ukrainian who has not acquired any other nationality." The protestors argued that the "practice of heaping indiscriminately all nationalities of the late Russian Empire into one class of Russians" was contrary to the League's role as the "protector of the Rights of nationalities."[52] Those without nationality did not want to just be lumped together for the sake of bureaucratic and political expediency. If they fell outside of the state system, they wanted the League to explicitly recognize their ethnolinguistic identity as a national status.

But former subjects of the Russian Empire were not the only large group of refugees in the interwar period. Armenians were the next major group of refugees to be offered Nansen passports. Soon thereafter the program was extended to Turks, Kurds, and Syrians (Assyrians and Assyro-Chaldeans). The agreement extending the Nansen regime to cover Armenian refugees made one somewhat significant change in eligibility. In contrast to the capacious political definition of Russian refugee, which included anyone who formerly resided in the Russian Empire, the definition that was adopted for Armenians was more narrowly tailored. The final agreement made the identification certificate available to "any person of Armenian origin, formerly a subject of the Ottoman Empire." Like its Russian counterpart, the Armenian definition was defined with reference to a political state, effectively making Ottoman nationality a prerequisite for obtaining an identity certificate. But unlike the definition of "Russian," the definition of "Armenian" was further limited to "any person of Armenian origin" and explicitly recognized a unique ethnic identity within a broader politically defined nationality. The trend continued in 1928 with the extension of the Nansen regime to Turks, Syrians, and Kurds. In the case of the Turks, the recipient must have been both of "Turkish origin" and have previously been a subject of the Ottoman Empire – requiring both a political and an ethnic status in order to acquire international documents. In the Syrian and Kurdish cases, no political status was required, only an ethnic status.[53] Unlike the Ukrainians whose ethnic identity was absent from their documentation, Armenians, Syrians, Kurds, and Turks had their ethnic identity explicitly recognized. But in all the implementations of the Nansen regime, some sort of prior status, either political or ethnic, was required. Indeed, when Nansen went to the League Council in 1927 to seek permission to generalize the refugee passport regime, the League Council demurred.[54] Such an extension, they argued, was problematic: "No attempt should be made to frame a definition, which would be difficult to establish." The Council specifically did not want to extend the regime to those who were merely stateless, telling Nansen, "The mere fact that certain classes of persons are without the protection of any national government is not sufficient to make them refugees; for on that theory all classes of persons without nationality and persons of doubtful nationality would have to be included."[55] The League Council was reluctant to move to a generalist, individual definition of refugee and hesitant to make the stateless person eligible for protection.[56] They instead stuck to political and ethnic definitions.

National politics continued to play out in the refugee regime more generally. By the late 1920s it became clear that many refugees could not return to their country of origin. The Russians had been denaturalized, and the Soviet government was unwilling to welcome back those who had refused to aid the revolution. Syrians and Armenians were also unlikely to want to return into the keep of those who had massacred so many of their kin. Naturalization and the regularization of legal status seemed to be the only permanent solution to the high commissioner. But, when Nansen made unofficial inquiries into the prospects of naturalization, he obtained some unexpected information. Some states were hesitant to naturalize a large number of relatively poor refugees out of concern for their own public purse. However, there were also states very willing to naturalize the refugees in their territory en masse. What was unexpected was that the refugees themselves often did not want to naturalize, they did not want to adopt a new legal nationality. There were two reasons for this reluctance.

First, like the Ukrainians who demanded that their national status be listed in their Nansen Passport, refugees residing in foreign lands were reluctant to adopt a new legal nationality as they still waited in hope for a state of their own.[57] Advocacy for the principle of national self-determination played out in the legal struggles over the very category of refugee.

In his report to the League Assembly, the high commissioner noted that assimilation had proved difficult, in part, because "the majority of the refugees, for reasons which it was difficult not to respect, did not wish to adopt other nationalities."[58] States complained that when offered naturalization, many refugees adamantly refused.[59] The British delegate to the Assembly agreed with the high commissioner, and observed, "Everyone sympathized with the feelings of men who, finding themselves in refugee colonies, hoped that the opportunity might arise for them to return to their native land and to resume their natural position."[60] Nevertheless, the delegate continued, "It was deplorable to think that children should be born refugees and that people should grow up from their earliest youth to think of the country in which they found themselves as a foreign country and be striving always to go back somewhere else."[61] Hannah Arendt, likewise, observed this phenomenon, writing:

> The Russian refugees were only the first to insist on their nationality and to defend themselves furiously against attempts to lump them together with other stateless people. Since them, not a single group of refugees or Displaced Persons has failed to develop a fierce, violent group consciousness and to clamor for rights as-and only as-Poles or Jews or Germans .... The stateless people were as convinced as the minorities that loss of national rights was identical' with loss of human rights, that the former inevitably entailed the latter. The more they were excluded from right in any form, the more they tended to look for a reintegration into a national, into their own national community.[62]

The Nansen passport, despite its quasi-international character, remained deeply tied up with nationality as a fundamental status. The great irony was that it was a document designed for those who had been deprived of nationality – yet it was only available to those who, in effect, had had a recognizable nationality. One had to prove that she had been a Russian national to receive a Nansen passport; one had to prove that he had been an Ottoman subject to receive a Nansen passport. Nationality, in its narrow juridical sense, was still a prerequisite for the document. Only the temporal boundaries had shifted. André Mandelstam, the Russian jurist who had been a staunch advocate of a passport for Russian émigrés, praised the regime specifically for not representing a type of international status. Rather, by being available only to Russians, Armenians, Syrians, Kurds, and Turks who had not yet acquired any other nationality, these passports were an explicit acknowledgement of their nationality.[63] It was this explicit acknowledgement that led Ukrainian activists to demand the inclusion of their distinctive identity within the passport.[64]

Second, naturalization would also deprive them of their personal legal status – subjecting them to the law of their new nationality for the determination of marriage rights and other personal relations. Both political and cultural nationalism thrived even in the legal limbo of statelessness.

Despite the conservative nature of the document and the imperial definition of nationality it adopted, the Nansen passport regime entered the international consciousness as a more robust document than it ever would end up being. Many believed that the document was, in fact, an international passport. The Legal Section of the League received reams of correspondence asking about the passport. "I have heard that the office of the League of Nations gives passports to persons who are 'staatenlose.' My friend finds himself in this situation," wrote a hopeful lawyer from Strasbourg to the League in 1923.[65]

Joost Van Hamel, the League's legal director, had to reply that the League could not and did not issue passports to anyone and corrected the record by stating, "You may be referring to the certificates of legitimation that many governments committed to delivering to *Russian* refugees as a result of the Geneva Agreement reached 5 July 1922 at the Intergovernmental Conference for the Russian Refugees, held under the auspices of the League of Nations."[66] The most common requests, of course, came from refugees writing in asking for a passport. The refugees in their letters almost always expressed their belief that the passports granted them the protection of the League itself – that is that these documents would be issued by the League and carry with them the same rights to legal and diplomatic protection that accompanied being a national of a recognized state willing to intervene on your behalf when abroad. So many of these letters were received that the legal section developed a form letter to send in response, which emphasized that the certificates were only available to *Russian* refugees and came complete with a blank space in which to place the name of the country's foreign office to which they needed to apply.[67]

But even international jurists, some of whom had been involved in and disappointed by the scheme ultimately adopted at Geneva in 1922, saw the Nansen passport as representing more than what it was in actuality – or at least they consciously mobilized the image of an international passport for their own political or intellectual purposes. Writing in the mid-1920s, André Mandelstam noted that because of the Nansen passport "it could be said that Russian and Armenian refugees have acquired an international character."[68] Egidio Reale, another international legal theorist, wrote that the Nansen Passport regime meant, "the international protection of the rights of the individual has become a task imposed upon the international community."[69] Many of the interwar legal revisionists, including Nicolas Politis, perhaps the most vocal supporter of the international recognition of the individual, agreed with Reale's sentiment.[70] The Nansen passport had created a discursive space that could be filled with visions of international citizenship. In 1924, a British delegate to the Assembly rhetorically adopted refugees as the League's first true citizens, asking, "Is there anyone who is likely to be a better friend of the League, a better child of the League, than he or she who has its international passport?" The delegate further added that "By the man in the street the refugees are in fact regarded as the League's children."[71] The high commissioner's implementation of the passport regime occurred amidst a broader debate about identity documents and their place in the interwar world.

In the years leading up to World War I, travel throughout Europe and the world was relatively free of bureaucratic formalities for Europeans. Stefan Zweig, a prominent Austrian writer, for example, nostalgically described the world as it was before the antagonisms unleashed by World War I had torn it asunder:

> Before 1914 the earth belonged to the entire human race. Everyone could go where he wanted and stay there was long as he liked. No permits or visas were necessary, and I am always enchanted by the amazement of young people when I tell them that before 1914 I travelled to India and America without a passport. Indeed, I had never set eyes on a passport. You boarded your means of transport and got off it again, without asking or being asked any questions; you didn't have to fill in a single one of the hundred forms required today. No permits, no visas, nothing to give you trouble; the borders that today, thanks to the pathological distrust felt by everyone for everyone else, are a tangled fence of red tape were then nothing but symbolic lines on the map, and you crossed them as unthinkingly as you can cross the meridian in Greenwich.[72]

The French academic and political writer André Siegfried also nostalgically recalled the openness of the pre-1914 world, writing, "I recall having made a tour of the world [around 1900] without having to produce a passport, a photograph, or a letter of sufficient credit and, at the majority of borders, nobody asked anything of you. The white man could go everywhere and, if he encountered an obstacle, he had only say: *civis Romanus sum*."[73]

Zweig and Siegfried's recollections are certainly selective.[74] Already by the late nineteenth century, states in Europe and the Americas had introduced many regulations on immigration. Health inspections and vaccinations for immigrants and third-class, or steerage, passengers were increasingly required at borders.[75] Bans or restrictions were placed on undesirable or suspect populations, and the requirement of a passport to travel from Asia was reintroduced.[76] Even in the 1850s, Herman Melville had observed economic inequalities when it came to free movement in his novel, *Moby Dick*. Aboard Captain Ahab's ship, Father Mapple sermonizes, "In this world, shipmates, sin that pays its way can travel freely, and without a passport; whereas Virtue, if a pauper, is stopped at all frontiers."[77]

The border regime was certainly not egalitarian in 1914, nor was the regulation of borders systematic. Europeans from privileged backgrounds, like Zweig and Siegfried, moved unchecked throughout much of Europe and the world. As a British consul in Suez reminded a hurried (and wealthy) Phileas Fogg on his voyage around the world, "You know that a visa is useless, and that no passport is required?"[78]

The law, as it was expressed at the time, was in harmony with Zweig's general observation. While always straddling the line between normative and descriptive, international law from Grotius onward was ambivalent about the sovereign power to regulate migration. Hospitality was an obligation of all Christian states. "To refuse to welcome strangers and foreigners is inherently evil," wrote Vittoria.[79] And likewise, Grotius (rather polemically) claimed, "The most famous jurists . . . deny that any state or any ruler can debar foreigners from having access to their subjects and trading with them."[80] Yet territorial sovereignty seemed to imply the absolute power to exclude.[81] The ambivalence continued well into the nineteenth century. However, the right to exclude made significant gains over the obligation to admit in the last few decades of that century, particularly as jurists struggled to reconcile Asian exclusion with the principles of international law.[82] Yet, even in the late nineteenth century, the international legal establishment continued to have difficulty resolving the two principles. The Institute of International Law, perhaps in reaction to increasing restrictions on migration, issued recommendations for a potential draft convention on migration that declared, "The Contracting States recognize the freedom to emigrate and to immigrate to isolated individuals or to a large number, irrespective of nationality." It further noted, "This freedom may be restricted only by a duly published decision of the governments and within the strict limits of the social and political necessities."[83] If restrictions were to exist, they could not be arbitrary and had to be necessary.

By the onset of World War I, territorial sovereignty firmly trumped the strictures of hospitality. Mandatory passports were reintroduced en masse during the war as a security measure. Germany, Britain, France, Italy, and the United States all either restored old or created new restrictions on the movement of people and goods and set up new checkpoints on their frontiers. These provisions were intended to be a temporary security measure. However, the war altered the logic and the priorities of European and American governments. Wartime restrictions remained in place long after the guns had gone silent. Mutual suspicion and new economic incentives made it politically difficult to dismantle the new border regimes.[84] That logic, however, did not go entirely unchallenged in the interwar world.

For a certain type of European intellectual, the passport and border regimes became tropes in their polemics (and particularly their polemical memoirs). The passport was a concrete and intimate manifestation of the illiberality of the interwar international order. It was an object that many readers had experience with, and it could provide them with a clear and personal contrast between the nineteenth and twentieth century worlds. As such, the passport, in particular, and the border regime, in general, were constantly mobilized in the rhetorical battle over the restoration of the pre-1914 world. British economist John Meynard Keynes, in his summary of nineteenth-century economic progress, observed that in addition to the integration of global markets, an average man before the war "could secure forthwith, if he wished it, cheap and comfortable means of transit to any country or climate without passport or other formality... and would consider himself greatly aggrieved and much surprised at the least interference."[85] Likewise, in 1925, Moritz Bonn, a noted German economist, political activist, occasional propagandist, occasional historian, and soon-to-be exile,[86] identified two particular changes that engendered anti-democratic nostalgia for the *Kaiserreich* (German Empire) among the average German. The first was, predictably, the interwar economic decline. The second, however, was the lack of mobility in the interwar world. Under the authoritarian Wilhelm II, Bonn explained, a German could "move freely about; nobody asked for a passport, and in most cases nobody balked his desire when bent on emigration." Under the democratic Weimar government, new regulations prevented him from going abroad. It was no wonder, Bonn observed, that some Germans had come to the conclusion that democracy's benefits were underwhelming.[87] André Siegfried mobilized the image of the passport, again to serve as a contrast between the triumphant nineteenth century and the disastrous twentieth century in his *La crise de l'Europe*. In the nineteenth century, Siegfried noted, "emigration was nearly free... and the formalities of passports were reduced to such a minimum, one could truly say they were nonexistent."[88] Likewise, Austrian writer Stefan Zweig, who we met recently above, in his sometimes-saccharine, yet perspicaciously nostalgic, sketch of prewar European life, identified the modern passport and border regime as the "petty" symptoms of the "intellectual epidemic" of xenophobia that swept through Europe between the wars. "We have been repeatedly questioned, registered with numbers, searched, rubber-stamped," wrote an indignant Zweig, "I regard every one of those rubber stamps in my passport as a brand."[89] In contrast to Phileas Fogg's (or Nellie Bly's) trip around the world in the 1870s for which "no passport [was] required,"[90] British writer Patrick Leigh Fermor's walk across Europe in the 1930s left him with a "faded, torn, dog-eared and travel-stained [passport], crammed with the visas of vanished kingdoms and entry- and exit-stamps in Latin, Greek and Cyrillic characters."[91]

Nor were commentaries on the absurdities and indignities of the modern regime restricted to memoirs, polemics, and nonfiction. German novelist B. Traven artfully captured the alienation and dislocation of the modern border regime in his macabre 1926 novel, *The Death Ship*.[92] As a police officer in that novel put it to the paperless protagonist, "The law is that anybody picked up without papers must be imprisoned for six months. We cannot shoot you like a dog with a disease, or drown you in the sea, although I am not so sure but that sooner or later such a law will be passed in every country, above all in every civilized country."[93] The novel's protagonist had earlier lamented, "Before the war nobody asked you for a passport."[94] Stefan Zweig, in a fictive mode, made a similar observation in his 1936 short story, *The Incident on Lake Geneva*. "A border means there's a foreign country on the other side. People won't let you through," said an Inn Manager to a marooned Russian soldier. "Why wouldn't they let me go back to my wife, if I ask them in Christ's name?" he asked. "People don't take any notice of the word of Christ any more" replied the manager. It's impossible to not feel Zweig's deep nostalgia for a borderless Christendom. With nowhere to go, the Russian soldier drowned himself in the lake.[95]

Reestablishing the mobility of the pre-1914 world was also on the minds of many of the statesmen meeting in Paris in 1919. The result was Article 23e of the League Covenant, which required that the League "make provision to secure and maintain freedom of communication and of transit."[96] To meet its obligations under the treaty, the League established the Provisional Committee on Communications and Transit, which organized the International Conference on Passports, Customs Formalities and Through Tickets in the autumn of 1920.[97] The conference convened with the expectation of drafting a plan for the gradual eradication of the passport regime. It soon became clear that those expectations were premature.[98]

There were serious objections to the reestablishment of the pre-1914 world articulated at the conference. First, the war had brought about a dramatic expansion in economic regulation as each belligerent attempted to fully mobilize human and material resources. By the end of the war in much of Europe, the "national economy" had become an object of intensive management by governments.[99] Moreover, the international economy in Europe had been brought to a virtual halt between the bellicose blocs of Europe. While the reestablishment of economic trade was attractive to business, cash-strapped continental governments wanted to increase their revenues and protect their expanded industries by maintaining or establishing new tariffs. They also jealously guarded their monetary resources by maintaining strict controls on the export of capital stowed away in the suitcases of travelers.[100] Second, states were concerned with political stability. Haunted by the specter of revolution, states in Eastern Europe strictly policed borders to keep out Bolshevik agents. As the Hungarian representative to the conference put it, "At the point of entry, control is indispensable for preventing contraband . . . for preventing the entry of Bolshevik couriers . . . and for impeding the importation of Bolshevik brochures and pamphlets. At the point of exit . . . to prevent Hungarian Bolsheviks from escaping justice and continuing their destructive propaganda campaign in neighboring countries."[101] The conference concluded that under the current geopolitical circumstances states were not yet ready to abandon the passport regime. Instead the conference redirected its efforts to the document – creating the booklet that is still the standard today. Despite creating a standard format, the final resolution of the conference expressed hope that pre-war conditions, including the "total abolition of restrictions" would be "gradually reestablished in the near future."[102]

That hope was not to be realized. Six years later the League Assembly passed another resolution convening another conference to look specifically into the question of eliminating passports. The International Chamber of Commerce (ICC), established in 1920 to promote the interests of international commerce, was one of several nongovernmental organizations present at the conference to come out strongly in favor of abolishing compulsory travel documents.[103] Other states supported the move, including Poland, which introduced the resolution proposing abolition. But Poland found few allies in the delegations from Western Europe.[104]

Several Western European states now actively opposed abolition. While security concerns were occasionally cited for opposing abolition, by 1926 the debate had shifted rather dramatically. Instead of focusing only upon controlling the entry of "undesirables" or the exit of financial resources, the conference was interested in the role of the passport as a protective instrument. Although the conference, like that in 1920, began with an acknowledgement that abolition was ultimately desirable, if still unachievable at the present, it quickly became apparent that there were new perspectives. The British delegate, for example, argued that up until now the discussion had "proceeded on the assumption that the abolition of all passports would be a sign of progress." That assumption, however, was one that the British government no longer shared. "The passport was one of the most useful possessions that a traveller abroad could possibly have," the British delegate argued, "it enabled him to claim to the protection of his diplomats and consular representatives if he got into any kind of difficulty."[105] Italy concurred, "The passport afforded immigrants a kind of social protection . . . it provided them with the protection they needed . . . and to obtain information as to the best locality for securing work."[106] The passport for many of the delegates had come to serve as a clear indication of the relationship between people and their foreign states for the purposes of diplomatic intervention – of knowing who was in as much as knowing who was out. It was the culmination of a trend that began with the reaction to the instrumentalization of nationality for the purposes of obtaining international protection.

The ICC representative acknowledged that passports were a useful document for travelers, especially for the British, "as it assured them of the protection of the British government, just as in time past the Roman Government protected those who could claim to be Roman Citizens." However, the representative asserted that neither Poland's nor the ICC's proposal advocated abolishing the passport as a document, but merely wanted to render their use optional, as it had been before the war. Despite the best efforts of the ICC and a few states, Britain's argument carried the day – the passport regime would remain in place. Although the president of the conference reminded the delegates that the Assembly and "public opinion . . . undoubtedly expects at least a step towards the abolition, to the widest extent possible, of the passport system," the majority of the delegates not only refused to consider abolishing the regime but also refused to insert even a prospective statement that the future abolition of passports "was desirable in itself," into the final act of the conference.[107] Just six years before, such a prospective statement found nearly unanimous support.[108]

The final act did have one notable success. In the preliminary meetings, it was widely recognized that because the Nansen passport regime was only available to certain categories of refugees, there were still large numbers of stateless persons who did not qualify for any identity document. Many refugees were still undocumented and unprotected from the standpoint of international law.[109] In recognition of this problem, the final act of the Passport Conference encouraged the League to prepare a plan to make a document available to other stateless peoples.[110]

But, by 1927, it was clear that the system was still hopelessly broken. In addition to the Passport Conference's directives, the high commissioner had received approximately 150,000 requests for passports on behalf of either refugees or stateless peoples who did not fit into the Nansen categories. Several organizations – including the *Comité unifié Juif*, the *Congrès de la Fédérations des Ligues des Droits de l'Homme*, and the International Council of Women – had contacted the high commissioner requesting that the Nansen passport regime be extended to everyone without a nationality. The *Verband der Staatenlosen*, which had met in Berlin earlier that year, voted unanimously to appeal to the League to establish a permanent commission and begin preparations for the "international regulation of the Stateless question."[111]

So, the League took up the broader issue of identity documents for all stateless people, not just those of a specific ethnic or defunct political identity. Athanasios Politis (the brother of Nicolas) chaired the committee charged with developing an identity document. The committee of experts worked tirelessly and drafted a comprehensive plan to at last solve the identification crisis. The plan would have made passports widely available to those with unclear nationality and to those, like Russian political refugees, unable to get a passport.[112]

Governments, however, criticized the plan for not making clear that the proposed passport neither created a right to protection nor made the bearer a national of the issuing country.[113] Politis shot back at the critics noting, "It should be made quite clear that the Committee's sole object has been to establish a document for the purposes of travel . . . it has in no way contemplated setting up an international system of protection."[114] But rather than leaving it there, Politis incredulously argued:

> It is difficult to see the value in a civilised country to-day of this right of protection which causes our critics such concern. Surely every individual, whatever his status, is or should be protected at all times by the laws and authorities of any country in which he happens to be? I cannot think that any civilised country in honour could claim the right to refuse protection to any individual even if only temporarily resident in the country . . . . Nor can I believe that nowadays the consular authorities accredited to civilized countries often have occasion to use this right of protection even for their own nationals, since they would thereby be recalling such countries to what, in my view, is an elementary duty. . . . Despite the reluctance to grant this right of protection to a certain category of persons, those persons will come to possess it, even without claiming it, as mankind in course of time attains to a clearer consciousness.[115]

Politis finished his comments by again reassuring the objecting governments that the proposed passport did not create any "legal consequences." Specifically, it did not "give the holder any right to protection," and it could not "in any way influence the official determination of his nationality."[116]

Despite Politis' impassioned clarifications and qualifications, governments continued to object. Romania, while agreeing with the humanitarian principles at the core of the proposed passport system, was concerned that regularizing the stateless would compromise its financial and public health. Poland objected to standardizing a passport regime for the stateless because they were concerned that half measures would regularize rather than eliminate statelessness. Much of the ire was reserved for Politis' moralizing tone, with the Italian delegation refusing to discuss what they deemed were political questions clothed in the "guise of humanitarian considerations."[117]

Generally, the proposal was criticized for going beyond its writ. The Passport Conference of 1926 had referred to the committee their assignment with the aim that "facilities for traveling should be granted to those without nationality." Instead, the Committee recommended that the passport be made available to three types of people: (1) persons without nationality, (2) persons with doubtful nationality, and (3) persons whose nationality was known but who cannot obtain a passport. This third category was limited to those whose consular authorities refused to issue a passport or for those who could not apply to their consular authorities for political or economic reasons. It was within this third category that most recipients of Nansen passports would fall.[118]

The first two groups were relatively uncontroversial. However, delegations strongly objected to the inclusion of the third group. The objecting delegations argued that making the passports available to individuals whose nationality was known would permit people to avoid obligations to their own country by giving a legal status to military deserters, political refugees, and those who refused to pay taxes or fees to their state to receive a passport. An Italian delegate noted, for example, that requiring hefty taxes or fees to receive a passport might be "... fully justified by the laws of the country of which the applicant for a passport is a national, in which case it is not easy to see how or why the authorities of the country of residence should be authorised to intervene," aiding and abetting what was, in effect, a type of tax evasion. The proposal died at the conference.[119]

These attitudes were emblematic of the continued anxiety that statesmen shared with regard to giving individuals any legal personality within international law. The concern expressed by the Italian delegate was not that permitting individuals an international status would limit Italy's freedom of action or bring its penal policies under greater international scrutiny. Rather, Italy's delegate argued that permitting individuals an international status, allowing them to run to the League whenever they might need a passport, would permit them to escape even the most basic of obligations to the state. The state's walls were often as much about keeping people in as they were in keeping people out. Permitting the League to issue an identity card or a passport further frayed the increasingly tenuous relationship between allegiance and protection that had been central to the relationship between sovereigns and their subjects.[120]

The Individual in Interwar International Legal Theory

Within international legal theory the place of the individual had been an open question, with support for individual subjectivity waning with the waxing of positivism. Grotius had made space for individuals in his system of thought.[121] Vattel, in contrast, strictly denied a direct subjectivity.[122] As a result, for much of the eighteenth and nineteenth centuries the individual had been excluded as a direct subject of international law within the writings of the most eminent publicists.[123]

But if one could not find much in the way of outright support for the proposition that individuals were subjects of international law, one could find hints, whispers, and muffled exclamations. In 1844, for example, August Wilhelm Heffter, the author of the most widely read German textbook on international law, adamantly argued that the purpose of law was first and foremost to protect the rights of the individual person and that the law of nations created rights and obligations for both individuals and states.[124] Heffter went so far as to explicitly reject the newly fashionable term, "international law," in favor of the more traditional and more comprehensive "law of nations" to better express his point.[125] Heffter's views, however, were controversial. Most commentators, and even his own glossator, quickly brushed aside his arguments in favor of the dominant view that states were the only subjects of international law.[126]

However, by the end of the century, the whispers had become audible conversations and the exclamations were no longer quickly muffled.[127] The new social theories and critiques that emerged out of the fledgling field of sociology provided the intellectual foundation upon which legal thinkers could build new models of law and its relationship to both the state and society. A whole new generation of legal scholars began to question the traditional exclusion. In the first place the sovereignty of the state had come under assault. Legal thinkers like Léon Duguit in France, Otto Gierke in Germany, and Harold Laski in England, along with broad-based syndicalist, corporatist, and anarchist political movements began to question, or outright deny, the personality and sovereignty of the state,[128] as Léon Duguit provocatively wrote in 1908, "The State is dead."[129]

The idea that individuals might be subjects of international law quickly took hold in the years following 1914. Quincy Wright, who would become one the world's premier political scientists, argued in his first ever publication, "Formerly states were almost the only subjects of conventional international law; now individuals and public officers are very frequently the immediate subjects of treaty stipulations."[130] Georges Scelle went further and argued, "An international society, like a state society, is a society of individuals, and nothing but individuals."[131] Nicolas Politis (brother of Athanasios) agreed with Scelle about individuals and also denied the sovereignty of states.[132] While many were not willing to go quite as far as Scelle and Politis, the idea that individuals *were* or *should be* considered subjects of international law was growing in popularity.[133]

Natural law, too, with its emphasis on the existence of an authority superior to that of the sovereign law giver, saw a comeback. James Brierly, Maurice Bourquin, Gabriele Salvioli, and Louis Le Fur all placed elements of natural law at the center of international jurisprudence in the courses they presented at the prestigious The Hague Academy of International Law in the interwar period.[134] And the idea produced so vast an amount of scholarly literature over the course of the 1920s and 1930s,[135] that it was possible for an international legal scholar to seriously claim that, "modern international lawyers have to a considerable extent left the old dogma [that only states are subjects of international law] behind."[136]

There were some theorists who held on to the old normative fiction that only states were properly subjects of international law.[137] However, critics of making individuals subjects of international law were often more tempered. Edwin Borchard, for example, opposed making individuals direct subjects because it might retard the growth of international law and international adjudication in general. Borchard, in an article entitled "The Access of Individuals to International Courts," rhetorically asked, "How many states are likely to sign a convention which proceeds from the assumption that aliens cannot be certain of justice when they sue the state in its local courts, because the local judges are apt to be biased against them?"[138] But Borchard acknowledged that the system as it stood had its flaws, particularly with regard to those with many nationalities and those with none at all.[139] He also understood that the requirement of a state espousing the claim was often pro-forma and that the reality was that individuals were, in effect, making claims.[140] However, he still found the fiction useful and proposed a middle-way of reform.[141] As with Borchard, it was increasingly recognized, even by more conservative jurists, that the descriptive reality was that individuals were increasingly at the center of international legal disputes. In a wonderful exchange during a forum held by the American Society of International Law in 1941, Alwyn Freeman criticized the degree to which theorists seemed to be building castles in the air with regard to the place of individuals in the international legal system and reasserted the need to acknowledge the theoretical primacy of states in the international legal world. That only states were the subject of international law, Freeman argued, was a fact derived from positivist international legal theory. He ended his screed by rhetorically asking, "Wouldn't you agree with that, Professor Dunn?"

Frederick Dunn, in a staccato cadence, retorted, "No, I don't." And then added, doubtlessly with a biting tone, that "it is unfortunate when a rule of law gets too far away from reality. . . . I think that when an established principle in fact gets so far away from what we know, or could know if we would only look and see what goes on in the world, that principle might well be subject to serious criticism. I am not denying for a moment that this is the way lawyers talk and will continue to talk."[142] For Dunn, as for many other theorists of international law, the concept of sovereignty as it had been briefly articulated around the turn of the twentieth century was, despite its positivist pretensions, far from a description of reality.[143] Sovereign equality and the absence of individuals from international law as practiced was a fiction, according to Dunn and, from a legal perspective, an overwrought, erroneous, and overly formalistic understanding of the world.

In addition, an international court was finally operational in which these legal philosophies and arguments could play out. For decades, peace activists had been pushing for the establishment of a permanent international court. While the Permanent Court of Arbitration had been established at The Hague in 1899, it was not a permanent sitting court (despite its name) but rather a list of arbitrators from which parties in a dispute could draw. It was a more institutionalized form of the arbitral practice that was characteristic of the nineteenth century. Peace activists wanted more. They wanted an institution that had both prestige and permanence. They wanted an institution that would build upon its own jurisprudence. In short, they wanted a "Supreme Court of the World."[144]

That dream became a reality in 1919. Article 14 of the Covenant charged the League with establishing a Permanent Court of International Justice (PCIJ). Toward that end, the League established a committee of jurists to draft a statute forming the court. The statute would define everything about the court's future operation – how judges would be appointed, how often it would convene, what types of cases it could hear, and its jurisdiction. Whether individuals should have access to international tribunals had been a question addressed in every major attempt to make an international court. In 1907, the world came close to getting its first international court explicitly open to individuals in the aborted International Prize Court. The short-lived Central American Court of Justice had been open to individuals, but the court blinked out of existence in 1918 after only ten years of service. So it was not surprising that as a committee of jurists convened to discuss the new PCIJ, several committee members submitted proposals that gave individuals and organizations access to the court.[145] Albert de Lapradelle, France's most eminent international legal mind, brought up the issue of criminal liability. As part of the peace settlements, the question of trying individuals for war crimes was being actively discussed. Lapradelle argued that if individuals might be held accountable by violations of international law, then they should reciprocally have rights in international courts.[146] The Inter-Parliamentary Union submitted a plan with Henri La Fontaine, president of the International Peace Bureau, that would have created a court competent to hear conflicts between private persons, conflicts between private persons and foreign states, conflicts related to administrative questions, and conflicts related to the circulation of persons.[147]

The committee debated the subject extensively during its hearings, and the subject turned on whether the older method of diplomatic protection was sufficient. Representatives argued that because everyone was a member of a state, whether individuals had access was irrelevant since their state could espouse their claim.[148] Clearly, the statelessness crisis had yet to become chronic enough for jurists to perceive the problem of making such an assumption. However, working from the minority paradigm that was so predominant in the League Covenant, several delegates countered that, at the very least, the competency of the proposed court could be extended to hear cases brought by protected minority groups.[149] Similarly, more alternatives were proposed to give other states the ability to bring a claim on behalf of a nonnational, effectively making states into advocates. Despite support from influential jurists, however, the argument that all complaints to the PCIJ should be brought by states on behalf of their own nationals won the day.[150] Although the PCIJ would hear disputes involving individuals and companies, it did so under the old Vattelian fiction.[151] A state was still required to espouse the claim.[152] Moreover, with a few exceptions for mandates and minorities, an individual or corporation had to have the nationality of the state that espoused it.[153] Despite this decision, during the first three years of its operation, the PCIJ continued to receive applications from stateless individuals pleading for the body to hear their case.[154]

The failure to get individual legal personality before the PCIJ did not end the movement in that direction within the interwar period. Over the course of the previous decade, several projects to define the rights and duties of states had been undertaken by various international law societies.[155] But the most prominent of the law societies, the Institute of International Law, had yet to issue its own declaration by the end of the war. In 1921, Lapradelle, the jurist who had taken a strong stance in favor of permitting individuals to bring cases before the PCIJ, drafted the proposed declaration. Previous efforts had focused primarily on the rights of nations to self-determination and enshrining the doctrine of sovereign equality.[156] Lapradelle's proposal went further, declaring that "states had obligations not only to other states, but to men."[157] In contrast to the earlier efforts, the Institute's draft would carefully avoid using "nation" and refer only to states to avoid the dangerous conflation that was already rampant within the international community.[158] But the members were intrigued by the recognition of individuals. André Mandelstam was particularly captivated, noting that he had a "very strong desire to give immediate and without reservation" his approval to the principles on the interdependence of states and the international recognition of the rights of man in de Lapradelle's draft. Although de Lapradelle's draft was not accepted, the Institute initiated a project, headed by Mandelstam, that would tackle both individual rights and minority protections and culminate in 1929 with the adoption of a Declaration of the International Rights of Man by the Institute and of a resolution recognizing "that there are cases in which it can be desirable that the law recognize individuals directly."[159]

Although the declaration issued by the Institute carried weight in intellectual communities and doubtlessly influenced the development of the Universal Declaration of Human Rights issued by the United Nations following World War II, it had little immediate legal impact beyond its ideological gesturing.[160]

There were some, albeit few, practical attempts to incorporate individuals more formally into international legal machinery. The Central American Court of Justice was permitted to hear the complaints of individuals. But as a body, it was rather geographically restricted and lasted only ten years – closing its doors in 1917.[161] While the Central American Court of Justice was beset with difficulties, it did serve, at least, as a practical instantiation the theory that individuals should be subjects of international law.[162] Poland and Germany had, by treaty, established a claims commission.[163] Individuals could bring their cases before the commission directly, and the body of jurisprudence developed by the court could serve as precedent in its own later proceedings. The commission was, at first, relatively generic – little different from the dozens of mixed claims commissions that states had established in the nineteenth century. But in 1928, a case came before the commission that challenged the assumed limits of that body. In *Steiner and Gross* v. *Polish State*, two plaintiffs, one Polish and one Czech, brought a claim before the commission alleging that Poland's establishment of a tobacco monopoly had, in effect, made it impossible for the pair to run their tobacco company. Poland objected to the claim, arguing that since one of the plaintiffs was a Polish national the claim should be dismissed. Under the old Vattelian fiction, where the individual's claim became that of his or her state, Poland's objection would have been decisive. But the Silesian Claims Commission noted that the convention that established the commission conferred jurisdiction on the Commission regardless of the nationality of the claimants. In effect, this decision made the Commission a court open to any individual from anywhere with a claim against either Poland or Germany resulting from the territorial adjustments after the war. Polish nationals, the Commission ruled, could indeed hale their own government before the court.[164] But it was a court with limited impact on the international system a whole. Its existence, like the Nansen passport, did more perhaps to fire the imagination and serve as an illustrative example for reform.[165]

The Limits of Internationalized Protection

The pragmatic efforts by the League to internationalize the protection of "stateless" refugees failed to escape the grasp that nationality had on the international legal system. Even the much-admired Nansen passport was still tied to a national status. Having to be a former Russian national to get a passport was not much different than having to be a Russian national, at least in terms of the role nationality played in the equation. Similarly, international legal theory was unable to shift the jurists on the PCIJ too far beyond their initial remit. Although hints of movement on the issue could be seen, states were still required to espouse claims.[166] Nationality was still an inescapable requirement of international existence for nearly every human being in the Atlantic world – and that was how nearly everyone wanted it to be.

Three sets of interests conspired to prevent effective solutions to the problem of nationality as it pertained to human beings.

The first was national politics. Even those in desperate need of some sort of international status still engaged in the politics of nationality. As with the petitions by Ukrainians, the praise heaped upon the Nansen regime by Mandelstam, and the concern over retaining nationality for the purposes of private international law illustrate, what many advocated for in the discursive spaces provided by the League and its associated organs was the international recognition and protection of nations, not of individuals. The Nansen passport's successes were, in some ways, attributable to its affirmation of nationality as the basis of international legal personality. It did little to undermine the sovereign authority of states to police their populations, and it could even serve the purposes of national politics – becoming a vehicle for national claims rather than an instrument of individual protection or liberation. Even André Mandelstam, whom some scholars have identified as an intellectual pioneer of the Universal Declaration, saw individual rights primarily as a less objectionable means through which the minority regime could be generalized.[167]

The second was the already well-trodden concern about sovereignty. States were not interested in giving individuals access to the PCIJ, allowing disputes over civil rights to be internationalized.

The third was anxiety that providing individual protection had the potential to undermine the reciprocal relationship between allegiance and protection. The failure to generalize the refugee passport regime had at its core the long-standing fear, anchored in a sort of persistent mercantilism, that emigration was a means of escaping the obligations owed to the state either in the form of military service or taxation. While states were certainly concerned about being haled in front of an international court, their objection to efforts to create a kind of international status for individuals was also anchored in a concern – acute in the interwar period – of the financial and military capacities of the state. Creating a "citizen of the world" would, without a global state of some sort, also create a person who had obligations nowhere.

***

Lieutenant I. S. K. Soboleff set out from Shanghai in November of 1928 on a motorcycle trip around the world with a Nansen passport in hand. Yet he soon realized that "the roads of the world did not seem so open and free" as he had assumed.[168] The French consul refused him a visa to travel through Indochina.[169] In Rangoon and India, he constantly had to check in with the local authorities, have his papers stamped, and suffer countless harassments.[170] It seemed as if every border was closed to him.

After crossing the Sind Desert, our hero happened upon a branch of the Ariel Motor Company, a British motorcycle manufacturer. In a gambit for publicity, Ariel presented Soboleff with a new motorcycle and a letter of introduction on Ariel stationary and a British license.[171] From that moment forward, Soboleff's travel was easy.[172] His bike was repaired at Ariel branches all over the world, free of charge.[173] He was provided gasoline at Shell stations all over the world, free of charge.[174] His tires were replaced at Firestone branches all over the world, free of charge.[175] And he traveled through the Middle East to Europe, across the Atlantic to America, from the East Coast to Los Angeles (where he did some minor acting),[176] from southern California up the coast to San Francisco (where he dined at what he considered to be the world's finest restaurants)[177] and the Russian River Valley, from California to Canada, from Canada to Japan, and finally back to Shanghai, all without ever being denied a visa.[178]

Soboleff began his book with a glowing summary of the Nansen passport program. He closed his tale with the observation that, "all over the world, I can always find others who speak my own language and who carry the Nansen passport, issued by the League of Nations to those who have no longer any country of their own."[179] He even entitled his book *Nansen Passport*. Running throughout his entire story was a triumphant vision of the Nansen passport as the international legitimation of the stateless person. It was a vision that was widely believed. But it was a vision that was certainly false, as the history of the document and Soboleff's early visa denials reveal.

In truth, Soboleff's journey was aided by another piece of paper – a piece of paper that seemingly did more to open the borders of the world to him than his Nansen passport – a letter of introduction from the Ariel Motor Company.[180] Once Soboleff was in possession of that letter (and a bit of global celebrity), he was never again harassed at a border.

5 Sovereign Commerce

> Let me just say one thing in conclusion: commerce is the subject of no State and it is the sovereign of all.
>
> R. S. Fraser, 1912[1]

Lena Goldfields, Ltd. was a strange being. Conjured in 1908, following a series of incantations, inscriptions, and signatures prescribed by English law, Lena Goldfields, Ltd. appeared in the world as a legal person. Unborn, unliving, undying, unfeeling, and unthinking, Lena Goldfields, Ltd. was nevertheless a person under the law and, like Don Pacifico, a British subject of sorts.[2] Through a similar set of incantations and inscriptions prescribed by English law, Lena Goldfields, Ltd. acquired 70 percent of the shares of Lenzoto,[3] a company conjured under Russian law in 1855 to mine for gold along the Lena River and its tributaries in the harsh expanse of Siberia.[4] Lena Goldfields, Ltd. was a British subject. Its shareholders, however, could be found in Britain, France, Germany, Russia, and the United States.[5] So Lena Goldfields, Ltd., like so many persons in the first decade of the twentieth century, had many potential nationalities and many states that could potentially come to its aid.

The year 1912 marked the first in a series of bad years for Lena Goldfields, Ltd. Workers struck against poor working conditions, and the gendarme of the Tsar massacred hundreds of the striking miners.[6] The massacre sparked a new wave of labor unrest and activism that swept the country, with strikes being called annually to mark the anniversary. Soon-to-be revolutionaries appropriated the Lena Goldfields Massacre into their propaganda.[7] Then came the Revolution and with the Revolution came expropriation. On June 28, 1918, Vladimir Lenin seized all industrial enterprises, including mining operations, on behalf of the Soviet state.[8] Soviet authorities seized the mining facilities at Lena, and the holding companies were rendered worthless. For what were they holding now that the equipment and rights to mine were gone? Thousands of investors from all over the world were left with nothing and wondering what, if anything, they could do.

The Economy after the War

In the years following the armistice and the peace, the markets of the world were still being tossed about by the economic turbulence of World War I. The storm had passed, but many merchants were still hesitant to brave the choppy seas of global trade. Exchange rates were fluctuating wildly, which created strong incentives to break contracts.[9] Moreover, wartime animosities continued to generate commercial frictions because trust proved a scarce commodity in the postwar period.[10] An economist at the International Financial Conference in 1920 noted that for all the economic damage done by the war, "that highly important intangible asset, good will, in its domestic and its international aspects, . . . had been destroyed in unexampled measure."[11] How, after four years of war, months of contentious peace negotiations, and a controversial and resented treaty, could courts and their various officers be trusted to render expedient and impartial decisions in commercial disputes between their own nationals and those of another state? Could a German manufacturer find justice in a French court over a breach of contract? Could a British trader get compensated in an Austrian court?

The war also brought with it a dramatic expansion of economic protectionism, which only added to the expanding conflicts of interest that could hinder the rendering of impartial decisions between nationals and foreigners. Adding to the confusion, the fracturing of empires brought not only the end of several large, ethnically heterogeneous polities but also the end of large and integrated markets in Eastern Europe and new economic hostility.[12] The twenty states that composed Europe in 1914 had become twenty-seven by 1919. New states meant more than 12,000 miles of new borders along with new customs formalities, new court systems, new rules regarding entry into the legal profession, and new judges.[13] Would an Estonian court, months after its birth, be competent to hear a case? What about new states in the Middle East where foreign businesses were gradually losing the long-held privilege of having disputes handled by their own consular courts? Could these new states and mandates be trusted? How would Soviet Russia be integrated into a global marketplace formed around private property and private business? How would Mexico? Could trade and investment be reestablished with governments that had begun their reigns with two of the largest expropriations of private property and sovereign debt repudiation in modern history?

Just as the breakdown of empires and the emergence of new states and nationalities rendered millions of refugees stateless and unprotected, so too did businessmen, investors, and corporations find themselves without reliable advocates in the new geopolitical arena. Whereas stateless people struggled to become subjects of international law, international capital and business were also busy searching for and crafting guardians less fickle than the state and more responsive to their global mobility.

As the nineteenth century gave way to the twentieth, the increased politicization of the international system and the reaffirmation of the principle of territorial sovereignty inherent within the League Covenant rendered diplomatic protection increasingly controversial.[14] As in so many other facets of international life, the intractable legal tension between nationality and territoriality, when combined with the scalability problems inherent within diplomatic protection, sent those engaged in international business searching for ways to eradicate both nationality and the support of a recognized state as a the defining status necessary for leading a secure international life. Like Hannah Arendt's stateless peoples, international businesses sought safety in the development of a group consciousness and the formation of their own metaphorical nation enabling them to live in the world under a system of laws of their own devising.[15] Global commercial interests worked to extricate themselves from an internationalism that put global investment and commerce at the mercy of foreign courts and foreign politics. However, unlike Arendt's stateless peoples and the foreign nationals of weak states, international businesses and capital crafted a robust, expansive, and comprehensive regime of protective institutions and apparatuses that substantially shaped the history of global capital and trade in the twentieth century.

Over the course of the early twentieth century, business interests sought to extricate themselves from the problems of nationality and to make themselves less reliant upon states for protection. This chapter makes four interrelated arguments. First, increasing anonymity within international trade and the increasing reluctance of states to intervene to protect the trade and investment of their nationals generated new commercial frictions. Commercial groups sought to smooth out those frictions by creating a new international legal system to suit their needs. Second, the politicization of economic issues at Versailles and the weak political mandate granted to the League created a vacuum. Commercial interest groups that could present themselves as neutral were in a strong position to fill that vacuum and substantially shape the agenda of both the League and its successor, the United Nations. Third, this commercial agenda was aimed at depoliticizing the application of European international commercial customs and reducing reliance upon states to protect investments abroad. Finally, commercial interest groups accomplished these goals by obtaining a globally recognized system of arbitration. While not completed by the outbreak of World War II, the institutional groundwork had been laid.

Trust and Distance

Forming trust over distance has been a recurring problem in international trade and investment.[16] The expansion of states and courts had been the traditional solution in the domestic arena. Internationally, traders and investors often used family, religious, or ethnic connections in which moral sanctions could be effective.[17] As trade relationships expanded beyond those connections, trade associations and other institutions were established for the dissemination of information and the regulation of reputation.[18]

But since the mid-nineteenth century, two particular problems have plagued international trade and investment. The first problem was at the level of the international transaction. If two people resident in different countries signed a contract and one of them violated that contract, where could either of them seek redress? They could go to their own courts. However, few states at the turn of the twentieth century would recognize or execute the judgments of a foreign court (to say nothing of their attitude toward foreign judgments at the end of the war), which made the recovery of any damage awards issued by their own courts unlikely. They could go to the courts in the other country. However, if navigating the legal system of one's own country is sometimes difficult, navigating that of another's is often impossible. Postwar territorial realignments further complicated this problem. Did ethnic Germans living in a resurrected Poland feel that they could obtain justice from a Polish court in a contract dispute against an ethnic Pole? Were those who had been transferred without their consent from one legal system to another able to expect that their business relations would be secure? Contractual certainty, the bedrock of trade, was increasingly hard to come by.

The second problem was inherent in the decision to sign a contract with a state. If a person, who was a national of country A, bought a bond issued by country B and country B decided not to pay, where could the national of country A go to seek redress? Could the national of country A stand as a creditor in front of the debtor's own agents of justice and expect just compensation? Could a German bondholder go into Soviet Russia and demand that the country meet its debt obligations? Beyond bonds, simple business relationships were problematic. The war had forged large-scale cooperation in many of the belligerent countries between the state and private industry. Businesses signed thousands upon thousands of contracts with both domestic and foreign governments. What were they to do when these states decided to alter their compensation?

Prior to the war, these two problems – of international contracts and contracts with states – led to different and somewhat unrelated institutional solutions. Some were industry specific. For instance, groups of merchants and traders worked to establish mercantile associations that could regulate trade, establish best practices, resolve disputes among their members, and, like the guilds from which they sprang, enforce the decisions of the association through moral sanctions. In contrast, investors established associations that were designed to disseminate information and to negotiate collectively in the event of a default, thereby protecting individual investors. Yet, as the volume of global trade and investment increased and the number of actors engaged in it multiplied during the decades surrounding the turn of the twentieth century, traditional methods of managing disputes and establishing trust over vast expanses of land and sea came under renewed strain. Domestically, the expansion of commerce and increasing anonymity in transactions had been coupled with a renewed role for national courts that could enforce contracts throughout the country. But internationally, enforcing a decision issued by a national court remained a problem. Instead, merchants, investors, and traders turned to the state to intervene diplomatically on their behalf to enforce claims against other states and in some cases the subjects of those states. However, that system had also been put under strain.

The Decline of Diplomatic Protection

In 1912, at the Fifth International Congress of Chambers of Commerce, Max Apt, a syndic of *Die Ältesten der Kaufmannschaft von Berlin* (the Berlin Chamber of Commerce), presented a report on what he considered to be a grave problem. Businessmen, he asserted, when they entered into a contract with a foreign state, had no way of defending their rights in the event of a breach of that contract. In 1910, the *Die Ältesten der Kaufmannschaft von Berlin* had sent a letter to the German Chancellor highlighting this very problem and Philipp Karl Ludwig Zorn, one of Germany's premier international jurists and that country's representative at The Hague Peace Conference in 1907, concurred in the report's assessment.[19]

It is true that no impartial or international court existed that could hear the claims of an individual against a foreign government.[20] But the problem did not merely involve questions of judicial impartiality either. In many countries at the end of the nineteenth century, there was no mechanism for suing a government, *either foreign or domestic*, for damages. Someone with a claim even against *their own government* had little recourse to the courts for complaint, let alone in a foreign land.[21] Moreover, the pervasive domestic legal principle of sovereign immunity limited the degree to which foreign sovereigns could be sued in domestic courts. In the nineteenth century, this had all been part of the broader debate about the types of protection a national could receive while abroad. Whether a state should intervene diplomatically to protect the wallets of its nationals abroad in addition to their bodies was an important standing question in international jurisprudence. State intervention remained one of the only ways through which an individual or business could find protection against a foreign government in the business realm.

However, if diplomatic protection and intervention was a matter of national discretion, then it created an uneven and arbitrary justice for claimants from varying countries.[22] Precisely which claims would be espoused became an issue of international politics, and those with "strong arms" to defend their interests found themselves in possession of greater investment security than those from states with fewer gunboats.[23] Among the many problems with this situation was the moral hazard it created. An investor or property owner could reap the benefits of high interest rates or low prices, while their state bore the burden of seeking compensation in the case of default, destruction, or expropriation – the likelihood of which was what produced the high interest rates and low prices.[24] Beyond moral hazard, it created a situation in which foreigners had recourse to a power beyond that of the state and the collective interest it could represent; thus, instantiating the nineteenth century normative liberal order in the international realm and subjecting all states to it.

Various nineteenth century utopian thinkers and Pan-European essayists had proposed the creation of fora in which individuals could bring complaints against foreign states without involving the political branches of the claimant government.[25] However, by the early twentieth century, the problem had shifted from the realm of utopian visions to pragmatic legal thought. In 1902, following Venezuela's refusal to compensate European nationals for damaged property and loans, Britain, Germany, and Italy launched a massive blockade and created a hemispheric diplomatic crisis.[26] In response to the European intervention, Luis Drago, the Argentinian minister to the United States, sent a note to President Theodore Roosevelt in which he articulated what would later become known as the Drago Doctrine:[27]

> The capitalist who lends money to a foreign state always takes into account the resources of the country and the probability, greater or less, that the obligations of the contract will be fulfilled without delay. All governments thus enjoy different credit according to their degree of civilization and culture and their conduct in business transactions; and these conditions are measured and weighed before making any loan, the terms more or less onerous in accordance with the precise data concerning them which the bankers always have on record.[28]

Drago articulated with precision the underlying problem with the collection of sovereign debt by force. Just as debtor's prisons had been eradicated from Europe and the Americas, so too, the argument of Drago and his sympathizers went, should armed intervention in the case of sovereign default. Collecting by force, as even Palmerston had acknowledged in his circular, had the potential to lead people into making imprudent investments. The intervention in Venezuela was controversial in Europe and was the subject of substantial criticism, particularly in Britain and France, where it served as a visible reminder of the growing and controversial influence of capital over the foreign policy of European states.[29] Indeed, a mere four years after the Venezuelan affair, Drago's doctrine was enshrined in one of the several multilateral legal instruments to come out of the Second International Peace Conference, held at The Hague in 1907. There, the assembled states signed the treaty for the Limitation of Employment of Force for Recovery of Contract Debts in which "the Contracting Powers agree[d] not to have recourse to armed force for the recovery of contract debts claimed from the Government of one country by the Government of another country as being due to its nationals."[30]

Although the convention never entered into force and many parties later withdrew from the convention, the principle was becoming so well-established that by 1912, when Max Apt delivered his report before the Fifth International Congress of Chambers of Commerce, he could lament that The Hague prohibition on armed collection "gives the private creditor not only no rights but it even deprives him of the possibility that his home State might declare war against the foreign State on his account."[31] Moreover, owing to the capriciousness of modern politics, Apt complained, "unless it is a quite extraordinary case, in which national questions come into play, [states] will find reasons for refusing diplomatic intervention."[32] Edwin Borchard, the foremost expert on the topic, likewise observed in 1913 that owing to the increasing "exploitation of backward countries by foreign capital," foreign offices had begun to differentiate between interventions involving torts – injuries to persons or physical property – and breaches of contract. Governments would increasingly decline to intervene to remedy a breach of contract or would "[exercise] more careful scrutiny" than they would in the case of a personal injury.[33] Like Apt, Borchard noted:

> The unpaid creditor has no individual right to bring about the adjustment of his claim. The action of his government in his behalf depends upon political considerations and is entirely a matter of expediency and policy. If his government for any reason declines to become interested in his case or to espouse his claim against the foreign government, the creditor is without a remedy. A legal right of the individual may therefore be sacrificed to the political expediency to the political expediency of his government.[34]

Even Joseph Conrad levied a critique against the uncertainty and insufficiency of diplomatic protection in his 1904 novel, *Nostromo*. Following a violent riot against the English proprietors of a South American silver mine and the mine's expropriation by a "gang in possession of the Presidential Palace," Conrad's fictional South American country was made to "pay a beggarly money compensation to the families of the victims, and then the matter dropped out of diplomatic dispatches."[35] And what statistics have been compiled bears this out. Whereas claims for tortious injuries to subjects were a common justification for war in the nineteenth century (and indeed peaked then), such claims fell precipitously at the turn of the twentieth century – to say nothing of claims made for the use of armed force (or the threat of armed force) outside of war.[36]

In contrast to the bellicose language of the mid-nineteenth century, the governments of Europe had begun to take a more cautious approach in the years following the Venezuela Blockade. French Foreign Minister Stephen-Jean-Marie Pichon, speaking before the Chamber of Deputies in support of the Drago Doctrine's implementation in The Hague Conventions of 1907, exclaimed before the entire Chamber, "There is no doubt, gentlemen, that diplomacy cannot simply follow behind all of the financiers who risk their capital in their more-or-less adventurous investments. We cannot risk the forces and engage the politics and the foreign relations of a country in all of the fortunate or unfortunate speculations of the great businessmen, the financiers and the bankers, who would allow themselves to be imprudently carried away."[37] His comments were answered with cheers and acclamation ("*Très bien! Très bien!*").[38] Across the Atlantic, Theodore Roosevelt struck a similar tone in a letter expressing concern over the activities of the San Domingo Improvement Company, a New York-based company, noting that he was "always afraid of seeming to back any big company which has financial interests in one of [the] South American states," since often they were, as in this case, involved in something unseemly.[39] Several treatise writers on diplomatic protection were also openly critical of the use of the principle in Latin America, with one poetically observing that often "under protection hides oppression."[40] Indeed, there were few international jurists who were not critical of the manner in which the principle of diplomatic protection had been abused in the support of large capital interests.

The time for change had arrived. Diplomatic protection had become increasingly unpopular and politically fraught. Discontentment with mobile capital and big industry had been growing in Atlantic politics over the previous twenty years.[41] Explicitly and unabashedly mobilizing the instruments of state for the benefit of wealthy investors and entrepreneurs was not as politically feasible in 1900 as it had been in 1850 – particularly when their nationality was dubious. That is not to say that it did not happen. The intervention in Venezuela dramatically illustrated that capital interests were not bereft of support. But the blowback over the intervention and the wide ratification of The Hague Convention on the Limitation of Employment of Force for Recovery of Contract Debts demonstrated that there were very real limits on how far governments would go to defend the foreign investments and property of their nationals.[42]

By the late 1930s, it was no longer enough for a business to appeal to its government for intervention. In the increasingly democratic states of Europe and North America, appeals also had to be made to a skeptical public.

Following Mexico's nationalization of the oil industry in the 1938, the Cowdry estate, which had significant holdings in Mexican petroleum, sponsored acclaimed writer Evelyn Waugh to travel to Mexico and write a popular polemic against expropriation, which the writer provocatively titled *Robbery Under Law*.[43] In that travelogue, Waugh explained to his readers the complex principles of international law surrounding expropriation and diplomatic protection, like the exhaustion of local remedies. Despite the corruption of the judiciary, Waugh opined, "The tedious and expensive farce had to be played out to satisfy the Mexican objection that a denial of justice [and diplomatic protection] could not be pleaded so long as there were legal means of appeal open."[44] Skeptical of the British Left to the point of being contemptuous, Waugh lamented that the British public had not yet been aroused by the injustice of the seizure because "the confiscations had been accompanied by a number of potent phrases about democracy," and because "the Mexicans had a Left Book Club vocabulary."[45]

Likewise, Standard Oil Company produced a series of pamphlets for wide public distribution about the law and politics of the expropriation. Some of the pamphlets had colorful titles, like "The Fine Art of

Squeezing," which was not at all about lemons. Others, with less provocative titles, covered subjects like "The Accustomed Practices in Cases of Expropriation and Confiscation," "The Question of Subsoil Rights in Mexico," and "Diplomatic Protection," among others.[46] The pamphlet on diplomatic protection drew heavily on Borchard's opus on the subject and was dedicated to explaining the law of diplomatic protection to lay readers. Nevertheless, the pamphlet covered the finer points of when protection was permissible, standards of justice, exhaustion of local remedies, denial of justice, the Drago Doctrine, the Calvo Doctrine, and the denationalization of corporations, all in an easily digestible fifteen pages. In its conclusion, the pamphlet exhorted the Department of State to not "too long delay in taking the necessary steps to meet Mexico's challenge to the principles of right and fair dealing between nations.[47]

So, with diplomatic protection becoming less certain, more dependent on public appeals, and more unwieldy for dealing with increasing numbers of international commercial disputes against sovereign states in the first decades of the twentieth century, international jurists and businessmen – particularly those of German extraction[48] – began to advocate for the establishment of a new international court.

Hans Wehberg, a prominent international lawyer and pacifist, wrote a treatise in 1911 advocating for an international tribunal to deal with, among other things, claims by private creditors against debtor states.[49]

The creation of such a court was one of the central issues discussed at the Fifth International Congress of Chambers of Commerce in 1912. There, Max Apt, following his lament that state intervention was no longer sufficient protection for business interest, argued, "There is only one way left, that of creating a neutral court of arbitration by State representation, which would have the right of deciding in cases which are brought by subjects of a contract State against another contract State."[50] Apt, therefore, proposed a resolution supporting "the establishment of an international court for suits between individuals and foreign states."[51] The introduction of his resolution was greeted with applause and was seconded by R. S. Fraser of the London Chamber of Commerce, who concluded his statement of support by noting that "commerce is the subject of no State and it is the sovereign of all."[52] Louis Varjassy, the secretary of the Hungarian Chamber of Commerce, likewise announced his support of the resolution, despite being from "debtor country."[53] Representatives from France, Italy, Germany, and others likewise supported the resolution.

The subject was then at the center of the proceedings of the 1912 Congress of the Inter-Parliamentary Union (IPU).[54] At the gathering in 1912, Henri La Fontaine noted, "Grave difficulties arise each moment between individuals belonging to one state and dealing directly with the government of another state."[55] Individuals engaged in business with foreign states were, he argued, being "forced to plead before the tribunals of [foreign] states, whose judges can be influenced by the political and economic environment." Fontaine continued with a plan, noting:

> There is a major interest in having a supreme court that can escape such influences. This [court] would be a considerable improvement, because it would permit our large European industrialists, who engage in lots of business with foreign countries, to undertake this business with full security, assured that they will find impartial judges on which they can depend."[56]

Philipp Karl Ludwig Zorn contributed a proposal for such a court, which he hoped could begin developing to a body of jurisprudence.[57] Working from this proposal, as well as La Fontaine's critique of it, the IPU declared that the time had come to examine the possibility of forming a permanent judiciary for the settlement of international disputes to complement the Permanent Court of Arbitration currently residing at The Hague and to examine the extent to which this new court might deal with "questions relating to private international law and to disputes interesting private persons whether in relations to foreign States or in questions regulated by international conventions."[58] Writing a few years later in 1916, La Fontaine, in his proposal for a postwar order, advocated for expanding the competence of international law and the courts and tribunals that applied it to include individuals either in disputes with foreign states or in disputes with each other.[59] "Nearly all jurists," he stressed, "have advocated for this enlarged competence."[60]

The League of Nations and the World League of Business

The reestablishment of the global economy was one of the many tasks facing those who took charge in planning for the postwar international order. President Woodrow Wilson, in his Fourteen Points speech of January 1918, had called for "the removal, so far as possible, of all economic barriers and the establishment of an equality of trade conditions among all the nations consenting to the peace."[61] Taking many of their early cues from Wilson, the delegates to the peace conference attempted to deal with what they called "economic disarmament." Representatives of the United States and Britain pushed hard in the earliest phases of the conference to enshrine principles of the equality of trade and the reduction of tariffs in the final peace settlement. Wilson's press secretary at the conference and later his biographer, Ray Stannard Baker, conjured the ghost of Richard Cobden by rhetorically asking, "How can there long be peace among nations which are employing against each other, without restriction, all the weapons of economic warfare?"[62] The French, for their part, even suggested that the powers go as far as requiring an unrestricted exchange of raw materials to eradicate the unequal distribution of resources throughout the world. These ambitious plans for a global regime of free trade, however, like so many other schemes dreamt up in the grand parlors and halls of Paris during the six months of the conference, came to naught. Tensions over the punitive economic measures to be imposed on Germany and the economic benefits demanded by France created too many paradoxical requirements – free trade was possible but only after a heavily regulated effort to rebuild the French economy that involved protecting French industry while simultaneously extracting a heavy economic toll on Germany. Moreover, the war created new constituencies and empowered European labor movements, many of which were skeptical of the value of free trade and demanded that their elected officials represent their interests accordingly. While the disagreements at Paris prevented the powers from crafting a detailed plan for the reconstruction of the postwar economy, they did enshrine in the ambiguously worded Article 23(e) of the Covenant of the League of Nations their collective desire for the League to take up the issue upon its establishment and to secure the "equitable treatment for the commerce of all Members of the League," albeit with a special caveat creating exceptions for the "regions devastated during the war."[63]

The wrangling over the shape of the League centered on general political concerns and on sketching the broad outlines of the organization. How the League would actually function on a day-to-day basis was the subject of only a few discussions during the Paris Peace Conference. Similarly, the Covenant's vision for the Secretariat, which was to be the bureaucratic arm of the League, was limited to oblique references in a half-dozen articles that focused primarily on regulations regarding the collection and distribution of treaties made between members.[64] During the meetings of the Organizing Committee, two visions of what the Secretariat should look like emerged. The first envisioned a secretariat along the lines of the International Postal Union, with national delegations in residence to support the aims of their own countries at periodic conferences. Eric Drummond, a member of the British delegation to the conference, strongly advocated for a second vision, which he described as a *permanent* "international Civil Service, in which men and women of various nationalities might unite in preparing and presenting to the members of the League an objective and common basis for discussion." Drummond, got his wish and was then appointed the League's first secretary-general.[65] With a substantial plan missing, it was left to Drummond to determine how the Secretariat would operate.[66]

During the League's first few months, Secretary General Drummond went about crafting an organization that would soon serve as a central hub for the accumulation and distribution of information through committees of experts and technical advisors. This expansive role created by Drummond encouraged the development of relationships between the League's Secretariat and various nongovernmental and intergovernmental organizations that could provide needed expertise and escape criticisms of national bias.[67] Consequently, the organizations that were in a position to work closely with the League had the potential of exerting significant influence on its agenda. One of these organizations that would significantly shape the agenda of the League was the International Labor Organization (ILO). Born in 1919 alongside the League of Nations, its role was to ensure that peace would be "based upon social justice" and, over the following two decades, it was active in shaping international economic and social policy by providing expertise and representatives to the League's technical committees from the many epistemic communities devoted to improving social welfare that had emerged in the late nineteenth and early twentieth centuries. The ILO's goal was to establish an internationalism of social rights designed to deal with the problems presented by the global spread of industry.[68] However, it was not the only organization that competed for the League's attention.

Across the sea from Paris, another organization that came to play a significant role in shaping the League's agenda formed in 1919. On the sandy boardwalk of Atlantic City, the International Chamber of Commerce (ICC) took its first breaths in 1919. The war had encouraged close cooperation between business interests and governments – John Bull, Der Deutsche Michel, Marianne, and Uncle Sam all danced with the "merchants of death." But, as the drumbeat of war abruptly stopped, private business interests and representatives from various chambers of commerce from the Allied and Associated powers came together at the International Trade Conference in October to discuss their plans for a postwar order and to mitigate the painful economic hangover that was already manifest.[69] Little of substance came out of the conference, which found itself still mired in the political concerns of the war. But the Chamber of Commerce of the United States, which had been responsible for planning the conference, successfully pushed its agenda to establish a "World League of Business" modeled on the International Congresses of Chambers of Commerce that had been popular before the outbreak of war.[70] By the end of 1920, the business leaders of the world, the self-styled "merchants of peace," had met again and drafted a constitution for the newly christened International Chamber of Commerce, which would be a "businessmen's league of nations."[71] Over the next twenty years, it would work closely with the League Secretariat and become by some measures the most powerful nongovernmental organization affiliated with the League and its various interwar economic projects.[72]

The League began its operations in Geneva with a weak economic mandate and a quasi-utopian Covenant that unfortunately had been embedded in a treaty critiqued for its economic revanchism. Following the conclusion of the Peace, however, a number of leading economists and political figures signed a petition advocating for international financial cooperation.[73] Among the many signatories was John Maynard Keynes, whose recently published *The Economic Consequences of the Peace* was a best-selling and damning critique of the Versailles settlement. In addition to Keynes, more than 150 leading figures, from a half-dozen countries, lent their names to the document, including Herbert Hoover, J. P. Morgan, Herbert Asquith, Gustav Ador, Lord Robert Cecil, Elihu Root, and Gustav Cassel. Cassel was then the world's most famous economist and had been a fierce advocate for convening an economic conference before the Versailles Treaty had even been signed.[74] The petition resulted in the recently formed Secretariat of the League of Nations being tasked with preparing an international financial conference that was set to meet in Brussels in the autumn of 1920.[75] In preparing for the conference, the League wanted to include more than just statesmen. So, in addition to the traditional cadre of diplomats, the League invited leading experts from industry, academia, both private and central banking, as well as national and international civil services.[76] Expertise, it was thought, could be apolitical and League partisans claimed well into the 1930s that "scientific impartiality" lent greater credibility to the League and provided an avenue of action for an organization that had little explicit power.[77] In the first months of the League's existence, the Secretariat began to push for the standardization of national statistics as part of Secretary Drummond's plan to make the Secretariat into a center of international expertise. In the lead up to the conference, the Secretariat's invited and consulted experts produced comprehensive surveys of the status of European currencies, exchanges, public finances, trade, retail prices, and coal prices. The ICC was among the organizations invited to provide expertise.

While many divergent views were represented at the conference, there was some consensus around a few general points, among which were prescriptions for "the widest possible application of freedom of trade; full resumption of trade relations on the freest possible basis with the outside world; universal recognition of rights of private property; and guarantee of equal treatment of subjects of all nations."[78] The gathering had few substantive outcomes. But, as Patricia Clavin noted, "The conference established [the League's] entitlement to engage in economic diplomacy," and gave rise to the Joint Provisional Economic and Financial Committee, which would play a substantial role in shaping the League's economic agenda.[79]

By 1921, the League Secretariat was stacked with proponents of free trade (many of whom were British) who found themselves in charge of an important hub for organizing economic expertise and advocating for an international economic policy.[80] Importantly the League had shown itself to be open to the influence of people and organizations from outside the halls of state and to be particularly interested in asserting its nascent influence through the mobilization of elite expertise drawn from nonnational sources.[81]

Importantly, the International Trade Conference in 1920 also marked the beginning of what would be the ICC's substantial participation in shaping an international economic agenda. Throughout the League's truncated existence, it often extended invitations to the ICC to participate in a consultative capacity. Representatives from the ICC regularly served on advisory and technical subcommittees for various projects undertaken by the League and played an active role in producing the information that the League used to craft international economic policy recommendations. In some cases, League conferences adopted, without modifications, the recommendations made by the Chamber's representatives during preparatory committee hearings. In instances where Chamber policies were not just implemented into an agenda verbatim, their recommendations still had tangible impacts. For example, while the Chamber's recommendations for the abolition of passports came to naught at the 1927 World Economic Conference, their secondary proposal, which called for a conference to be held dealing with the issue of the rights of foreigners, was adopted and led directly to the 1929 Conference on the Treatment of Foreigners. The ICC was directly represented on the Economic Consultative Committee of the League. By 1933 the ICC decided to maintain a permanent representative in Geneva to handle the organization's business with the League.[82] Between 1927 and 1932 alone, the ICC was represented at twenty-nine official conferences in either a consultative capacity or, occasionally, as a voting member.[83]

The ICC's powerful spot within the League's various economic apparatuses drew sharp criticism. In 1930, the International Cooperative Alliance complained:

Our attention has been drawn to the extraordinary claims which have been publicly made that the organized private traders of the world had not only succeeded in entrenching themselves at Geneva in the authorities of the League on a basis of equality of voice and voting with the National Governments, but wielded such influence on behalf of their clients – the capitalist private traders – that they practically dominated the situation and were even able to repudiate their own National Governments.[84]

Throughout the early years of its existence, supporters of the ICC attempted to establish its reputation as an independent and nonpartisan organization staffed by experts who could claim to sit above the petty national disputes that were disruptive to world commerce and consequently world peace. The reputation of many of the Chamber's spokesmen, as well as their special role in advancing the so-conceived science of standardizing international economic statistics, contributed to that image of impartiality, as did their multinational character. The ICC itself cultivated in its organizational structure the type of expertise that would be attractive to the League Secretariat by creating committees that specialized in specific trade policies.[85] The neutral mask of the expert was a potent guise in the interwar period, and the Chamber wore it often and wore it well. The ICC's appearance of political neutrality and its nonnational organizational structure enabled it to effectively insinuate itself into a League that was desperate to navigate the murky waters of international cooperation through the mobilization of experts and by avoiding national politics. By making their nonnational expertise readily available to the League, the ICC was able to push for policies that were "of interest mainly to international traders themselves, and only indirectly to the public benefitting from increased world trade."[86]

Arthur Balfour, an occasional member of the British Delegation to the League and a supporter of the ICC's role in shaping interwar economic policy, happily summed up the relationship of the two international organizations: "The League of Nations was prompt to realize the value of the assistance of such a diversity of important economic interests, and from the beginning, it has always been in close touch with the Chamber in connection with economic matters."[87] That "close touch" described by Balfour meant occasionally going as far as directly following the ICC's policy initiatives or incorporating their recommendations verbatim into reports and treaties.[88] As Kurt Will noted in his assessment of the ICC's influence on League activities, it was in the area of international commercial arbitration that the impact of the Chamber's advocacy could be most directly observed.[89] Similarly, George L. Ridgeway, the official biographer of the ICC, himself claimed that the establishment of an "extensive system of international arbitration" was "perhaps the most definite and indisputable achievement directly attributable to the ICC."[90]

At the center of that extensive system of international arbitration was the ICC's Court of Arbitration in Paris. The court was a private affair. As the arbitral court of the ICC, it was designed to serve the needs and interests of international commerce. Etienne Clémentel, France's wartime minister of Commerce, a prominent member of the French political establishment, and the first president of the ICC, had (in addition to his duties as a senator in France) taken the helm of the ICC's nascent court. The court had opened its doors to the public in 1923 to widespread acclaim. At the inaugural dinner, Joost Van Hamel, director of the League's Legal Section, gave a speech on behalf of the secretary general of the League in which he acknowledged the challenges presented to international arbitration by national laws and customs opposed to the recognition and enforcement of arbitration. Because the League's agenda was at the mercy of its state members, Van Hamel told his audience, the League's work in the area of international arbitration depended upon the efforts of the Chamber.[91] Over the next several years, the ICC and the League would together craft a system of arbitration that could solve the international commercial disputes of individuals.

Commercial Arbitration

Arbitration by disinterested specialists is one of the world's oldest mechanisms of dispute resolution and for this reason was adopted by merchants to decide disputes among their own far-flung communities. By the middle ages, guilds, merchants, or other corporate bodies of traders would sit in tribunals in order to resolve commercial disputes, often with the explicit sanction of the local prince or courts.[92] Yet, by the end of the eighteenth century, such arbitration had begun to decline in much of Europe as a result of five interrelated processes. First, state-building efforts had consolidated the medieval patchwork of dispute–resolution mechanisms into a public judicial system staffed by jealous judges. Second, the expansion of rights regimes increasingly included guaranteed access to courts that substantially reduced the legitimacy and finality of private dispute resolution mechanisms. Third, the expansion of commerce within states increased the anonymity of transactions and thus reduced the effectiveness of informal forms of contract enforcement and arbitration. Fourth, and finally, the rise of mercantile empires limited the amount of extra-jurisdictional trade that was actually happening. So long as British traders kept their business to wherever the King's writ ran, and likewise with

French, Spanish, and Dutch traders, there was little need for a solution that could span judicial systems.[93]

The collapse of those mercantile empires created new trading nightmares as the Americas gradually fractured from four empires into more than twenty countries by 1865.[94] An English tea merchant, for example, sending his wares to Virginia, could no longer count on being heard by a conational judge after 1776, a situation which led to the establishment of the first modern claims commission to settle contract disputes between British and American traders.[95] Claims commissions and diplomatic protection were increasingly used by states to mediate disputes. But private solutions also became more elaborate. Trade organizations began to require arbitration clauses be included within contracts among their members.[96] The London Corn Merchants Association, the Liverpool Cotton Association, the *Union Lyonnaise de Marchands de Soie*, and numerous others maintained their own institutional methods for solving disputes among members regardless of nationality. Enforcement was handled internally through blacklisting and expulsion from the trade organization.[97] Similarly, if a member sought enforcement outside of the association, via the public courts for example, the same sets of penalties could apply, which put a high cost on noncompliance with the arbitral tribunals of these trade organizations.

By the outbreak of World War I, commercial arbitration within trade organizations was exceedingly regular. In one year alone, the Incorporated Oil-Seed Association (a relatively tiny organization) arbitrated 6,386 disputes among its members. One legal observer called that number "enormous" and estimated that the London Corn Trade Association or the Liverpool Cotton Association undoubtedly had decided more.[98] The same observer imagined "that the disputes settled by commercial arbitrations in England in a year probably exceed[ed] the total number of civil actions . . . by a very large figure."[99] These trade organizations, moreover, were geographically widespread. A slump in the international economy following the conclusion of World War I also brought with it new import on the arbitral process. The American Arbitration Association (AAA), for example, handled 150 cases in 1921 alone between British and New York Merchants. Governments, too, were arbitrating. In 1920, the New York Chamber of Commerce (NYCC) was responsible for arbitrating a dispute between the French government and a private New York party, as well as seventeen cases between the French and the British governments. Greece, of course, also made an appearance among the NYCC's docket because the body heard a dispute between a US corporation and the Greek government.[100]

By 1924, at least thirty-three countries, more than two-thirds of those recognized by European diplomacy as being "sovereign," had some sort of committee tied to a chamber of commerce or one of its variants that dealt with the resolution of commercial disputes.[101] The US Department of State estimated in 1926 that there were at least 1,250 trade organizations, both national and international, with operations in the United States.[102] In 1927, the AAA surveyed and detailed all of the arbitration associations in the United States and classified them into 30 trades that took more than 800 pages to give just the basic details of each association's facilities for arbitration.[103] In addition to international trade organizations that revolved around specific industries, beginning in the early twentieth century, several chambers of commerce started entering into bilateral agreements with one another urging their respective members to insert a clause into all contracts that required the arbitration of any dispute. While many of these clauses were not recognized as binding by domestic courts, these bilateral agreements, like those of the trade organizations, relied upon customary enforcement mechanisms and stipulated that people who failed to comply with the terms of an award would have a notice served to their local chamber of commerce, which would be expected to ostracize the member. To this end, the chambers were expected to publish bulletins containing all information regarding the disputes settled via an arbitration agreement and "contain the firm name of any party refusing to comply with an award."[104]

These international trade institutions had developed in a highly globalized world, but a highly globalized world that was in a sense somewhat parochial and familiar. Trade was global but only among a select group of players and in a select set of geographic locations overseen by a select group of trade organizations that enabled effective blacklisting.[105] Geographically, all of this large volume of trade flowed through specific global centers. For example, nearly a quarter of all the wool in the world flowed through the city of Bradford, England. Consequently, the arbitration commission established by the Bradford Chamber of Commerce to supervise the woolen trade had the ability to prevent anyone who failed to comply with their decisions and procedures from participating in a substantial part in the woolen trade that happened to be under their moral influence.[106] Much of the rest of the wool trade moved through Leipzig, Germany, or Roubaix–Tourcoing, France, all of which had arbitral committees that were in regular contact with one another.[107] For the time being, international trade could function with customary forms of dispute resolution and enforcement outside of the law. The same was not true for *domestic* trade.

The expansion of the distance and volume of domestic trade in many countries by the middle of the nineteenth century had begun to challenge the traditional forms of pressure that mercantile and business associations could exert, especially as anonymity within business relations had become more common. Thus, it was increasingly the compulsive power of the state that ensured compliance. But litigation in national courts was also increasingly expensive with the expansion and increased professionalization of the legal system. More lawyers meant more procedural hurdles and maneuvers that added to the slowness of the law. Businesses operating at the national level needed the enforcement that could be provided by the state in order to continue to engage in increasingly anonymous business transactions, but they also sought to avoid the increasing costs of litigation. The solution, for many, was the legal recognition of contracts containing arbitration clauses. Recognition of the clauses would prevent parties from seeking the intervention of the courts before they engaged in arbitration, as per the contractual agreement; moreover, it would encourage the execution of the awards rendered by these tribunals by the legal authorities of the state.

In 1889, after years of advocacy by mercantile organizations and the London Chamber of Commerce, the British Parliament passed the Arbitration Act, which recognized the validity of clauses of arbitration, thus overturning centuries of common law rulings that had forbade people from ousting the courts from their disputes.[108] The law paved the way for the foundation of the City of London Chamber of Arbitration, the precursor of one of today's premier institutions for the arbitration of commercial disputes, the London Court of International Arbitration (LCIA). The United States also had its advocates of arbitration. By the late 1910s, two prominent members of the NYCC, Charles L. Bernheimer, chairman of the Committee on Arbitration of the NYCC, and Julius Henry Cohen, general counsel of the NYCC, together pursued via their ties to the NYCC, AAA, the International Congress of the Chambers of Commerce, and, later, the ICC, a three-pronged agenda to expand the practice of commercial arbitration in the United States and around the world. The first prong was to encourage the passage of state statutes. The second was to push for a federal statute (which would pass in 1925). And the third was to advocate for an international treaty.[109]

The gradual erosion of empire brought with it an alteration in global trading patterns. As the ICC observed, after 1919, "The producing and the consuming countries tended more and more to trade directly. As a result, a much greater number of individuals and private firms than ever before participated in international trade."[110] Not all cotton continued to flow through Bradford. Not all raw materials made their way to central imperial hubs where they were then redistributed. Global trade, like domestic trade during the previous century, was becoming more anonymous and punishing broken promises was becoming more difficult.

Consequently, the agenda of many international conferences and governmental organizations in the 1910s and 1920s featured the expansion of international commercial arbitration. Several of the Pan-American conferences called for the establishment and expansion of international commercial arbitration. The first Pan-American Financial Conference in 1915 featured commercial arbitration prominently among its resolutions, and it encouraged the International High Commission to study the problem.[111] The International Law Association had placed the expansion of international commercial arbitration on its agenda at its meetings in both 1910 and 1912. The Inter-Parliamentary Union had discussed it at its congress in 1912.[112] Nearly two decades earlier, the British Board of Trade had also looked into establishing courts all over the world to arbitrate commercial disputes.[113] Extensive support for the expansion of commercial arbitration was expressed at the International Congress of Chambers of Commerce held in 1912 and 1914, and in the latter year, a resolution was passed requesting that France call together an international conference for the purpose of drafting "an international agreement with respect to arbitration for the settlement of disputes between citizens of different countries."[114]

But enforcement of all of these decisions depended upon the goodwill of the parties and the sanction of financial markets. There was still limited or no judicial recognition.

Advocates for expanding judicial recognition of arbitration in Britain, France, the United States, and elsewhere all made similar claims. Arbitration, it was argued, would reduce commercial friction by preventing disputes from spinning out of control and devolving into contentious, distasteful, extended, and costly litigation.[115] Upon the establishment of the London Chamber of Arbitration, Edward Manson wrote that arbitration "is to have all the virtues which the law lacks. It is to be expeditious where the law is slow, cheap where the law is costly, simple where the law is technical, a peacemaker instead of a stirrer-up of strife."[116] It was supposed to produce better, more predictable, and more equitable decisions than did courts of law, since the judge and jury were peers in business. Judges, they claimed, were not experts on the ins and outs of the woolen trade, nor were they versed in the traditions of merchants. It was thought, arbitrators who were experts in the commercial subject at hand rather than in the complexities of the law would provide quicker and better decisions. It also put dispute resolutions on the timetable of business rather than on the timetable of the state. By removing the procedural barriers, commercial arbitration promised to be available when businessmen needed it. "In the past," noted R. S. Fraser, a prominent solicitor in London and a member of both the London Chamber of Commerce and the London Court of Arbitration,[117] "it has been a matter for rulers to decree whether they would open their courts during three of the most important months of the year. In arbitration I hope we will have forever put a stop to that abuse."[118]

Support also grew out of ideas of freedom of contract and a reaction against judicial paternalism. "Men of commercial experience," argued Julius Henry Cohen, "need[ed] no guardianship for determining . . . whether they prefer the opinions of their own trade upon technical questions, or the hazardous judgment of a jury of the vicinage."[119] It is not difficult to hear the echoes of Justice Peckham who, in a landmark 1906 US Supreme Court ruling reaffirming the liberty of contract, declared that bakers were "able to assert their rights and care for themselves without the protecting arm of the state, interfering with their independence of judgment and of action."[120] In this way, the commercial arbitration movement was related to the expansion of a widespread sensibility in the first half of the twentieth century that the contract was a sacred pact with which courts should refrain from interfering. Businesses wanted the state to stay out of their business.

While much of the commercial world was pushing for judicial recognition of arbitration clauses, critics were not entirely absent. In the 1880s, *The Economist*, which was a strong supporter of commercial arbitration, was hesitant to endorse those who wanted to make it more than just a customary practice. The vast majority of the cases were settled by friendly arbitration already, and the cases that did come before the courts often turned on points of law that could only, in fact, be decided by a court of law.[121] One merchant, while acknowledging the difficulties that court systems presented to the mediation of business disputes, noted that the trend toward commercial arbitration was eliminating the "highly useful curb of the law . . . and the highly trained intellects who administer it. Mercantile disputes [now] get settled, often with great individual injustice, by private associations, strong enough to coerce their brother traders." This trend, he thought, was "distinctively dangerous."[122]

The strongest critiques warned of the damage that expansion of the practice could do to long-sought civil rights.[123] The fundamental cause for the common law prohibition on clauses of arbitration, stated Cohen in testimony before the US Congress, "was that at the time this rule was made people were not able to take care of themselves . . . and the stronger men would take advantage of the weaker, and the courts had to come in and protect them. And the courts said, 'If you let the people sign away their rights, the powerful people will come in and take away the rights of the weaker ones.' And that still is true to a certain extent."[124] Roberto Pozzi, one of the drafters of the rules for the ICC's court of arbitration and the legal advisor to the Italian Cotton Association, noted that he could easily understand why most courts and treatise drafters had refused to recognize the validity of the clause because to do so represented "the renunciation of a fundamental right of the citizen and of the principle of personal liberty itself."[125] Arthur Nussbaum, another adamant supporter, cautioned that the "increase of arbitration might endanger state jurisdiction and the high ideals of impartial justice, if legislative measures for the remedy of abuses were not provided."[126] It is perhaps unsurprising that France, replete with its national tradition of civil protection and rights embodied in a singular state entity, resisted the impulse to grant recognition to the clauses until 1925, despite a long history of advocacy and the awkward fact that Paris was the headquarters of the ICC and its new court.[127] The French were hesitant because the recognition of a clause threatened to extract justice from the normative order and control of the state. It had been one of the sought-after aims of the French Revolution to open the courts to the common man. Article 14 of the French Civil Code had guaranteed all French citizens access to their courts, and it seemed anathema to the purposes of the state to permit others to oust its jurisdiction. For decades French treatises on civil procedure had written that to speak too highly of the benefits of commercial arbitration was "to prefer the shadow of justice to the brilliance which shines from the seat of the judiciary."[128]

Suspicions of foreign lands as well as international politics also plagued the cause of arbitration. Cohen reported the following to Congress: "A judge told me recently – one who is in sympathy with this measure and who approves it, but in the privacy of his own chambers he told me recently – 'Cohen you understand what this difficulty in this matter is; when England is in possession of shipping, you can understand why our people do not want to go over there and arbitrate their differences over there.'"[129] But it was Emmanuel Gounot, a lawyer for the Court of Appeals and a professor of law strongly opposed to the change, who best summed up the concerns when he claimed that the expansion of commercial arbitration would result in "imposing upon the French the arbitration of 'corporations' of foreign countries" that would leave the French a "feudal justice of great trusts or foreign cartels."[130] Of course, at the time of Gounot's protest, the ICC had already established the seat of its private court in Paris.[131]

The League of Nations and the Protection of Investments

When the League of Nations convened the Advisory Committee of Jurists to establish the Permanent Court of International Justice (PCIJ) in 1920, they debated the competency of the proposed court in this context. The plan submitted to the Advisory Committee of Jurists by La Fontaine and the Inter-Parliamentary Union would have created a court competent to hear conflicts between private persons, conflicts between private persons and foreign states, conflicts related to administrative questions, and conflicts related to the circulation of persons.[132] Albert Geouffre de Lapradelle, a member of the advisory committee spoke up when the issue of competency was raised. "It might be considered," Lapradelle urged, "whether the right to have recourse to the Court should not be given to some extent to private individuals, that is to say, in cases of denial of justice." By way of example, Lapradelle noted, "It sometimes happens that a private individual who has made a contract with a State, finds it impossible to obtain justice against it." He proposed that the PCIJ be given competency over cases brought by private individuals so long as the case was "not of a political nature."[133] In the realm of "commercial relations," Lapradelle argued, "a certain equality exists between the State and the individual."[134] Bernard Loder, then a member of the Supreme Court of the Netherlands and soon-to-be first president of the PCIJ, agreed with Lapradelle. Loder opined that he "saw no reason for limiting the competence of the Court by stipulating that private individuals must be represented by their Governments to have access to the Court."[135]

Like the proposal to open the court to minorities, the proposals to open the court to individual claims in general – and thus to creditors and international business interests – failed. The argument that all complaints to the PCIJ should be brought by states won the day.[136] As was mentioned before, the PCIJ would hear cases involving companies, breached contracts, and sovereign defaults, but it would only do so under the old Vattelian fiction.[137] A state was still required to espouse the claim.[138]

While the legal internationalization of disputes by individuals lost out, at least temporarily, in the creation of the PCIJ, there was still a flurry of activity to protect holders of sovereign debt. Many of the League's efforts focused on expanding the practice and enforcement of arbitration.

In 1922, the Czechoslovakian government contracted a loan with the London banking house, Baring Brothers, for 50 million USD. Part of the loan agreement stipulated that in the event of a default the Council of the League of Nations through its financial committee "will be empowered to make the best arrangement for the protection of the bondholders."[139] Whereas Russian refugees were not entitled to the protection of the

League, the investors in sovereign debt facilitated by Baring Brothers certainly were. In a letter addressed to Secretary General Drummond, Frank Nixon wrote that the arbitration of investment disputes seemed to be "one of the most useful things" that the League could do.[140] The League agreed to the terms and passed a resolution authorizing the Council to nominate either the Financial Committee or another committee or representative to make arrangements to protect the bondholders in the event of a dispute.[141] Over the next several years, the League would likewise apply this system to loans made to Austria, Bulgaria, Danzig, Estonia, Greece, and Hungary.[142] Investors had found a way to shift the burden of demanding the arbitration of disputes regarding sovereign debt from their own diplomatic corps to the Council of the League. Financiers and businessmen had found another avenue to overcoming the increasing reluctance of states to protect the foreign investments of their subjects. However, the success should not be overstated. Despite the League Council's decision to protect the purchasers of bonds to fund the development of Czechoslovakia, there was hesitancy on the part of the League to agree automatically to protect the interests of all creditors to sovereign League members, particularly those lending to South American states.[143] Like with states, international politics played a significant role in determining whether the League Council would agree to protect bondholders.[144] While the League Council's guarantee of investments was another avenue through which individuals could seek some kind of protection,[145] it was an avenue still fraught with uncertainty and limited by the political interests of the League Council.

The League, however, did not stop with the League Loans. For one, the League Council moved to ensure that contracts and titles to property would be valid in the mandated territories. In 1925, the League Council declared that contracts and titles to property assumed by a mandate would still be valid following the dissolution of a mandate.[146] There would be no mass expropriations or mass repudiations of debts or concessions in a former mandate, as there had been in Russia and Mexico. Mandatory Powers, such as Britain and France, would be free to obligate their mandates, and independence from the mandate system would be predicated on honoring those obligations. The sanctity of the contract continued its global march.[147]

More importantly, perhaps, the same year that the League Council agreed to guarantee the loans to Czechoslovakia, Frank Nixon, acting head of the Economic and Financial Committee, wrote to Ronald Vaughan Williams,[148] who was then a member of the Anglo-German tribunal in London. The Anglo-German tribunal had been established after the war to deal with the claims of individuals who had been harmed in the course of the conflict. Many viewed the tribunal as a success, and Nixon was interested in Williams' thoughts on the operation of mixed tribunals that dealt with contract and property disputes. In the event that the states of Europe began to recognize the Bolshevik government in Russia, Nixon wanted to be prepared. "If the European countries," Nixon wrote, "establish relations with Russia, one of the most important questions will be the settlement of property, rights, contracts, etc."[149] In his reply, Williams supported the idea of establishing a Russian claims tribunal and thought it would be best managed under the League.[150] Nixon was sniffing around ways in which the League could aid in the resolution of disputes pertaining to contracts, property, and investments.[151]

In 1922, thirty-two countries gathered together in Genoa for the second major economic conference of the interwar period and the first in which a Soviet delegation was invited to participate. The aim of the conference, which had been proposed by Lloyd George, was to reconstruct economic relations within central and eastern Europe, particularly with Soviet Russia and the new "fringe of States on the western frontier of Russia" that had been born out of the shattered remains of the Russian Empire.[152] The conference had been kicked off by Soviet interests in an economic rapprochement with the West in order to encourage much-needed foreign investment and aid.[153]

In preparing for the conference, Claude Schuster, then the permanent secretary to the Lord Chancellor's Office, noted in a letter to Frank Douglass MacKinnon that two major obstacles stood in the way of resumption of trade with central and eastern Europe. The first obstacle was the problem of credit, a problem that was quickly passed over in the correspondence. The second and most significant obstacle was, according to Schuster, "the reluctance which British traders feel to submitting their disputes arising between themselves and their customers to the tribunals of these semi-civilised states."[154] The solution advocated by the Chamber of Commerce and the Board of Trade was that the countries at the Genoa conference should agree that the presence of an arbitration clause in a contract should "oust absolutely" the jurisdiction of the "semi-civilised" courts.[155]

Although the Genoa conference broke down and little of note was achieved, Article 14 of the Resolutions of the Genoa Economic Commission declared, "It is desirable that the enquiries now being made by the League of Nations, as to the best means of safeguarding the validity of voluntary agreements to refer to arbitration disputes arising out of commercial contracts, should be continued."[156] The expansion of commercial arbitration was seen as a vital means through which the international economy could be stabilized. "It is no exaggeration," wrote

Julius Henry Cohen in 1921, "to say that at the present moment commerce and trade are passing through one of the greatest crises in their history, and, as the Federal Reserve Bank is acting as a stabilizer for money conditions, existing systems of commercial arbitration are acting as stabilizers of commercial relations."[157]

Hubert Llewellyn Smith had worked to expand the collaboration between British Chambers of Commerce and the Board of Trade while he was the permanent secretary at the latter and took the concerns of the Chamber seriously.[158] By 1920, he was the chief economic advisor to the British government, and by March of 1922, he had put commercial arbitration on the agenda of the League's Economic and Financial Committee. In a statement to the committee, Llewellyn Smith extolled the oft-recited virtues of commercial arbitration. "The Clause has been found of great value in avoiding litigation and promoting commercial honesty, and the commercial world attaches great importance to its general recognition," he wrote. "There have been some recent cases, however, in which arbitration clauses in contracts between nationals of different countries have been ignored by one of the parties." Drawing upon statements made by the ICC that singled out nonrecognition of the clause as a troublesome barrier to trade, he noted the many difficulties encountered when states refused to recognize the validity of the arbitral clause. Llewellyn Smith closed his statement by hoping he had illustrated the importance "of the subject, not only in relation to trade with countries in which the Courts cannot be trusted but also in relation to international commerce generally."[159] The idea that commercial arbitration would be of value in countries where the courts could not be trusted was an age-old concern, and the language certainly echoes that of Schuster's letter to MacKinnon from the same month. In several of the regions in the world where formal empire had not held sway, commercial arbitration had been used to prevent contract disputes from entering into what Western Europeans considered to be questionable jurisdictions. The system of commercial arbitration fit well into Britain's informal imperial strategies.[160]

While at the British Board of Trade, both as comptroller-general of the commercial, labor, and statistical branch and then later as permanent secretary, Llewellyn Smith had engaged in a number of bureaucratic turf war to wrest control of international commercial issues from the hands of the Foreign Office.[161] Commercial arbitration, no doubt, served as a proxy in this continued struggle, since the expansion of commercial arbitration promised to reduce the influence that the Foreign Office had in shaping international commerce through its sometimes-idiosyncratic exercise of diplomatic protection, intervention, and most-favored-nation treaty negotiations. In effect, Llewellyn Smith's advocacy for the greater recognition of international commercial arbitration had the potential to reduce the influence of the political and judicial branches of government in shaping the priorities and policies of global trade. By removing the Foreign Office from disputes, the interests of business, rather than those of the state generally, would shape the manner in which international commercial disputes between individuals could be resolved. Individuals (at least those engaged in business) could finally seek protection (primarily for their property) without relying upon increasingly reluctant foreign ministries.

On the urging of Llewellyn Smith, the League's Economic and Financial Committee formed a subcommittee of commercial and legal experts drawn from the Latin, Scandinavian, Central European, Asian, German, and South American systems of law to explore the problem and draft a series of recommendations for expanding the scope and potency of international commercial arbitration in the resolution of international commercial disputes. MacKinnon was appointed as the British representative. As both "the chairman and the most active member of the committee," MacKinnon was responsible for drafting much of the language that made its way into the final draft of the proposed protocol, which itself was thought of as a "very largely British" proposal that had been "badly wanted by the commercial community of [Britain]."[162] Schuster, Llewelyn Smith, and MacKinnon, all either under pressure from the their local chambers of commerce or with the aid of the ICC's increasing influence in League activities, had managed to get international commercial arbitration placed front and center on the agenda of the Economic and Financial Committee of the League during the first years of its existence.

The subcommittee's report gave its resounding support to the project declaring that "the system of commercial arbitration [was] of essential importance." Subcommittee members further noted, "We think it is clearly a matter for regret when a man who is breaking his contract is assisted in doing so by the provisions of the law of his own country upon which he can rely." The report continued, "The claims of nationality or of a national legal system, are too dearly vindicated when the price of that vindication is private immorality and the dishonour of the citizen."[163] Making use of a judicial system that had recently evolved to protect the interests and rights of citizens was coded by an expert committee of the League as privately immoral without any acknowledgement of any benefits of judicial or even political oversight.

By the autumn of 1923, the drafting committee had finished its work and the Geneva Protocol on Arbitration Clauses was signed at a meeting of the Assembly of the League. The Geneva Protocol entered force the following year on July 28, and by the end of 1931, more than thirty countries and jurisdictions had ratified it.[164] Albania, Austria, Czechoslovakia, Estonia, Finland, Iraq, Poland, and Romania all were among those who ratified and submitted their ratification to the League. In addition Bolivia, Chile, Latvia, Lithuania, Nicaragua, Panama, Paraguay, Peru, Salvador, and Uruguay all signed the convention and made use of its provisions.[165]

With the relative success of the Geneva Protocol, the League again took up the issue of making decisions rendered by arbitral tribunals abroad enforceable, efforts that culminated in the drafting of the 1927 Geneva Convention on the Enforcement of Arbitral Awards. By 1931, twenty-four countries had ratified the 1927 Convention with a further five signing. Nearly every new eastern European country, with the exceptions of Hungary and the Kingdom of the Serbs, Slovenes and Croats, were signatories. Several of the new mandates also made an appearance, notably Iraq.

Despite the best efforts of its champions at the ICC and the League, however, the Geneva Protocol and Convention remained flawed instruments. While they had many powerful advocates and they were certainly a step toward the goals of arbitration's proponents, they also had some harsh critics who condemned the treaties for being "exceedingly vague."[166] For example, the treaties only applied to contracts "between parties subject respectively to the jurisdiction of different contracting states."[167] What did that mean? Would two parties currently in the same country but of different nationality be considered to be "subject" to the same jurisdiction? If states were free to determine their jurisdictional powers, then could they simply "assume" unilaterally that they had jurisdiction over both parties? This so-called diversity-of-citizenship clause introduced into the project of international commercial arbitration the very tension that partisans of arbitration sought to escape. It put all the vagaries and problems inherent to questions of an individual's relationship to a state, of an individual's *nationality*, front and center in the first sentence of the first article of the 1923 Protocol.

The British architects of the Protocol had come across this problem as well. In the earliest versions of the treaty drafted by MacKinnon, the diversity-of-citizenship clause had required that the parties be of different "nationalities." The committee, in what they considered their most important departure from the original text, had substituted "jurisdiction" for "nationality." Their stated reason for doing so was to avoid the problems that would arise if, for example, "a British merchant in London makes a contract including an arbitration clause with an Englishman carrying on business in Paris," since the Englishman in Paris would have been able to bring an action in a French court against his co-national despite the presence of an arbitration clause. It was thus necessary to have an agreement with France to ensure that its courts would refuse to hear a dispute involving an arbitration clause.[168]

Arthur Nussbaum, in his survey of the criticism of the treaties, thought that this vague requirement was the most "particularly troublesome."[169] Despite the efforts of the drafters, the old and intractable debate between domicile and nationality was causing problems almost from the treaty's inception, Nussbaum noted, as the Italians had already "read their traditional nationality principle into the clause," and "German and English courts would probably prefer domicile." [170] Comte Giorgio Balladore Pallieri, a prominent Italian professor of international law, warned in his exegesis on the two treaties that, based on its language, "if the State submits to its jurisdiction a large number of people, the parties to the arbitral agreement will almost always be under the jurisdiction of a single state; and we will thus render useless the convention which aims to resist these exaggerated pretensions of states."[171] He also noted that it was unclear whether individuals who were part of the British Empire, or who were residents in one of the newly created mandates, would be able to be properly assumed to be "under the jurisdiction" of the state that was in control of the mandate. Would, for instance, a British merchant resident in Britain and an Iraqi merchant resident in Iraq, then a British mandate, both be considered to be "under the jurisdiction" of Britain?[172]

The 1927 Convention, moreover, did not go as far as the Chamber would have liked in ensuring the enforcement of arbitral awards. It had some fatal flaws as well, the most basic of which was that it was still bound to the law of the jurisdiction in which the arbitration was conducted. Throughout the 1920s and 1930s, moreover, many domestic jurisdictions continued to be jealous of their powers generally but also remained reluctant to execute arbitral sentences rendered abroad especially as more European states shifted toward autarky.[173] Van Hamel, in a letter to Frank Nixon, argued that because the recognition of foreign judicial and arbitral judgments implied "the abandonment of a part of national sovereignty," most countries were not prepared to agree to a general enforcement treaty.[174] Likewise, Ernest Lorenzen, in his survey of the global landscape, was pessimistic that the problems of enforcement would be solved anytime soon via the methods pursued by the League.[175]

The International Institute of Rome for the Unification of Private Law agreed that the "only road likely to put an end to these difficulties [was the] unification of the national laws relative to arbitration."[176]

Arthur Nussbaum, one of arbitration's most tireless supporters, concluded in 1942 while surveying the treaties that they had been relatively unsuccessful. Moreover, the arbitral courts of international organizations like the ICC had far fewer cases brought to them than had originally been expected.[177]

There were some who disagreed. Few disputes over the use of arbitration ended up in court, a fact that Nussbaum interpreted as a lack of success. The German emigré lawyer, Heinrich Kronstein, in contrast, saw that as evidence of exactly the opposite – that arbitration had been so successful that disputes were simply not ending up in the courts – private or public.[178]

But the problem was also one of a changed international environment. The economic collapse of 1929 brought with it a dramatic reduction in the volume of international trade. As the Great Depression set in, the shift toward autarky exacerbated the decline in global trade, which by the mid-1930s was only a third of what it had been in 1929. But the collapse also brought with it a dramatic increase in sovereign default, expropriation, and renewed capital controls. In response, the League Assembly resolved to established a committee of experts to "examine the means for improving contracts relating to international loans issued by Governments or other public authorities in the future, and, in particular, to prepare model provisions – if necessary, with a system of arbitration – which could, if the parties so desired, be inserted in such contracts."[179] After several years of study, the committee issued its report in May 1939. The question of what law should apply to resolve disputes between states and individuals was difficult to answer As the Committee wrote, "Where, as in the case of international loans, the parties concerned are of different nationalities and domicile . . . questions arise which are among the most difficult in the whole field of legal science."[180] It appeared to the Committee "that the only way of dealing with [the problem] would be to embody into an international convention a code of rules applicable to international loans, thus removing the subject from the field of municipal law into that of international law."[181] The question of what body would be competent to hear such a case was also taken up by the Committee:

> The courts of countries other than the debtor State and, in particular, those of the country or countries in which the service of the loan is effected generally declare themselves incompetent ; on the other hand, an action before the national courts of the debtor State is not always calculated to yield the results which the bondholder is entitled to expect. It is not generally possible to apply to an international

tribunal. The Permanent Court of International Justice, to which it would seem natural to have recourse, is by its Statute only empowered to take cognisance of disputes between States, It cannot therefore be seized by bondholders or their representatives.[182]

The solution, the Committee argued, was "that loan contracts should in all cases include at least a clause providing for arbitration on matters of interpretation of the contract" and that "a manifest improvement in international loan contracts would . . . be, while laying down in every contract the manner in which legal disputes are to be settled, also to provide for the appointment of arbitrators by some international body."[183] As per the League Assembly's instruction, the committee provided a draft clause.[184]

World War II broke out shortly after the report was issued. In December, the League decamped from Geneva to wait out the war. In exile it worked on, among other things, examining the conditions of private investment.[185]

***

The reader might recall that at the beginning of this chapter we were left with the shareholders of Lena Goldfields, Ltd. wondering what, if anything, they could do following the mass nationalization of the mines by Vladimir Lenin. Like many foreigners who owned property or who had invested in Russia, Lena Goldfields, Ltd. lodged a formal complaint against the Soviet government with the Russian Claims Department in the United Kingdom's Board of Trade.[186] By 1923, things had changed. The Soviet government, more secure with the end of the Russian Civil War, was attempting to rebuild the economy. Desperate for capital and foreign expertise, Lenin instituted the New Economic Policy in 1921, which permitted a degree of private ownership and slowly reversed some of the nationalizations that had taken place during the Civil War. In 1923, rather than continue to press for monetary reparation, Lena Goldfields, Ltd. sought to regain their concessions from a Soviet government that seemed increasingly cooperative.[187]

By 1925, Lena Goldfields Ltd. and the USSR had signed a new concession agreement. In exchange for waiving any claims upon the Soviet Union for the nationalization, Lena Goldfields, Ltd. gained the exclusive right to mine in the Urals and other parts of Siberia.[188] But Lena Goldfields, Ltd. was, understandably, wary of investing further in a territory controlled by a regime that had expropriated all of their property and interests a mere seven years earlier ("fool me once . . ." and all that). Moreover, Soviet Russia had an untested and irregular justice system. And so, as part of their concession agreement, Lena Goldfields, Ltd.

demanded the inclusion of a clause that provided that the Soviet government and Lena Goldfields, Ltd. would submit any dispute concerning the agreement to a court of arbitration.[189]

For five years, Lena Goldfields Ltd. ran its operation. But by 1929, the relationship between Lena Goldfields, Ltd. and the Soviet Union had begun to sour.[190] Following a series of financial mishaps, the Joint State Political Directorate carried out a series of raids on Lena's offices, seizing papers and arresting officers.[191] Lena Goldfields, Ltd.'s manager in Moscow was tried and convicted for permitting the late payment of wages.[192] Things looked bad for Lena Goldfields, Ltd.

By 1930, Lena Goldfields, Ltd. felt that it could no longer continue its operations and invoked the arbitration clause.[193] An arbitral tribunal met in London in 1930 to hear the case. The British press closely followed the proceedings.[194] And the tribunal eventually awarded Lena Goldfields, Ltd. the handsome sum of 12,965,000 GBP plus 12 percent interest from the date of the award.[195]

But the Soviet Union failed to honor the award. Nor was the Soviet Union yet a member of the 1927 Convention on the Execution of Foreign Arbitral Awards (which might have permitted Lena Goldfields, Ltd. to seek execution of the award elsewhere). Progress had been made from the perspective of investors and investor-state arbitration was now, at least, a more visible and more recognized process.[196] The procedure was increasingly apparent. All that was left was to find a better way of binding states. The 1923 Geneva Protocol and the 1927 Geneva Convention were a start. But they were imperfect instruments. Better ones would need to be crafted to finally bring states to heal and to truly make commerce "the sovereign of all."[197]

Part III

Mise-en-scène

The International Legal World, 1945–Present

> Everyone is entitled to all the rights and freedoms set forth in this Declaration, without distinction of any kind, such as race, colour, sex, language, religion, political or other opinion, national or social origin, property, birth or other status. Furthermore, no distinction shall be made on the basis of the political, jurisdictional or international status of the country or territory to which a person belongs, whether it be independent, trust, non-self-governing or under any other limitation of sovereignty.
>
> Universal Declaration of Human Rights, 1948.

For more than half a decade, Geneva had been silent. In December of 1939, the Twentieth Assembly of the League of Nations had decided not to close its session but rather to adjourn. The Palace of Nations, the home of the League, shut its doors and shuttered its windows. The vast and sun-soaked interiors of the second-largest building complex in Europe (after Versailles) were darkened. The chattering halls were silenced. The building would remain empty for more than six years as war raged around the globe.

In the spring of 1946, international life slowly began to return to Geneva. Footsteps echoed through the Palace of Nations again. The shutters were opened, the curtains drawn, and the facilities prepared to welcome back delegates to the League. In April the delegates gathered, and the tone was somber and quiet. In his address to close the Twentieth and open the Twenty-First Ordinary Session of the League, the president of the Assembly addressed the delegations. "This is a solemn occasion for you will be invited to decide to dissolve the League of Nations as such and to dissolve the Permanent Court of International Justice, and to declare this twenty-first session of the Assembly of the League of Nations to be its last one."[1] The president then welcomed the delegates present in the room from the new United Nations (UN). He then quickly dismissed with many of the usual formalities of procedure and began to walk the

Assembly through the process of liquidating the League's assets and hand them over along with the rest of the League's real property – including its headquarters, library, and archives at Geneva – to the UN.[2]

Robert Cecil, one of the few remaining stalwarts from the early days of the League, gave an assessment of the League:

> We saw a new world centre, imperfect materially, but enshrining great hopes, an assembly representing some fifty peace-loving nations, a Council, an international civil service, a World Court of International Justice, so often before planned but never created, an International Labour Office to promote better conditions for the workers. And very soon there followed that great apparatus of committees and conferences, striving for an improved civilisation, better international co-operation, a larger redress of grievances and the protection of the helpless and oppressed.' . . . But, as we know, it failed in the essential condition of its existence—namely, the preservation of peace.[3]

Cecil closed his *relatively* brief speech with an exclamation, "The League is dead; long live the United Nations."[4]

The close of World War II had brought with it the close of the League of Nations. The new United Nations, born from a charter in San Francisco instead of a covenant in Paris and soon-to-be headquartered in a high-rise in New York instead of a palace in Geneva, was set to take the League's place. Yet, despite the changes, much (as usual) remained the same. The UN had an Assembly, a Council, and a Secretariat – as had the League. Great Power interests were anchored in a council, as they had been in the League, while developing countries found a voice in the Assembly, as they had in the League.

Indeed, many of the institutions developed by the League, particularly as they pertained to international law, continued. The Committee of Experts for the Progressive Codification of International Law saw much of their work continue under the guise of the International Law Commission (ILC), which was established to fulfill the UN Assembly's obligation "to initiate studies and make recommendations for the purpose of . . . encouraging the progressive development of international law and its codification."[5] Yet the United Nations was far less legalistic than its predecessor. Law, as one postwar jurist observed, had "a secondary position in the Charter . . . . The emphasis is now upon the prevention of the use of force between nations, rather than upon settlement in accordance with law."[6] If the League displaced its popular juridical alternatives in favor of politics,[7] the United Nations continued that tradition with a renewed vigor. The League's flirtations with alternative bases of sovereignty were nowhere to be found in the UN Charter. Instead, it reaffirmed "the principle of the sovereign equality of all its Members."[8]

Whereas the League had put the protection of minorities near the center of its agenda, such concerns were absent from the UN's remit. There was no "minority" section. Instead, alongside the UN Charter was the Universal Declaration of Human Rights – a document which placed the individual, rather than a group, at its center. But as any international lawyer knows, most declarations have no legal force. Declarations detail a world that the drafters hope will emerge and duties they think are important, but that they don't want to assume. They're a persuasive argument about how international society should be, not how it is. While not quite a castle in the air, declarations only have soft power. Conventions, in contrast, are descriptive. As legally binding documents, once ratified, they describe the legal world that the drafters have created. Conventions are a statement of what international society is. The UN Charter was a legally binding convention; the Universal Declaration, a wish. And lawyers in the postwar years recognized this.[9]

Nevertheless, over the next half-century, human rights would gradually become a legal language which would challenge the state's monopoly on sovereignty and international legal subjectivity. The UN Charter, even more than the League, had reaffirmed the principle of sovereign equality.[10] Yet the Universal Declaration presented rhetorical, if not legal, challenges to that reaffirmation by the late twentieth century.

The Permanent Court of International Justice (PCIJ) had been dissolved with the League, but the International Court of Justice (ICJ) was established in its place. The new court was almost identical to the old in structure, and it adopted the PCIJ's jurisprudence and its docket, ensuring a continuity of international legal thought and process.[11] The ICJ was joined over the next several decades by more and more international judicial institutions. Regional human rights courts, like the European Court of Human Rights and the Inter-American Court of Human Rights, sprung up and were occasionally capable of issuing binding decisions and giving standing to individuals and not just states.

And individuals were also increasingly subject to, and not just subjects of, international law. The League had made some sporadic and incomplete efforts toward the establishment of international criminal tribunals, particularly for terrorism.[12] But following World War II, the International Military Tribunals in Nuremberg and Tokyo tried individuals for crimes against the peace and crimes against humanity, and both issued and carried out sentences. The development of international criminal law paused during the Cold War but came back strong in the 1990s, culminating with the establishment of the International Criminal Court at The Hague in 2002.[13]

Other institutions in the legal world continued. Books and journals on international law proliferated. Law schools expanded in size and scope. Law firms, those from the United States in particular, increased the size of their staffs, established new offices around the globe, and dramatically expanded their global influence in the field of international law – often taking charge of public international disputes where they represented states as clients before international fora, as well as the more expected private international legal disputes.

More interestingly, though, the number of states in the world exploded as formal colonization gradually came to an end. The United Nations in 1945 counted fifty-one countries among its members. Twenty years later, in 1965 there were 117, more than double the original number. By 2011 there were 193 members, or nearly four times the number of sovereign state members in 1945. These "new" states all had new governments, new court systems, new laws, and new sovereignty. And new borders meant even more potential for international transactions and international boundary crossings. As formal imperialism gave way and extraterritorial concessions became a thing of the past, international law bore the weight of the need to provide legal certainty. But more states also meant more nationalities and more persons, real and fictive, moving and living abroad. Just how would the international legal apparatus adapt?

The year 1919 had been a time in which all sorts of international configurations seemed possible – sovereign nations, sovereign peoples, sovereign persons, sovereign labor. The year 1945, in contrast, narrowed the field of possibility dramatically. States were sovereign – full stop. However, slowly over the succeeding decades it became clear that, perhaps, so were persons.

6 Cosmopolitans and Capitalists

> The protection of minorities in the future should consist primarily in the defense of human democratic rights and not of national rights. Minorities in individual states must never again be given the character of internationally recognized political and legal units, with the possibility of again becoming sources of disturbance.[1]
>
> Eduard Benes, 1942

In 1881, Friedrich Nottebohm, a man whose name shouts, "German!," was birthed into the world a subject of Kaiser Wilhelm I. He owed the kaiser allegiance and, in return, the Kaiser swaddled him with Sovereign protection. When he was a young man, Nottebohm steamed across the Atlantic to join his brothers' business, Nottebohm Hermanos, a banking and trading house that would soon become the second largest producer of coffee in Guatemala.[2] For more than thirty years, Nottebohm spent most of his time in Guatemala, only occasionally returning to Germany for business. Like countless transatlantic migrants in the nineteenth and early twentieth centuries, Nottebohm never obtained Guatemalan nationality, but rather retained his status as a German national. Who wouldn't? As we saw in Chapter 2, being a foreigner[3] could be an advantage when it came with the ability to appeal any injustice beyond the domestic courts to one's own consul. So, of course, Nottebohm retained his link to Germany and, as long as he did so, his property would be relatively safe from arbitrary confiscation or expropriation. He retained his German nationality until it became a liability. In October 1939, a month after German troops marched into Poland and set in motion World War II, Mr. Nottebohm marched into tiny Liechtenstein and set in motion events that would lead to one of the more controversial opinions of the International Court of Justice.[4]

Mr. Nottebohm had come to Liechtenstein with a single purpose: to obtain a certificate of naturalization and the passport of a *neutral power*, a process that took him less than a week.[5] He applied for naturalization on October 9 and four days later, owing to a bureaucratic efficiency that is only possible in a country that is (a) German, and (b) has a population of just over 10,000 people, Mr. Nottebohm became a national of the Principality of Liechtenstein, or, to use the whimsical demonym, Mr. Nottebohm became a Liechtensteiner.[6] In exchange for his naturalization, Mr. Nottebohm agreed to pay the somewhat-exorbitant sum of 40,500 Swiss Francs in fees for naturalization and to deposit 30,000 Swiss Francs as a deposit. Moreover, he agreed to pay 1,000 Swiss Francs annually while out of the country.[7] As the proud new owner of a Lichtenstein passport, Mr. Nottebohm renounced his German nationality, tore up his German passport,[8] and did what any newly naturalized citizen[9] of Liechtenstein seems to do – he got the hell out of Liechtenstein.

In 1940, Mr. Nottebohm returned to Guatemala, the country where he had spent the vast majority of his life. Three years later, our poor protagonist was arrested by the Guatemalan authorities and turned over to the armed forces of the United States on suspicion of being a German national – apparently his Lichtenstein passport just wasn't convincing enough. He was confined as an enemy alien in the United States, where he divided his time between the scorching summers of Camp Kenedy in Texas[10] and the frigid winters of Fort Lincoln in North Dakota,[11] until 1946.[12] While he was an involuntary guest at Camp Kenedy and Ford Lincoln, more than fifty suits were filed against him in the Guatemalan courts. Soon all of his property in Guatemala was confiscated by the Guatemalan government. After his release, poor, beleaguered, and nearly propertyless Mr. Nottebohm was denied entry to Guatemala. And so he returned "home" to Liechtenstein.[13]

Five years later, tiny Liechtenstein brought a complaint against Guatemala before the International Court of Justice (ICJ) on behalf of Mr. Nottebohm. The complaint sought upwards of 10 million Swiss Francs in damages.[14] The hearing before the ICJ was somewhat scandalous, as Guatemala accused (albeit to varying degrees) Mr. Nottebohm and little Liechtenstein of fraud. Henri Rolin, a prominent professor of international law and future judge at the European Court of Human Rights, served as one of Guatemala's counsels in the case. Rolin's overarching claim was that Mr. Nottebohm was not a Liechtenstein national from the perspective of international law. Specifically, Rolin pointed to the manifest absurdity that a man who, before coming to Guatemala in 1940, had never lived in Liechtenstein, had no home in Liechtenstein, and had spent almost no time even visiting Liechtenstein, could be considered a Liechtensteiner and seek Liechtenstein's protection and intervention against the state where the same man had lived for 35 years, made his home, built his business, and kept many of his assets.[15]

To support its case, Guatemala argued "that Mr. Nottebohm appear[ed] to have solicited Liechtenstein nationality fraudulently... with the sole object of acquiring the status of a neutral national before returning to Guatemala, and without any genuine intention to establish a durable link... between the Principality and himself."[16] And this is where the case gets a bit scandalous. Germany had, Rolin claimed, encouraged its nationals to do that. Rolin produced a circular issued by the German foreign ministry in 1939, on the eve of the war, that encouraged Germans outside the country to try and naturalize elsewhere to avoid being confined or having their property confiscated. The circular went so far as to offer easy reintegration into Germany after the war, should the renunciation of German nationality be required for a naturalization (as it was in the case of Liechtenstein).[17] Rolin additionally presented a memorandum from the Ambassador of the United States in Guatemala that Mr. Nottebohm, "although individually inactive within the sphere of the Nazi Party, were as affectively pro-German in their educational background, their business connections and their every action as the staunchest Nazi Party member could be."[18]

The accusations of scurrilous behavior did not stop with poor Mr. Nottebohm. Guatemala went so far as to accuse Liechtenstein itself of an abuse of rights and even fraud. Rather than taking Liechtenstein's word that Mr. Nottebohm had been duly naturalized, Guatemala demanded that Liechtenstein produce:

> all original documents in the archives relating to the naturalization of Nottebohm and, in particular, the convocations of members of the Diet to the sitting on 14 October 1939, and those of the Assembly of Mauren citizens on 15 October 1939, the agenda and minutes of the aforesaid sittings, together with the instrument conferring naturalization allegedly signed by His Highness the Prince Regnant.[19]

Additionally, Rolin alluded to the unsavory character of the transaction. "Does it need to be said," he asked in a rejoinder, "that these naturalization fees appear to be much higher than those levied by every other State and that they are, notably, more than four times the amount demanded by the Canton of Berne at that time?"[20]

Still, Nazi connections and conspiracies aside, it looked grim for Guatemala. As you, dear reader, already know if you've stuck with me for this long, the assignment of nationality is part of the "reserved domain." Or put another way, it's (almost) nobody's business how a state chooses its nationals. The reader might recall that this was one of the centerpieces of the failed Convention on Certain Questions Relating to the Conflict of Nationality Law. Chapter I, Article 1, the *very first provision* of that convention, declared, "It is for each State to determine under its own law who are its nationals. This law shall be recognised by other States in so far as it is consistent with international conventions, international custom, and the principles of law generally recognised with regard to nationality."[21] The qualifications laid out in the second sentence were few in number in 1930. In general, the only restriction on a state's conferral of nationality was that it had to be consensual. A state could not impose its nationality on a person without that person's consent.[22] But how and why a state chose to admit a person to its polity was its business alone. As Judge Klaestad put it in his dissent from the Court's majority opinion, "It is generally recognized that questions of naturalization of aliens are, in the absence of conventional rules, in principle within the exclusive competence of States, and that international law has left it to the States themselves to regulate in what manner and under what conditions their nationality may be conferred upon aliens."[23]

But the Court surprised many when it held that Liechtenstein could not press its claim against Guatemala. The Court agreed, among other things, that Mr. Nottebohm's naturalization "was lacking in the *genuineness* requisite to an act of such importance."[24] In what is probably dicta,[25] but has nevertheless become the decision's most cited passage, the ICJ declared:

> According to the practice of States, to arbitral and judicial decisions and to the opinions of writers, nationality is a legal bond having as its basis a social fact of attachment, a genuine connection of existence, interests and sentiments, together with the existence of reciprocal rights and duties. It may be said to constitute the juridical expression of the fact that the individual upon whom it is conferred... is in fact more closely connected with the population of the State conferring nationality than with that of any other State.[26]

The ICJ, it seemed, had taken nationality – at least in part – out of the reserved domain. Liechtenstein was told flatly that it had no legal basis to press a claim against Guatemala because Mr. Nottebohm was not a *genuine* Liechtensteiner.

Despite the ICJ majority's attempt to limit the scope of its decision, the reasoning had far-reaching effects over the subsequent half century, provoking extensive commentary and citation in modern international cases.[27] More than fifty years on, the *Nottebohm* principle is still debated and contested.[28]

The point of this, perhaps, over-long story of Mr. Nottebohm is to highlight what is one of the central trajectories of postwar international law – the revolt against nationality as a basis for protection. The contradictions and tensions inherent in nationality as a legal status could no longer be fully reconciled with an orderly world. And the reasons are obvious. The protection of nationals abroad, the claims of special rights by states to protect peoples living beyond their borders had wrought havoc on the world twice in a half-century – most recently when Hitler had moved to protect the *Auslandsdeutsche* in central and eastern Europe. The international legal community would no longer permit nationality to be instrumentalized and used as a mere pretext for intervention – diplomatic or otherwise.

Eduard Benes, the once and future president of Czechoslovakia and a victim of the principle of nationality and the right of diplomatic protection, when thinking about the organization of postwar Europe, opined, "The protection of minorities in the future should consist primarily in the defense of human democratic rights and not of national rights. Minorities in individual states must never again be given the character of internationally recognized political and legal units, with the possibility of again becoming sources of disturbance."[29] Benes' prescription was more or less adopted by the postwar international system. In Eastern Europe, empire reasserted itself in the form of a dramatically expanded Soviet Union. There would be no minority treaties with Stalin. And none of the major postwar planning documents, the Atlantic Charter, the Moscow Declaration, or the Declaration of Liberated Europe made any mention of minority rights or protections.[30]

Instead, as Benes put it, the international system should "facilitate emigration from one state to another, so that if national minorities do not want to live in a foreign state they may gradually unite with their own people in neighboring state."[31] Echoing Benes, Anthony Eden, the British foreign secretary, confided to a reporter in 1942, "I certainly don't want any more minorities and minorities treaties.... They are a constant source of grievances and friction and they will always be used by some other Power to ferment trouble. That's what happened after 1919 and it would happen again. Therefore transference – voluntary transference – is the remedy."[32]

And, indeed, population transfers were the remedy employed after the war. The Allied Powers vigorously supported a great "unmixing" of populations.[33] The German minorities scattered throughout Eastern Europe, many of whom had made effective use of the interwar language of minority rights, were forcibly returned to Germany in one of the great ethnic cleansings of the twentieth century.[34] The Soviet Union, likewise, accelerated their own – already robust – program of internal mass population transfers and continued to participate in exchange programs with their neighbors in the Polish-Ukrainian borderlands.[35] Instead of conforming borders to people, as the League had attempted in principle (if not always in practice), people were conformed to borders.[36]

When reviewing whether or not the minority treaties were still in force, the United Nations concluded in the first few years of its existence, "that between 1939 and 1947 circumstances as a whole changed to such an extent that, generally speaking, the [League of Nations] system [of international protection of minorities] should be considered as having ceased to exist."[37]

The Nottebohm case, then, should be read in this broader context: one in which jurists were suspicious of intervention on behalf of nationals abroad. The doctrine had been stained by the minorities system of the interwar period and by the German instrumentalization of that system, most famously at Munich. In one decision, the ICJ did what years of preparation for the Hague Conference for the Progressive Codification of International Law in 1930 had failed to do – impose some restraints on the sovereign prerogative to decide just who was a national and whom would be entitled to those protections. This change certainly has not prevented the claiming of nationals abroad. But it has reduced the legitimacy of doing so from the standpoint of the postwar international legal institutions. The decision certainly did not solve the nationality problem. And some contemporary scholars have even taken issue with the long-standing interpretation of the "genuine link" principle, arguing that the *Nottebohm* majority "atomized nationality by function and scrutinized one of these functions: authorizing a person's state of nationality judicially to espouse a diplomatic claim in international fora."[38]

The Decline of Nationality in the International System

Assessing the Hague Codification Conference's work on nationality, Richard W. Flournoy, one of the early twentieth century's more prolific scholars of international law and nationality, observed in 1930:

> A century ago international law was regarded as having little or nothing to do with nationality, but as movements of populations from country to country and acquisition of new nationalities through naturalization have greatly increased in modern times, problems concerning the nationality of persons, involving conflicting claims between states, have correspondingly increased. This movement of people from country to country, for permanent or temporary residence, has entailed problems. . . . Increase in facilities for travel, especially through the development of the airplane, will, no doubt cause a further increase in movements of people from country to country and still greater multiplication of nationality problems, and these problems must be settled sooner or later by international agreements, tacit or express.[39]

In the nearly ninety years that have passed since Flournoy penned that assessment and prognostication, there has been no tacit or express global agreement to reduce or eliminate dual nationality. In fact, dual nationality has proliferated since the 1970s. While the erosion of coverture globally has, for the most part, eliminated the problems faced by married women with regard to their nationality,[40] little other progress has been made on the subject. In the recent report on diplomatic protection undertaken by the UN's International Law Commission, the rapporteur reiterated the nineteenth-century doctrine, "It is for each State to determine under its own law who are its nationals," and that despite the majority's opinion in *Nottebohm*, "A State's determination that an individual possesses its nationality is not lightly to be questioned."[41]

In the postwar world, the international legal system shifted away from nationality and protection by states – embracing instead an individualist paradigm. As Benes said, "The protection of minorities in the future should consist primarily in the defense of human democratic rights." And so, alongside the Charter of the United Nations was born the Universal Declaration of Human Rights.[42] René Cassin, one of the drafters of the Universal Declaration, like Benes, was dubious and, at times, scornful of the minorities regime – specifically because of Nazi Germany's effective use of the regime to legitimize international aggression.[43] The Universal Declaration as a set of legal norms and principles, thus, should be read in the context of the rejection of group-based rights systems – particularly those dependent upon nationality as a legal status.[44]

And the associated legal regimes followed suit. The system of refugee support as it emerged in the 1920s had defined its subjects by their nationality *qua* political allegiance (in the case of the Russians) or their nationality *qua* ethnic, cultural, or linguistic background (in the case of the Assyrians and Armenians).[45] Refugees had presented the League with difficult political problems since to define a group of people, to name them, and to convey a special status – even in something as basic as a travel document – had the potential to provoke extensive controversy. What would it mean – as the reader might recall – for the League to identify Russian refugees as Ukrainians when there was no longer a Ukrainian state? What would it mean politically for the League to identify Ruthenians as Ruthenians when a Ruthenian state was a political fantasy? But, when it came time to draft a new convention to deal with the displaced persons of World War II, the drafters instead adopted an individual approach.[46] The 1951 Convention Relating to the Status of Refugees defined a "refugee" as a person who, "owing to well-founded fear of being persecuted for reasons of race, religion, nationality, membership of a particular social group or political opinion, is outside the country of his nationality and is unable or, owing to such fear, is unwilling to avail himself of the protection of that country."[47] The analysis applied was "any person," that is to any individual.[48] Applicants for protection under the convention had to (and must) individually demonstrate their own "well-founded fear of being persecuted."[49] Each *individual* person was (and is) evaluated and scrutinized.[50] And the requirement was that they be without the formal protection of a state – that is that they be stateless in either law or fact.[51]

The gradual emergence of international "human," or more accurately in this case, "individual" rights, rather than "national" rights as the foundational principle of the international legal order presented challenges for the right of diplomatic protection and the law surrounding the responsibility of states. As human rights agreements and treaties protecting the rights of traders and investments proliferated, the necessity of having a state – and thus a valid nationality – to intervene became less necessary. Following the war, the International Law Commission, like its predecessor in the interwar period, identified the laws regarding state responsibility for injury to foreigners as one of the fourteen topics most ripe for discussion by the newly established body.[52] Between 1956 and 1961, the first special rapporteur of the International Law Commission on the subject of state responsibility, Francisco V. Garcia-Amador of Cuba, delivered a series of reports on the subject. In them, he argued that the traditional system of state responsibility and diplomatic protection was incompatible with the postwar emphasis on human rights:

> Aliens, and so stateless persons, are on a par with nationals in that all enjoy these rights not by virtue of their particular status but purely and simply as human beings. In the recent international recognition of the right of the individual, nationality does not enter into consideration. This means that the alien has been internationally recognized as a legal person independently of his State: he is a true subject of international rights.[53]

In Garcia-Amador's view, diplomatic protection and espousal were no longer necessary. The radical legal theories of Nicolas Politis, Georges Scelle, André Mandelstam, and other interwar legal theorists had come into their own in the postwar world. Individuals, whether they be real, flesh-and-blood human persons, or the soulless wraiths conjured under the law as juridical persons, were to be protected not because of their status as a member of a particular state – not because of their nationality – but rather because they were human (or human adjacent). And the International Court of Justice (ICJ), the body in which states can (and have) bring disputes over the protection of the person and property of foreign nationals, has been an unfriendly forum for diplomatic protection and espousal. This chapter began with *Nottebohm* case and the ICJ's dismissal of Liechtenstein's claim for compensation for his injuries.

Since then, there have been few cases before the ICJ involving diplomatic protection, most of which found against the intervening state. In contrast to the arbitral tribunals of the nineteenth and early twentieth century, whose work made "the international law governing the responsibility of states for injuries to aliens . . . one of the most highly developed branches of [international] law,"[54] the ICJ has made "little contribution to the law of expropriation."[55]

Under the individualized rights model that has been at the center of "modern" international law, people would, ideally, be subjects of international law. They would be able to stand for themselves as individuals and not as members of a state, nation, or minority. But the institutional development on the ground has been thin. Some regional courts, like the European Court of Human Rights and the Inter-American Court of Human Rights, permit individuals to hale states before the court for violations of fundamental rights. Some domestic courts have opened themselves up to individual claimants from around the world, permitting, for example in the American case, an alien to bring a complaint before a federal district court for a tort "committed in violation of the law of nations."[56] But such access has been rare and fleeting.[57] There is no world court for the aggrieved victim of arbitrary detainment, political violence, or religious persecution – that is, for the loss of life or liberty.

The New York Convention

There has been one exception to the relative lack of global institutional success in the international rights realm – property. The protection of property has been the unsurprising and unqualified success story of international rights in the twentieth century and has generated pervasive and powerful institutions designed for the protection of those rights.

As with the League, the United Nations carefully maneuvered in international politics through the mobilization of experts provided by nongovernmental organizations. And just as with the League, the International Chamber of Commerce (ICC) was front and center in the postwar order. Representatives from the ICC were present at Bretton Woods, the first session of the Preparatory Committee for an international trade organization in 1946 (where the representative sat immediately to the left of the representative of the International Monetary Fund), and continued to participate in every subsequent round of negotiations involving the General Agreement on Tariffs and Trade (GATT). The ICC was also one of the first organizations that the new UN Economic and Social Council granted General or "Level A" Consultative Status.[58] And over the second half of the twentieth century, the organization has loomed large in efforts to defend property rights globally and to provide for expeditious dispute resolution.

In 1950, twenty-three years and a second global war after the Geneva Convention on the Enforcement of Arbitral Awards of 1927 entered into force, the ICC's Commission on International Arbitration was tasked with evaluating the convention's effectiveness. The main defect, according to the ICC, was that the 1927 treaty only recognized awards that were in strict compliance with the national laws of the location where the award was made. In other words, there was no mechanism for the enforcement of truly international awards divorced of a national context. "There could be no progress," noted the ICC, "without the full recognition of the concept of international awards." It was further noted, "an advance is possible only to the extent that international arbitral awards are made more independent of the law of the country in which the arbitration takes place."[59] National laws still mattered and hence the resolution of commercial disputes was still firmly anchored to the national politics of a location. It was hard, as the Commission put it, "to imagine the sense of frontier and sovereignty disappearing" under the current treaty regime. The Commission made it explicit that the will of the parties needed to be the paramount concern of contract law globally if enforcement was to be the same everywhere.[60]

Following the advice of the commission, the ICC approached the UN Economic and Social Council to advocate for a new treaty that would fix the problems of the Geneva Protocol and Convention. Among the alterations proposed in the ICC's preliminary draft (which formed the core of the final treaty)[61] were changes in the wording of the diversity-of-citizenship clause that had so vexed jurists in the 1920s and 1930s. The clause, which had required that the contract be between "persons subject to the jurisdiction of different states," remained, but with the added alternate criterion: "or involving legal relationships arising on the territories of different states."[62] The commission charged with drafting the new treaty agreed that the diversity-of-citizenship clause had been a problem but it still was not quite sure how to solve it. Negotiations over the wording of the first article of the draft treaty, which defined its scope and limit, were the most controversial.[63] Negotiations proceeded slowly, but in 1958 the UN Convention on the Recognition and Enforcement of Foreign Arbitral Awards, more popularly known as the "New York Convention," was opened for signature. The final version of the treaty omitted language relating to the jurisdictional status of the parties involved in the dispute, which the UN commission thought was "vague and ambiguous" and would lead to "different interpretations in different countries."[64]

Instead, the final text required the recognition and enforcement of arbitral agreements and awards that were "not considered as domestic awards."[65] The change incorporated a stricter principle of territorial location than had the original ICC proposal. Or, to put it another way, the change created room for a strictly territorial approach to determining whether the dispute was truly international and provided a way out of the *nationality*-v.-*domicile* and the *jus sanguinus*-v.-*jus soli* debates that had raged for a century among international jurists and had complicated nearly every question surrounding individuals and their relationships to private and public international law.[66]

The New York Convention also overcame the barriers to enforcement that had hindered the 1927 Geneva Convention. Under the Geneva Convention, awards were only enforceable if they conformed to the law of the territory upon which the award was issued. The ICC instead shaped the New York Convention such that awards would be "international," that is awards would be valid so long as they conformed to the will of the parties regardless of whether they conformed strictly with the law of the place where the arbitration physically happened to take place. For example, if two parties decided to arbitrate their dispute in France under the rules of the ICC's Court of Arbitration, the procedure did not have to conform with France's procedural requirements, so long as the procedure conformed with the "will" of the parties.[67]

Moreover, the New York Convention provided, "Each Contracting State shall recognize arbitral awards as binding and enforce them in accordance with the rules of procedure of the territory where the award is relied upon."[68] That is, a successful plaintiff could take her award to any state party to the treaty and demand its courts enforce the award against any assets the defendant might have in that jurisdiction. The New York Convention, in short, truly internationalized arbitration, taking disputes out of Courts and requiring enforcement by all members. The right to contract had become internationalized.

The Washington Convention

The short twentieth century had been an age of expropriation. Even a cursory survey from 1917 to 1960 reveals just how expansive the government seizure of private property was. Russia, Bolivia, Mexico, Turkey, Estonia, Latvia, Lithuania, Bulgaria, France, the Netherlands, Czechoslovakia, Hungary, Poland, Austria, Britain, Romania, Burma, New Zealand, China, Iran, Guatemala, India, Yugoslavia, Egypt, Indonesia, Iraq, Cuba, and Brazil all had seized private property en masse during that forty-three-year period.[69] Likewise, the nineteenth and twentieth centuries had been ages of foreign ownership.[70] Investors and businesses, which the reader might recall had decried the waning interest in intervention for the protection of assets, also decried the increasing toleration of mass expropriations. The formalist sovereignty of the twentieth century gave rise to new legal principles by which domestic courts were reluctant to judge the sovereign acts of foreign governments.[71]

States had become reluctant to intervene diplomatically and many states had grown weary and wary of intervention on behalf of nationals abroad. Yet capital still wanted property protections. After World War II, business organizations[72] and academics[73] began advocating for expanded investor protections.[74] The Charter of the International Trade Organization (ITO), which was to be one of the pillars of the postwar economic order, had contained provisions for the protection of foreign investment.[75] Despite the failure of the ITO, advocacy for a sweeping multilateral treaty for investment protection continued apace. In 1958, for example, Herman Josef Abs, the director of Deutsche Bank and the personal advisor to Germany's Economic Minister, delivered a speech before the International Industrial Development Conference in San Francisco[76] entitled "The Safety of Capital," in which he advocated for "the creation of an International Convention, backed by an international Court of Arbitration, which would establish an effective and enforceable rule of law for private foreign investment, protecting investors and recipient nations alike."[77] *Time* referred to the proposal as "The Capitalist Magna Carta."[78] With the President of Deutsche Bank behind such an idea, it wasn't long before major international institutions began to take note.[79]

The International Bank on Reconstruction and Development, better known as the World Bank, had been established following the end of World War II to finance Europe's reconstruction efforts. But, by the mid-1950s, the World Bank had begun to pivot away from Europe and toward the recently decolonized Global South. The Bank was faced with the tricky question of how, precisely, to encourage foreign investment in an age of expropriations.[80] In 1961, the General Counsel of the World Bank, Aron Broches, wrote the Bank's General Directors about the problem. Investors, he argued, were usually left at the mercy of local courts in the event of an investment dispute. Diplomatic protection had become difficult and was far from guaranteed:

> The necessity of espousal of his case by his national Government before an international claim can be lodged, introduces a political element. An investor may well find that his national Government refuses to espouse a meritorious case because it fears that to do so would be regarded as an unfriendly act by the host

Government. And this consideration is even more likely to cause the national Government to refrain from acting if the merits of the investor's case are not wholly clear in its view, thus withholding from the investor an opportunity to have his case judged by an impartial tribunal.[81]

Not much had changed since 1912 when similar complaints were lodged at the International Congress of Chambers of Commerce.[82] The problem, in Broches' view, was that investors were generally unable to bring claims against foreign governments directly.[83] The solution to the problem, he argued, was to create an international tribunal in which individuals would have direct access and that was empowered to issue binding decisions.[84] Later that year, the president of the World Bank, Eugene R. Black, broached the subject in his annual address to the Bank's Board of Governors and recommended that a new institution be established and that the bank should "undertake an active study of the possibilities... [that] would facilitate the settlement of investment disputes by means of arbitration or conciliation procedures."[85]

The ICC's Court of Arbitration featured prominently in the debate. Many delegates were familiar with the organization's Court and many states had already made agreements with foreign investors that contained clauses that empowered the ICC to resolve any disputes that might have arisen.[86] The experience with the Court undoubtedly made establishing a similar (albeit more powerful) institution more palatable. And the ICC's Court was, in many ways, used as a model.[87] When thinking about the rules of arbitration that would be employed, for example, Broches noted, "there was no lack of sources to which reference could be made when formulating the rules, e.g. the rules of the International Chamber of Commerce."[88] The Spanish representative, likewise, cited the rules developed "by the International Chamber of Commerce, which dealt with disputes between individuals."[89] Even the representative of Nepal looked to the ICC's rules for reference and inspiration.[90] Likewise, when the problem of obtaining neutral legal expertise arose, the German representative wondered whether the proposed arbitral center "might be given the right to draw upon the unrivaled experience and large staff of available arbitrators of the International Chamber of Commerce."[91]

The result of the numerous hearings, conferences, and surveys of UN member nations was the 1965 Convention on the Settlement of Disputes Between States and Nationals of Other States, known as the Washington Convention. The Convention established the International Centre for the Settlement of Investment Disputes (ICSID) at the World Bank headquarters in Washington "to provide facilities for conciliation and arbitration of investment disputes between Contracting States and nationals of other Contracting States."[92]

Like the New York Convention, the Washington Convention provided for binding enforcement of any decision issued under its provisions. Article 58 provided, "Each Contracting State shall recognize an award rendered pursuant to this Convention as binding and enforce the pecuniary obligations imposed by that award within its territories as if it were a final judgment of a court in that State." Like under the New York Convention, enforcement did (and does) not depend on the good will of the defendant state. A plaintiff could take a valid award to any contracting state have a court enforce the judgment against a defendant states' assets.

While nationality as a legal category was not altogether absent from the Washington Convention (as its title indicates it only applies to disputes "Between States and Nationals of Other States"), all that mattered was that one wasn't a national of the state against which one brought a complaint. A relationship with a state was not a necessity. Indeed, even a stateless investor could bring a claim.

International Rights and Property

The New York and Washington Conventions have been astonishing successes and enabled the explosion of international commercial arbitration that has taken place since the 1970s. By 2010, more than 150 states had signed the pair of Conventions. Moreover, the explosion in the number of bilateral investment treaties (BITs), many of which created dispute resolution mechanisms for individuals against foreign states, topped 2,000 by the end of the century.[93] Regional trade and investment treaties, like the North American Free Trade Agreement (NAFTA), which proliferated in the last decades of the twentieth century, likewise included enforceable investment dispute mechanisms open to individual claims. The International Chamber of Commerce remains the preeminent institution for the resolution of disputes between individuals as well as between individuals and states and their public enterprises. And its use began to dramatically increase in from the 1970s onward – from the time when the most recent age of globalization commenced.[94] Between 1976 and 1986 the Court of Arbitration heard more cases than in its previous fifty years of existence.[95] And since 1986, the caseload has increased at an extraordinary rate.

Because of the interpenetration of capital and investment, decisions rendered by private arbitral institutions are easily enforced through the seizure of assets almost everywhere in the world. In 1922, Van Hamel wrote to Frank Nixon as the League began to take on the question of Arbitration clauses. He noted, "from a legal point of view, the recognition of foreign judicial decisions implies to a certain extent the abandonment of a part of national sovereignty which most countries, for the present, are not prepared to undertake. The execution in one country of judgments and arbitral decisions made in another country can only be established, if ever, by particular conventions between particular countries." Van Hamel was only partially right. States have now abandoned part of their sovereignty in their recognition of decisions rendered by private arbitral tribunals. However, compared to the progress made toward the enforcement of judgments issued by foreign *courts*, the success of the New York Convention is astonishing. As of 2013, 149 parties had signed the New York Convention, while only *five* had signed the Hague Convention on the Recognition of Foreign Judgments. States are still more willing to enforce the decisions rendered by foreign private courts than foreign public ones.[96]

In 2007, the ICJ heard preliminary objections in a case regarding whether Guinea was entitled to compensation for the arbitrary arrest and detainment of one of its nationals in the Democratic Republic of the Congo.[97] In its judgment on the preliminary objections, the Court noted that modern international law had less need for diplomatic protection, writing:

> The Court is bound to note that, in contemporary international law, the protection of the rights of companies and the rights of their shareholders, and the settlement of the associated disputes, are essentially governed by bilateral or multilateral agreements for the protection of foreign investments, such as the treaties for the promotion and protection of foreign investments, and the Washington Convention of 18 March 1965 on the Settlement of Investment Disputes between States and Nationals of Other States, which created an International Centre for Settlement of Investment Disputes (ICSID), and also by contracts between States and foreign investors. In that context, the role of diplomatic protection somewhat faded, as in practice recourse is only made to it in rare cases where treaty régimes do not exist or have proved inoperative.[98]

And state practice has provided support for the Court's observation. States have intervened far less often in the fifty years after World War II than they had in the fifty years before World War I.[99]

Property Rights in an Age of Human Rights

Nineteenth-century international commercial arbitration functioned well. It was able to function in part because the networks of traders who established their own courts of arbitration were at once both global and yet familiar. In many ways, global trade in the nineteenth century was less anonymous than national trade. Blacklisting members could work when most of the global exchange happened in commodities that flowed through specific global hubs and everyone knew everyone else and when, as the critic of arbitration in the 1890s made clear, trade was conducted "by private associations, strong enough to coerce their brother traders."[100] But as international trade became more varied, more expansive, less industry-specific, and altogether increasingly anonymous, the enforcement of decisions rendered via commercial arbitration became increasingly problematic. While there remain some examples today of this narrow globalism that allows for nonstate pressures to compel compliance,[101] the world by the early twentieth century was becoming too anonymous for that to form the core means of regulating global trade and disputes. The ICC's establishment of its court of commercial arbitration, in contrast to all of the others used over the nineteenth century to regulate their own trade, was representative of the commercial community's response to the greater variation and anonymity in trade.

George L. Ridgeway, when discussing the genesis of international commercial arbitration under the auspices of the ICC, firmly declared that the practice of arbitration had grown up "without government aid" and that the role of the state was limited merely to the recognition of arbitration as a practice. The business community wanted nothing more because international commercial arbitration had "never been primarily dependent upon legal sanctions."[102] The increasing anonymity of global trade challenged that pattern. While commercial arbitration worked hard to "oust the courts" from the disputes of merchants and to push aside the accumulated wisdom and interests of jurisprudence and public policy, by the end of the 1920s they had begun to work hard to insert the executive functions of government into their disputes – to command the compulsive power of the state without engaging with its judicial and legislative functions and oversight. Jan Paulsson, one of the leading practitioners and scholars of arbitration, observed, "Arbitration paradoxically seeks the cooperation of the very public authorities from which it wants to free itself."[103] The state, particularly the compulsive power of the state, contrary to so much of the literature on globalization, is an integral part of the global marketplace today. And the state is far from retreating.[104] What global capital interests have instead done is ousted legislative and judicial contemplation. In 1885, the arbitral tribunal in the Venezuelan Claims Commission Case, *Albino Abiatti* v. *The Republic of Venezuela* firmly stated that the "plaintiff State is not a claims agent."[105] At the time it was true. But the institutional developments of the last century have insured that the executive branches of the various states that have become a party to the New York and Washington Conventions have indeed become the claims agents of international commercial interests.[106]

Recently judicial scholars have begun to ask if "a World Court has finally been created by modern arbitration?"[107] While there is disagreement, many have begun to answer the question in the affirmative.[108]

The Permanent Court of International Justice and its successor the International Court of Justice have remained *mostly* closed to the pleas of individuals and nonstate entities. In the realm of human rights courts, the European Court of Human Rights has made inroads, but its participants are still only European states and it is certainly in no sense global. There is no global institution open to the complaints of individuals against sovereign states which arrest them arbitrarily, which torture them, which deprive them of the basic rights declared to be universal by the Universal Declaration of Human Rights. As John Dugard, the International Law Commission's special rapporteur on diplomatic protection and author of the draft articles on diplomatic protection, observed:

> The sad truth is that only a handful of individuals, in the limited number of states that accept the right of individual petition to the monitoring bodies of these conventions, have obtained or will obtain satisfactory remedies from these conventions. The position of the alien abroad is no better. Universal and regional human rights conventions do extend protection to all individuals – national and alien alike – within the territory of states parties. But there is no multilateral convention that seeks to provide the alien with remedies for the protection of her rights outside the field of foreign investment.[109]

"Outside the field of foreign investment," indeed. As Dugard obliquely noted, there are today global institutions open to the complaints of individuals against sovereign states which appropriate their property and their investments or which fail to meet their contractual obligations. Decisions rendered in these investment tribunals are often executable in 158 countries around the world.

Nor are such remedies restricted to the realm of investment tribunals. The European Court of Human Rights is often regarded as the most successful international human rights court.[110] It is open to individuals to bring complaints against governments from Lisbon to Moscow and from Stockholm to Ankara. Every year it hears nearly a thousand cases and protects those who have had their speech constrained, their religious freedoms curtailed, and their bodily autonomy threatened. In his fantastic study on the origins of the European Convention on Human Rights, Marco Duranti argues that the European Convention was an inherently conservative project.[111] Certainly the convention was novel insofar as it permitted individuals to bring complaints before an international tribunal that was, over the course of the latter half of the twentieth century, empowered to make binding decisions. But the supporters of the Convention also saw it as a bulwark against the postwar march of social and economic rights.[112] Rather than mirroring the Universal Declaration, the European Convention left out social and economic rights and instead, in its very first protocol, enshrined the protection of property. The European Court of Human Rights could, and to a degree did, challenge the policies of nationalization and expropriation that had been at the center of French, British, and German progressive social politics in the immediate postwar period.[113] In July of 2014, the European Court of Human Rights issued its largest and most sweeping award for a mass human rights violation: 1.9 billion euros.[114] Who were the victims? They were the shareholders of the Russian Oil Company Yukos.[115]

In 1912, R. S. Fraser declared that "commerce is the subject of no State and it is the sovereign of all."[116] Forty years later, Wilhelm Röpke lamented the decline of the liberal order which had separated the economic from the political. "The sovereign called the 'market,' since it belongs to the unpolitical sphere of private actions, [had] no political boundaries," Röpke wrote. The boundaries of "the new sovereign," in contrast were "identical with the power of the national government itself."[117] Sovereignty, for Röpke, had shifted from commerce to the state and, because of that shift, boundaries had proliferated and the international order had fractured. But he needn't have fretted. The state's triumph was short-lived and exceptional.[118] By the 1970s, the end of Bretton Woods, the ratification of the New York and Washington Conventions, and the spread of bilateral investment treaties had liberated international commerce from the state while simultaneously putting the executive organs of the state at the command of the private commercial courts of the world. Both the League of Nations and the United Nations attempted to enshrine within their respective international orders the principle of sovereignty, to make their members immune from the interpenetration of disruptive legal orders and foreign influence which had characterized nineteenth-century legal imperialisms. Yet the ICC and other commercial interests were ready and willing to use the organs of these international organizations to advance the cause of subjecting the sovereign state to the proclaimed sovereign will of commerce.

Whereas capital interests had relied upon their relationship through their nationality to sovereigns who could serve as champions in the nineteenth century (even if those sovereigns could, at times, be reluctant champions), in the twentieth those same interests relied instead upon an international law that gave to individuals outlets in which they could directly bring their claims.

***

This chapter began with the *Nottebohm* case and the principle of the "genuine link." The Majority there was concerned with what was an obvious attempt to instrumentalize Liechtenstein's naturalization laws to escape the wartime security regimes of sovereign states (although, put another way, he was trying to escape being placed in a concentration camp and having his property extrajudicially seized). But the dicta requiring a "genuine link" has not been so easy to apply in practice. Just what is a "genuine link?" The ICJ has never made it clear and it seems increasingly impossible to justify. Indeed, there are many absurdities inherent in the ICJ's opinion. If Mr. Nottebohm was not a Liechtensteiner for the purposes of protection but also not a Guatemalan or a German, then what was he? Was he effectively stateless? What state could have intervened on his behalf if not Liechtenstein? The *Nottebohm* principle has been influential, but contested, and the International Law Commission's work on diplomatic protection has noted, "A State's determination that an individual possesses its nationality is not lightly to be questioned,"[119] and has explicitly declined to extend the principle expressed in the *Nottebohm* decision beyond the facts of that case.[120] The determination of nationality is still very much left to the determination of states themselves.

It would be wrong to say that nationality is less central in the modern international legal regime. The Washington Convention, for example, puts nationality front and center in its official name – Convention on the Settlement of Investment Disputes between States *and Nationals of Other States*. And figuring out just how to deal with nationality was one of the difficulties encountered in drafting the convention.[121] The spectre of *Nottebohm* – the suspicion of nationalities of convenience and dual nationals – marked much of the negotiations as delegates worried about how people might take advantage of their national identity to gain access to this new international dispute resolution system.[122] As the architect of the agreement put it, "It is quite possible that the nationality requirement may prove to be troublesome in some cases – principally because of the many uncertainties surrounding the concept of 'nationality'"[123] The problem was compounded in the case of juridical persons. Those wraiths almost always had multiple nationalities since the method for determining the nationality of a corporation had always been difficult – was it the place of incorporation, the primary place of business, the place of effective control, the place of the shareholders (collectively, or by majority)?[124] Likewise, the Refugee Convention took note of nationality. That convention, in its definition of "refugee," required that the person be "outside the country of his nationality."[125] The bonds between abstract states and flesh-and-blood human beings continued to be a central part of international law and international life.

Yet, while nationality is still an important part of international life, it's hardly the point of international consternation that it had been. Whereas traditionally regimes required an affirmative determination of a nationality in order to gain international protection, now one merely has to be a "national of another state." In the first half of the twentieth century, the rhetorical and political assault on dual nationals was fierce.[126] Dual nationals were equated with bigamists.[127] Many states in Europe and the Americas, likewise, automatically denaturalized those who naturalized elsewhere, married, or resided abroad for extended periods of time.[128] In 1930, the Hague Conference declared, "It [was] in the general interest of the international community to secure that all its members should recognize that every person should have a nationality and should have one nationality only."[129]

Despite all the rumblings, we are farther away today from realizing the early twentieth century ideal of a mutually exclusive principle of nationality than ever before.[130] After World War II, dual nationality became increasingly acceptable. France, the United States, and the United Kingdom all began to permit their nationals to naturalize elsewhere without immediately losing their nationality.[131] In recent years, the trend has only continued, as states in Asia, Latin America, Africa, and Eastern Europe have embraced dual citizenship.[132] The improvement of the status of women and the end of coverture has led to the proliferation of plural nationality as a married woman no longer loses her nationality and often gains a second.[133] Children, as a result, now often inherit the nationality of both parents – creating the potential for geometric growth in the number of nationalities a person might have from one generation to another.[134] One study from the turn of the twenty-first century estimated that more than 500,000 children were born in the United States alone every year with potentially more than one nationality.[135]And, in 1997, the Council of Europe drafted the European Convention on Nationality, which explicitly accepts and even promotes plural nationality.[136] Taken altogether, the trend has been toward permissiveness.

What this chapter has argued is that the shift toward an individually focused regime of protection – for persons and their property – has led to a decline in the use of diplomatic protection and intervention. As the International Law Commission, the International Court of Justice, and others have argued, human rights treaties, investment treaties, and other international agreements increasingly permit individuals to stand before international tribunals. Whereas sovereign default brought the threat of gunboats in the nineteenth century and whereas discrimination against ethnic conationals brought the threat of invasion in the early twentieth century, both brought the threat of litigation before an international tribunal in the late twentieth century. States no longer have to be involved in the disputes of their nationals abroad. While the monetary damages that come with an ICSID decision can be substantial, the absence of state interest renders questions about nationality less vital. That's not to say there haven't been armed interventions to protect nationals abroad since 1945. But there have been far fewer than in the past.[137]

This book has been about migration, nationality, and the changing subjects of international law. The interwar period was filled with alternatives to state sovereignty. Might there be sovereign nations, sovereign labor, sovereign persons, sovereign commerce? What community might provide protection in a mobile world? In the postwar liberal order, the person became (in theory) an increasingly central component of the international system. But it has been an uneven victory. International protections for the rights of life and liberty have been halting and humble. But in the realm of property, individuals have truly come into their own as subjects of international law. Now, the individual has not displaced the state, which still has the vital duty of enforcing international arbitral awards. But the individual cosmopolitan or capitalist rarely needs the state to serve as a champion with a "strong arm" when abroad – she can instead stand herself before an international investment court and demand compensation for expropriation or breach of contract.

Conclusion

People still move, states still don't. In the eighteenth and nineteenth centuries, the states of the Atlantic world dealt with that fact through the legal formalization of protection abroad. But that system proved difficult at a time when incipient nationalism demanded that spaces of identity conform to spaces of politics. It was simply too dangerous for states to be active claimants on the literal and metaphorical bodies of their real and fictive nationals abroad. Beginning in the 1920s and accelerating in the decades after 1945, an individualist paradigm emerged in force. Individuals, it was thought, should be able to stand before international tribunals and have their rights protected by the international order and, importantly, nationality should no longer be determinative of the kinds of protection persons, real or fictive, receive. Refugees should not be determined based upon their nationality, but rather their individual well-founded fear of persecution. Investors should not receive greater protection because they were British or French or American with the political power such nationality could mobilize.

But this individual paradigm has emerged unevenly. Multiple institutions handle individual claims at the international level. Some institutions handle criminal charges, others handle investment disputes against sovereigns, still others handle human rights claims against states. The subject matter of the courts is split and scattered. Complaints against states concerning violations of life, liberty, and property are heard in different courts by different judiciaries operating under different charters with different jurisdictions.

E. P. Thompson began his celebrated book, *Whigs and Hunters*, with the observation that the British state in the eighteenth century "existed to preserve the property and, incidentally, the lives and liberties, of the propertied."[1] For Thompson, the first two parts of Locke's trinity were merely incidental to the preservation of the third. The father, the son, and the holy spirit were not equal in stature or import. And I find, after having written this book, that international law – in many ways – has come to share that emphasis. Among the fundamental rights protected by international institutions, it is the right to property that has been the most successfully secured in the twentieth century. What are we to make of the incredible success of property rights in the international realm, especially when placed alongside the humble (some might say minor) successes of other international rights regimes?

The propertied, it seems, are often the powerful. They're often able to mold institutions to suit their ends. In negotiations, even with foreign states, the propertied often have the upper hand. For Thompson, the law concealed shams and inequities and supported the hegemony of the gentry. Nevertheless, much to the consternation of his fellow Marxists, Thompson declared, "The rule of law itself... seems to me to be an unqualified human good."[2] And his reasons were that, despite all of the work that the law did at maintaining the hegemony,[3] the law imposed *some* restraints upon the powerful.[4] The law protected property, but in doing so sometimes protected life and liberty as well. Professions of law's sanctity, however hollow, "gave rise to a vision, in the minds of some men, of an ideal aspiration towards universal values of law."[5] It might also be argued that tying life and liberty to property ensured that the propertied class had incentives to support the legal system and its incidental protections of life and liberty.

But what, we might ask, would have happened if courts had overspecialized in the early modern period? What would the justice systems of Europe and the United States look like if the institutions championing property rights had become independent of those protecting life and liberty? What would domestic law have looked like if the courts that dealt with property claims, and the bodies legislating property law, had been distinct from those dealing with laws and rights concerned with the protection of life and liberty? One can only speculate, but I think it would look a lot like the international legal order today.

The European Court of Human Rights, as the reader might remember from the last chapter, has been far and away the most successful human rights court in the world. There are many different reasons for the success. For one thing, it lies at the heart of a continent moving toward ever-greater political integration (until recently, at least). While not an institution of the European Union, compliance with the court's decisions by western European states is certainly enhanced by a political project of international unity among many of the court's more powerful members. But, importantly, the European Court of Human Rights and the European Convention on Human Rights have served as a means of securing property.[6] The powerful have an incentive to "buy in" to the court.

But if the limited subject-matter jurisdiction of many human rights institutions has, perhaps, weakened them, the same cannot be said for international investment protections – which have been astonishingly effective in the past half century and their prevalence has been increasing at a dramatic pace. Owing to the secrecy of the system (a benefit from the perspective of investors and business management), there is no way to know precisely how this private arbitral system is used. However, between 1987 and 2015, there were nearly 700 known Investor-State Dispute Settlement (ISDS) cases. Seventy of those, nearly 10 percent of the total, were from 2015 alone.[7] Nor do those numbers include all of the hundreds of decisions made under regional trade agreements that provide for their own ISDS institutions.

But the success has not gone without criticism. Near the end of the 2000s, ISDS faced a backlash following a number of high-profile awards made to companies in the tens of millions of dollars. The companies were all from the Global North, while the countries were almost entirely from the Global South.[8] As a result, Bolivia, Ecuador, and Venezuela announced their intention to withdraw from the Convention on the Settlement of Investment Disputes Between States and Nationals of other States (Washington Convention). Despite these withdrawals, however, the web of arbitral treaties runs deep, and the three countries are still subject to the numerous Bilateral Investment Treaties (BITs) they've signed with various capital exporting countries around the world. And, anyway, ISDS would hardly be in trouble simply because Bolivia, Ecuador, and Venezuela began to object.

Pushback, however, has started coming from more than just a few states in the Global South. Activists, scholars, judges, and average citizens in the Global North, on both sides of the Atlantic, have begun to protest what they interpret as the erosion of state sovereignty and the burdensome restrictions placed upon democracy by strict property protections that limit the capacity of states to regulate for the public good. Advocates of ISDS and its supporting legal structures wanted to discourage the expropriation of private property, which, in the mid-twentieth century, meant the physical seizure of private property. But in the past four decades, ideas about just what constitutes expropriation have expanded considerably.

In the 1970s, Richard Epstein, a legal scholar at the University of Chicago, began to argue that laws that indirectly deprived someone of the full use of their property constituted an "indirect regulatory taking," known outside of the American context as an "indirect expropriation" or a "regulatory expropriation."[9] Epstein's theory rode to prominence in the era of Milton Friedman, the Chicago school of economics, and the Law and Economics revolution in the American legal academy.

In 1999, the State of California (where much of this book was written and where its author finds his home) banned the gasoline additive MTBE. Methanex, a Canadian corporation, sued the state of California for nearly a billion dollars under the North American Free Trade Agreement (NAFTA) dispute resolution mechanism, arguing that the ban of MTBE was, in effect, an expropriation of its MTBE production facilities in California and was thus a violation of NAFTA.[10] The arbitral panel found in favor of the State of California.[11] But the specter of billion-dollar suits in response to regulatory expropriation increasingly haunts the Global North.

José E. Alvarez observed, "Under the NAFTA investment chapter, corporate and natural investors have gained direct access to binding denationalized adjudication of any governmental measure that interferes with their ample rights." He went on to note that NAFTA's investor protections drew upon the language contained in many of the most prominent human rights documents, including "rights against discrimination, to security, to recognition of a legal person, to nationality, to freedom of movement, and to own property and not be arbitrarily deprived of it." NAFTA, he argued, was "the most bizarre human rights treaty ever conceived."[12] Indeed, despite the claim that the ISDS regime has been another way in which the capital exporting Global North has taken advantage of the poor, capital importing Global South, the regime has become almost universalized, with developing countries signing such agreements between themselves.[13]

In 2014, the Supreme Court of the United States heard arguments in *BG Group* v. *Republic of Argentina*, a case in which a group of investors were furious at Argentinian emergency law.[14] That law, enacted in 2002 during a major economic crisis, had dramatically impacted the return on an investment made by BG Group in the early 1990s.[15] BG Group filed a complaint with Argentina under the terms of a bilateral investment treaty between the United Kingdom and Argentina and submitted the case to an arbitral tribunal, which convened in Washington, D.C.[16] The arbitral tribunal found that Argentina had denied BG Group "fair and equitable treatment" and awarded BG Group 185 million USD in damages. BG Group subsequently took the award to a US court to have its award executed against Argentina's assets under the New York Convention.[17] Argentina attempted to set aside the award on the grounds that the arbitration violated the treaty between the United Kingdom and Argentina.[18] The question before the court was a narrow one – whether US courts or private arbitrators bore the responsibility for interpreting the scope of a treaty agreement.[19] The court held that the arbitrators were charged with determining the scope of the treaty and thus the arbitral award was likely valid.[20]

While the majority provided a victory for proponents of arbitration and investment, John Roberts, the Chief Justice of the US Supreme Court, launched an assault on ISDS. In his dissent, Roberts argued that the majority opinion "trivialize[d] the significance to a sovereign nation of subjecting itself to arbitration anywhere in the world, solely at the option of private parties."[21] Roberts described the stakes in strong terms: "Substantively, by acquiescing to arbitration, a state permits private adjudicators to review its public policies and effectively annul the authoritative acts of its legislature, executive, and judiciary."[22]

The Roberts argument is just one example of what has become a cacophonous revolt against ISDS in the past decade. Lawyers and academics have penned scathing critiques,[23] and journalists have unearthed disturbing abuses of the system.[24] And citizens are beginning to protest. In the spring of 2016, *Der Spiegel* reported, "An unprecedented protest movement of a scope not seen since the Iraq war in Germany has pushed negotiations over the T-TIP trans-Atlantic free trade agreement to the brink of collapse."[25] Many of the protestors carried signs singling out ISDS as one of the more noxious provisions. Cecilia Malmström, the European Union's trade commissioner, opined that ISDS seemed to have become "the most toxic acronym in Europe."[26]

And legislators and policy makers have taken note. In response to popular protest over the inclusion of ISDS provisions in the proposed Transatlantic Trade and Investment Partnership, the European Union produced a series of plans to create public investment courts that would be more transparent than the currently opaque system. The inclusion of ISDS provisions in the Trans-Pacific Partnership likewise drew resistance in the United States and was one of the many provisions that doomed that country's participation in the trade agreement.[27]

Jan Paulsson, in defending the modern arbitral regime, argued that "most human beings living on this planet today do not have the remotest chance of obtaining decent justice from their courts." Linking "the informal pronouncements by trusted elders in poor Anatolian villages . . . " to the "elaborate arbitral awards rendered in the context of vast business dealings," Paulsson argues, "those who would seek to prohibit such alternatives in order to preserve the primacy of public courts should first consider whether the public systems to which they command their fellows to cast their fate are dysfunctional."[28] Fair enough. But Paulsson would do well to pay attention to the power differential between those living in "poor Anatolian villages" and those engaged in "vast business dealings" and the different legal force of an "elaborate arbitral award" and the "pronouncements [of] trusted elders." The pronouncements of trusted Anatolian elders are, after all, not enforceable with only limited review in 158 countries around the world. And, moreover, the trusted elder probably lives amongst those she is advising.

ISDS emerged alongside the modern human rights regime and, indeed, adopted its institutional practices and language. It is based upon a universalist system of law and principles that, like the nineteenth century's standards of civilization, limit a state's sovereignty and the range of democratic expression. In the past twenty years, political theorists have written at length about the decreasing sovereignty of states in the face of "growing transnational flows of capital, people, ideas, goods, violence, and political and religious fealty," along with "neoliberal rationality" and the "steady growth of international economic and governance institutions such as the International Monetary Fund and the World Trade Organization."[29] Wendy Brown, for example, argues that the spate of wall building in the 2000s was a symptom of waning sovereignty. Building barriers against transnational rather than international threats seems to her a mere theatrical display designed to assuage fears and anxieties over the uncertainties of the modern global world.[30] Moria Paz, in a *slightly* more optimistic mode, similarly argues that the construction of fences and walls bespeaks the success of the "human rights tradition." States are building barriers, she claims, because physically preventing migrants from reaching a state's territory is often the only way to prevent them from gaining the benefit of human rights protections.[31] Perhaps they're right. But the walls have come alongside the somewhat-successful attack on ISDS and other politically effective criticisms of international trade, human rights, supranational institutions, international law, and international migration.

The postwar "embrace" of plural nationality has also been subject to increasing criticism. Some have approached the issue from the standpoint of traditional conservative anxieties about dual nationals.[32] But others have argued persuasively that plural nationality increases inequality. First, these critics point to the increasing incidence of "investor citizenship" – the practice of selling nationality to those willing (and able) to make a substantial investment in the state.[33] In effect, the practice enables the already wealthy to acquire access to lucrative employment markets.[34] Second, by undermining the affective bonds between nationals, nominal nationality enables nominal citizenship and erodes feelings of solidarity that originally bore the burden of economic redistribution,[35] especially as elite professional classes begin to inhabit multiple national spaces for tax or wealth management purposes.[36]

Meanwhile, states have taken a renewed interest in their populations abroad. Since the 1980s, more and more states have established offices and ministries dedicated to promoting closer ties between states and their (increasingly wealthy) nationals abroad with efforts that include providing parliamentary representation and investment advice.[37]

Modern international law, among other innovations, was founded on recognizing that individuals, and not just states, participate and shape the international legal order.[38] Many individual international rights institutions of the twentieth century emerged out of the political impossibility of states intervening to protect increasingly mobile nationals and their even more mobile property. International rights emerged to depoliticize what seemed politically irresolvable in an increasingly global world – the correlation of allegiance and protection. But there is, it seems, a vocal and effective resistance to the institutions of this regime afoot. ISDS was, perhaps, the most successful and pervasive international individual rights institution of the twentieth century. It was supported by many of the most powerful nonstate interests in the world. Yet, even it has found itself under threat with the world's politicians, jurists, administrators, and people, looking for new ways to navigate the relationship between people who move and states that don't.

Notes

Introduction

1 See, e.g., research on endurance running and evolutionary biology. Dennis M. Bramble and Daniel E. Lieberman, "Endurance Running and the Evolution of Homo," *Nature* 432 (November 2004): 345–352.

2 Poland, for example, when it reappeared in 1919 had not moved from Eastern Europe to the Upper Midwest of North America, as had much of Poland's population. Warsaw is in the same place today that it was in 1795 when Poland was partitioned out of existence by Russia, Prussia, and Austria.

3 For a summary of some different conceptions of human systems of rule, see John Gerard Ruggie, "Territoriality and Beyond: Problematizing Modernity in International Relations," *International Organization* 47, no. 1 (1993): 149; Robert D. Sack, *Human Territoriality: Its Theory and History* (New Haven, CT: Yale University Press, 1986).

4 See, e.g., W. R. Jones, "The Court of the Verge: The Jurisdiction of the Steward and the Marshal of the Household in Later Medieval England," *Journal of British Studies* 10, no. 1 (1970): 1–29; Jason R. Rozumalski, "Lords of All They Survey: The Social and Economic Origins of the English State" (Dissertation, University of California, Berkeley, 2017), chap. 4.

5 This common definition was most clearly articulated in the Montevideo Convention on the Rights and Duties of States, art. 1, December 26, 1933, 165 LNTS 19. The definition was likely inspired, in part, by Robert Phillimore, one of the leading anglophone jurists of the nineteenth century, who earlier had defined a state as "a people permanently occupying a fixed territory (*certam sedem*), bound together by common laws, habits, and customs into one body politic, exercising, through the medium of an organized Government, independent sovereignty and control over all persons and things within its boundaries, capable of making war and peace, and of entering into all international relations with the other communities of the globe." Robert Phillimore, *Commentaries Upon International Law*, 2nd ed. (London: Butterworth, 1871), 81 (§ LXIII).

6 During my research, I could not find anyone, since the nineteenth century, who has seriously argued that a state can exist without people (or at least a single person). But scholars, governing officials, and others have argued that entities that have no territory could potentially be considered states. See, e.g., Robert Lansing, "Notes on Sovereignty in a State," *American*

Journal of International Law 1, no. 1 (January 1907): 108; Philip Marshall Brown, "The Theory of the Independence and Equality of States," *American Journal of International Law* 9 (1915): 317; Hans Kelsen, *Das Problem der Souveränität und die Theorie des Völkerrechts* (Tübingen: J. C. B. Mohr (P. Siebeck), 1920), 70–76; Donato Donati, *Stato e territorio* (Rome: Athenaeum, 1924), 27–30; John W. Salmond, *Jurisprudence*, 6th ed. (London: Sweet & Maxwell, 1920), 99 (§ 38): "But we cannot say that [territory] is essential to the existence of a state. A state without a fixed territory – a nomadic tribe for example – is perfectly possible."

7 This last criterion, the capacity to enter into relations with other states in order to be considered a state, is still a sore subject for political scientists and international relations scholars. For a brief summary of the difference between the "declaratory" and "constitutive" theories of statehood, see James R. Crawford, *The Creation of States in International Law* (Oxford: Oxford University Press, 2007), 17–26.

8 Survey for English, French, and Spanish from Google One Million. Survey for German from "Ausland," bereitgestellt durch das Digitale Wörterbuch der deutschen Sprache, https://books.google.com/ngrams and www.dwds.de/d/zitieren.

9 Particularly for the millions of slaves brought to the Americas in the course of the seventeenth, eighteenth, and nineteenth centuries.

10 For a study of the efforts to protect private international creditors prior to the nineteenth century, see H. Neufeld, *The International Protection of Private Creditors from the Treaties of Westphalia to the Congress of Vienna* (Leiden: A. W. Sijthoff, 1971).

11 See, e.g., Thomas Hobbes, *Leviathan* (Oxford: Clarendon Press, 1909), 85 ("The finall Cause, End, or Designe of men, (who naturally love Liberty, and Dominion over others,) in the introduction of that restraint upon themselves, (in which wee see them live in Common-wealths,) is the foresight of their own preservation . . . ."); John Locke, *Two Treatises of Civil Government*, ed. Thomas Hollis (London: A. Millar et al., 1764), § 222 ("The reason why men enter into society, is the preservation of their property; and the end why they chuse and authorize a legislative, is, that there may be laws made, and rules set, as guards and fences to the properties of all the members of the society, to limit the power, and moderate the dominion, of every part and member of the society . . . ."); Heinrich von Treitschke, *Politics*, trans. Blanche Dugdale and Torben de Bille (New York: Macmillan, 1916), 1: 65 ("Without war no State could be. All those we know arose through war, and the protection of their members by armed force remains their primary and essential task."). Despite his emphasis on war and protection, Treitshke was less convinced that the state existed *solely* for the protection of life and property. Treitschke, *Politics*, 1: 73.

12 Clifford Geertz, *Meaning and Order in Moroccan Society* (Cambridge: Cambridge University Press, 1979), 137.

13 Emer de Vattel, *The Law of Nations, Or, Principles of the Law of Nature, Applied to the Conduct and Affairs of Nations and Sovereigns*, eds. Béla Kapossy and Richard Whitmore (Indianapolis, IN: Liberty Fund, 2008), 298 (bk. ii, § 71).

14 We the people formed a more perfect union. The King of France became the King of the French. The Mexican nation threw off its oppressor. The representatives of the United Provinces of South America by the authority of the people they represented declared their independence.
15 Ernest Renan, *Qu'est-ce qu'une nation?*, 2nd ed. (Paris: Calmann-Lévy, 1882); Ernest Gellner, *Nations and Nationalism*, 2nd ed. (Ithaca, NY: Cornell University Press, 2009); Benedict Anderson, *Imagined Communities: Reflections on the Origin and Spread of Nationalism*, revised ed. (New York: Verso, 2006).
16 See, e.g., Eugen Weber, *Peasants into Frenchmen: The Modernization of Rural France, 1870–1914* (Stanford, CA: Stanford University Press, 1976); Gellner, *Nations and Nationalism*; Anderson, *Imagined Communities*.
17 Charles Maier periodizes the age of territoriality as roughly 1850 to 1970. Charles S. Maier, "Consigning the Twentieth Century to History: Alternative Narratives for the Modern Era," *American Historical Review* 105, no. 3 (June 2000): 808, 823. Jordan Branch pushes it back slightly: "In early-nineteenth-century Europe, rule came to be defined exclusively in terms of territories with boundaries between homogenous spatial authority claims." Jordan Branch, "Mapping the Sovereign State: Technology, Authority, and Systemic Change," *International Organization* 65 (2011): 6. There are, of course, naysaying early modernists who push the centrality of territorial conceptions of the state back into the early modern. See, e.g., Ruggie, "Territoriality and Beyond;" Stuart Elden, *The Birth of Territory* (Chicago: University of Chicago Press, 2013), and, especially, Rozumalski, "Lords of All They Survey."
18 Maier, "Consigning the Twentieth Century to History," 818.
19 Edwin M. Borchard, "Basic Elements of Diplomatic Protection of Citizens Abroad," *American Journal of International Law* 7, no. 3 (1913): 497.
20 And so, perhaps, the King of the French was in many ways more the King of France than his predecessors had been.
21 Carl Schmitt, "The Plight of European Jurisprudence," trans. G. L. Ulmen, *Telos* 83 (1990): 35–70; William E. Scheuerman, *Liberal Democracy and the Social Acceleration of Time* (Baltimore, MD: Johns Hopkins University Press, 2004).
22 We might even see Maier's "identity space" and "decision space" as different ways of saying "national unit" and "political unit," as in Gellner. Compare Maier, "Consigning the Twentieth Century to History," 818, with Gellner, *Nations and Nationalism*, 1.
23 Anderson, *Imagined Communities*.
24 Owing to the idiosyncrasies of the law, *person* in this context can mean either a *real* person or a *juridical* person, the former being a human being made of flesh and blood and the latter being a fictional legal construct, like a corporation.
25 For great recent work on this subject with a legal rather than a historical focus (albeit with excellent histories), see Kate Parlett, *The Individual in the International Legal System* (Cambridge: Cambridge University Press, 2011); Anne Peters, *Beyond Human Rights: The Legal Status of the Individual*

in International Law, trans. Jonathan Huston, Cambridge Studies in International and Comparative Law (Cambridge: Cambridge University Press, 2016), chap. 2.

26 See, e.g., Paul Gordon Lauren, *The Evolution of International Human Rights: Visions Seen* (Philadelphia: University of Pennsylvania Press, 1998); Lynn Hunt, *Inventing Human Rights* (New York: W. W. Norton, 2008); Stefan-Ludwig Hoffmann, ed., *Human Rights in the Twentieth Century* (Cambridge: Cambridge University Press, 2010); Samuel Moyn, *The Last Utopia* (Cambridge, MA: Belknap, 2010); Pamela Slotte and Miia Halme-Tuomisaari, eds., *Revisiting the Origins of Human Rights* (Cambridge: Cambridge University Press, 2015).

27 See, e.g., M. N. Barnett, "Bringing in the New World Order: Liberalism, Legitimacy, and the United Nations," *World Politics* 49 (1997): 526–551; Didier Fassin, *Humanitarian Reason: A Moral History of the Present* (Berkeley, CA: University of Chicago Press, 2011), 2009.

28 But see the fantastic recent work by Marco Duranti. Marco Duranti, *The Conservative Human Rights Revolution: European Identity, Transnational Politics, and the Origins of the European Convention* (Oxford: Oxford University Press, 2017). Senator Bourke B. Hickenlooper made a similar observation in 1967 when he complained, "In our great concern with . . . rights we have far too often ignored one of the most basic of the bundle of rights – the right to hold property." Bourke B. Hickenlooper, "The International Rights of Property – Some Observations," *International Lawyer* 2, no. 1 (October 1967): 51.

29 See, e.g., UDHR, art. 17.

30 Ibid., art. 4.

31 Ibid., art. 5.

32 Ibid., art. 7.

33 Ibid., art. 3.

34 UDHR, art. 17(2).

35 Fedor Fedorovich Martens, *Traité de droit international*, trans. Alfred Léo (Paris: Librairie Marescq Ainé, 1883), 428, 440–441.

36 Reproduced in André N. Mandelstam, "La protection internationale des droits de l'homme," *Recueil des cours de l'Académie de Droit International de la Haye* 38 (1931): 205. On Mandelstam and the Declaration's influence on the UDHR, see Helmut Philipp Aust, "From Diplomat to Academic Activist: André Mandelstam and the History of Human Rights," *European Journal of International Law* 25, no. 4 (November 2014): 1105–1121; Jan Herman Burgers, "The Road to San Francisco: The Revival of the Human Rights Idea in the Twentieth Century," *Human Rights Quarterly* 14, no. 4 (November 1992): 447–477.

37 On the history of capitalism, see Eric Hilt, "Economic History, Historical Analysis, and the 'New History of Capitalism'," *Journal of Economic History* 77, no. 2 (June 2017): 511–536.

38 But see Duranti, *Conservative Human Rights Revolution*.

39 Samuel Moyn, "Giuseppe Mazzini in (and beyond) the History of Human Rights," in *Revisiting the Origins of Human Rights*, eds. Pamela Slotte and

Miia Halme-Tuomisaari (Cambridge: Cambridge University Press, 2015), 53.

40 Jenny S. Martinez, *The Slave Trade and the Origins of International Human Rights Law* (Oxford: Oxford University Press, 2012); Kathryn Sikkink, *The Justice Crusade: How Human Rights Prosecutions Are Changing World Politics* (New York: W. W. Norton, 2011).

41 Moyn, "Giuseppe Mazzini in (and beyond) the History of Human Rights," 68.

42 Ibid.

43 Moyn, *Last Utopia*; Hoffmann, *Human Rights in the Twentieth Century*.

44 Stefan-Ludwig Hoffmann, "Human Rights and History," *Past and Present* (August 2016); Samuel Moyn, "The End of Human Rights History," *Past and Present* 233, no. 1 (November 2016): 307–322.

45 See, e.g., Talbot Imlay, "International Socialism and Decolonization during the 1950s: Competing Rights and the Postcolonial Order," *American Historical Review* 118, no. 4 (October 2013): 1105–1132: "European and Asian socialists framed their exchanges in terms of competing rights: national rights, minority rights, and human rights." See also Rachel Sturman, "Indian Indentured Labor and the History of International Rights Regimes," *American Historical Review* 119, no. 5 (December 2014): 1439–1465.

46 In doing so, it contributes to a growing body of literature that explore the ways in which business interests and business organizations are involved in the formal development of intergovernmental law and policy. See, e.g., Steve Charnovitz, "Nongovernmental Organizations and International Law," *American Journal of International Law* 100, no. 2 (April 2006): 348–372; Peter J. Spiro, "Accounting for NGOs," *Chicago Journal of International Law* 3, no. 1 (2002): 161–169; David Gartner, "Beyond the Monopoly of States," *University of Pennsylvania Journal of International Law* 32, no. 2 (2010): 595–641; Edith Brown Weiss, "The Rise or the Fall of International Law," *Fordham Law Review* 69, no. 2 (2000): 345–372; Markus Wagner, "Regulatory Space in International Trade Law and International Investment Law," *University of Pennsylvania Journal of International Law* 36, no. 1 (2014): 1–87; Tim Büthe and Walter Mattli, *The New Global Rulers: The Privatization of Regulation in the World Economy* (Princeton, NJ: Princeton University Press, 2011).

47 I take Manu Goswami's criticism of Charles Maier's periodization of the age of territoriality seriously (in some ways, this project is also an extended criticism of that periodization). Manu Goswami et al., "AHR Conversation: History after the End of History: Reconceptualizing the Twentieth Century," *American Historical Review* 121, no. 5 (December 2016): 1572. Until 1960, the majority of the world's population lived under the rule of empires and not states. And, as will be made clear in the first chapter, that was one of the ways in which European state policy attempted to elide legal difference.

Part I

1 Emer de Vattel, *The Law of Nations, Or, Principles of the Law of Nature, Applied to the Conduct and Affairs of Nations and Sovereigns*, eds. Béla Kapossy and Richard Whitmore (Indianapolis, IN: Liberty Fund, 2008), 67, italics in original.

2 David Kennedy, for example, observed, "For today's international lawyer, the nineteenth century seems long ago and far away, in many ways more distant from current problems and reflections than the great publicists of the seventeenth and eighteenth centuries – Hugo Grotius, Franciscus Suarez, Emmerich de Vattel and the rest." David Kennedy, "International Law and the Nineteenth Century: History of an Illusion," *Quarterly Law Review* 17 (1997): 100.

3 See Anthony Carty, "19th Century Textbooks and International Law" (Dissertation, Jesus College, University of Cambridge, 1972); A. W. B. Simpson, "The Rise and Fall of the Legal Treatise: Legal Principles and the Forms of Legal Literature," *University of Chicago Law Review* 48, no. 3 (1981): 632–679.

4 For another take on the shift away from scripture and morality in international legal writing in the 1850s, see Casper Sylvest, "The Foundations of Victorian International Law," in *Victorian Visions of Global Order: Empire and International Relations in Nineteenth-Century Political Thought*, ed. Duncan Bell, *Ideas in Context* (Cambridge: Cambridge University Press, 2007), 51.

5 See Mark W. Huddleston and William W. Boyer, *The Higher Civil Service in the United States: Quest for Reform* (Pittsburgh, PA: University of Pittsburgh Press, 1996); Ari Hoogenboom, *Outlawing the Spoils: A History of the Civil Service Reform Movement, 1865–1883* (Champaign: University of Illinois Press, 1961).

6 The U.K. Foreign Office began consulting regularly with the Law Officers of the Crown in 1835, and in 1876 the office appointed its first permanent legal under-secretary. UKNA: FO 834; The U.S. Department of State formally created a position for a chief legal advisor in 1891. Richard B. Bilder, "The Office of the Legal Advisor," in *International Law in the Twentieth Century*, ed. Leo Gross (New York: Appleton, 1969), 786.

7 Aimee M. Genell, "The Well-Defended Domains: Eurocentric International Law and the Making of the Ottoman Office of Legal Counsel," *Journal of the Ottoman and Turkish Studies Association* 3, no. 2 (November 2016): 255–275.

8 See Paul Laity, *The British Peace Movement, 1870–1914* (Oxford: Clarendon Press, 2001); Alexander Tyrrell, "Making the Millennium: The Mid-Nineteenth Century Peace Movement," *The Historical Journal* 21, no. 1 (1978): 75–95; A. C. F. Beales, *The History of Peace: A Short Account of the Organised Movements for International Peace* (New York: MacVeagh, 1931).

9 For a statistical breakdown of nineteenth-century arbitrations, see Henri La Fontaine, *Pasicrisie internationale* (Berne: Stämpfli, 1902).

10 On the Alabama Claims, see Adrian Cook, *The Alabama Claims* (Ithaca, NY: Cornell University Press, 1975); Tom Bingham, "The Alabama Claims

Arbitration," *International and Comparative Law Quarterly* 54, no. 1 (January 2005): 1–25.

11 To put it into perspective that sum would equate to roughly 4 billion 2015 GBP if measured against national income, or the equivalent of about 150 billion 1995 GBP if measured in comparison to the size of the annual budget. Bingham, "The Alabama Claims Arbitration," 1–25. Using an alternative measure, that sum would equate to 33 billion USD in terms of economic power in 2015. See Samuel H. Williamson, "Seven Ways to Compute the Relative Value of a U.S. Dollar Amount, 1774 to present," MeasuringWorth, 2016, www.measuringworth.com/calculators/uscompare/, accessed on October 31, 2016.

12 James Brown Scott, ed., *The Proceedings of the Hague Peace Conferences: The Conference of 1907* (Oxford: Oxford University Press, 1921), 1: 812–819; Martha Finnemore, *The Purpose of Intervention: Changing Beliefs about the Use of Force* (Ithaca, NY: Cornell University Press, 2003), 44.

13 For some expansive coverage of the formation of these institutions, see Irwin Abrams, "The Emergence of the International Law Societies," *The Review of Politics* 19, no. 3 (July 1957): 361–380. For a great introduction to the Institute of International Law specifically, see Martti Koskenniemi, *The Gentle Civilizer of Nations: The Rise and Fall of International Law 1870–1960*, Hersch Lauterpacht Memorial lectures (Cambridge: Cambridge University Press, 2001).

14 See, e.g., The Arrest and Expulsion of Ben Tillet and Arbitration, UKNA: FO 10/771, FO 10/772; Convention between Belgium and Great Britain Referring to Arbitration the Case of Mr. Ben Tillett, March 19, 1898, 186 CTS 193, XC BSP 5.

15 ILA 1/1; See also Abrams, "The Emergence of the International Law Societies," 377–378.

Chapter 1

1 Stephen Mitchell, trans., *Gilgamesh: A New English Version* (New York: Atria Books, 2004), 70–71.

2 For a description of Athens at the time, see Bayard Taylor, *Travels in Greece and Russia* (New York: G.P. Putnam, 1859).

3 For the facts as laid out in a subsequent international case, see Alfred Lapradelle and Nicolas Politis, *Recueil des arbitrages internationaux* (Paris: A. Pedone, 1905), 581. Lord Stanley also discusses the traditional "burning of the Jew" in a speech before the House of Lords. House of Lords, Debates, June 17, 1850, Hansard Third Series, vol. 111, cols. 1293–1404. This is a tradition that continued until at least 2006. U.S. Department of State, Bureau of Democracy, Human Rights, and Labor, *International Religious Freedom Report 2006*.

4 M. Pacifico to Edmund Lyons, April 7, 1847, UKNA: FO 881/413.

5 A brief note on terminology: Emer de Vattel used the words "subject" and "citizen" somewhat (although not totally) interchangeably to denote individuals bound to a sovereign. For the purposes of his international legal

theory, there was none of the domestic content that we today associate with the word "citizen." To avoid confusion henceforth, I will use the word "subject" or "national" to denote individuals bound through some relationship to a sovereign. "National" is also a word with baggage, a topic which will be discussed in the next chapter. Briefly, however, despite its myriad connotations within English and the Romance languages, within the language of international law "nationality" merely denotes the relationship between an individual "national" and a state or sovereign. It is usually free from ethnic, historic, or linguistic content. For a discussion of the continual linguistic confusion this causes, see Maximilian Koessler, "'Subject,' 'Citizen,' 'National,' and 'Permanent Allegiance'," *The Yale Law Journal* 56, no. 1 (November 1946): 58–76; B. Akzin, "La sociologie de la nationalité," in *La Nationalité dans la science sociale et dans le droit contemporain* (Paris: Recueil Sirey, 1933), 3–23.

6 M. Pacifico to Edmund Lyons, April 7, 1847. UKNA: FO 881/413.

7 M. Glarakis to Edmund Lyons, December 17, 1847. UKNA: FO 881/413.

8 For a detailed account of the French perspective of the Pacifico affair, see Lynn M. Case, *Edouard Thouvenel et la diplomatie du Second Empire* (Paris: Pedone, 1976), 34–51.

9 I should note here that Pacifico's claims were not the only complaints the British government had against the Greek government. Tensions had been building for years over disputes related to the Ionian islands. For a survey of British grievances in the years leading up to the Pacifico Affair, see Edouard Driault and Michel Lhéritier, *Histoire diplomatique de la Grèce de 1821 à nos jours* (Paris: Les Presses Universitaires de France, 1925), 327–340; Lauren Benton and Lisa Ford, *Rage for Order: The British Empire and the Origins of International Law, 1800–1850* (Cambridge, MA: Harvard University Press, 2016), 112–116. Indeed, in Palmerston's famous speech (discussed below), he brought the treatment of the Ionians in support of his actions: ". . . there have always been in every town in Greece a great number of persons whom we are bound to protect—Maltese, Ionians, and a certain number of British subjects. It became the practice of this Greek police to make no distinction between the Maltese and Ionians, and their own fellow-subjects." House of Commons, Debates, June 25, 1850, Hansard Third Series, vol. 112.

10 For an example of the concern for Pacifico's nationality, see House of Commons, Debates, February 4, 1850, Hansard Third Series, vol. 108, col. 285.

11 Lord Stanley, speaking in the House of Lords, enumerated many of the items Pacifico had claimed were destroyed: "Why, the house of this M. Pacifico, this petty usurer, who, as I have said, was trading on a borrowed capital of 30l., is represented to have been furnished as luxuriously as it might have been if he had been another Aladdin with full command of the Genii of the ring and of the lamp. Now listen to the amount of a single couch in his drawing room: –1 large couch in solid mahogany, British work, with double bottom, one of which is Indian cane for summer, 70l.; 1 bottom for the winter for the above, a cushion in tapestry embroidered in real gold (Royal work), 25l.; 2 pillows and cushion also, for the back of the whole length of the couch, in silk and wool covering, embroidered in real gold, as the

bottom of the above couch, 75l. Total for one couch 170l. Now, I doubt if many of your Lordships have in your houses (I am sure I have not in mine) furniture of this gorgeous description." House of Lords, Debates, June 17, 1850, Hansard Third Series, vol. 111, col. 1316. Alexander Cockburn took note of the rampant anti-Semitic rhetoric used to indict Pacifico's claim: "According to these authorities, M. Pacifico is a species of Jew broker–a Jew usurer–a Jew trafficker–a hybrid Jew. And then, Sir, forsooth, we are told in the same breath as that in which such phrases are employed, that they are not used to prejudice the individual to whom they are applied. For what purpose, then, I ask, are they used?" House of Commons, Debates, June 28, 1850, Hansard Third Series, vol. 112, col. 619.

12 House of Commons, Debates, June 27, 1850, Hansard Third Series, vol. 112, col. 569. Also available in Arthur Tilney Bassett, ed., *Gladstone's Speeches* (London: Methuen, 1916), 134.

13 This critique was at the center of the entire Pacifico affair specifically and of Lord Palmerston's foreign policy generally. As one Member of Parliament put it: "The noble Lord pressed upon the consideration of the House the obligation and duty imposed on the Government to afford protection to British subjects in every nation of the world; and, as it appeared to him, they would constitute the British Government not merely a court of appeal, but a sort of court of premiere instance, totally setting aside the laws and tribunals of all foreign States. No doctrine could be more dangerous, or could more infallibly lead to collision with great States, or to aggressive movements on small ones." House of Commons, Debates, June 27, 1850, Hansard Third Series, vol. 112, col. 480.

14 Cockburn would eventually become Chief Justice of the Queens Bench and author a special study on British nationality reform, making his opinions in this case particularly interesting. Alexander Cockburn, *Nationality: Or the Law Relating to Subjects and Aliens Considered with a view to Future Legislation* (London: William Ridgway, 1869).

15 House of Commons, Debates, June 24, 1850, Hansard Third Series, vol. 112, cols. 249–250.

16 Qtd. in John Morley, *The Life of William Ewart Gladstone* (New York: Macmillan, 1904), 1:369.

17 House of Commons, Debates, June 25, 1850, Hansard Third Series, vol. 112, col. 444. Palmerston (and, indeed a faction of the British governing class) had a long history of saber rattling for the benefit of wronged individuals. Nine years earlier, in 1841, the State of New York indicted Alexander McLeod, a British militiaman, for the murder of an American during a minor border kerfuffle (known as the Caroline Affair). Britain was outraged that a soldier would be arrested for murder while acting in his official capacity. Palmerston, who was foreign secretary, instructed the British minister to Washington to prepare for war. John Fabian Witt, *Lincoln's Code* (New York: Free Press, 2012), 114–115. In a letter to his brother, Palmerston confided, "If [New York] were to hang McLeod we could not stand it, and war would be the inevitable result." Henry Lytton Bulwer, *The Life of Henry John Temple, Viscount Palmerston*, ed. Evelyn Ashley (London: Richard Bentley, 1874), 3:46. Luckily, a jury acquitted McLeod. Witt, *Lincoln's Code*, 116.

18 Convention Between Greece and Great Britain Relating to Don Pacifico's Claims, July 18, 1850. UKNA: FO 94/429.

19 Addington to Pacifico, August 1, 1851, Correspondence Respecting the Mixed Commission Appointed to Investigate the Claims of M. Pacifico Upon the Government of Greece... (London: Harrison and Son, 1851). For overviews of the Don Pacifico Affair, see Muriel E. Chamberlain, *Pax Britannica?: British Foreign Policy 1789–1914* (London: Routledge, 2014), 98–100; David Hannell, "Lord Palmerston and the 'Don Pacifico Affair' of 1850: The Ionian Connection," *European History Quarterly* 19, no. 4 (October 1989): 495–508; Geoffrey Hicks, "Don Pacifico, Democracy, and Danger: The Protectionist Party Critique of British Foreign Policy, 1850–1852," *International History Review* 26, no. 3 (September 2004): 515–540.

20 Eric Hobsbawm, *The Age of Capital* (New York: Vintage, 2006), 210. For references to the late nineteenth century as the "first age of globalization," see, e.g., Frederic S. Mishkin, *The Next Great Globalization* (Princeton, NJ: Princeton University Press, 2006), 2; Harold James and Kevin H. O'Rourke, "Italy and the First Age of Globalization, 1861–1940," in *The Oxford Handbook of the Italian Economy since Unification*, ed. Gianni Toniolo (Oxford: Oxford University Press, 2013), 37–68. On late nineteenth-century globalization compared with other epochs from an economic perspective, see Kevin H. O'Rourke and Jeffrey G. Williamson, *Globalization and History* (Cambridge, MA: MIT Press, 1999); Christopher Chase-Dunn, Yukio Kawana, and Benjamin D. Brewer, "Trade Globalization since 1795: Waves of Integration in the World-System," *American Sociological Review* 65, no. 1 (February 2000): 77–95; Angus Maddison, *Monitoring the World Economy, 1820–1992* (Paris: Development Centre of the Organisation for Economic Co-operation/Development, 1995). On late nineteenth-century globalization in general, see Jürgen Osterhammel, *The Transformation of the World: A Global History of the Nineteenth Century* (Princeton, NJ: Princeton University Press, 2014); Jürgen Osterhammel and Niels P. Petersson, *Globalization: A Short History* (Princeton, NJ: Princeton University Press, 2009). For an excellent overview of the literature on globalization up until 2006, see Michael Lang, "Globalization and Its History," *Journal of Modern History* 78, no. 4 (December 2006): 899–931.

21 See Jules Verne, *Le tour du monde en quatre-vingts jours* (Paris: Pierre-Jules Hetzel, 1873); Nellie Bly, *Around the World in Seventy-Two Days* (New York: Pictorial Weeklies, 1890); see also Joyce E. Chaplin, *Round About the Earth* (New York: Simon/Schuster, 2012), chap. 6.

22 O'Rourke and Williamson, *Globalization and History*, 119–120; Timothy J. Hatton and Jeffrey G. Williamson, *The Age of Mass Migration* (Oxford: Oxford University Press, 1998), fig. 2.1; see also J. D. Gould, "European Inter-Continental Emigration: The Road Home: Return Migration from the U.S.A.," *Journal of European Economic History* 9, no. 1 (1980): 41–113; Walter Nugent, *Crossings: The Great Atlantic Migrations, 1870–1914* (Bloomington: University of Indiana Press, 1992); Mark Wyman, *Round-Trip to America: The Immigrants Return to Europe 1880–1930* (Ithaca, NY: Cornell

University Press, 1993); Donna R. Gabaccia, *Foreign Relations: American Immigration in Global Perspective* (Princeton, NJ: Princeton University Press, 2012), 26.

23 Richard Baldwin and Philippe Martin, "Two Waves of Globalization: Superficial Similarities, Fundamental Differences," NBER Working Paper No. 6904 (1999), 19. In 2015, by way of contrast, migrants only accounted for 3.3 percent of the global population. UN Department of Economic and Social Affairs, International Migration Report 2015, UN Doc. ST/ESA/SER.A/375, p. 21.

24 See, e.g., nearly the *entire* corpora of Henry James and Edith Wharton. But also William Dean Howells, *Indian Summer* (New York: New York Review Books, 2004); or, for a transcontinental version, Edward Morgan Forster, *A Room with a View* (New York: Penguin, 2000). The number of Atlantic crossings could be quite impressive; for example, Wharton crossed the Atlantic more than 60 times in the course of her life. A feat reflected accordingly in her novels. Edith Wharton, *Edith Wharton Abroad: Selected Travel Writings, 1888–1920*, revised ed., ed. Sarah Bird Wright (New York: St. Martin's Griffin, 1996), xvii–xviii.

25 Henry Pratt Judson, "American Politics: A Study of Four Careers," *Review of Reviews and World's Work* 7, no. 37 (February 1893): 160.

26 Peter Gay, *Weimar Culture: The Outsider as Insider* (New York: W. W. Norton, 2001), 6–7. See also, Daniel T. Rodgers, *Atlantic Crossings* (Cambridge, MA: Belknap, 1998), chap. 5. A fine example of this with respect to architects is the career and work of the University of California's architect, John Galen Howard, who brought the Beaux Arts of Paris to the shores of the Pacific. Joan Draper, "The Ecole des Beaux-Arts and the Architectural Profession in the United States: The Case of John Galen Howard," in *The Architect: Chapters in the History of the Profession*, ed. Spiro Kostof (Berkeley: University of California Press, 2000), 209–237.

27 Hobsbawm, *Age of Capital*, 50; O'Rourke and Williamson, *Globalization and History*, 30, 36, 52, and chap. 2.

28 Baldwin and Martin, "Two Waves of Globalization," 1–2.

29 Eric Hobsbawm, *Industry and Empire* (New York: Pantheon Books, 1968), 161; O'Rourke and Williamson, *Globalization and History*, 208–209.

30 Baldwin and Martin, "Two Waves of Globalization" (), 8; Kevin H. O'Rourke, "Globalization and Inequality: Historical Trends," NBER Working Paper No. 8339 (2001), 9–11.

31 On the use of these other methods of forming trust over distance in the early modern Atlantic world, see Lynden Macassey, "International Commercial Arbitration: Its Origin, Development and Importance," *Transactions of the Grotius Society* 24 (January 1938): 179–202; Peter Mathias, "Risk, Credit, and Kinship in Early Modern Enterprise," in *The Early Modern Atlantic Economy*, eds. John H. McCusker and Kenneth Morgan (Cambridge: Cambridge University Press, 2001), 15–35; Douglass C. North, "Institutions," *Journal of Economic Perspectives* 5, no. 1 (January 1991): 97–112; Francesca Trivellato, *The Familiarity of Strangers: The Sephardic Diaspora, Livorno, and Cross-Cultural Trade in the Early Modern Period* (New Haven, CT: Yale University Press, 2009).

32 See Benton and Ford, *Rage for Order*.

33 See Pär Kristoffer Cassel, *Grounds of Judgment: Extraterritoriality and Imperial Power in Nineteenth-Century China and Japan* (Oxford: Oxford University Press, 2012); Turan Kayaoglu, *Legal Imperialism: Sovereignty and Extraterritoriality in Japan, the Ottoman Empire, and China* (Cambridge: Cambridge University Press, 2012); Turan Kayaoglu, "The Extension of Westphalian Sovereignty: State Building and the Abolition of Extraterritoriality," *International Studies Quarterly* 51, no. 3 (September 2007): 649–675.

34 The classic work on informal empire is John Gallagher and Ronald Robinson, "The Imperialism of Free Trade," *Economic History Review* 6, no. 1 (1953): 1–15.

35 According to Carl Schmitt, "The expansion and distention of international law from a specifically European order to the spacelessness of a general universalism was evident in the fact that, toward the end of the 19th century, European authors also ceased to write textbooks on European international law and began customarily to speak only of international law." Carl Schmitt, *The Nomos of the Earth* (New York: Telos Press, 2003), 230.

36 Carlos Calvo, Latin America's premier scholar of international law in the nineteenth century, explicitly disagreed with the idea. Arnulf Becker Lorca, *Mestizo International Law: A Global Intellectual History, 1842–1933*, Cambridge Studies in International and Comparative Law (Cambridge: Cambridge University Press, 2015), 99; Liliana Obregón, "Regionalism Constructed: A Short History of 'Latin American International Law'," in *5th Biennial Conference*, Valencia (Spain), September 13–15, 2012, eds. Nico Krisch and Anne van Aaken and Mario Prost, vol. 2, Conference Paper Series 1 (European Society of International Law, 2012), 2–3. At the turn of the twentieth century the claim became more common. At both the Third and Fourth Latin American Scientific Conferences, claims were made for the existence of an international law that was distinct to the states of Latin America. Alejandro Álvarez, Latin America's premier scholar of international law in the twentieth century, was the idea's foremost advocate – although he included the United States in some of his geographic delimitations. See, e.g., Alejandro Álvarez, "Le droit international américain, son origine et son évolution," *Revue générale de droit international public* 14 (1907): 393; Alejandro Álvarez, *Le droit international américain: son fondement, sa nature: d'après l'histoire diplomatique des états du nouveau monde et leur vie politique et économique* (Paris: A. Pedone, 1910). Álvarez held onto this idea for decades. See, e.g., Alejandro Álvarez, "The New International Law," *Transactions of the Grotius Society* 15 (1929): 39. Yet, the conceptualization never became widely accepted even among Latin American jurists. See generally Sá Vianna, *De la non existence d'un droit international américain* (Rio de Janeiro: L. Figueredo, 1912). Nor did Álvarez himself ever conceive "American international law" as entirely distinct from what he termed "universal international law." Rather, he saw it as a kind of regional variation that included practices peculiar to the States of the Western Hemisphere in relations amongst themselves. Asylum Case (Colombia v. Peru) 1950 ICJ Rep. 266, 290, 293 (November 20) (dissenting opinion by Judge Álvarez). See

also Kennedy, "International Law and the Nineteenth Century: History of an Illusion," 127–128.

37 Vianna, *De la non existence d'un droit international américain*; See also Schmitt, *Nomos of the Earth*, 228–229, 232–235, 287.

38 Lorca, *Mestizo International Law*, 128–140.

39 Philip Lindsley, *The Works of Philip Lindsley* (Philadelphia, PA: J.B. Lippincott, 1866), 1:536. The American Minister at Copenhagen expressed similar sentiments in 1867, noting that for the Roman, "*civis Romanus sum* was his passport and his shield. American citizenship is as noble as Roman and should command no less deference among nations." U.S. Congress, House, *Message of the President of the United States and Accompanying Documents*, 40th Cong., 2d sess., Ex. Doc. 1, 671. A half century later, the American novelist and intellectual, John Dos Passos argued, "'I am an American citizen' should carry with it at least as much respect and impressiveness as '*civis Romanus sum*,' which was a passport under the Commonwealth of Rome of protection, privilege and honor over the world." John R. Dos Passos, "Citizenship in a Federation," *Yale Law Journal* 23, no. 6 (April 1914): 485.

40 Canada, *Senate Debates*, April 26, 1888 (Hon. Mr. Miller), 422. Ten years later, in analyzing why Canada had not yet separated from Britain, a German scholar provided another fine example of the phrase being used, although in its patriotic rather than legal register: "Modern science has brought the colonies together with their mother country, to a point that nobody could have suspected just a few years ago. Aided by the economic development of the colonies, [science] has helped to inspire every subject of *her most graceful Majesty*, in whatever far-off corner of our globe that they find themselves, the same sentiment of pride that the Roman of the ancient word expressed with these three words: *civis Romanus sum.*" Günther Kurt Anton, "Parallèle entre la colonisation moderne et la colonisation soul l'ancien régime démontrée par l'exemple des colonisations Française et Anglaise au Canada (Fin)," *Questions Diplomatiques et Coloniales: Revue de Politique Extérieure* (January 1898): 491.

41 On Francesco Crispi and his politics, see Federico Chabod, *Italian Foreign Policy*, Giovanni Angelli Foundation Series in Italian History (Princeton, NJ: Princeton University Press, 1996), 243–245; Elizabeth Brett White, "The Foreign Policy of Francesco Crispi" (master's thesis, University of Wisconsin, Madison, 1917). For the text of the speech in which he expresses those sentiments, see "A Palermo" given on October 14, 1889 in *Scritti e discorsi politici di Francesco Crispi (1849–1890)* (Rome: Unione cooperative editrice, 1890), 713–744, 737.

42 Kaiser Wilhelm had taken a personal interest in the excavation and reconstruction of the Roman Fort. The speech was given on the occasion of the Fort's grand reopening (of sorts). News coverage of the speech and a transcript can be found in *Journal officiel de la République française* (Paris) October 14, 1900, 6752. The speech was given on October 11 at the Roman Fort in Saalburg, which had been reconstructed under orders from the Kaiser and opened to the public – an example of the age's continued preoccupation with antiquity. See Hartwig Schmidt, *Wiederaufbau* (Stuttgart:

K. Theiss, 1993), 203; See also Suzanne L. Marchand, *Down from Olympus: Archaeology and Philhellenism in Germany, 1750–1970* (Princeton, NJ: Princeton University Press, 1997).

43 Enrique Tocornal to the Cámara de Diputados, 36th Extraordinary Session, December 11, 1875, 670; For a brief comparison of Palmerston with Tocornal, see Thomas M. Bader, "A 'Second Field' for Historians of Latin America: An Application of the Theories of Bolton, Turner, and Webb," *Journal of Inter-American Studies and World Affairs* 12, no. 1 (January 1970): 51.

44 See, e.g., André Siegfried, *La Crise de l'Europe* (Paris: Calmann-Lévy, 1935), 39; André Siegfried, *L'âme des peuples* (Paris: Librairie Hachette, 1950), 19–20; André Siegfried, "Les nationalismes asiatiques et l'Occident," *Revue française de science politique* 1, nos. 1–2 (1951): 11. See also Yannick Muet, *Les géographes et l'Europe: L'idée européenne dans la pensée géopolitique française de 1919 à 1939* (Geneva: Europa, Institut européen de l'Université de Genève, 1996), 32.

45 This excerpt is drawn from the second edition of Joseph Story's groundbreaking and internationally renown *Commentaries on the Conflict of Laws* and was not in the first edition. Compare Joseph Story, *Commentaries on the Conflict of Laws*, 2nd ed. (London: A. Maxwell, 1841), 286n1/291 with Joseph Story, *Commentaries on the Conflict of Laws*, 1st ed. (Hilliard, Graytory, 1834).

46 Bassett, *Gladstone's Speeches*, 122.

47 *A Few Words to Mr. Bull on His Return from the Continent* 46 (1852): 591.

48 Edmund Burke, for example, based his prosecution of Warren Hastings on Cicero's Verrine Orations. Elizabeth D. Samet, "A Prosecutor and a Gentleman: Edmund Burke's Idiom of Impeachment," *English Literary History* 68, no. 2 (June 2001): 397–418.

49 Acts 16:38; For a reference made directly to the exclamation by St. Paul, see Paul Charlton, "Naturalization and Citizenship in the Insular Possessions of the United States," *Annals of the American Academy of Political and Social Science* 30 (July 1907): 106.

50 For reference to Italians in the United States, see J. Tchernoff, *Protection des nationaux résidant à l'étranger, avec introduction sur la souveraineté des états en droit international* (Paris: A. Pedone, 1899), 190; see also Elihu Root, "The Basis of Protection to Citizens Residing Abroad," *Proceedings of the American Society of International Law at Its Annual Meeting (1907–1917)* 4 (April 1910): 16–27. For Americans in Austria and Mexico, see Edwin M. Borchard, *The Diplomatic Protection of Citizens Abroad, Or, The Law of International Claims* (New York: Banks Law Publishing, 1915).

51 Stephen Mitchell, *Gilgamesh: A New English Version* (New York: Free Press, 2004), 68.

52 Schmitt, *Nomos of the Earth*, 67–79; Hannah Arendt, *The Human Condition*, 2nd ed. (Chicago, IL: University of Chicago Press, 1998), 63–64, 63n62, 64n64.

53 The oldest surviving treaty was preserved via this method and is currently in the collection of Fondation Bodmer, Geneva, Switzerland, Inv. 37 (Clou d'argile avec inscription cunéiforme, règne du roi Gudea, sumérien

nouveau, env. 2144–2124 av. J.C.). For a general treatment of clay nails, see J. T. Hooker, *Reading the Past: Ancient Writing from Cuneiform to the Alphabet* (Berkeley: University of California Press, 1990) and I. J. Gelb, "A New Clay-Nail of Hammurabi," *Journal of Near Eastern Studies* 7, no. 4 (October 1948): 267–268.

54 Arendt, *Human Condition*, 63.

55 See the work done on the fiscal-military state, e.g., Geoffrey Parker, *The Military Revolution: Military Innovation and the Rise of the West, 1500–1800* (Cambridge: Cambridge University Press, 1996); John Brewer, *The Sinews of Power: War, Money, and the English State, 1688–1783* (Cambridge, MA: Harvard University Press, 1990). For a classic and telling description of a naval force as a "wooden wall," see Herodotus, *The Histories*, ed. Tom Holland (Penguin, 2015), 496–497, 550.

56 Yair Mintzker, *The Defortification of the German City* (Cambridge: Cambridge University Press, 2012), 53; see also Mack Walker, *German Home Towns: Community, State, and General Estate, 1648–1817* (Ithaca, NY: Cornell University Press, 1971). Just to put a contemporary spin on the relationship between states and walls, at the time of the writing of this book, walls became a central part of the 2016 American presidential campaign with the Republican party making the construction of a wall along the United States–Mexico border part of its party platform. Republican National Convention, 2016 Republican Platform (2016), 26. See also David Smith, "Trump Supporters Say Terrorist Attacks Strengthen Case for Mexico Wall," *The Guardian* (July 18, 2016). A political activist, perhaps, best illustrated the continued sense of connection between states and walls when, in explaining his support for building a wall on the United States–Mexico border, he said, "We believe that to have a country, you have to have a wall." Jamie Ferrell and Samantha Wilson, "Trump Supporters are Building a Wall at Sather Gate," *Tab* (September 12, 2016).

57 Hugo Grotius, *The Rights of War and Peace* (Indianapolis, IN: Liberty Fund, 2005), 1:162 (bk. i, chap. i, ¶ xiv).

58 Thomas Hobbes, *The English Works of Thomas Hobbes of Mamesbury*, ed. William Molesworth, vol. 3 (*Leviathan*) (London: John Bohn, 1839), 158 (pt. II, chap. 17).

59 Vattel, *The Law of Nations, Or, Principles of the Law of Nature, Applied to the Conduct and Affairs of Nations and Sovereigns*, 67.

60 John Bouvier, *A Law Dictionary Adapted to the Constitution and Laws of the United States of America, and of the Several States of the American Union; with References to the Civil and Other Systems of Foreign Law* (Philadelphia, PA: T./J. W. Johnson, 1839), 2:410.

61 The English legal aphorism describing this limitation was that the king's power reached to "where the King's writs could ride." On this idea generally, see Jason R. Rozumalski, "Lords of All They Survey: The Social and Economic Origins of the English State" (Dissertation, University of California, Berkeley, 2017); F. A. Mann, "The Doctrine of Jurisdiction in International Law," *Recueil des cours de l'Académie de Droit International de la Haye* 111 (1964): 25–26; Max Gutzwiller, "Le développement historique du droit international privé," *Recueil des cours de l'Académie de Droit International de la Haye* 29 (1929): 324.

62 On the century from 1850 to 1950 as an age of territoriality, see Charles S. Maier, "Consigning the Twentieth Century to History: Alternative Narratives for the Modern Era." On the definition of territoriality used here and by Maier in the aforementioned article, see Robert D. Sack, "Human Territoriality: A Theory," *Annals of the Association of American Geographers* 73, no. 1 (March 1983): 55–74. On the turn of the twentieth century as a period when "sovereignty described a relation to territory parallel to the contemporaneous understanding of the relationship between individuals and their property," and "International law did not regulate the use of territory, it registered an absolute and exclusive jurisdiction whose boundaries were territorial," see Kennedy, "International Law and the Nineteenth Century" 124.

63 Robert Phillimore, *Commentaries Upon International Law*, 2nd ed. (London: Butterworth, 1871), 81, emphasis added.

64 Max Weber, "Politics as a Vocation," in *From Max Weber: Essays in Sociology*, eds. H. H. Gerth and C. Wright Mills (London: Routledge, 2005), 77–78, emphasis added.

65 On territoriality in the law, see, e.g., Story, *Commentaries on the Conflict of Laws*; Friedrich Carl von Savigny, *System des heutigen römischen Rechts* (Berlin: Veit und comp., 1840–1849), 8: § 348; For an example of the forward march of territoriality with regard to law being applied, see the classic American case *Pennoyer* v. *Neff*, 95 U.S. 714 (1878); See also Joseph H. Beale's interpretation of the basic principle behind the Conflict of Laws/Private International Law, in which he argues, "The jurisdiction of a state is absolute within its territory.... [And] a state can exercise no jurisdiction over persons or things in the territory of another state, or overt acts done there." *Restatement of the Law of Conflict of Laws as Adopted and Promulgated by the American Law Institute*, Washington, DC, *May 11, 1934* (St. Paul, MN: American Law Institute, 1934), 1–2, § 1, ¶¶ 4–5. For secondary scholarship that argues that territory was integral to late nineteenth- and early twentieth-century definitions of sovereignty in international law, see Kennedy, "International Law and the Nineteenth Century":124; Anthony Carty, *The Decay of International Law? A Reappraisal of the Limits of Legal Imagination in International Affairs* (London: Manchester University Press, 1986).

66 Weber, "Politics as a Vocation," 77–78. Weber uses the German *gebiet*, which has been translated here as territory, but could more generally mean area. Charles Maier offers a brief dissection of the original German articulation of this definition in Charles S. Maier, *Once Within Borders: Territories of Power, Wealth, and Belonging since 1500* (Cambridge, MA: Belknap, 2016), 2n4. There is obviously much evidence in opposition to this theory. For example, see Phillimore, *Commentaries Upon International Law*, 1:81 ("a State may be defined to be a people permanently occupying a fixed territory (*certam sedam*), bound together by common laws, habits, and customs into one body politic, exercising through the medium of an organized government, independent sovereignty and control over all things within its boundaries.") and, in general, Maier, "Consigning the Twentieth Century to History," 818. However, in Phillimore's definition the state, "a people

occupying a fixed territory," "people," had primacy of place, with territory being a mere modifier. Moreover, frontiers were understudied to such an extent that it's hard to accept territoriality as being unequivocally central to the idea of the nineteenth-century state. Lord Curzon, for example, made this lack of study explicit in 1907 when he wrote, "Frontiers are the chief anxiety of nearly every Foreign Office in the civilized world, and are the subject of four out of every five political treaties or conventions that are now concluded... [yet there is] no work or treatise in any language which, so far as I know, affects to treat the subject as a whole." George Nathaniel Curzon, *Frontiers*, 2nd ed. (Oxford: Clarendon Press, 1908), 4. Territory and frontiers were undoubtedly becoming increasingly important in how the state was defined, but, again, it was hardly a self-evident characteristic in the late nineteenth and early twentieth century. However, Lord Curzon's declaration could be read as an early example of the obnoxious scholarly shibboleth of decrying the oft-imagined neglect of a topic by one's forebears while proclaiming one's own virtue for both recognizing the neglect and fixing it. Harold Bloom remarked upon a similar practice by poets "misreading one another, so as to clear imaginative space for themselves." Harold Bloom, *The Anxiety of Influence: A Theory of Poetry*, 2nd ed. (Oxford: Oxford University Press, 1997), 10. For examples of this practice, one need only look at nearly every article published in the *American Historical Review* for the past twenty years and at this author's own introduction.

67 Robert Lansing, "Notes on Sovereignty in a State," *American Journal of International Law* 1, no. 1 (January 1907): 108.

68 Mintzker, *Defortification of the German City*, 53; Rachel St. John, *Line in the Sand: A History of the Western United States–Mexico Border*, eds. Sven Beckert and Jeremi Suri (Princeton, NJ: Princeton University Press, 2011), chap. 5.

69 For example, in 1851, the United States and Mexico as well as France and Spain decided to more firmly fix their territorial boundaries and established commissions to survey and demarcate their lines. See St. John, *Line in the Sand*, chap. 1; Peter Sahlins, *Boundaries: The Making of France and Spain in the Pyranees* Peter Sahlins, *Boundaries: The Making of France and Spain in the Pyranees* (Berkeley: University of California Press, 1989), chap. 7.

70 Friedrich Carl von Savigny, *Private International Law: A Tratise on Conflict of Laws, and the Limits of Their Operation in Respect of Place and time*, ed. William Guthrie (London: Stevens/Sons, 1869), 27 (§ 348).

71 *The Appollon*, 22 U.S. 362, 370 (1824); See also Story, *Commentaries on the Conflict of Laws*. Story, in his groundbreaking treatise on the conflict of laws, adopted the strict territorial principle with a carve-out for foreign subjects in the set of "general maxims or axioms which constitute the basis upon which all reasonings on the subject must necessarily rest." Ibid. Joseph Story, despite being an American, was one of the nineteenth century's preeminent legal scholars. Indeed, one scholar has declared, "At the time of their publication, in 1834, Story's *Commentaries* were without question the most remarkable and outstanding work on the conflict of laws [also known as private international law] which had appeared since the thirteenth century in any country and in any language." Ernest Gustav Lorenzen, *Selected Articles on the Conflict of Laws* (New Haven, CT: Yale University Press, 1947),

193–194. Indeed the eminent German jurist Savigny praised Story's work and acknowledged Story's tremendous influence on his own work. Gerhard Kegel, "Story and Savigny," *American Journal of Comparative Law* 37, no. 1 (1989): 39–66. On Story's unequaled influence on the development of European Conflict of Laws/Private International Law jurisprudence, see Joseph Henry Beale, *A Treatise on the Conflict of Laws or Private International Law*, vol. 1 (Cambridge, MA: Harvard University Press, 1916), 51–52 (§ 40). For a more recent assessment on the importance of Savigny and Story in conflicts jurisprudence generally, see James Gordley, *The Jurists: A Critical History* (Oxford: Oxford University Press, 2013), 217–219. Story's language mirrored that of Justice Marshall's declaration, "It is conceded that the legislation of every country is territorial; that beyond its own territory, it can only affect its own subjects or citizens." *Rose* v. *Himley* 8 U.S. 241, 279 (1808).

72 An international regime, as defined by a prominent theorist of international relations, is a set of "principles, norms, rules, and decision-making procedures around which actor expectations converge in a given area." Stephen D. Krasner, "Structural Causes and Regime Consequences: Regimes as Intervening Variables," *International Organization* 36, no. 2 (April 1982): 186.

73 Vattel, *Law of Nations*, 85 (bk. i, chap. ii, § 12).

74 Hospitality usually includes the guarantee of protection by the host. A failure to live up to this responsibility in international law is considered a violation. Anthropologists have noted this principle in an array of nonlegal contexts. Ian Whitaker, for example, observed that in late twentieth-century Albania it was still the rule that "with hospitality went protection, and a man who did not avenge a guest... would be universally despised." Ian Whitaker, "Tribal Structure and National Politics in Albania," in *History and Social Anthropology*, ed. I. M. Lewis (London: Routledge, 2013), 269.

75 This principle is at the foundation of, for example, long-distance trading regimes in North Africa. See, e.g., Geertz, *Meaning and Order in Moroccan Society*, (Cambridge: Cambridge University Press, 1979).

76 Lev. 19:33–34. See also Exod. 22:21; Deut. 10:19.

77 This principle can be found in the work of many political theorists. Samuel Pufendorf noted, "If, for example, some one should come as a stranger to a state which is in the habit of treating outsiders in a friendly manner, the stranger, although he has never expressly pledged his good faith, is, nevertheless, regarded as having pledged his good faith, both tacitly and by the act of coming, to a willingness to accommodate himself to the laws of that state in accordance with his status. And so he in his turn has tacitly stipulated for his own temporary protection on the part of the same state." Samuel von Pufendorf, *Two Books of the Elements of Universal Jurisprudence*, ed. Thomas Behme (Indianapolis, IN: Liberty Fund, 2009), 140. It is also one of the principles at the foundation of legal territoriality within international law (both public and private). See, e.g., Ulrich Huber's principle that "[the laws of each State] bind all persons found within the territory, whether permanently or temporarily." Ulrich Huber, "De conflictu legum diversarum in diversis imperiis," in *Praelectiones Juris Romani et hodierni*

(Henricus Amama/Zacharias Taedama, 1689). It was Huber's articulation of this principle that Joseph Story incorporated it into his territorially based principles on the conflict of laws. Story, *Commentaries on the Conflict of Laws*, 19, 21. The principle that a state's laws bound and protected foreigners was articulated in English jurisprudence by Edward Coke who described such allegiance as *ligentia localis*, or local allegiance. See *Calvin's Case*, 77 E.R. 377 (1608). The principle was likewise articulated in English political theory by John Locke, who observed, "[There is] a local protection and homage due to and from all those, who, not being in a state of war, come within the territories belonging to any government, to all parts whereof the force of its laws extends." Locke, *Two Treatises of Civil Government*, ed. Thomas Hollis (London: A. Millar et al., 1764), 304–305 (bk. II, § 122). By 1804, a reciprocal version of the principle had found its way into the first civil code in France, which declared, "A foreigner shall enjoy in France the same civil rights as are or shall be accorded to Frenchmen by the treaties of that nation to which such foreigner shall belong." George Spence, *Code Napoleon; or, The French Civil Code. Literally Translated from the Original and Official Edition, Published at Paris, in 1804* (London: William Benning, 1827), 4 (bk 1, title 1, chap. 1, art. 11). Although, reciprocity was not required if the Government had permitted the foreigner to make France his domicile. Ibid., 4 (bk 1, title 1, chap. 1, art. 13).

78 For an example of this principle as it is applied in a contemporary code, see Civil Code, art. 11 (Fr., 1 July 2016): "A foreigner shall enjoy in France the same civil rights as are or shall be accorded to Frenchmen by the treaties of that nation to which such foreigner shall belong."

79 This, rather than the "minimum standards" required by the "standards of civilization," are what even critics of nineteenth-century jurisprudence on intervention adhered to. See, e.g., Carlos Calvo, *Droit International* (Paris: Nouvelle de droit et de jurisprudence, 1896); Carlos Calvo, *Le droit international: théorie et pratique précédé d'un historique des gens* (Paris: Rousseau, 1896).

80 Samuel von Pufendorf located the foundation of such a principle in the Old Testament agreement between God and the "People of Israel" in which God granted protection and governance in exchange for the observation of His commandments: "The Conditions of this Covenant strictly taken on the Part of God were a particular Protection, and the Supream Government over that People.... The Conditions of this Covenant on the Part of the People were a peculiar Sanctity of Life and Manners, by which they might be distinguish'd from the Impurity of other Nations." Samuel von Pufendorf, *The Divine Feudal Law: Or, Covenants with Mankind, Represented*, eds. Simone Zurbruchen (Indianapolis, IN: Liberty Fund, 2002), 83 (§§ 31). Pufendorf's own articulation of the principle can also be found in Samuel von Pufendorf, *The Whole Duty of Man According to the Law of Nature*, eds. Ian Hunter and David Saunders (Indianapolis, IN: Liberty Fund, 2003), 44. The principle can be found in Roman law as well as in the early Germanic bond of allegiance described as the *comitatus* by Tacitus and called *mund* by the Germans from the Germanic word for hand or protection. See Tacitus, *Agricola, Germania, Dialogus*, eds. R. M. Ogilivie, E. H.

Warmington, and Michael Winterbottom (Cambridge, MA: Harvard University Press, 1914); *Deutsches Rechtswörterbuch, s.v.* "mund;" *Etymologisches Wörterbuch der deutschen Sprache*, 22nd ed., s.v. "mund." The German was latinized *mundium*, which evolved into various legal institutions in German, French, and Italian Law. *Black's Law Dictionary*, for example, defines *mundium* as "a tribute paid by a church or monastery to their seignorial avoués and vidames, as the price of protecting them." *Black's Law Dictionary*, 2nd ed., s.v. *mundium*. On the early *mund* and *mundium* see *Pouvoirs et institutions dans la France médiévale: Des origines à l'époque féodale* (Paris: Armand Colin, 1994), 1:41; Carlo Calisse, *A History of Italian Law* (Boston, MA: Little, Brown, 1928), 2:566–567.

81 William Blackstone, *Commentaries on the Laws of England*, ed. George Sharswood (Philadelphia, PA: J.B. Lippincott, 1893), 366. See also Pufendorf, *Whole Duty of Man According to the Law of Nature*, 44.

82 In the eighteenth century, the failure of the sovereign to provide protection or to withdraw its protection was seen as a valid reason for rebellion. See Declaration of Independence (1776).

83 Marc Bloch, *Feudal Society* (Chicago, IL: University of Chicago Press, 1961), 145–147.

84 Grotius, *Rights of War and Peace*, 2:1151 (bk. ii, chap. xxv, pt. i, ¶ 2). This idea is also partially, and famously, illustrated in the Frontispiece of Thomas Hobbes' *Leviathan*. See Quentin Skinner, *Hobbes and Republican Liberty* (Cambridge: Cambridge University Press, 2008), 183–198.

85 Grotius, *Rights of War and Peace*, 2:1151 (bk. ii, chap. xxv, pt. i, ¶ 2).

86 Geertz, *Meaning and Order in Moroccan Society*, 137.

87 *Protection diplomatique* in French, *Protezione Diplomatica* in Italian, and *Diplomatischer Schutz* in German.

88 Vattel, *Law of Nations*, 298 (bk. ii, § 71).

89 Ibid.

90 Ibid., 464 (bk. ii, § 350).

91 On Vattel's importance to eighteenth- and nineteenth-century legal thought, see David Armitage, *Foundations of Modern International Thought* (Cambridge: Cambridge University Press, 2013), 222–223; Maurizio Isabella, *Risorgimento in Exile: Italian Émigrés and the Liberal International in the Post-Napoleonic Era* (Oxford: Oxford University Press, 2009), 99–100; Lisa Ford, *Settler Sovereignty: Jurisdiction and Indigenous People in America and Australia, 1788–1836* (Cambridge, MA: Harvard University Press, 2010), 9, 27–28; Philip Allott, *The Health of Nations: Society and Law beyond the State* (Cambridge: Cambridge University Press, 2004), 416; Jennifer Pitts, *Boundaries of the International: Law and Empire* (Cambridge, MA: Harvard University Press, 2018), 70; For a nineteenth-century reference to his importance within international jurisprudence, see Henry Sumner Maine, *International Law, A Series of Lectures Delivered Before the University of Cambridge, 1887*, 2nd ed. (London: John Murray, 1915), 1.

92 Benjamin Franklin, "Benjamin Franklin to Charles-Guillaume-Frédéric Dumas," in *Papers of Benjamin Franklin*, ed. William B. Willcox, vol. 22 (New Haven, CT: Yale University Press, 1959). For a general assessment of Vattel's influence in America, see Jesse S. Reeves, "The Influence of the

Law of Nature Upon International Law in the United States," *American Journal of International Law* 3, no. 3 (July 1909): 549, who argues that although Vattel was perhaps not the most authoritative international legal thinker of the eighteenth century, by the nineteenth century he was quoted more frequently than any of his predecessors. For a critique of the contemporary view that Vattel's work was of *singular* importance to early American international jurisprudence, while simultaneously acknowledging the work's general popularity and importance, see Brian Richardson, "The Use of Vattel in the American Law of Nations," *American Journal of International Law* 106, no. 3 (July 2012): 547–571.

93 Alison Flood, "George Washington's library book returned, 221 years later," *The Guardian*, May 20, 2010.

94 Lapradelle and Politis, *Recueil des arbitrages internationaux*, 3:xli–xlii.

95 Alfred Chrétien, *Principes de droit international public* (Paris: Librairie Marescq Ainé, 1893), 58–59. Martti Koskenniemi has also noted "The continued widespread use" of Vattel in the nineteenth century. Martti Koskenniemi, "The Legacy of the Nineteenth Century," in *Routledge Handbook of International Law*, ed. David Armstrong (London: Routledge, 2009). For some excellent examples of nineteenth-century criticism of Vattel, particularly by Jeremy Bentham, see Pitts, *Boundaries of the International*, 120.

96 Alexander Hamilton, James Madison, and John Jay, *The Federalist Papers*, ed. Clinton Rossiter (New York: Signet Classics, 2003), 475 (no. 80).

97 House of Lords, Debates, June 17, 1850, vol. 111, col. 1353. See also ibid., at 1341; House of Commons, Debates, June 4, 1850, vol. 111, col. 716; Bassett, *Gladstone's Speeches*, 122.

98 House of Lords, Debates, June 17, 1850, vol. 111, cols. 1341–1342.

99 House of Lords, Debates, June 17, 1850, vol. 111, col. 1353.

100 Lapradelle and Politis, *Recueil des arbitrages internationaux*, 3: xlvii–xlviii.

101 Mavrommatis Palestine Concessions (*Greece* v. *Gr. Brit.*), 1924 P.C.IJ. (ser. A) No. 2, 12. N.B. This was also a case involving Greece and Great Britain.

102 On the use of "Vattelian Fiction," see Philip C. Jessup, "Responsibility of States for Injuries to Individuals," *Columbia Law Review* 46, no. 6 (November 1946): 923; Annemarieke Vermeer-Künzli, "As If: The Legal Fiction in Diplomatic Protection," *European Journal of International Law* 18, no. 1 (February 2007): 37–68; Noura Karazivan, "Diplomatic Protection: Taking Human Rights Extraterritorially," in *Canadian Yearbook of International Law*, ed. D. M. McRae, vol. 44 (Vancouver: University of British Columbia Press, 2008), 299–352.

103 Neufeld, *The International Protection of Private Creditors from the Treaties of Westphalia to the Congress of Vienna*, 51.

104 Vattel, *Law of Nations*, 451–452 (bk. ii, chap. xviii, § 329).

105 Jackson H. Ralston, *The Law and Procedure of International Tribunals*, revised ed. (Stanford, CA: Stanford University Press, 1926), chap. 3.

106 Ibid., xxvi.

107 The traditional historiography on the subject dated the start of the modern era of arbitration to the Jay Treaty. As one representative historian on the

subject wrote, "The modern era of arbitral or judicial settlement of international disputes, by common accord among all writers upon the subject, dates from the signing on November 19, 1794, of the Jay Treaty between Great Britain and the United States. Prior to this time arbitrations were irregular and spasmodic; from this time forward they assumed a certain regularity and system." Jackson H. Ralston, *International Arbitration from Athens to Locarno* (Stanford, CA: Stanford University Press, 1929), 191. However, historians have questioned this emphasis. See, e.g., Cornelis G. Roelofsen, "International Arbitration and Courts," in *Oxford Handbook on the History of International Law* (Oxford: Oxford University Press, 2012), 160–161; Cornelis G. Roelofsen, "The Jay Treaty and All That," in *International Arbitration: Past and Prospects*, ed. A. H. A. Soons (Dordecht: Kluwer, 1990), 204; Karl-Heinz Lingens, *Internationale Schiedsgerichtbarkeit und Jus Publicum Europaeum 1648–1794* (Berlin: Duncker/Humboldt, 1988), 74–78.

108 "Au sixième protocole de la séance des cinq Puissances, du 10 février 1815; Procès-verbal de la commission de redaction, donnant l'indication de 29 projets d'articles" in Comte d'Angeberg, *Le Congrès de Vienne et Les Traités de 1815* (Paris: Archives Diplomatiques, 1864), 4:1888.

109 Mark Jarrett, *The Congress of Vienna and Its Legacy* (London: I.B. Tauris, 2013), 148.

110 Lingens, *Internationale Schiedsgerichtbarkeit und Jus Publicum Europaeum 1648–1794*, 74–78.

111 "Convention between Great Britain and France, relative to the Claims of British Subjects," *British Foreign and State Papers, 1814–15*, 3:342–358.

112 This shift toward territoriality began in the seventeenth century when land became a commodity, and the purpose of government came to be the defense and preservation of that commodity. Rozumalski, "Lords of All They Survey.".

113 Stephen D. Krasner has defined an international regime "as sets of implicit or explicit principles, norms, rules, and decision-making procedures around which actors' expectations converge in a given area of international relations." He adds, "Regimes must be understood as something more than temporary arrangements that change with every shift in power or interest." Krasner, "Structural Causes and Regime Consequences," 185–186. Using this definition, the pattern of international arbitration in the latter half of the nineteenth century certainly qualifies. While each tribunal was composed in an ad hoc manner and there was no central authority at the center of the regime, international arbitration and the procedures involved formed a persistent sense of "principles, norms, rules, and decisions-making procedures." While I have no compiled hard data on the level of compliance with this regime, in almost every case I encountered, the parties complied with the outcome of the arbitration. There is some theoretical work, and there are surveys of contemporary behavior which indicate high levels of compliance with the decisions of international tribunals of all sorts. See, e.g., Andrew T. Guzman, "Why LDCs Sign Treaties That Hurt Them: Explaining the Popularity of Bilateral Investment Treaties," *Virginia Journal of International*

Law 38 (1997): esp. 197; Frans Viljoen and Lirette Louw, "State Compliance with the Recommendations of the African Commission on Human and Peoples' Rights, 1994–2004," *American Journal of International Law* 101, no. 1 (January 2007): 1–34.

114 Cicero, *In Verrem*, II.5.167-8.

115 For information about the role of the consulate today, see Vienna Convention on Consular Relations, art. 5, April 24, 1963, 596 UNTS 261.

116 Jörg Ulbert, "A History of the French Consular Services," in *Consular Affairs and Diplomacy*, eds. Jan Melissen and Ana Mar Fernández, Diplomatic Studies (Leiden: Martinus Nijhoff, 2011), 308.

117 See, e.g., An Act Concerning Consuls and Vice Consuls, April 14, 1792, 1 Stat. 254. See also an assessment of the Act made in 1906 by Jones Lloyd Chester in which he noted, "The duties of the consuls are thus by this act almost wholly the protection of the interests of American citizens, especially seamen." *The Consular Service of the United States, Its History and Activities* (Philadelphia: University of Pennsylvania Press, 1906), 5.

118 Richard Henry Dana, *Two Years Before the Mast and Twenty-Four Years After*, ed. William Charles Eliot, The Harvard Classics (New York: P.F. Collier, 1909-14), chap. 14; Richard Henry Dana, *The Seaman's Friend*, 5th ed. (Boston, MA: Thomas Groom, 1847), 190–191; For an example of a law establishing the duties of consuls, see An Act Concerning Consuls and Vice Consuls, April 14, 1792, 1 Stat. 254.

119 Dana, *Two Years Before the Mast and Twenty-Four Years After*, chap. 14. Richard Henry Dana, Jr. was no stranger to international law in his long career following his service at sea. He would eventually serve on an international arbitral commission and serve as an editor of the eighth edition of Henry Wheaton's classic textbook on international law as well.

120 Act for the Relief and Protection of American Seamen, May 28, 1796, 1 Stat. 477.

121 See especially the discussion of the rule of reimbursement for medical expenses and the care of foreign poor in Fedor Fedorovich Martens, *Traité de droit international*, trans. Alfred Léo (Paris: Librairie Marescq Ainé, 1886), 2:257–267, 2:288–289. See also William Henry Rattigan, *Private International Law* (London: Stevens/Sons, 1895), 32; Ludwig von Bar, *The Theory and Practice of Private International Law*, 2nd ed. (Edinburgh: William Green, 1892), 138n7, 139, 139n9; For an example of the recognition of this principle being considered in practice by governing officials, see Peter G. Parkhurst, *Ships of Peace: A Record of Some of the Problems Which Came Before the Board of Trade in Connection with the British Mercantile Marine from the Early Days to the Year 1885: Compiled from Official Records*, vol. 9, pp. 15–16, National Maritime Museum and Archive, Greenwich: PKT/9/1.

122 *My Consulship* (New York: Cornish, Lamport, 1853), 2:292. Emphasis in original.

123 President Ulysses S. Grant, Fourth Annual Message to Congress in *Cong. Globe*, 42nd Cong., 3rd Sess. 5 (1872). This theme was hit upon a number

of other times throughout the 1870s and 1880s, and for more references and citations to comments on this problem by various members of government, see Francis Wharton, *A Digest of International Law of the United States*, 2nd ed., vol. 2 (Washington, DC: W.H. Lowdermilk, 1888), chap. 7, § 190a (454).

124 Martens, *Traité de droit international*, 2:257–267. See also Rattigan, *Private International Law*, 32; Bar, *The Theory and Practice of Private International Law*, 138n7, 139, 139n9; Tara Zahra, *The Great Departure: Mass Migration from Eastern Europe and the Making of the Free World* (New York: W. W. Norton, 2016), 98.

125 Qtd. in Ralston, *Law and Procedure of International Tribunals*, 76.

126 House of Commons, Debates, July 6, 1847, Hansard Third Series, vol. 93, cols. 1305–1306. The use of discretion in deciding which claims to press proved particularly hazardous to British Prime Minister Spencer Perceval. John Bellingham, a shipbroker, was detained in Russia in 1804 based on claims that he was liable for a debt. Bellingham fiercely denied the claims and spent years petitioning the British government to intervene on his behalf. They continually refused. After his release in 1809, Bellingham returned to Britain and, again, pressed the British government for compensation. The British government refused. Finally, on Monday, May 11, 1812, Bellingham entered the Houses of Parliament and shot Perceval through the heart. As Bellingham described it at his trial, "I was detained in durance for near two years, in spite of all my endeavours to induce the British Minister to interfere with the Emperor of Russia for an investigation of my case. At length, however, after being banded from prison to prison . . . and frequently marched through the streets under a military guard with felons and criminals of the most atrocious description, even before the residence of the British Minister, who might view from his window, this degrading severity towards a British subject who had committed no crime to the disgrace and insult of the British nation." *R.* v. *Bellingham*, Session Papers, Justice Hall, Old Bailey, 1811–1813, Fifth Session, 268.

127 Zara S. Steiner, *The Foreign Office and Foreign Policy, 1898–1914* (London: Cambridge University Press, 1969), 3–4.

128 Reports of the Law Officers of the Crown, 1861–1921, UKNA: FO 834/3 – FO 834/30.

129 Ulbert, "A History of the French Consular Services," 306; Jean Baillou, ed., *Les affaires étrangères et le corps diplomatique français* (Paris: Editions du CNRS, 1984), 2:80. See also Paul Gordon Lauren, *Diplomats and Bureaucrats: The First Institutional Response to Twentieth-Century Diplomacy in France and Germany* (Stanford, CA: Hoover Institution Press, 1976).

130 Indeed a rarity within the State Department legal records, which are otherwise scattered throughout the National Archive and Records Administration (NARA). Register of International Claims, ca. 1900 – ca. 1936; Records of Boundary and Claims Commissions and Arbitrations, 1716–1994; Record Group 76. In the process of retrieving these records for me one day, NARA personnel dropped the tome, which then broke open. As such, the pages have been removed from the ledger and placed in a more manageable series of boxes.

131 Department of State, *Outline of the Organization and Work of the Department of State* (Washington, DC: Government Printing Office, 1911), 28–50.
132 Ibid.
133 See also Benjamin Allen Coates, "Transatlantic Advocates: American International Law and U.S. Foreign Relations, 1898–1919" (PhD diss., Columbia University, 2010), 246.
134 See, e.g., Steiner, *Foreign Office and Foreign Policy, 1898–1914*, 3–4. There has recently been interesting work on the Ottoman Foreign Ministry's Office of the Legal Advisor, which saw its role within Ottoman foreign policy dramatically increase in the decades before 1914. See Aimee M. Genell, "The Well-Defended Domains: Eurocentric International Law and the Making of the Ottoman Office of Legal Counsel," *Journal of the Ottoman and Turkish Studies Association* 3, no. 2 (November 2016): 255–275.
135 See, e.g., the hundreds of examples contained within both Borchard, *Diplomatic Protection of Citizens Abroad*, and Frederick Sherwood Dunn, *The Protection of Nationals: A Study in the Application of International Law* (Baltimore, MD: Johns Hopkins University Press, 1932). The Supreme Court of the United States, looking back over the previous century, eloquently noted the danger: "One of the most important and delicate of all international relationships, recognized immemorially as a responsibility of government, has to do with the protection of the just rights of a country's own nationals when those nationals are in another country. Experience has shown that international controversies of the gravest moment, sometimes even leading to war, may arise from real or imagined wrongs to another's subjects inflicted, or permitted, by a government." *Hines* v. *Davidowitz*, 312 U.S. 52, 64 (1941).
136 Ellen C. Collier, *Instances of Use of United States Forces Abroad, 1798–1993* (Washington, DC: Congressional Research Service, 1993). The size of the forces used could range from "a dozen seamen" to more than "three thousand men . . . engaged in long campaigns." For more details on these interventions, see the fairly exhaustive Milton Offutt, *The Protection of Citizens Abroad by the Armed Forces of the United States* (Baltimore, MD: Johns Hopkins University Press, 1928), 1. Unfortunately, no similar set of official numbers has been compiled for any European power.
137 D. C. M. Platt, *Finance, Trade and Politics in British Foreign Policy, 1815–1914* (Oxford: Oxford University Press, 1968). Oona Hathaway and her colleagues, in their analysis of "war manifestos" issued from the late fifteenth century to World War II, found that 45.2 percent of manifestos in their collection justified war to collect compensation for tortious wrongs, namely "injuries to property or life, including injuries to the issuing sovereign and to its citizens." Twenty-one percent of the manifestos identified the tortious wrongs as the manifesto's primary justification for war. Such claims peaked in the nineteenth century, they note, then fall off precipitously in the twentieth century. Additionally, 27.4 percent of all manifestos in their collection made religious claims, at least some of which were premised on protecting the religious liberty of their subjects abroad. However, such claims were uncommon by the nineteenth century. Scott J. Shapiro, Oona A. Hathaway, William S. Holste, Lisa Wang Lachowicz, and Jacqueline Van De Velde,

"War Manifestos," *University of Chicago Law Review* 85, no. 5 (September 20018): 1188–1189, 1192, 1203; Scott J. Shapiro Oona A. Hathaway, *The Internationalists* (New York: Simon/Schuster, 2017), 43.

138 Qtd. in John Bassett Moore, *A Digest of International Law* (Washington, DC: Government Printing Office, 1906), 6: 211–223.

139 Kif Augustine-Adams, "Constructing Mexico: Marriage, Law and Women's Dependent Citizenship in the Late-Nineteenth and Early-Twentieth Centuries," *Gender and History* 18, no. 1 (April 2006): 28.

140 Based on a survey of: A. M. Stuyt, *Survey of International Arbitrations, 1794–1938* (The Hague: Martinus Nijhoff, 1939); Lapradelle and Politis, *Recueil des arbitrages internationaux*; Henri La Fontaine, *Pasicrisie internationale* (Berne: Stämpfli, 1902); William Evans Darby, *International Tribunals*, 4th ed. (London: J.M. Dent, 1904).

141 [1902–2001] The Pious Fund of the Californias (*The United States of America* v. *The United Mexican States*), [1902–2002] Japanese House Tax (*Germany, France, and Great Britain* v. *Japan*), [1903–2001] Preferential Treatment of Claims of Blockading Powers against Venezuela (*Germany, Great Britain and Italy* v. *Venezuela*), [1908–2002] Deserters of Casablanca (*France* v. *Germany*), [1909–2002] The Orinoco Steamship Company case (*United States of America* v. *Venezuela*), [1910–2001] Canevaro claim (*Italy* v. *Peru*), [1910–2002] Russian Claim for Interest on Indemnities (*Russia* v. *Turkey*), [1912–2001] French Postal Vessel "Manouba," [1912–2001] The Carthage (*France* v. *Italy*).

142 General Claims Commission (Convention of September 8, 1923) (United Mexican States, United States of America), February 4, 1926–July 23, 1927, RIAA 4, p. 3. To place this number in perspective, the caseload of this commission alone was greater than that of the 2014 caseload for the European Court of Human Rights, the most active international court in the world as of this writing. That court issued 2,388 judgments in 2014, about 2/3 of the 1923 claims commission's 3,617. European Court of Human Rights, Analysis of Statistics 2014 (January 2015), p. 5. Similarly, the caseload of the ten largest international arbitral institutions plus International Centre for Settlement of Investment Disputes (ICSID) in 2008 numbered 3,328. ICSID, The ICSID Caseload Statistics, Issue 2016-2; Other numbers compiled from statistics available from the Hong Kong International Arbitration Centre.

143 Jessup, "Responsibility of States for Injuries to Individuals," 904.

144 For statistics on the increase in international arbitration around mid-century, see Fontaine, *Pasicrisie internationale.*

145 See Edmond Pittard, *La protection des nationaux à l'étranger* (Geneva: W. Kündig, 1896).

146 See, e.g., *Le droit de protection exercé par un état à l'égard de ses nationaux résidant a l'étranger* (Paris: A. Pedone, 1898); P. Pradier-Fodéré, *Cours de droit diplomatique* (Paris: A. Pedone, 1899); Gaston de Leval, *De la protection diplomatique des nationaux à l'étranger* (Brussels: Émile Bruylant, 1907).

147 See Dionisio Anzilotti, *Teoria generalla della responnsabilita dello stato nel diritto internazionale* (Florence: F. Lumachi, 1902).

148 See Borchard, *Diplomatic Protection of Citizens Abroad.*

149 Most of these projects were undertaken in response to the increasing successes of peace advocacy in favor of arbitration, culminating in the establishment of the Permanent Court of Arbitration as a result of the Peace Conference held at The Hague in 1899. These tomes, it was thought, could provide a set of jurisprudence whence the new court could draw. See, e.g., Darby, *International Tribunals* (Darby's tome was compiled explicitly at the request of the International Law Association in 1895 to study the feasibility of an international court.); Moore, *Digest of International Law*; Fontaine, *Pasicrisie internationale*; Lapradelle and Politis, *Recueil des arbitrages internationaux*.

150 Costa Rica Packet Arbitration, UKNA: FO 37/792; FO 37/793; FO 37/794; FO 37/795; FO 37/796; FO 37/804; FO 37/815; FO 881/6389X; FO 881/6532; FO 881/6677; FO 881/6685; FO 881/6829X; FO 881/6963; Convention Between Great Britain and the Netherlands for the Arbitration of the Costa Rica Packet Claim, May 16, 1895, 181 CTS 253, 87 BSP 21; Award of the Czar of Russia in the Arbitration of the Costa Rica Packet Case Between Great Britain and the Netherlands, February 25, 1895, 184 CTS 240, 89 BSP 1284.

151 The Arrest and Expulsion of Ben Tillet and Arbitration, UKNA: FO 10/771, FO 10/772; Convention Between Belgium and Great Britain Referring to Arbitration the Case of Mr. Ben Tillett, March 19, 1898, 186 CTS 193, XC BSP 5.

152 Root, "Basis of Protection to Citizens Residing Abroad" 24.

153 See, e.g., the cases illustrated in Marjorie M. Whiteman, *Damages in International Law* (Washington, DC: Government Printing Office, 1937).

154 Manley O. Hudson took note of the systematic nature of these ad hoc tribunals: "Claims made by individuals or private companies against States have long been fruitful of international litigation. Numerous international tribunals have been created to deal directly or indirectly with such claims, and their jurisprudence has had a formative influence on the development of international law with respect to state responsibility. The circumstances in which such tribunals should be created, the precise law which they should apply, and the execution of their decisions, are all matters on which controversy surges. Yet to some extent practices have been evolved which constitute a systematic approach to these problems, and on the basis of which constructive effort must proceed for the future." Manley O. Hudson, *International Tribunals: Past and Future* (Washington, DC: Carnegie Endowment for International Peace, 1944), 187. Similarly, in reviewing Borchard's *Diplomatic Protection*, Philip Marshall Brown observed that Borchard's tome revealed "that the field of international law is infinitely more extended and involves much more definite subject matter than has been heretofore realized . . . [and that] . . . the attempt to classify as matters of Private International Law, or mere Conflict of Law such questions as relate to rights of nationality, domicile, etc., which at any moment may properly give rise to diplomatic intervention, is illogical and preposterous." Philip Marshall Brown, "The Theory of the Independence and Equality of States," *American Journal of International Law* 9 (1915): 305–335.

155 Felix Stoerk, "Staatsunterthanen und Fremde," in *Handbuch des Völkerrechts*, ed. Franz von Holtzendorff (Berlin: Carl Habel, 1887).
156 Borchard, *Diplomatic Protection of Citizens Abroad*, 25.
157 Howard Thayer Kingsbury, "The 'Act of State' Doctrine," *American Journal of International Law* 4, no. 2 (April 1910): 359–372.
158 Pittard, *La protection des nationaux à l'étranger*, 333–334.
159 Pradier-Fodéré, *Cours de droit diplomatique*, 108.
160 For a geographic survey of the complaints, see Fontaine, *Pasicrisie internationale*.
161 For an overview of the "Standards of Civilization," see Gerrit W. Gong, *The Standard of "Civilization" in International Society* (Oxford: Oxford University Press, 1984).
162 Borchard, *Diplomatic Protection of Citizens Abroad*, 27–28.
163 On the "Standards of Civilization" and their application in the nineteenth century, see Gong, *The Standard of "Civilization" in International Society*.
164 On the Calvo Doctrine, see Amos S. Hershey, "The Calvo and Drago Doctrines," *American Journal of International Law* 1, no. 1 (January 1907): 26–45; Donald Richard Shea, *The Calvo Clause: A Problem of Inter-American and International Law and Diplomacy* (Minneapolis: University of Minnesota Press, 1955); Calvo, *Le droit international: théorie et pratique précédé d'un historique des gens*, 195–197, 253–255. Lord Palmerston had specifically argued against the principle, which would become known as "national treatment," in his famous "*civis Romanus sum*" speech discussed above, arguing, "It became the practice of this Greek police to make no distinction between the Maltese and Ionians, and their own fellow-subjects. We shall be told, perhaps, as we have already been told, that if the people of the country are liable to have heavy stones placed upon their breasts, and police officers to dance upon them . . . [then] foreigners have no right to be better treated than the natives, and have no business to complain if the same things are practised upon them. We may be told this, but that is not my opinion, nor do I believe it is the opinion of any reasonable man." House of Commons, Debates, June 25, 1850, Hansard Third Series, vol. 112.
165 Grotius, *Rights of War and Peace*, 2:1151 (bk. ii, chap. xxv, pt. i, ¶ 2).
166 Vattel, *Law of Nations*, 298 (bk. ii, § 71).

Chapter 2

1 George Bancroft to Lord Palmerston, reprinted in U.S. Congress, Senate, *Messages of the President of the United States, communicating, in compliance with resolutions of the Senate, information relative to the compulsory enlistment of American Citizens in the army of Prussia, etc.* 36th Cong., 2nd sess., 1860. Sen. Ex. Doc. 38, p. 164.
2 To be fair, I do not know that the snow "crunched." This is pure literary license. Herzen indicated that there was snow and that he left his sledge, so I'm assuming that the snow crunched, since it usually does. But it could have been slushy and merely "slurped;" or it could have been icy and made

almost no sound at all; or it could have been exceptionally powdery and "scrunched."

3 Alexander Herzen, *My Past and Thoughts: The Memoirs of Alexander Herzen* (London: Chatto/Windus, 1868), 598–599.
4 Herzen, *My Past and Thoughts*, 642.
5 Edward Hallett Carr, *The Romantic Exiles: A Nineteenth Century Portrait Gallery* (London: V. Gollancz, 1933), 11; Martin Malia, *Alexander Herzen and the Birth of Russian Socialism, 1812–1855* (London: Oxford University Press, 1961), 335–337; Judith E. Zimmerman, *Midpassage: Alexander Herzen and European Revolution, 1847–1852* (Pittsburgh, PA: University of Pittsburgh Press, 1989).
6 Alexander Herzen, *From the Other Shore, and the Russian People and Socialism* (Cleveland, OH: World Publishing Company, 1963), 15.
7 Herzen, *My Past and Thoughts*, 2:783.
8 Ibid.
9 Ibid., 2:786
10 Herzen, *My Past and Thoughts*, 2:786.
11 Ibid.
12 Malia, *Alexander Herzen and the Birth of Russian Socialism, 1812–1855*, 390, 472, n. 6.
13 Ibid., 390.
14 Herzen, *My Past and Thoughts*, 2:801.
15 Ibid., 2:798.
16 Herzen, *My Past and Thoughts: The Memoirs of Alexander Herzen*, 2:797.
17 Malia, *Alexander Herzen and the Birth of Russian Socialism, 1812–1855*, 390, 472, n. 6.
18 See David Cook-Martin, *The Scramble for Citizens: Dual Nationality and State Competition for Migrants* (Stanford, CA: Stanford University Press, 2013); See the surveys of nationality laws contained in Laws bearing upon nationality and naturalisation of foreign countries, answers to circular of October 13, 1892, UKNA: FO 83/1291–83/1293 (1892). See also Richard W. Flournoy and Manley O. Hudson, eds., *A Collection of Nationality Laws of Various Countries As Contained in Constitutions, Statutes, and Treaties* (Oxford: Oxford University Press, 1929).
19 For example, throughout the nineteenth century, aliens in the majority of the states of the United States had the right to vote. It would not be until 1928 that aliens could no longer participate in national elections. See Leon E. Aylsworth, "The Passing of Alien Suffrage," *American Political Science Review* 25, no. 1 (February 1931): 114–116.
20 See Gerrit W. Gong, *The Standard of "Civilization" in International Society* (Oxford: Oxford University Press, 1984).
21 See, e.g., Carlos Calvo, *Le droit international: théorie et pratique précédé d'un historique des gens* (Paris: Rousseau, 1896). In international legal jargon this principle is known as "national treatment."
22 Maybe even most.
23 Indeed, it was said by some of the earliest scholars of "diplomatic protection" that protection was merely a pretextual veil for oppression. See, e.g., Edmond Pittard, *La protection des nationaux à l'étranger* (Geneva:

W. Kündig, 1896), 333–334; P. Pradier-Fodéré, *Cours de droit diplomatique* (Paris: A. Pedone, 1899), 108. See also the discussion of diplomatic protection literature toward the end of Chapter 1.

24 It is fair to say that this is similar to the role that human rights plays in international politics today. As several observers have noted, human rights violations have provided what is, perhaps, the only "legitimate" pretext for intervention absent a direct violation of territorial sovereignty. See the "responsibility to protect" principle established at the UN World Summit in 2005 and its implementation plan: Implementing the responsibility to protect, Report of the Secretary-General, United Nations, General Assembly, 63rd sess., UN Doc. A/63/677 (January 12, 2009); see also Stefan-Ludwig Hoffmann, "Human Rights and History," *Past and Present* (August 2016).

25 Although, as the reader is by now well aware, in the twentieth century, in a particular academic context, nationality came to denote the link in its purest sense – but, again, only a particular academic context. This point is repeated in more detail below.

26 The difficulty persists in assigning a word to describe the person on the receiving end of such protection. "Citizen," "subject," "national," like their counterparts "citizenship," "subjecthood," "nationality," all have connotations that extend beyond the reciprocal relationship of allegiance and protection. The German *staatsangehöriger*, like its counterpart *staatsangehörigkeit*, is probably the most neutral term, although the French *ressortissant* is a strong runner-up, despite the fact it was not used regularly until the turn of the twentieth century. The use of *ressortissant* as a term that was more expansive than the French *national* but roughly equivalent to the international legal definition of the English "national" led to several headaches for jurists in the 1920s who had to decide the appropriate scope of the word, particularly since the French *nationaux* and *ressortissants* seem to have been used almost interchangeably within the Versailles Treaty. For cases dealing with the confusion, see *Recueil des decisions des Tribunaux Arbitral Mixte institués par les Traités de Paix* (Buffalo, NY: William S. Hein, 2006), 2:798–799, 3:239. For a discussion of the difference between the French *ressortissant* and the French *national*, see Georg Schwarzenberger, *International Law* (London: Stevens, 1945), 1:155–156; Louis Cavaré, *Le droit international public positif* (Paris: A. Pedone, 1951), 228. Scholars at the time did understand and argue that the English "national" and the French *nationaux*, from the standpoint of international law, were to be interpreted in an expansive way, like the French *ressorissant* and the German *staatsangehorigkeit*. This became particularly apparent based upon the text of the Versailles treaties. The French version used *ressortissant* and *national* interchangeably where the English version used only *national*. See, e.g., Hermann Isay, *Die privaten Rechte un Interessen im Friedensvertrag*, 3rd ed. (Franz Vahlen, 1923), 46–48. Ernest Satow, in his *A Guide to Diplomatic Practice* warned (although a *tad* too late) against importing even the word "national" into English. But he defined *ressortissant* as "one who is subject to a particular jurisdiction" and used as his example residents of Tunis or Morocco who are not French citizens, but are French *ressortissants* insofar as they are entitled to French protection. Ernest Satow, *A Guide to Diplomatic Practice* (Longmans: Green,

1917), 1:167. On the difference between nationality as a politco-legal term and a ethno-sociological term, see H. F. van Panhuys, *The Role of Nationality in International Law: An Outline* (Leiden: A. W. Sythoff, 1959), 37.

27 Edwin M. Borchard, *The Diplomatic Protection of Citizens Abroad, Or, The Law of International Claims* (New York: Banks Law Publishing, 1915), 457. See also, e.g., David Dudley Field, *Oulines of an International Code*, 2nd ed. (New York: Baker, Voorhis, 1876), 129–131; George Cogordan, *La nationalité au point de vue des rapports internationaux* (Paris: L. Larose, 1879); "The Harvard Research on International Law: Nationality," *American Journal of International Law* 23, no. 2, Supplement: Codification of International law (April 1929): 23.

28 Paul Weis, *Nationality and Statelessness in International Law*, 2nd ed. (Germantown, MD: Sijthoff/Noordhoff, 1979), 5. See also Josef L. Kunz, "The Nottebohm Judgment," *American Journal of International Law* 54, no. 3 (July 1960): 546. For a sharp illustration of the distinction, as one American observer noted, "Dred Scott [an american slave] was not an alien; he was a national, but he was not, under the famous decision, a citizen." Frederic R. Coudert, "Our New Peoples: Citizens, Subjects, Nationals or Aliens," *Columbia Law Review* 3, no. 1 (January 1903): 13–32.

29 Cogordan, *La nationalité au point de vue des rapports internationaux*, 2.

30 The *Oxford English Dictionary* (OED) defines "nationality" as: "National origin or identity; (Law) the status of being a citizen or subject of a particular state; the legal relationship between a citizen and his or her state, usually involving obligations of support and protection; a particular national identity. Also: the legal relationship between a ship, aircraft, company, etc., and the state in which it is registered." The earliest example of "nationality" provided by the OED is in a letter from 1763 in which one J. Fothergill writes, "Are they not daily reproaching the English for invidious distinctions, and are they not daily giving the English too obvious instances of their own nationality (excuse a new coined word)." No other example is cited until 1828. The number of examples begins to increase in the mid-nineteenth century. *Oxford English Dictionary*, 3rd ed., s.v. "Nationality." This is consistent with a frequency survey conducted using Google's One Million English corpus for the word "nationality" (case insensitive) from 1800–2000. Use remains low until the mid-nineteenth century and peaks in the years surrounding World War I. For information on the corpus and on the methodologies used in selecting the texts, see Jean-Baptiste Michel et al., "Quantitative Analysis of Culture Using Millions of Digitized Books," *Science* 331, no. 6014 (January 2011): 176–182.

31 H. J. Randall, "Nationality and Naturalization: A Study in the Relativity of the Law," *Law Quarterly Review* 40 (1924): 18–39.

32 Weil, *How to Be French*, 258.

33 Randall, "Nationality and Naturalization," 21.

34 Satow, *A Guide to Diplomatic Practice*, 167. In his retirement, Satow compiled his *Guide to Diplomatic Practice* and it quickly became the standard English textbook on the subject. See Joachim Schwietzke, "Ernest Satow's Guides to Diplomatic Practice: From the First Edition in 1917 to the Sixth Edition (2009)," *Journal of the History of International Law* 13, no.

1 (2011): 235–245. The book is still periodically updated, see Ivor Roberts, ed., *Satow's Diplomatic Practice*, 6th ed. (Oxford: Oxford University Press, 2011), and the 2011 edition was, according to one reviewer, "still a beacon of orientation, a reliable guide to, and authoritative commentary on, the world of diplomacy." Christian J. Tams, review of *Satow's Diplomatic Practice*, ed. Ivor Roberts, *Edinburgh Law Review* 15, no. 1 (January 2011): 156–157. Satow, however, was a snobbish grammatical prescriptivist (he spent part of his spare time compiling dictionaries), which indicates that while "national" may have been of relatively recent vintage in 1917 (having begun to enter use in the mid-nineteenth century), it probably could not be considered a "neologism." His characterization of the word as such was probably more of a performance of strict lexicography and less of a statement of objective reality. For more on Satow, see Bernard M. Allen, *The Rt. Hon. Sir Ernest Mason Satow G.C.M.G.: A Memoir* (London: K. Paul, Trench, Trubner, 1933).

35 See, e.g., Emer de Vattel, *The Law of Nations, Or, Principles of the Law of Nature, Applied to the Conduct and Affairs of Nations and Sovereigns*, eds. Béla Kapossy and Richard Whitmore (Indianapolis, IN: Liberty Fund, 2008):"Subjects then have no right, in doubtful cases, to examine the wisdom or justice of their sovereign's commands; this examination belongs to the prince: his subjects ought to suppose (if there be a possibility of supposing it) that all his orders are just and salutary: he alone is accountable for the evil that may result from them." Although Vattel, himself from the Swiss canton of Neuchâtel and a "citizen" amidst the European sea of subjects, used "citizen" and "subject" somewhat interchangeably.

36 See, e.g., Fisher, *Americanus Examined, and his Principles*, 8: "The power of making war, of protecting and defending British subjects, in every part of the world, and of forming, directing and executing that protection, is constitutionally vested in the crown alone. The subject has a right to demand it whenever he is in danger. This right is purchased by his allegiance, which is the reciprocal consideration daily paid for it."

37 This manner of describing the relationship is rendered very clear by the language invoked in the documents produced by the American colonies and colonists justifying their separation. See, e.g., the Pennsylvania, Rhode Island, Massachusetts Constitutions in Francis Newton Thorpe, ed., *The Federal and State Constitutions, Colonial Charters, and Other Organic Laws of the States, Territories, and Colonies Now or Heretofore Forming the United States of America* (Washington, DC: Government Printing Office, 1909). See also Vattel, *Law of Nations*.

38 Excepting those fortunate enough to be born in Switzerland or the Dutch Republic.

39 A condition the unfortunate souls of a damp island in northern Europe had to endure until embarrassingly late into the twentieth century.

40 James H. Kettner, *The Development of American Citizenship, 1608–1870* (Chapel Hill: University of North Carolina Press, 1978), 17.

41 William Blackstone, *Commentaries on the Laws of England*, ed. George Sharswood (Philadelphia, PA: J.B. Lippincott, 1893), 1:369. Blackstone's inflexible and immutable rendering of the principle is true primarily of the

English rule. The French, too, had a particularly inflexible conception of the rule through the seventeenth century. But beginning in the eighteenth century, the French conception became more flexible. Continental law in general by the late eighteenth century recognized de facto cancellation whenever a subject left the kingdom without the intention of return or when a subject had spent a long time, in a far off place. But this recognition was just as much a recognition that the sovereign was also deciding to no longer protect someone who had been far outside of the sovereign's realm for a lengthy amount of time – the circularity of the bilateral contract continues. See Robert Kiefé, "L'allégeance," chap. 3 in *La Nationalité dans la science sociale et dans le droit contemporain* (Paris: Recueil Sirey, 1933), 64–67.

42 On this subject in general, see Peter J. Spiro, "Dual Nationality and the Meaning of Citizenship," *Emory Law Journal* 46, no. 4 (1997): 491–565; Thomas S. Martin, "Nemo Potest Exuere Patriam: Indelibility of Allegiance and the American Revolution," *American Journal of Legal History* 35, no. 2 (April 1991): 205–218; Kettner, *Development of American Citizenship, 1608–1870*, 17. Protection, however, could be withheld by the sovereign in the event a subject violated their obligations of allegiance. See, e.g., Letters Patent to Humfrey Gylberte in Thorpe, ed., *Federal and State Constitutions*, 1: 52: "And if the saide Sir Humfrey, his heires and assignes, shall not [. . . obey us . . .] then it shall be lawfull to us, our heires and successours, to put the said Sir Humfrey, his heires and assignes, and adherents, and all the inhabitants of the said places to be discovered as is aforesaide, or any of them out of our allegiance and protection, and that from and after such time of putting out of protection the saide Sir Humfrey, and his heires, assignes, adherents and others so to be put out, and the said places within their habitation, possession and rule, shall be out of our protection and allegiance, and free for all princes and others to pursue with hostilitie as being not our Subjects, nor by us any way to be advowed, maintained or defended, nor to be holden as any of ours, nor to our protection, dominion or allegiance any way belonging, for that expresse mention, [etc.]."

43 Aristide R. Zolberg, "The Exit Revolution," in *Citizenship and Those Who Leave*, eds. Nancy L. Green and Francois Weil (Champaign: University of Illinois Press, 2007), 34–35; John Duncan Brite, "The Attitude of European States Toward Emigration to the American Colonies and the United States, 1607–1820" (Dissertation, University of Chicago, 1937), 195–223; See also Roger Mols, "Population in Europe, 1500–1700," in *The Fontana Economic History of Europe*, eds. Carlo M. Cipolla (London: Collins, 1973). For wonderfully brief summaries of Grotius, Pufendorf, Wolff, Blackstone, and Vattel's views toward emigration, see Frederick G. Whelan, "Citizenship and the Right to Leave," *American Political Science Review* 75, no. 3 (September 1981): 648–649. What can be said is that Grotius, Pufendorf, and Vattel all recognized some right to expatriation, although Grotius and Pufendorf heavily qualified that right. Ibid. Vattel, writing in the middle of the eighteenth century, was the most supportive of an individual natural right to expatriation, although even he tried to balance that right against the necessary recognition that children are "bound by natural ties to the society in which they were born: they are under an obligation to shew themselves

grateful for the protection it has afforded to their fathers, and are in a great measure indebted to it for their birth and education." For that reason expatriation was a right only after "making [the state] a compensation for what it has done in his favour, and preserving, as far as his new engagements will allow him, the sentiments of love and gratitude he owes it." Vattel, *Law of Nations*, 220–221 (bk. 1, chap. 19, § 220). See also Whelan, "Citizenship and the Right to Leave," 649.

44 John H. Elliott, *Empires of the Atlantic World: Britain and Spain in America, 1492–1830* (New Haven, CT: Yale University Press, 2006), 110–113.

45 On trading restrictions within the age of mercantilism, see Elise S. Brezis, "Mercantalism" in *The Oxford Encyclopedia of Economic History*, ed. Joel Mokyr (Oxford: Oxford University Press, 2003); Fernand Braudel, *Civilization and Capitalism, 15th–18th Century* (London: William Collins, 1982), 2:542–549; Ronald Findlay and Kevin H. O'Rourke, *Power and Plenty: Trade, War, and the World Economy in the Second Millennium* (Princeton, NJ: Princeton University Press, 2007), 227–228; See also Immanuel Weallerstein, *The Modern World System II: Mercantilism and the Consolidation of the European World-Economy, 1600–1750* (Berkeley: University of California Press, 2011). On Britain and Spain, see Elliott, *Empires of the Atlantic World*. On France, see James Pritchard, *In Search of Empire: The French in the Americas, 1670–1730* (Cambridge: Cambridge University Press, 2004); Charles Woolsey Cole, *Colbert and a Century of French Mercantilism* (Hamden, CT: Archon, 1964); Pierre H. Boulle, "French Mercantilism, Commercial Companies, and Colonial Profitability," in *Companies and Trade: Essays on Overseas Trading Companies during the Ancien Regime*, eds. Leonard Blussé and Femme Gaastra (The Hague: Martinus Nijhoff, 1981), 97–117. On the history of mercantilism as a concept, see Steve Pincus, "Rethinking Mercantilism: Political Economy, the British Empire, and the Atlantic World in the Seventeenth and Eighteenth Centuries," *William and Mary Quarterly* 69, no. 1 (January 2012): 3–34. For an example of the highly restrictive measures that could be taken against "foreigners" in the Spanish Empire during the age of mercantilism, see Tamar Herzog, "'A Stranger in a Strange Land': The Conversion of Foreigners into Community Members in Colonial Latin America (17th–18th Centuries)," *Social Identities: Journal for the Study of Race, Nation and Culture* 3, no. 2 (1997): 156.

46 Nathan Perl-Rosenthal, *Citizen Sailors* (Cambridge, MA: Harvard University Press, 2015), 16–44. On ships as particularly cosmopolitan spaces, see Marcus Rediker, *Between the Devil and the Deep Blue Sea: Merchant Seamen, Pirates and the Anglo-American Maritime World, 1700–1750* (Cambridge: Cambridge University Press, 1993).

47 Perl-Rosenthal, *Citizen Sailors*, 16–44.

48 There were exceptions. On imperial peripheries, fluid identities and loyalties foreshadowed problems that would become central in the nineteenth and twentieth centuries. Maya Jasanoff, for example, provides a compelling story of competing legal identities in eighteenth-century Ottoman Alexandria, in her account of Etienne Roboly, the chief interpreter for the French Consulate of Alexandria. Maya Jasanoff, "Cosmopolitan: A Tale of Identity from Ottoman Alexandria," *Common Knowledge* 11, no. 3 (2005): 393–

409, doi:10.1215/0961754X-11-3-393. Roboly worked for the consulate for nearly three decades. He had an Italian wife and was claimed by the French consulate as French. Yet, when he was arrested by Ottoman authorities for tax evasion in 1767, they claimed he was an Armenian and an Ottoman subject. "Born in Constantinople—perhaps of mixed parentage, perhaps never having visited France at all. The French called Roboly French, and the Ottomans called him Ottoman." The French tried to intervene, demanding that as a French subject he was entitled to a hearing in a French consular court. The protests, however, were in vain. Roboly died as a slave following nearly a year of torture. His widow, however, was provided a pension from the king of France. Ibid., 405–406. For more on the flexibility of identity on imperial peripheries, see Robert Ilbert, *Alexandrie 1830–1930: Histoire d'une communauté citadine* (Cairo: Institut Français d'Archéologie orientale, 1996), 72–98; Ziad Fahmy, "Jurisdictional Borderlands: Extraterritoriality and 'Legal Chameleons' in Precolonial Alexandria, 1840–1870," *Comparative Studies in Society and History* 55, no. 2 (2013): 305–329, doi:10.1017/S0010417513000042.

49 See, e.g., Letter Patent to Humphrey Gylberte in Thorpe, 1:53; Charter to Walter Raleigh in Ibid., 1:56–57; Charter of Connecticut in Thorpe, *The Federal and State Constitutions, Colonial Charters, and Other Organic Laws of the States, Territories, and Colonies Now or Heretofore Forming the United States of America*, 1:528–536: "If the said Person or Persons who shall commit any such Robbery or Spoil shall not make Satisfaction accordingly, within such Time so to be limited, that then it shall and may be lawful for Us, Our Heirs and Successors, to put such Person or Persons out of Our Allegiance and Protection." This formula was repeated almost verbatim in: The Charter for New England, Ibid., 3:1839; The Charter for Massachusetts Bay, Ibid., 3:1859; The Charter of Rhode Island and Providence Plantation, Ibid., 6:3219. The First Charter of Virginia, Ibid., 7:3788. See also Arthur Ashley Sykes' use of the principle to argue that when "*Papists* refuse the Tests of *Allegiance* they have a Right to be refused *Protection*" *An Enquiry How Far Papists Ought to Be Treated Here as Good Subjects and, How Far They Are Chargeable with the Tenets Commonlty Imputed to Them* (London: J./P. Knapton, 1756), 9.

50 This was particularly true in English legal doctrine, in which Edward Coke famously applied the latin maxim: "*nemo patriam, in qua natus est, exuere, nec ligeantiae debitum ejurare possit.*" The maxim, however, was usually shortened to: "*nemo potest exuere patriam*" or "No man may renounce [his] country." Edward Coke, *First Part of the Institutes of the Laws of England; or, a Commentary upon Littleton*, eds. Francis Hargrave and Charles Butler (Philadelphia, PA: Robert H. Small, 1853), 129a. See also I-Mien Tsiang, *The Question of Expatriation in America Prior to 1907* (Baltimore, MD: Johns Hopkins University Press, 1942), 11; Kiefé, "L'allégeance," 47–50; John W. Salmond, "Citizenship and Allegiance," *Law Quarterly Review* 18 (1902): 49–63.

51 Kiefé, "L'allégeance," 66. Beyond the practical, there was also the persistent idea that travel was transformative and "individualizing." See Eric J. Leed, *The Mind of the Traveler: From Gilgamesh to Global Tourism* (New York: Basic Books, 1991). Travel was also sometimes seen as a type of death. See Ibid.,

224–227. To travel too far outside the domain of one's sovereign was, perhaps, to be metaphorically reborn abroad and thus outside of a sovereign's allegiance and protection.

52 John Locke, *Two Treatises of Civil Government*, ed. Thomas Hollis (London: A. Millar et al., 1764), 389–417. See also James H. Kettner, "Subjects or Citizens? A Note on British Views Respecting the Legal Effects of American Independence," *Virginia Law Review* 62, no. 5 (June 1976): 948–951; Kettner, *The Development of American Citizenship, 1608–1870*, 9.

53 Vattel, *Law of Nations*, 223 (bk. 1, chap. 19, § 223).

54 Ibid.

55 Ibid.

56 On the legal debates over the separation and allegiance, see James H. Kettner, "The Development of American Citizenship in the Revolutionary Era: The Idea of Volitional Allegiance," *American Journal of Legal History* 18, no. 3 (July 1974): 208–242; Kettner, "Subjects or Citizens?"; Kettner, *Development of American Citizenship, 1608–1870*; Tsiang, *Question of Expatriation in America Prior to 1907*; Salmond, "Citizenship and Allegiance."

57 See, e.g., James Otis, *The Rights of the British Colonies Asserted and Proved* (London: J. Almon, 1764), 110–111; James Otis, *Considerations on Behalf of the Colonists: In a Letter to a Noble Lord*, 2nd ed. (London: J. Almon, 1765), 11; Fisher, *Americanus Examined, and his Principles*, 8. See also Martin, "Nemo Potest Exuere Patriam," 212–213; Kettner, *Development of American Citizenship, 1608–1870*, 9.

58 16 Geo. III., c. 5. (1775).

59 Declaration of Independence (1776). Commenting on the Prohibitory Acts, John Adams argued, "It throws thirteen Colonies out of the Royal Protection, levels all Distinctions and makes us independent in Spight [sic] of all our supplications and Entreaties." John Adams to Horatio Gates, March 23, 1776.

60 Thorpe, *Federal and State Constitutions*, 5:2594.

61 Ibid., 5:2789. See also Rhode Island's An Act for repealing an act entitled "An Act for the more effectually securing to His Majesty the allegiance of his subjects in this his colony and dominions of Rhode Island and Providence Plantation;" Constitution of Pennsylvania; the Constitution of Massachusetts, Constitution of Vermont available in Thorpe, *The Federal and State Constitutions, Colonial Charters, and Other Organic Laws of the States, Territories, and Colonies Now or Heretofore Forming the United States of America*, 6:3737. Constitution of Virginia, Ibid., 7:3815. See also Salem Dutcher, "The Right of Expatriation," *American Law Review* 11 (1877): 447–479.

62 Thomas Jefferson himself wrote, "I hold that the right of expatriation to be inherent in every man by the laws of nature." Thomas Jefferson, *The Works of Thomas Jefferson*, Correspondence and Papers 1804–1807, vol. 10 (New York: Cosimo Classics, 2009), 273.

63 Douglas Bradburn, *The Citizenship Revolution* (Charlottesville: University of Virginia Press, 2009), 105.

64 Antoine Louis Claude, *A Treatise on Political Economy: To Which Is Prefixed a Supplement to a Preceding Work on the Understanding or Elements of*

Ideology; with an Analytical Table, and an Introduction on the Faculty of the Will (Georgetown, DC: Joseph Milligan, 1817), 223. Claude's argument for expatriation, in contrast to Jefferson's was pretty dark. Rather than basing the principle on some natural freedom or right or on some abstract contractualism, Claude's basis was purely economic. According to Claude, expatriation was the only way to ensure that poor men could go "exercise their feeble talent wherever it would be the most profitable." However, to end this note on a better note, I thought I'd point out to the reader that Thomas Jefferson was the editor of the English translation of Claude's work and made many corrections to the translation itself. So in a small way both of these quotes on expatriation are the product of Jefferson's hand.

65 On expatriation and the influence of the United States on the development of the principle, see Tsiang, *Question of Expatriation in America Prior to 1907*; Nancy L. Green, "Expatriation, Expatriates, and Expats: The American Transformation of a Concept," *American Historical Review* 114, no. 2 (April 2009): 307–328. On the particular debates over expatriation in the United States following the War for Independence, see Bradburn, *Citizenship Revolution*, 101–138.

66 George Spence, *Code Napoleon; or, the French Civil Code: Literally Translated from the Original and Official Edition, Published at Paris, in 1804* (London: William Benning, 1827), 5–6(bk. 1, title 1, chap. 2, § 1, arts. 17–21.) This provision is still in effect today. See Civil Code, art. 11 (Fr., 1 July 2016).

67 Dutcher, "The Right of Expatriation," 477; Tsiang, *Question of Expatriation in America Prior to 1907*, 94. Although high ranking officials did hold that expatriation was a natural right in official documents and the United States did not actively pursue those who had left. See FRUS 1866, pt. i, p. 69. Congress declared expatriation a right with the Expatriation Act of 27 July 1868, 15 Stat. 223 (1868).

68 Herzog, "'A Stranger in a Strange Land';" E. S. Zeballos, *La nationalité* (Recueil Sirey, 1914), 2:82–85.

69 Brite, "Attitude of European States toward Emigration to the American Colonies and the United States, 1607–1820," 195–223.

70 See Frank George Franklin, "The Legislative History of Naturalization in the United States" (Dissertation, University of Chicago, 1906).

71 An act to establish an uniform rule of naturalisation, 1 Stat. 103 (1790).

72 An act to establish an uniform rule of naturalisation; and to repeal the act heretofore passed on that subject, 1 Stat. 414 (1795).

73 Ibid.

74 U.S. Congress, House, Report to the President of the Commission on Naturalization, 59th Cong., 1st sess., H.Doc 46 (Washington, DC: GPO, 1905), 13.

75 1 Stat. 414 (1795).

76 Ibid.

77 Report to the President of the Commission on Naturalization, 16; See also the details of the Koszta Affair. Andor Klay, *Daring Diplomacy: The Case of the First American Ultimatum* (Minneapolis: University of Minnesota Press, 1957).

78 For a survey of naturalization procedures in the Western Hemisphere, see generally Zeballos, *La nationalité*, vol. 2. For an overview of the negotiations for peace and recognition between the Spanish-speaking republics and Spain, including that of nationality, see William Spence Robertson, "The Recognition of the Spanish Colonies by the Motherland," *Hispanic American Historical Review* 1, no. 1 (February 1918): 70–91.

79 See José C. Moya, "A Continent of Immigrants: Postcolonial Shifts in the Western Hemisphere," *Hispanic American Historical Review* 86, no. 1 (February 2006): 3. On Mexico, see Charles A. Hale, *The Transformation of Liberalism in Late Nineteenth-Century Mexico* (Princeton, NJ: Princeton University Press, 2014), 236–238; On Brazil, see Herbert S. Klein, "European and Asian Migration to Brazil," in *The Cambridge Survey of World Migration*, ed. Robin Cohen (Cambridge: Cambridge University Press, 1995), 208; On Argentina and Chile, see Carl Solberg, *Immigration and Nationalism: Argentina and Chile, 1890–1914* (Austin: University of Texas Press, 2014). While nearly every state in Latin America implemented a number of policies to attract European immigrants, few of them were successful. As José C. Moya notes, "more Europeans arrived in the United States in a busy week than arrived in Mexico during the entire 35-year-long *Porfiriato*. The *cientifco*'s contempt for the indigenous masses and their efforts to attract Europeans were echoed by politicians from Guatemala to Bolivia. But all of these countries together received fewer immigrants in a century of national history than a single Argentine province in a month." Moya, "A Continent of Immigrants":3.

80 Zolberg, "Exit Revolution."

81 For more examples, see Zolberg, "The Exit Revolution," 49–51.

82 Adam M. McKeown, "Global Migration 1846–1940," *Journal of World History* 15, no. 2 (June 2004): 156.

83 Moya, "A Continent of Immigrants," 2.

84 Samuel L. Baily, *Immigrants in the Lands of Promise: Italians in Buenos Aires and New York City, 1870–1914* (Ithaca, NY: Cornell University Press, 1999), 58–59, 81.

85 McKeown, "Global Migration 1846–1940," 156. Much of the Indian migration in the region was driven by British imperial policies to provide labor to Burma and Malaya. See Amarjit Kaur, "Indian Ocean Crossings: Indian Labor Migration and Settlement in Southeast Asia, 1870–1940," in *Connecting Seas and Connected Ocean Rims: Indian, Atlantic, and Pacific Oceans and China Seas Migrations from the 1830s to the 1930s*, eds. Donna R. Gabaccia and Dirk Hoerder, Studies in Global Social History (Leiden: Brill, 2011), 134–166. While the vast majority of the migration was within the British Empire, see McKeown, "Global Migration 1846–1940," 157, a small number travelled to places outside of the imperial domains – an important (although not important enough to note in the main text) fact that will be discussed later in this chapter. Michael Mann, "Migration – Re-Migration – Circulation: South Asian Kulis in the Indian Ocean and Beyond, 1840–1940," in *Connecting Seas and Connected Ocean Rims: Indian, Atlantic, and Pacific Oceans and China Seas Migrations from the 1830s to the*

1930s, eds. Donna R. Gabaccia and Dirk Hoerder, Studies in Global Social History (Leiden: Brill, 2011), 119.

86 See, Ibid.; Robert C. Smith, "Diasporic Memberships in Historical Perspective: Comparative Insights from the Mexican, Italian and Polish Cases," *International Migration Review* 37, no. 3 (2003): 737–740; For steamship fares, see Mark Wyman, *Round-Trip to America: The Immigrants Return to Europe 1880–1930* (Ithaca, NY: Cornell University Press, 1993), 24.

87 Wyman, *Round-Trip to America: The Immigrants Return to Europe 1880–1930*, 24. For price calculations, see Samuel H. Williamson, "Seven Ways to Compute the Relative Value of a U.S. Dollar Amount, 1774 to present," MeasuringWorth, 2016, available at www.measuringworth.com/calculators/uscompare3/, accessed on October 31, 2016.

88 Donna R. Gabaccia, *Foreign Relations: American Immigration in Global Perspective* (Princeton, NJ: Princeton University Press, 2012), 25; citing Peter B. Harris, "Some Teachable Ironies about the Alfred Stieglitz Photo *The Steerage* (1907), on the Cover of *The Heath Anthology of American Literature*, 3/e, Volume 2," available at http://college.cengage.com/english/heath/harris.htm.

89 Fernando J. Devoto, *Del crisol al pluralismo: treinta años de estudios sobre las migraciones europeas a la Argentina* (Buenos Aires: Instituto Torcuato Di Tella, Centro de Investigaciones Sociales, 1992), 235.

90 For a fine example of this timing, see Michael Whitaker Dean, "'What the Heart Unites, the Sea Shall not Divide': Claiming Overseas Czechs for the Nation" (Dissertation, University of California, Berkeley, 2014), xxii.

91 Herzen, *My Past and Thoughts*, 2:786.

92 Qtd. in Nancy L. Green, "The Politics of Exit: Reversing the Immigration Paradigm," *Journal of Modern History* 77, no. 2 (June 2005): 284; Donna R. Gabaccia, *Italy's Many Diasporas* (Seattle: University of Washington Press, 2000), 139.

93 Peter Marschalck, *Deutsche Überseewanderung im 19. Jahrhundert: ein Beitrag zur soziologischen Theorie der Bevölkerung* (Stuttgart: E. Klett, 1973), 35.

94 Many of the speeches made use of the phrase "*civis Romanus sum*." Mack Walker, *Germany and the Emigration, 1816–1885* (Cambridge, MA: Harvard University Press, 1964), 139.

95 Bradley D. Naranch, "Inventing the Auslandsdeutsche: Emigration, Colonial Fantasy, and German National Identity, 1848–71," in *Germany's Colonial Pasts*, eds. Eric Ames, Marcia Klotz, and Lora Wildenthal (Lincoln: University of Nebraska Press, 2005), 21–40; Walker, *Germany and the Emigration, 1816–1885*; Günter Wollstein, *Das "Grossdeutschland" der Paulskirche: Nationale Ziele in der bürgerlichen Revolution 1848/49* (Düsseldorf: Droste, 1977). See the law: Gesetz für den Schutz und die Fürsorge des Reichs für deutsche überseeische Auswanderung betreffend in Franz Wigard, eds., *Stenographischer Bericht über die Verhandlungen der deutschen constituirenden Nationalversammlung zu Frankfurt am Main* (Frankfurt am Main: Johann David Sauerländer, 1849), 8: 5716. For a volume written at the time of the emigration that surveys the legal questions involved in emigration, particularly those questions involving the responsibility of a state

for their emigrants, see Alexander Müller, *Die deutschen Auswanderungs-, Freizugigkeits-, und Heimatsverhältnisse* (Leipzig: Adolph Wienbrad, 1841).

96 Mack Walker, *German Home Towns: Community, State, and General Estate, 1648–1817* (Ithaca, NY: Cornell University Press, 1971), 146–152. On German "colonialism" in America, see Susanne Zantop, *Colonial Fantasies: Conquest, Family, and Nation in Precolonial Germany, 1770–1870* (Durham, NC: Duke University Press, 1997); For a survey of just how closely towns recreated themselves in America, see Walter D. Kamphoefner, *The Westfalians* (Princeton, NJ: Princeton University Press, 1987), 70–105. On Czech "colonialism," as well as a wonderful etymological history of the word "colony," see Dean, "'What the Heart Unites, the Sea Shall not Divide'." On Austrian in general, see Zahra, *The Great Departure: Mass Migration from Eastern Europe and the Making of the Free World*, chap. 2.

97 Naranch, "Inventing the Auslandsdeutsche;" 26.

98 See Eli Nathans, *The Politics of Citizenship in Germany: Ethnicity, Utility, and Nationalism* (New York: Berg, 2004). For comparative perspectives, see Andreas Fahrmeir, *Citizens and Aliens: Foreigners and the Law in Britain and the German States 1789–1870* (New York: Berghahn Books, 2000); Rogers Brubaker, *Citizenship and Nationhood in France and Germany* (Cambridge, MA: Harvard University Press, 1992). For the Wilhelmine policy on the German diaspora in general, see Stegan Manz, "Diaspora and Weltpolitik in Wilhelmine Germany," in *Germans as Minorities during the First World War: A Global Comparative Perspective*, ed. Panikos Panayi (London: Routledge, 2017), 27–46.

99 On Germany, see generally Walker, *Germany and the Emigration, 1816–1885*, chaps. 4–6; Naranch, "Inventing the Auslandsdeutsche;" On Austrians and Eastern Europeans, see Zahra, *Great Departure*, 65–104; For Czechs, see the fantastic dissertation by a fellow Berkeley alum, Dean, "'What the Heart Unites, the Sea Shall not Divide'" (PhD diss.). On Italians, see Baily, *Immigrants in the Lands of Promise*; Caroline Douki, "The Liberal Italian State and Mass Emigration, 1860–1914," in *Citizenship and Those Who Leave*, eds. Nancy L. Green and Francois Weil (Champaign: University of Illinois Press, 2007), 91–113; Mark Choate, *Emigrant Nation* (Cambridge, MA: Harvard University Press, 2008). For some contemporary sources explicitly talking about the Italian colonization of Latin America, see Luigi Einaudi, *Un principe mercante: Studio sulla espansione coloniale italiana* (Turin: Bocca, 1900); Leone Carpi, *Delle colonie e dell'emigrazione d'Italiani all'estero sotto l'aspetto dell'industria, commercio, agricoltura, e contrattazione d'importanti questioni sociali* (Milan: Lombarda, 1874).

100 See, e.g., Choate, *Emigrant Nation*, 93; Doreen S. Goyer and Gera E. Draaijer, *The Handbook of National Population Censuses* (New York: Greenwood Press, 1992).

101 Sabina Donati, *A Political History of National Citizenship and Identity in Italy, 1861–1950* (Stanford, CA: Stanford University Press, 2013).

102 For an example of the state increasing regulation on passenger transit and emigration agents, see Caroline Douki, "Protection sociale et mobilité transatlantique: les migrants italiens au début du XXe siècle," *Annales: Histoire, Sciences Sociales* 66, no. 2 (April 2011): 375–410.

103 Zahra, *Great Departure*, 70–72, 80–84.

104 For the best overview of nation building and its relationship to mass emigration, see Donna R. Gabaccia, Dirk Hoerder, and Adam Walaszek, "Emigration and Nation Building during the Mass Migrations from Europe," in *Citizenship and Those Who Leave*, eds. Nancy L. Green and Francois Weil (Champaign: University of Illinois Press, 2007), 63–90.

105 Pasquale Mancini, *Della nazionalità come fondamento del diritto delle genti* (Turin: Eredi Botta, 1851).

106 Ibid., 41.

107 Ibid.

108 Pasquale Mancini, *Diritto Internazionale* (Naples: Giuseppe Marghieri, 1873), 201–205.

109 Qtd. in Donati, *Political History of National Citizenship and Identity in Italy, 1861–1950*, 27. See also David Laven, "Italy," in *What Is a Nation?: Europe 1789–1914*, eds. Timothy Baycroft and Mark Hewitson (Oxford: Oxford University Press, 2006), 259.

110 Angelo Piero Sereni, *The Italian Conception of International Law* (New York: Columbia University Press, 1943), 166–169.

111 There are many theoretical problems with the distinction. For a wonderful Marxist critique of the division, see A. Claire Cutler, "Artifice, Ideology and Paradox: The Public/Private Distinction in International Law," *Review of International Political Economy* 4, no. 2 (1997): 261–285. Nevertheless, the division is a widely used convention that I will use here both for convenience and because the distinction within the field was well-established by the late nineteenth century.

112 Pasquale Mancini, "De l'utilité de rendre obligatoires pour tous les Etats, sous la forme d'un ou de plusieurs tratés internationaux, un certain nombre de règles générales du Droit international privé pour assurer la décision uniforme des conflits entre les différentes législations civiles et criminelles," *Journal du droit international privé et de la jurisprudence comparée* 1, no. 4 (July 1874): 224–225.

113 Legally at least, although the French *éleveur de boeuf* in our scenario probably thinks that the German *metzger* is generally incompetent.

114 Pasquale Mancini, "De l'utilité de rendre obligatoires pour tous les Etats, sous la forme d'un ou de plusieurs tratés internationaux, un certain nombre de règles générales du Droit international privé pour assurer la décision uniforme des conflits entre les différentes législations civiles et criminelles," *Journal du droit international privé et de la jurisprudence comparée* 1, no. 4 (July 1874): 293.

115 For a great summary of Mancini's influence on other continental jurists, see Angelo Piero Sereni, *The Italian Conception of International Law* (New York: Columbia University Press, 1943), 177–179. See also Beale, *A Treatise on the Conflict of Laws or Private International Law*, 71–72. Not all of Mancini's

ideas with regard to private international law were popular. Mancini, believing that private law existed to serve the individual persons who made use of it, advocated for the acceptance of choice of law clauses in contracts. This allows two parties who were contracting with one another to choose which law was to govern the provisions of their contract. To go back to our cattle farmer and sausage maker example, the pair could have agreed that the law of New York (or, if they were alive today, the Southern District of New York) would govern the transaction. But states were unwilling to fully recognize the autonomy of the parties with regard to choice of law, a problem that will be explored (albeit somewhat tangentially) in Chapter 5.

116 By 1904, the Conventions, which adopted nationality as their governing principle, had been ratified by Germany, Austria, Belgium, Spain, France, Hungary, Italy, Luxembourg, and the Netherlands. See, e.g., Convention pour régler les conflits de lois en matière de mariage, art. 1, June 12, 1902 ("Le droit de contracter mariage est réglé par la loi nationale de chacun des futurs époux [. . .]."); Convention pour régler les conflits de lois et de juridictions en matière de divorce et de séparations de corps, art. 1, June 12, 1902 ("Les époux ne peuvent former une demande en divorce que si leur loi nationale et la loi du lieu où la demande est formée admettent le divorce l'une et l'autre."); Convention pour régler la tutelle des mineurs, art. 1, June 12, 1902 ("La tutelle d'un mineur est réglée par sa loi nationale."). See also F. Meili and Arthur Mamelok, *Das internationale Privat- und Zivilprozessrecht auf Grund der Haager Konventionen* (Zürich: O. Füssli, 1911); John Westlake, *A Treatise on Private International Law* (London: Sweet/Maxwell, 1905), § 27; Borchard, *Diplomatic Protection of Citizens Abroad*, 24.

117 See Cook-Martin, *Scramble for Citizens*.

118 It still generally is. See Satvinder S. Juss, "Nationality Law, Sovereignty, and the Doctrine of Exclusive Domestic Jurisdiction," *Florida Journal of International Law* 9, no. 2 (1994): 219–240. However, the principle was held to be subject to some international scrutiny by the Permanent Court of International Justice in 1923. *Advisory Opinion No. 4, Nationality Decrees Issued in Tunis and Morocco*, 4, Permanent Court of International Justice, February 7, 1923. See also Nathaniel Berman, "The Nationality Decrees Case, or, Of Intimacy and Consent," *Leiden Journal of International Law* 13 (2000): 265–295.

119 Qtd. in Cook-Martin, *Scramble for Citizens*, 3.

120 See, e.g., Nottebohm Case (second phase), Judgment of April 6, 1955: ICJ Reports 1955.

121 See, e.g., Charles S. Maier, "Consigning the Twentieth Century to History: Alternative Narratives for the Modern Era."

122 Neither were Englishmen (technically). The inhabitants of that damp island in the North Sea would remain "subjects" (in the domestic sense) until the British Nationality Act of 1948, which had to pass with *Royal Assent*, finally gave to those subjects of the King the title of "citizens." But before then, they were *technically* subjects with political rights.

123 Some good work has gone against this binary characterization. Suaknya Banerjee, for example, has argued that the line was not quite so stark. Banerjee tracks "the contours of anticolonial critique [and] the formation of

colonial subjectivities along the category of citizenship." That is, she argues that Indians sometimes performed the role of citizen even if they were technically legally excluded from political citizenship. See Sukanya Banerjee, *Becoming Imperial Citizens* (Durham, NC: Duke University Press, 2010), 4–5. However, I am not concerned with domestic rights, but rather with the spectrum of statuses that span between the domestic and international legal realms. Some other work on this, albeit in the early nineteenth century focused on the inhabitants of the Ionian islands. As a territory under British protection, the status of Ionians subjects was a source of debate within Britain for decades as was whether Britain would intervene on their behalf abroad. Lauren Benton and Lisa Ford, *Rage for Order: The British Empire and the Origins of International Law, 1800–1850* (Cambridge, MA: Harvard University Press, 2016), 102–116. Such questions, however, were generally settled by the latter half of the nineteenth.

124 According to one source, upwards of 250 traders arrived in Zanzibar in 1872 alone. Around 4,000 Indians lived in Zanzibar by the late nineteenth century. Thomas Metcalf, *Imperial Connections: India and the Indian Ocean Arena, 1860–1920* (Berkeley: University of California Press, 2007), 167.

125 See John E. Sandrock, "A Monetary History of German East Africa," *Numismatics International* 37, no. 9 (September 2002): 255–283.

126 See, e.g., Report on Application made to H. M. Vice-Consul of Alexandria for a Grant of British Protection [. . .], October 23, 1867, UKNA: FO 96/316; Circular on Aliens Naturalized in Colonies, May 18, 1882, UKNA: FO 372/24.

127 Note by Legal Advisor, India Office, May 13, 1904, UKNA: FO 83/2110.

128 In 1906, for example, three Indians found themselves without money and without help in Port Said. The British Consul there provided them temporary relief amounting to 1 pound, 11 shillings, 6 pence, a sum that equates to (in terms of economic status of that income) to 966.10 GBP in 2015. Distressed Indians and Port Said, September 25, 1906, UKNA: FO 369/15/419; See Lawrence H. Officer and Samuel H. Williamson, "Five Ways to Compute the Relative Value of a U.K. Pound Amount, 1270 to Present," MeasuringWorth, 2016.

129 For example, in 1905, the Secretary of State for Foreign Affairs, Henry Petty-Fitzmaurice, issued a circular confidently declaring, "When the whole control of the foreign relations of a state has been assumed by His Majesty's Government, it is apparent that the duty of protecting the natives of subjects of that State in other countries must also be assumed." UKNA: FO 83/2110.

130 On the subject of international labor protections and Indian indentured labor, see Rachel Sturman, "Indian Indentured Labor and the History of International Rights Regimes," *American Historical Review* 119, no. 5 (December 2014): 1439–1465. For an example of debate over extending emigration from India to French territories, see *Report by Mr. George Geoghegan on Coolie Emigration from India*, Parliamentary Paper (July 21, 1874), p. 30. See also, Convention Between Great Britain and France, relative to the Emigration of Labourers from India to the Colony of Réunion, July 25, 1860.

131 Qtd. in Sturman, "Indian Indentured Labor and the History of International Rights Regimes," 1459.
132 Weil, *How to Be French*, 209; Michael Brett, "Legislating for Inequality in Algeria: The Senatus-Consulte of 14 July 1865," *Bulletin of the School of Oriental and African Studies, University of London* 51, no. 3 (1988): 441.
133 Circular of January 20, 1869, Protection des Algeriens en Pays Étranger, Archives-Corneuve, Sous-Direction des Affaires Consulaire, box 403.
134 Ibid.
135 Ibid.
136 Ibid.
137 See, e.g., Mr. Leishman to Mr. Hay in United States Department of State, *Foreign Relations of the United States, 1900* (Washington, DC: Government Printing Office, 1902), 905.
138 The Supreme Court of the United States would resolve the domestic question in 1904, see *Gonzales* v. *Williams*, 192 U.S. 1 (1904).
139 The only matter up for serious debate was whether it would be better if they were labeled as "nationals" or "subjects" under domestic law. See Coudert, "Our New Peoples":32.
140 *Official Opinions of the Attorneys-General of the United States*, vol. 23 (Government Printing Office, 1902), 402. See also Coudert, "Our New Peoples," 32: "The Attorney-General of the United States in his argument in the Insular Cases suggested and ably maintained that the Islanders were American subjects. That term, however, is one which is foreign to our legal system and alien to our trend of political thought. The term 'National' fits the case more accurately and bears with it no unpleasant inference of political inferiority or servitude to an individual."
141 An act temporarily to provide for the administration of the affairs of civil government in the Philippine Islands, and for other purposes, 32 Stat. 691 (1902). This act's language with regard to protection closely followed that of An Act temporarily to provide revenues and a civil government for Porto Rico, and for other purposes, 31 Stat. 77 (1900). For more examples of the United States intervening on behalf of Filipinos abroad, see NARA, General Records Relating to More Than One Island Possession, Record Group 350, Box 1268.
142 Being equal under the law internationally does not mean, necessarily, that European states pursued the claims of colonial subjects with the same vigor that they did for domestic bondholders or white nationals. A claim made by a pukka sahib like John Flory would probably have been taken up more readily by the Foreign Office than one made by an Indian like Dr. Veraswami. That said, as mentioned above, there were often geopolitical reasons for vigorously pursuing the claims of colonial subjects.
143 That is real, flesh and blood and bone, human persons.
144 The word "corporation" is itself derived from the Latin *corporare*, which means "to embody." Corporations/juridical persons are also metaphorically assigned corporeal parts all the time, as in the following example: "We conclude that the phrase 'principal place of business' refers to the place where the corporation's high level officers direct, control, and coordinate the corporation's activities. Lower federal courts have often metaphorically called

that place the corporation's 'nerve center.'" *Hertz Corp.* v. *Friend*, 559 U.S. 77, 80–81 (2010).

145 The nationality of British Petroleum, Royal Dutch Petroleum (before its merger with the British Shell Transport and Trading), The American Broadcasting Corporation, Amway, etc., while now sometimes complicated, in the mid-twentieth century was certainly more clear.

146 This is despite Robert Reich's argument that multinational firms were increasingly becoming stateless. As Geoffrey Jones put it, in responding to Reich, "If you look at the historical evidence on the nationality of firms, the opposite conclusion seems more plausible: The nationality of global companies may actually have become clearer and more important in recent decades." Geoffrey Jones, *Nationality and Multinationals in Historical Perspective*, Harvard Business School Working Paper, No. 06-052, 2006. To give some perspective, Mervyn Jones, writing in 1949, was able to look back and say, "The era of foreign investment on a large scale reached its height during the fifty years or so preceding the First World War." Mervyn Jones, "Claims on Behalf of Foreign Nationals Who Are Shareholders in Foreign Companies;" *British Yearbook of International Law* 26 (1949): 225–258.

147 Of course, there is still the problem of long chains of subsidiaries that muddle the general question of nationality, particularly when plaintiffs occasionally try to "pierce the veil" that separates, say, Shell Petroleum Development Company of Nigeria, Ltd. (Nigerian) from Royal Dutch Shell (British, despite the "Dutch" in the name). Also, some legal systems use the location of the company's central administration, or "nerve center." Nevertheless, under the nineteenth-century legal order we'd not only have to inquire into the relationships between various companies, but it would not be clear that Shell Petroleum Development Company of Nigeria was even Nigerian based upon its ownership structure. The point is, the nineteenth century was hardly a simpler time in terms of the question of a juridical person's nationality.

148 Jones, *Nationality and Multinationals in Historical Perspective*, 29; See also Geoffrey Jones, "The End of Nationality? Global Firms and 'Borderless Worlds'," *Zeitschrift für Unternehmensgeschichte/Journal of Business History* 51, no. 2 (2006): 149–165; Geoffrey Jones, *Merchants to Multinationals: British Trading Companies in the Nineteenth and Twentieth Centuries* (Oxford: Oxford University Press, 2002); Mira Wilkins, "European and North American Multinationals, 1870–1914: Comparisons and Contrasts," *Business History* 30, no. 1 (1988): 8–45.

149 In 1906, Georges Marais in a report before the International Law Association identified three theories – place of incorporation, the nationality of the members that composed the corporation, place of domicile. Georges Marais and Gaston de Leval, "De la nationalité des sociétés anonymes en droit international;" *International Law Association, Conference Report* 23 (1906): 362–363. For a fine summary of two theories on the status of foreign corporations, see Borchard, *Diplomatic Protection of Citizens Abroad*, 41. For summaries of the manner in which various European countries determined the nationality of a corporation and an assessment of the complexities of

the issue, see Prince Cassano, "De la nationalité des sociétés par actions," *International Law Association, Conference Report* 19 (1900): 330–338.

150 François Laurent, *Droit Civil International* (Paris: Librairie Marescq Ainé, 1880), 4: 231–232 (§ 119).

151 See, e.g., *Long's Case*, 2 Knapp's Privy Council Reports 51 (holding that a corporation, although composed of British subjects, must be considered a foreign corporation if it exists in a foreign country under the consent of the foreign government). See also *Great Britain* v. *United States*, 29 RIAA 11, 15 (1853).

152 Heinrich Kronstein, "The Nationality of International Enterprises," *Columbia Law Review* 52, no. 8 (December 1952): 985.

153 See Ibid., 985–990.

154 Borchard, *Diplomatic Protection of Citizens Abroad*, 41–42.

155 *Daimler Co.* v. *Continental Tyre and Rubber Co.* [1916] 2 A.C. 307 (H. L.); Kronstein, "Nationality of International Enterprises":986.

156 Marais and Leval, "De la nationalité des sociétés anonymes en droit international;" 363.

157 See Jones, "Claims on Behalf of Foreign Nationals Who Are Shareholders in Foreign Companies;" Wilkins, "European and North American Multinationals, 1870–1914."

158 "Death of Colonel McMurdo," *South Africa Magazine*, May 11, 1889.

159 UKNA: FO 63/1261–1267; FO 63/1305; FO 63/1326; FO 63/1358; FO 63/1371; FO 93/24/9; See also John Bassett Moore, *A Digest of International Law* (Washington, DC: Government Printing Office, 1906), 1865; Jones, "Claims on Behalf of Foreign Nationals Who Are Shareholders in Foreign Companies;" 228–230; Gleider I. Hernández, "Delagoa Bay Railway Arbitration," *Max Planck Encyclopedia of Public International Law* (April 2009).

160 The economic power of 599,816,198 GBP equates to roughly 778,400,000,000 GBP (or two spell it out – more than three-quarters of a *trillion* pounds, which should indicate just how laughably large the sum was. See Lawrence H. Officer and Samuel H. Williamson, "Five Ways to Compute the Relative Value of a U.K. Pound Amount, 1270 to Present," MeasuringWorth, 2016, available at www.measuringworth.com/calculators/ukcompare/, accessed on October 31, 2016.

161 See, e.g., Marais and Leval, "De la nationalité des sociétés anonymes en droit international;" Cassano, "De la nationalité des sociétés par actions."

162 This comment appeared in a report submitted in support of a bill to amend the American Espionage Act, which would have made it a crime to submit a false claim for protection to the Department of State. U.S. Congress, House, *Amendment to Espionage Act, Report*, 65th Cong., 2nd sess., 1918, H.Rep. 667. The report continued on incredulously noting, "It appears that in at least one case the [State] department was recently called upon to protect the interests of a certain American concern which, as subsequently developed, appeared to be acting as a cloak for the interests of agents of the German Government in the United States."

163 William Edward Hall, *A Treatise on International Law*, 3rd ed. (Oxford: Clarendon Press, 1890), 236.

164 Addington to Waddington, March 7, 1854, UKNA: HO 45/5740.

165 As noted above, Maya Jasanoff has written a compelling account of the fluidity of identity through the account of Etienne Roboly, the chief interpreter for the French Consulate of Alexandria. Jasanoff, "Cosmopolitan."

166 British Legation, Addis Ababa to the Foreign Office, February 28, 1914, UKNA: FO 141/796.

167 Circular of January 20, 1869, Protection des Algeriens en Pays Étranger, Archives-Corneuve, Sous-Direction des Affaires Consulaire, box 403.

168 Archives-Corneuve, Sous-Direction des Affaires Consulaire, box 403.

169 Débats parlementaires, Chambre des députés, Journal official de la République française, 7 June 1907, p. 1231.

170 Ulysses S. Grant: "Sixth Annual Message," December 7, 1874. The best surveys of America's relationship with dual nationality are Spiro, "Dual Nationality and the Meaning of Citizenship" and the longer (and more comprehensive). Peter J. Spiro, *At Home in Two Countries: The Past and Future of Dual Citizenship* (New York: New York University Press, 2016).

171 U.S. Congress, House, *Foreign Relations*, December 1, 1879, 46th Cong., 2nd sess., 1879, H.Exdoc.1/2, serial 1902, 143.

172 Elihu Root, "The Basis of Protection to Citizens Residing Abroad," *Proceedings of the American Society of International Law at Its Annual Meeting (1907–1917)* 4 (April 1910): 19. For more detail on the problems faced in Morocco, see George Edmund Holt, *Morocco the Piquant* (London: William Heinemann, 1914), 56–74.

173 Ibid., 70.

174 Theodore Roosevelt, "Americanization Day," *Metropolitan* 42, no. 3 (July 1915): 59.

175 See Perl-Rosenthal, *Citizen Sailors*; Paul A. Gilje, *Free Trade and Sailors' Rights in the War of 1812* (Cambridge: Cambridge University Press, 2013), chap. 8; Matthew Taylor Raffety, *The Republic Afloat: Law, Honor, and Citizenship in Maritime America* (Chicago, IL: University of Chicago Press, 2013), chap. 8.

176 Rising Lake Morrow, "The Negotiation of the Anglo-American Treaty of 1870," *American Historical Review* 39, no. 4 (July 1934): 663–681. See also David Sim, *A Union Forever: The Irish Question and U.S. Foreign Relations in the Victorian Age* (Ithaca, NY: Cornell University Press, 2013), 98; Lucy E. Salyer, *Under the Starry Flag* (Cambridge, MA: Belknap, 2018), 188.

177 See, e.g., Minutes of the Royal Commission for Inquiry into the Laws of Naturalization and Allegiance, 1868, UKNA: FO 317/1; Analysis of the Report of the Royal Commission for Inquiring into the Laws of Naturalization and Allegiance, April 17, 1869, UKNA: FO 881/1659.

178 See George H. Yeaman, *Allegiance and Citizenship: An Inquiry into the Claim of European Governments to Exact Military Service of Naturalized Citizens of the United States* (Copenhagen: Fritz Moller, 1867). For an account of the negotiation of the Anglo-American Treaty of 1870, see Morrow, "Negotiation of the Anglo-American Treaty of 1870."

179 George Bancroft to Lord Palmerston, reprinted in U.S. Congress, Senate, *Messages of the President of the United States, communicating, in compliance with resolutions of the Senate, information relative to the compulsory enlistment of American Citizens in the army of Prussia, etc.* 36th Cong., 2nd sess., 1860. Sen. Ex. Doc. 38, p. 164; see also Salyer, *Under the Starry Flag*, 189–195.

180 Analysis of the Report of the Royal Commission for Inquiring into the Laws of Naturalization and Allegiance, April 17, 1869, UKNA: FO 881/1659.

181 Alexander Cockburn, *Nationality: Or the Law Relating to Subjects and Aliens Considered with a view to Future Legislation* (London: William Ridgway, 1869), 187.

182 André Weiss, "La proposition de loi sur la nationalité au Sénat," *Critique legislative et jurisprudence* 16 (1887): 492. Countries even went further than law and tried to sever affective allegiances. Following the 1906 San Francisco earthquake, countries around the world offered to send financial assistance to the United States and President Roosevelt, a staunch opponent of "hyphenated-americanism" and concerned that the assistance would only serve to strengthen ties between immigrants and their sending states, refused any aid. Erica Anne Lee, "Sanctuaries into Fortresses: Refugees and the Limits of Social Obligation in Progressive Era America" (Dissertation, University of California, Berkeley, 2017), 67–74. Reactions to Roosevelt's policy were mixed, but the California Club of Women announced, "We hold that the denial of the right to contribute on the ground of nationality is wrong, harmful, and without precedent," and concluded that foreign donors "unquestionably had in mind the fact that thousands upon thousands of their nationality will require assistance." Qtd. in Ibid., 73–74.

183 See Act of March 2, 1907, 34 Stat. 1228 (1907).

184 Patrick Weil, "From Conditional to Secured and Sovereign: The New Strategic Link between the Citizen and the Nation-State in a Globalized World," *Journal of International Constitutional Law* 9, nos. 3–4 (2011): 626.

185 See, e.g., F. Llewellyn-Jones, "The Nationality of Married Women," *Transactions of the Grotius Society* 15 (1929): 121–138; Jesse S. Reeves, "Nationality of Married Women;" *American Journal of International Law* 17, no. 1 (1923): 97–100; Raymond Hubert, *L'Influence du mariage sur la nationalité* (Paris: Bureaux des lois nouvelles, 1908). See also M. Page Baldwin, "Subject to Empire: Married Women and the British Nationality and Status of Aliens Act," *Journal of British Studies* 40, no. 4 (2001): 522–556; Ann Marie Nicolosi, "'We Do Not Want Our Girls to Marry Foreigners': Gender, Race, and American Citizenship," *NWSA Journal* 13, no. 3 (2001): 1–21.

186 See, e.g., Reeves, "Nationality of Married Women;" Hubert, *L'Influence du mariage sur la nationalité.* When the world finally came together to draft a convention on refugees and the reduction of statelessness in the decade after 1945, delegates noted the urgency of addressing statelessness had declined – in part because states had begun to end the forcible expatriation of women. See, e.g., UN General Assembly, Convention on the Nationality of Married Women, January 29, 1957, 309 UNTS 65.

187 Mexican Constitution of 1917, art. 27(1).

188 Kif Augustine-Adams, "Constructing Mexico: Marriage, Law and Women's Dependent Citizenship in the Late-Nineteenth and Early-Twentieth Centuries," *Gender and History* 18, no. 1 (April 2006): 28.
189 Institute of International Law, Principes relatifs aux conflits de lois en matière de nationalité, Session de Cambridge, 1895. James Brown Scott, ed., *Resolutions of the Institute of International Law* (Oxford: Oxford University Press, 1916).
190 Institute of International Law, Résolutions relatives aux conflits de lois en matière de nationalité, Session de Venice, 1895. Scott, ed., *Resolutions of the Institute of International Law* (Oxford).
191 Qtd. in Zahra, *Great Departure*, 98.
192 Edwin M. Borchard, "Decadence of the American Doctrine of Voluntary Expatriation," *American Journal of International Law* 25, no. 2 (April 1931): 315–316.
193 Qtd. in Hannah Arendt, *The Origins of Totalitarianism* (New York: Meridian, 1962), 279, n. 25.
194 Francis Piggott, *Nationality* (London: William Clowes, 1907).
195 Malia, *Alexander Herzen and the Birth of Russian Socialism, 1812–1855*, 284, 294.
196 Ibid., 290.
197 M. K. Dziewanowski, "Herzen, Bakunin and the Polish Insurrection of 1863," *Journal of Central European Affairs* 8 (April 1948): 58–78; Aviel Roshwald, *Ethnic Nationalism and the Fall of Empires* (New York: Routledge, 2001), 232, n.24.

Part II

1 Nicolas Politis, *The New Aspects of International Law* (Washington, DC: Carnegie Endowment for International Peace, 1928), 1–2.
2 See Ronald F. Roxburgh's preface in Lassa Oppenheim, *International Law: A Treatise*, 3rd ed., ed. Ronald F. Roxburgh (London: Longmans, 1920-1921), 2:v. The newly created League of Nations featured in both volumes of Oppenheim's postwar treatise, but in no way was it the central or defining feature. In part, this can be attributed to the ill health of Oppenheim himself in the last few months before his death. But it can also be attributed to an idea held among many – but by no means all – jurists that the League was not so much a repudiation of prewar law, but rather an organization for the cooperation of states in general as well as a forum for the further refinement of the law in existence before the war.
3 Lassa Oppenheim, *The League of Nations and Its Problems: Three Lectures* (London: Longmans, Green, 1919), 6.
4 Ibid., 6–12.
5 Oppenheim, *International Law*, 1:269. For more on Oppenheim, see Hatsue Shinohara, *US International Lawyers in the Interwar Years: A Forgotten Crusade* (Cambridge: Cambridge University Press, 2012), 37–39.
6 One might compare this sense of newness to Peter Gay's argument that "the Weimar style was born before the Weimar Republic" and that the war

simply gave it "a political cast and a strident tone, and saddled it with a deadly quarrel." Peter Gay, *Weimar Culture: The Outsider as Insider* (New York: W. W. Norton, 2001), 4–6.

7 On the importance of Geneva as a space for talking, see Susan Pedersen, *The Guardians: The League of Nations and the Crisis of Empire* (Oxford: Oxford University Press, 2015), chap. 3. On the importance of Geneva as a space for making claims about the international order visible, see Susan Pedersen, "Samoa on the World Stage: Petitions and Peoples before the Mandates Commission of the League of Nations," *The Journal of Imperial and Commonwealth History* 40, no. 2 (2014): 231–261, doi:10.1080/03086534.2012.697612.

8 Quoted in Frederick W. Haberman, ed., *Nobel Lectures, Peace 1926–1950* (Amsterdam: Elsevier, 1972); For the full text of Cecil's address, see League of Nations, *The Records of the First Assembly, Plenary Meetings* (Geneva, 1920), 93–99.

9 Statute of the Permanent Court of International Justice, art. 59, December 16, 1920, 6 LNTS 389.

10 Oppenheim, *The League of Nations and Its Problems*, 6.

11 Alejandro Álvarez, "The New International Law," *Transactions of the Grotius Society* 15 (1929): 87.

12 See, e.g., Politis, *The New Aspects of International Law*, 12; Álvarez, "The New International Law," 46–47: "It is impossible to abolish politics as some jurists pretend."

13 Politis, *The New Aspects of International Law*, 12.

14 See, e.g., the so-called role "standards of civilization" as played in nineteenth-century international law and the practices of informal empire. Gong, *The Standard of "Civilization" in International Society*. Nor was this conception of absolute sovereignty entirely dominant in the theoretical literature. Henry Maine, one of the most popular jurists of the latter nineteenth century, argued that, far from being absolute and indivisible, "the powers of sovereigns are a bundle or collection of powers, and they may be separated from one another." Henry Sumner Maine, *International Law* (London: John Murray, 1890), chap. 3.

15 States themselves had once not necessarily been subjects of the law, with Sovereign Princes being the primary subjects. See Jan Schröder, "Die Entstehung des modernen V ölkerrechtsbegriffs im Naturrecht der frühen Neuzeit," *Jahrbuch für Recht und Ethik* 8 (2000): 59–61.

16 Pitts, *Boundaries of the International: Law and Empire*.

17 Politis, *New Aspects of International Law*, chap. 2.

18 Politis, *The New Aspects of International Law*, 23.

19 Carl Brinkman, *Recent Theories of Citizenship In its Relation to Government* (New Haven, CT: Yale University Press, 1927), 116.

20 Daniel Gorman, *The Emergence of International Society in the 1920s* (Cambridge: Cambridge University Press, 2012); Hedley Bull, *The Anarchical Society*, 3rd ed. (New York: Columbia University Press, 2002).

21 See, e.g., Natasha Wheatley's two excellent articles on the subjects of differing visions of international legal subjectivity and the role of petitioning in the League, Natasha Wheatley, "New Subjects in International Law and

Order," in *Internationalisms: A Twentieth Century History*, eds. Glenda Sluga and Patricia Clavin (Cambridge University Press, 2017), 265–286; Natasha Wheatley, "Mandatory Interpretation: Legal Hermeneutics and the New International Order in Arab and Jewish Petitions to the League of Nations," *Past and Present*, no. 227 (May 2015): 205–248.

22 Or sometime in the early-modern period if you ask a nay-saying early modernist.

23 Finnemore, *The Purpose of Intervention: Changing Beliefs about the Use of Force*, 43 n.54.

24 Laurence Lafore, *The Long Fuse: An Interpretation of the Origins of World War I* (Long Grove, IL: Waveland Press, 1997).

Chapter 3

1 G. M. W. Jellinghaus and R. S. Fraser, "The Status of the Individual in International Law," in *Report of the Conference of the International Law Association*, vol. 30 (International Law Association, 1921), 289–313.

2 U.S. Congress, Senate, *Treaty of Peace with Germany, Hearings before the Committee on Foreign Relations*, 66th Cong., 1st sess., S.Doc. 106 (Washington, DC: GPO, 1919), 835–838.

3 On the problems of national self-determination and the minorities problem in the nineteenth century and the interwar period, see Eric D. Weitz, "From the Vienna to the Paris System: International Politics and the Entangled Histories of Human Rights, Forced Deportations, and Civilizing Missions," *American Historical Review* 113, no. 5 (December 2008): 1313–1343; Nathaniel Berman, "'But the Alternative Is Despair:' European Nationalism and the Modernist Renewal of International Law," *Harvard Law Review* 106, no. 8 (June 1993): 1792–1903; Erez Manela, *The Wilsonian Moment: Self-Determination and the International Origins of Anticolonial Nationalism* (Oxford: Oxford University Press, 2009); Mark Mazower, "The Strange Triumph of Human Rights," *Historical Journal* 47, no. 2 (June 2004): 379–398; Inis L. Claude, *National Minorities: An International Problem* (Cambridge, MA: Harvard University Press, 1955); Matthew Frank, *Making Minorities History: Population Transfer in Twentieth-Century Europe* (Oxford: Oxford University Press, 2017), chaps. 1–2.

4 Carlos Calvo, *Droit International* (Paris: Nouvelle de droit et de jurisprudence, 1896), 1:24, 169: La plupart des auteurs moderns ont definé le mot *nation* comme Cicéron: "*Respublica est coetus multitudinis, juris consensu et utilitatis communion sociatus*." See also Lassa Oppenheim, *International Law: A Treatise*, 2nd ed. (London: Longmans, 1912), 1:369; William Edward Hall, *A Treatise on International Law*, 3rd ed. (Oxford: Clarendon Press, 1890), 220. Even after the complexities and tragedies of the 1930s and 1940s, it was (and is) still claimed, "The word 'national,' as used in international law, has a technical meaning .... The word national is used in connection with a state and then means a member or subject of such a State. An individual who is a national of a state is internationally only known

through the state to which he belongs. Nationality, that is to say, membership of a State, is the link through which an individual can enjoy the benefits of the law of nations." W. R. Bisschop, "Nationality in International Law," *American Journal of International Law* 37, no. 2 (April 1943): 320–321.

5 "Mixed Claims Commission – United States and Germany: Opinion Dealing with Germany's Obligations and the Jurisdiction of the Commission as Determined by the Nationality of Claims and Administrative Decision No. V," *American Journal of International Law* 19, no. 3 (July 1925): 624. See also B. Akzin, "La sociologie de la nationalité," chap. 1 in *La Nationalité dans la science sociale et dans le droit contemporain* (Paris: Recueil Sirey, 1933), 4–5.

6 Martin Malia eloquently explains the double character of the Russian word for nationality, *narodnost*. "In the usage of the day, this slippery notion could signify at least two contradictory things." For some it meant primarily "'that which is national,' in the sense of the distinctive historic institutions of the Russian state . . . ." For others, however, it meant primarily "'that which is of the nation as a whole,' a concept which tended to set the people apart from the government." Martin Malia, *Alexander Herzen and the Birth of Russian Socialism, 1812–1855* (London: Oxford University Press, 1961), 284.

7 See, e.g., Ernest Renan, *Qu'est-ce qu'une nation?*, 2nd ed. (Paris: Calmann-Lévy, 1882); John Emerich Edward Dalberg, "Nationality," in *The History of Freedom and Other Essays*, eds. John Neville Figgis and Reginald Vere Laurence (London: Macmillan, 1907), 270–300; Pasquale Mancini, *Della nazionalità come fondamento del diritto delle genti* (Turin: Eredi Botta, 1851); George Cogordan, *La nationalité au point de vue des rapports internationaux* (Paris: L. Larose, 1879), 3.

8 A professor of history at the University of California, Berkeley, for whom Stephens Hall is named – a relic of an age when buildings, quadrangles, fountains, and courtyards were named after faculty administrators and important local personages in addition to (and not only) wealthy donors.

9 Henry Morse Stephens, "Nationality and History," *American Historical Review* 21, no. 2 (January 1916): 225–236. Stephens also implicates the historical profession in the reinvigoration of the nationalism of the "small nationalities" and chastises historians for their part in the rise of nationalist rivalry, exclaiming, "Woe unto us! professional historians, professional historical students, professional teachers of history, if we cannot see, written in blood, in the dying civilization of Europe, the dreadful result of exaggerated nationalism as set forth in the patriotic histories of some of the most eloquent historians of the nineteenth century." Ibid., 236. He makes an interesting point, and perhaps some enterprising graduate student might add to the voluminous literature apportioning blame for the First World War a tome further exploring his claim as to the damage historians can do.

10 Akzin, "Sociologie de la nationalité," 4–5. On Russian, see Malia, *Herzen*, 284.

11 Mancini, *Della nazionalità*. For the best English language summary of his work, see Sereni, *The Italian Conception of International Law*, 160–172.

12 Calvo, *Droit International*, 169.

13 Ibid., Vattel, *The Law of Nations, Or, Principles of the Law of Nature, Applied to the Conduct and Affairs of Nations and Sovereigns*, 67 (Prel., § 1.)
14 For an example of such a discussion, see B. Akzin, ed., *La Nationalité dans la science sociale et dans le droit contemporain* (Paris: Recueil Sirey, 1933). See especially Akzin, "Sociologie de la nationalité," 4–5.
15 Oppenheim, *International Law*, 370.
16 See, e.g., Mancini, *Della nazionalità*; Giuseppe Mazzini, *A Cosmopolitanism of Nations: Giuseppe Mazzini's Writings on Democracy, Nation Building, and International Relations*, eds. Stefano Recchia and Nadia Urbinati, trans. Stefano Recchia (Princeton, NJ: Princeton University Press, 2009), 53–65.
17 Samuel Moyn notes, "Nationalism had only one real nineteenth-century competitor as a contributor to rights language, namely the defense of contractual freedom and unregulated property." Samuel Moyn, "Giuseppe Mazzini in (and beyond) the History of Human Rights," in *Revisiting the Origins of Human Rights*, eds. Pamela Slotte and Miia Halme-Tuomisaari (Cambridge: Cambridge University Press, 2015), 121.
18 Mazzini, *Cosmopolitanism of Nations*, 61.
19 Mancini, *Della nazionalità*.
20 Mazzini, *Cosmopolitanism of Nations*, 134.
21 Cogordan, Nationalité au point de vue, 3–4.
22 Dalberg, "Nationality," 297–298.
23 Milton J. Esman has defined irredentas (those who engage in irredentism) as "territorially based minorities continuous to a state controlled by their co-ethnics." Milton J. Esman, "Ethnic Pluralism and International Relations," *Canadian Review of Studies in Nationalism* 17, nos. 1–2 (1990): 83.
24 For an argument about how this activity brought about World War I, see Laurence Lafore, *The Long Fuse: An Interpretation of the Origins of World War I* (Long Grove, IL: Waveland Press, 1997), chaps. 1–2. For a survey of irredentist claims prior to World War I, see Markus Kornprobst, *Irredentism in European Politics* (Cambridge: Cambridge University Press, 2008), 13. For excellent work on nationalist activism in the European land empires (particularly Austria-Hungary) prior to the First World War, see Pieter M. Judson, *Guardians of the Nation: Activists on the Language Frontiers of Imperial Austria* (Cambridge, MA: Harvard University Press, 2008); Jeremy King, *Budweisers into Czechs and Germans: A Local History of Bohemian Politics, 1848–1948* (Princeton, NJ: Princeton University Press, 2005); Tara Zahra, *Kidnapped Souls: National Indifference and the Battle for Children in the Bohemian Lands, 1900–1948* (Ithaca, NY: Cornell University Press, 2008); Tara Zahra, "Imagined Noncommunities: National Indifference as a Category of Analysis," *Slavic Review* 69, no. 1 (2010): 93–119. For Serbian irredentism and the First World War, see Christopher M. Clark, *The Sleepwalkers: How Europe Went to War in 1914* (London: Allen Lane, 2012), 20–27. For a survey of the role that nationalism played on the engendering of interstate conflict, see Gretchen Schrock-Jacobson, "The Violent Consequences of the Nation: Nationalism and the Initiation of Interstate War," *The Journal of Conflict Resolution* 56, no. 5 (October 2012): 825–852. But, for a different take, downplaying the role of ethnolinguistic politics

in geopolitics, see Denis Vovchenko, *Containing Balkan Nationalism: Imperial Russia and Ottoman Christians, 1856–1914* (Oxford: Oxford University Press, 2016).

25 For work on national indifference and ambiguity in the borderlands, see Zahra, "Imagined Noncommunities;" Zahra, *Kidnapped Souls*; Judson, *Guardians of the Nation*; Peter Sahlins, *Boundaries: The Making of France and Spain in the Pyranees* (Berkeley: University of California Press, 1989). For works on the politics of nationality and national identity on the border, see Judson, *Guardians of the Nation*; King, *Budweisers into Czechs and Germans*; Andrés Reséndez, *Changing National Identities at the Frontier: Texas and New Mexico, 1800–1850* (Cambridge: Cambridge University Press, 2004).

26 See, e.g., King, *Budweisers into Czechs and Germans*; Zahra, *Kidnapped Souls*. For PCIJ cases, see, e.g., Rights of Minorities in Upper Silesia (*Germ.* v. *Pol.*), 1928 PCIJ (ser. A) No. 15 (April 26); Minority Schools in Albania, Advisory Opinion, 1935 PCIJ (ser. A/B) No. 64 (April 6).

27 See A. Mitchell Palmer, "Why We Seized German Property," *The Forum* (December 1919): 584–592.

28 Eric Lohr, for example, argues that the Russian government's treatment of Kunst and Al'bers, a company owned and managed by naturalized Russian citizens, "demonstrated how the campaign [against enemy subjects] could spill over from a focus on enemy subjects to include long-naturalized Russian subjects and their enterprises. It was also quite typical in that while on the surface the main issue was security, upon closer inspection, the real issue becomes the attempt to shift economic power to *ethnic* Russians." Eric Lohr, *Nationalizing the Russian Empire: The Campaign against Enemy Aliens during World War I* (Cambridge, MA: Harvard University Press, 2003), 77–79, emphasis added.

29 Donald Bloxham, *The Final Solution: A Genocide* (Oxford: Oxford University Press, 2009), 73; Although it was hardly just Great Power intrigue. Emigré nationalists used the war and the interests of the Great Powers to push their own agenda. See the efforts of organizations like the League of Non-Russian Peoples. Alfred Erich Senn, "Garlawa: A Study in Émigré Intrigue, 1915–1917," *The Slavonic and East European Review* 45, no. 105 (July 1967): 411–424.

30 Vladimir Ilyich Lenin, "The Right of Nations to Self-Determination," in *Lenin's Collected Works*, vol. 20 (Moscow: Progress Publishers, 1972), 393–454; Ibid.

31 Ibid.

32 Ibid.

33 Vladimir Ilyich Lenin, "The Socialist Revolution and the Right of Nations to Self-Determination," in *Lenin's Collected Works*, vol. 22 (Moscow: Progress Publishers, 1972), 143–156.

34 See Manela, *Wilsonian Moment*, chaps. 2–3. See also Arno J. Mayer, *Wilson vs. Lenin: Political Origins of the New Diplomacy 1917–1918* (Cleveland, OH: World, 1964).

35 See Woodrow Wilson, *American and the League of Nations: Addresses in Europe*, eds. Lyman P. Powell and Fred B. Hodgins (New York: Rand McNally, 1919), 120–121.

36 President Wilson's Message to Congress, January 8, 1918. Wilson, in one of his earlier drafts for the League of Nations, had empowered the delegates to the body with the power to adjust territorial boundaries whenever such an adjustment became necessary "pursuant to the principle of self-determination." David Hunter Miller, *The Drafting of the Covenant* (New York: Putnam, 1928), 2:70. Scholars more familiar with irredentist agitation in Europe heavily critiqued such provisions. Ibid., 1:53.

37 For a fuller elaboration of Wilson's ideas about the state, see Woodrow Wilson, *The State: Elements of Historical and Practical Politics* (Boston, MA: D.C. Heath, 1889).

38 U.S. Congress, Senate, *Treaty of Peace with Germany*, 835–838. Also qtd. in H. M. V. Temperley, *A History of the Peace Conference of Paris* (London: Henry Frowde/Haughtier/Stoughton, 1924), 4:429.

39 Robert Lansing, *The Peace Negotiations: A Personal Narrative* (New York: Houghton Mifflin, 1921), 97.

40 On the efforts of ethnographers and for examples of the confusing results of plebiscites in which communities voted to belong to a state different from that of their self-identified ethnolinguistic background, see Sarah Wambaugh, *Plebiscites since the World War, with a Collection of Official Documents* (Washington, DC: Carnegie Endowment for International Peace, 1933), 1:99–205, 300. For a survey of the geo-political problems that the management of the minority problem caused, see Carole Fink, *Defending the Rights of Others: The Great Powers, the Jews, and International Minority Protection, 1878–1938* (Cambridge: Cambridge University Press, 2004), chaps. 7–8.

41 Ibid., 267. Opposition to these minority treaties, however, was fierce. Representatives of the new states claimed that by making national minorities aware "of the fact that the liberties which they enjoy are not guaranteed to them by the state to which they belong, but by the protection of a foreign state," the minority guarantees would endanger the integrity of the new states that the Great Powers were crafting at Versailles. Qtd. in Ibid., 233. The states initially subject to the minority regime were Poland, Czechoslovakia, Yugoslavia, Austria, Hungary, Bulgaria, Greece, and Romania. By agreement, the regime was later extended to encompass Turkey, Iraq, and German Upper Silesia. Additionally, Romania, Albania, Finland, Latvia, Estonia, and Lithuania accepted obligations with regard to minorities. LNA: CPDI 2, pp. 5–6.

42 See, e.g., Minorities Treaty between the Principal Allied and Associate Powers and Poland, June 28, 1919, 112 BSP 232, arts. 3, 4.

43 Ibid.

44 Treaty of Versailles, art. 91.

45 B. Traven, *The Death Ship* (Chicago, IL: Chicago Review Press, 1991), 254.

46 Treaty of Versailles, art. 91.

47 Traven, *Death Ship*, 256.

48 See Frank, *Making Minorities History*, chaps. 1–2.

49 Michael Robert Marrus, *The Unwanted* (Oxford: Oxford University Press, 1985), 71.

50 Ibid., 72.

51 R. M. Douglas, *Orderly and Humane: The Expulsion of the Germans after the Second World War* (New Haven, CT: Yale University Press, 2013).
52 Ibid.; Frank, *Making Minorities History*.
53 Reproduced in LN Doc. C.8 M.6.1931.1. 240–242.
54 See, LNOJ 7 (1926), 138. For another example, see the Polish proposal in LNOJ Special Supplement 120 (1933), 30.
55 See, e.g., LNOJ Special Supplement 73 (1929); LNOJ Special Supplement 120 (1933), 42–44.
56 Ibid., 23. See especially Carole Fink, "Defender of Minorities: Germany in the League of Nations, 1926–1933," *Central European History* 5, no. 4 (December 1972): 330–357.
57 LNOJ Special Supplement 120 (1933), 24.
58 Gesetz zur Wiederherstellung des Berufsbeamtentums, April 7, 1933, RGBL, Part I, 171–174; Gesetz über die Zulassung zur Rechtsanwaltschaft, April 7, 1933, RGBL, Part I, 188. See also Saul Friedländer, *Nazi Germany and the Jews*, vol. 1 (New York: HarperCollins, 1997).
59 Convention between Germany and Poland relating to Upper Silesia, May 15, 1922, 9 LNTS 465. For background to the convention, see Georges Silvain François Charles Kaeckenbeeck, "The Character and Work of the Arbitral Tribunal of Upper Silesia," *Transactions of the Grotius Society* 21 (1935): 27–29.
60 J. W. Brugel, "The Bernheim Petition: A Challenge to Nazi Germany in 1933," *Patterns of Prejudice* 17, no. 3 (1983): 17–19; Fink, *Defending the Rights of Others*, 330–333.
61 LNOJ Special Supplement 120 (1933), 29. See also Howard B. Calderwood, "The Proposed Generalization of the Minorities Régime," *American Political Science Review* 28 (1934): 1096.
62 LNOJ Special Supplement 120 (1933), 31.
63 Ibid., 24.
64 Greg Burgess has written a particularly fine article on the Bernheim petition and its influence on discrediting the minorities regime. Greg Burgess, "The Human Rights Dilemma in Anti-Nazi Protest: The Bernheim Petition, Minorities Protection, and the 1933 Sessions of the League of Nations," *CERC Working Papers Series*, no. 2 (2002). See also Greg Burgess, *The League of Nations and the Refugees from Nazi Germany: James G. McDonald and Hitler's Victims* (London: Bloomsbury Academic, 2016).
65 Burgess, "Human Rights Dilemma in Anti-Nazi Protest":3–4. See also René Cassin, "Les droits de l'homme," *Recueil des cours de l'Académie de Droit International de la Haye* 140 (1974): 324–325. This was in part because by the 1930s German officials refused to acknowledge that the Jewish population in Germany was a minority within the legal sense of the term.
66 LNOJ Special Supplement 120 (1933), 23.
67 LNOJ Special Supplement 109 (1932), 43–44.
68 Susan Pedersen, *The Guardians: The League of Nations and the Crisis of Empire* (Oxford: Oxford University Press, 2015), 71.
69 Treaty of Peace between the Allied and Associated Powers and Germany ("Versailles Treaty"), art. 127, June 28, 1919, 225 CTS 189.
70 Covenant of the League of Nations, art. 22.

71 See Iraqi Nationality Law of October 9, 1924 (Law 42/1924).
72 James C. Hales, "Some Legal Aspects of the Mandate System: Sovereignty-Nationality-Termination and Transfer," *Transactions of the Grotius Society* 23 (1937): 97–98.
73 Ibid., 101.
74 Covenant of the League of Nations, art. 22.
75 Ibid.
76 "Appendix 5: Report of the Discussions with the Belgian Government Representatives of the Mandates Sub-Committee Appointed to Investigate the Question of the Nationality of Subjects in Mandated Territories,"*LNOJ* 3 (1922): 600.
77 "Record of an Interview with the High Commissioner for the Union of South Africa,"*LNOJ* 3 (1922): 598–599.
78 "Appendix 5: Report of the Discussions," 602.
79 See, e.g., National Status of the Mandated Territories, LNA: 1/17831/16844 box R57 (1921).
80 "Appendix 5: Report of the Discussions," 602.
81 See, e.g., National Status of the Mandated Territories, LNA: 1/17831/16844 box R57 (1921).
82 Ibid. See also "Appendix 5: Report of the Discussions," 600–601.
83 "Appendix 5: Report of the Discussions," 602.
84 See, e.g., The proposal of Jan Smuts with regard to South West Africa and the proposal of Belgium with regard to Ruanda-Urundi, "Appendix 4: Record of an Interview with the High Commissioner for the Union of South Africa," *LNOJ* 3 (1922): 598–599; "Appendix 5: Report of the Discussions," 600; National Status of the Mandated Territories, LNA: 1/17831/16844 box R57 (1921); See generally Pedersen, *Guardians*, 71; P. Lampué, "De la nationalité des habitants des pays à mandat de la Société des Nations," *Journal du droit international* 52 (1925): 54–61.
85 See National Status of the Mandated Territories, LNA: 1/17831/16844 box R57 (1921).
86 "Appendix 5: Report of the Discussions," 604. While Rappard was probably concerned with disguised annexation, the Japanese arguments to the sub-committee of the Permanent Mandates Commission illustrate the counter-point that giving the inhabitants of a mandate the nationality of the Mandatory Power would be "contrary to the spirit of Article 22 . . ." because of the indigenous people's lower state of development. "[I]t would not be possible," the Japanese representative argued, "to give the populations under mandate the nationality of the Mandatory Power without abandoning the fundamental principle of the mandate itself [that of normative development and statehood]." National Status of the Mandated Territories, LNA: 1/17831/16844 box R57 (1921).
87 P. Lampué, "De la nationalité des habitants des pays à mandat de la Société des Nations," *Journal du droit international* 52 (1925): 57.
88 Qtd. in Hales, "Some Legal Aspects of the Mandate System":105; See Council Resolution of April 23, 1923.
89 Qtd. in Ibid.

90 Qtd. in Hales, "Some Legal Aspects of the Mandate System: Sovereignty-Nationality-Termination and Transfer," 107.
91 Ibid., 108–109.
92 Council Resolution of March 5, 1928.
93 Hales, "Some Legal Aspects of the Mandate System," 111.
94 By far the best article ever written on the Nationality Decrees Case was by the incomparable Nathaniel Berman. See Berman, "The Nationality Decrees Case, or, Of Intimacy and Consent."
95 Pierre Winkler, *Essai sur la nationalité dans les protectorats de Tunisie et du Maroc* (Paris: Jouve, 1926), 187.
96 LNA: 19/22787/22587, box R1280.
97 Ibid.
98 Ibid.
99 William Latey, "The Anglo-French Tunis Dispute," *Transactions of the Grotius Society* 9 (1923): 49–60.
100 Ibid.
101 *Advisory Opinion No. 4, Nationality Decrees Issued in Tunis and Morocco*, 4, Permanent Court of International Justice, February 7, 1923.
102 Ibid.
103 Institute of International Law, Résolutions relatives aux conflits de lois en matière de nationalité, Session de Venice, 1895. James Brown Scott, ed., *Resolutions of the Institute of International Law* (Oxford: Oxford University Press, 1916). This dream of making nationality mutually exclusive persisted through the interwar period as this chapter will discuss. But as the reader is surely aware by now, those draft treaties came to nothing. But it's worth pointing out now that still, in 1928, a report circulated in the British Home Office articulating many of the principles at the heart of those draft conventions: "In an ideal world everyone should acquire a nationality at birth and should retain that nationality until he voluntarily acquires another . . . ." Memorandum on the Deprivation of Nationality, April 20, 1928, UKNA: HO 45/15683.
104 League of Nations, Committee of Experts for the Progressive Codification of International Law, Opening Speech by the Chairman, LNA: CPDI 7, p. 8.
105 See the list of members, Committee of Experts for the Progressive Codification of International Law, Revised List of Members, LNA: CPDI 1. Hjalmar Hammarskjöld, Diena, Brierly, Fromageot, Guerrero, Loder, Kosters, Barbosa de Magalhaes, Mastny, Matsuda, Rafique, Rundstein, Schücking, Suarez, De Visscher, Chung-Hui, and Wickersham all served on the committee.
106 See, e.g., Provisional lists of matters presented by Hammarskjöld, J. G. Guerrero, Barboza, Mastny. Rundstein and Wickersham also include Nationality, although only behind Responsibility of States. League of Nations, Committee of Experts for the Progressive Codification of International Law, Provisional List of Matters, Presented by the President of the Committee (Hammarskjold), LNA: CPDI 10; League of Nations, Committee of Experts for the Progressive Codification of International Law, Provisional Lists of Matters Presented by Members of the Committee,

LNA: CPDI 11. See also League of Nations, Committee of Experts for the Codification of International Law, Note of Dr. Jose Leon Suarez, LNA: CPDI 12.

107 James Brown Scott and Victor M. Maúrtua, *Observations on Nationality* (Oxford: Oxford University Press, 1930), 2; James Brown Scott, "Nationality: Jus Soli or Jus Sanguinis," *American Journal of International Law* 24, no. 1 (January 1930): 58.

108 With the possible exceptions of Henri Fromageot and Charles de Visscher. The former had written quite extensively on the problems of nationality and had more than three decades earlier been skeptical that a solution could ever be reached based on the issues facing states then. Since the issues had not changed, he probably saw little reason for optimism. Henry Fromageot, *De la double nationalité des individus et des sociétés* (Paris: Librairie Nouvelle de Droit et de Jurisprudence, 1892), 111–112. The latter was Belgian and thus could likely not help but be pessimistic about the politics of nationality.

109 J. L. Brierly to Cecil, February 1, 1926, UKNA: HO 45/15681/8.

110 Scott, "Nationality: Jus Soli or Jus Sanguinis," 58–59.

111 "The Harvard Research on International Law: Nationality," *American Journal of International Law* 23, no. 2, Supplement: Codification of International law (April 1929): 21.

112 LN Doc. 1930.V.15.; LN Doc. C.351(a).M.145(a).1930.V., p. 50; Shabtai Rosenne, ed., *Conference for the Codification of International Law* (Dobbs Ferry, NY: Oceana, 1975), 3: 930.

113 See, e.g., Fromageot, *De la double nationalité des individus et des sociétés.*

114 Convention on Certain Questions relating to the Conflict of Nationality Laws, April 12, 1930, 179 LNTS 89.

115 M. R. Standaert (Belgium) in Acts of the Conference for the Codification of International Law, Meetings of the Committees, Vol. II, Minutes of the First Committee, Nationality. LN Doc. 1930.V.15.; LN Doc. C.351(a).M.145(a).1930.V., p. 50; Rosenne, *Conference for the Codification of International Law*, 3: 930.

116 Ibid.

117 Manley O. Hudson, "The First Conference for the Codification of International Law," *American Journal of International Law* 24, no. 3 (July 1930): 447–466.

118 U.S. Congress, Senate, *Treaty of Peace with Germany*, 835–838.

119 Miller, *Drafting of the Covenant*, 1:53, 2:71. Miller had instead advocated for a generalized system of protection of the rights of minorities.

120 *Sitzungsbericht des Kongresses der Organisierten Nationalen Gruppen in den Staaten Europas, Genf, 26. bis 28. August 1929*, vol. 5 (Vienna: Wilhelm Braumüller, 1930), 72. See also Jacob Robinson et al., *Were the Minorities Treaties a Failure* (New York: Institute of Jewish Affairs of the American Jewish Congress/the World Jewish Congress, 1943), 257.

121 For background on Ferenczi, see Ira De Augustine Reid, 1901–1968, Memorandum on Dr. Imre Ferenczi, ca. February 13, 1941, W. E. B. Du Bois Papers (MS 312), Special Collections and University Archives, University of Massachusetts Amherst Libraries.

122 Imre Ferenczi, "Aliens in the World and Nationals Abroad," *Social Service Review* 11, no. 4 (December 1937): 694.

123 Ibid.

Chapter 4

1 Henry Morse Stephens, "Nationality and History," *American Historical Review* 21, no. 2 (January 1916): 236.

2 I. S. K. Soboleff, *Nansen Passport: Round the World on a Motorcycle* (London: G. Bell, 1936), 35, 44–45.

3 Ibid., 81, 86, 88.

4 Soboleff, *Nansen Passport*, 88–89.

5 Ibid. 91–93.

6 Amélie Rorty, *Essays on Aristotle's Poetics* (Princeton, NJ: Princeton University Press, 1992), 1.

7 Edward Everett Hale, *The Man Without a Country* (Boston, MA: Roberts Brothers, 1891).

8 See, e.g., John William Burgess, *Political Science and Comparative Constitutional Law* (London: Ginn, 1893), 1:52: "Political science and public law do not recognize in principle the existence of any stateless persons within the territory of the state."

9 Marc Bloch, *Feudal Society* (Chicago, IL: University of Chicago Press, 1961), 224.

10 Michel Foucher dates the total compartmentalization of the world's territory to sometime in late nineteenth, probably between 1892 and 1914. Michel Foucher, *Fronts et frontières: Un tour du monde géopolitique* (Paris: Fayard, 1988), 29–31.

11 Joseph Conrad, *Heart of Darkness and Other Tales*, Oxford World's Classics (Oxford: Oxford University Press, 1992), 108.

12 See Frederick Jackson Turner, "The Significance of the Frontier in American History," *Annual Report of the American Historical Association* (1894): 119–227.

13 See Hale, *Man Without a Country*; Even the language used to describe the stateless had maritime overtones with jurists describing the stateless as "adrift." Piggott, *Nationality*, 1.

14 Or, rather, in a large lake in the case of Zweig. But not on dry land. Stefan Zweig, *The Collected Stories of Stefan Zweig*, trans. Anthea Bell (London: Pushkin Press, 2013), 587; B. Traven, *The Death Ship* (Chicago, IL: Chicago Review Press, 1991).

15 See John Torpey, *The Invention of the Passport* (Cambridge: Cambridge University Press, 2000).

16 See Anthony Giddens, *A Contemporary Critique of Historical Materialism*, vol. 2, The Nation State and Violence (Cambridge: Polity, 1985).

17 *Oxford English Dictionary*, 3rd ed., s.v. "stateless."

18 Based on a survey of texts contained in the digital archives of the Bibliothèque nationale de France, gallica.bnf.fr, which includes many major French periodicals in circulation in the nineteenth century.

19 Based on a survey of texts contained on gallica.bnf.fr, which includes most major French periodicals in circulation in the nineteenth century. *Nationalité* was itself of fairly recent vintage at the time, coming into use only in the nineteenth century. See Patrick Weil, *How to be French* (Durham, NC: Duke University Press, 2008).

20 *Staatentlos* first begins to appear in German in the late nineteenth century, often denoting those within the German Reich without a domicile, but occasionally being appropriated by international jurists (and often in French usage) to denote those without a state. See, e.g., *Annuaire de l'Institut de Droit International* 13 (1894): 163. But it does not become a regular fixture of the language to describe an international status until the early twentieth century. See also Kathrin Kollmeier, "Staatenlos in einer staatlich geordneten Welt. Eine politische Signatur des 20. Jahrhunderts im Spannungsfeld von Souveränität, Menschenrechten und Zugehörigkeit," *Neue Politische Literatur* 57 (2012): 49–66.

21 See, e.g., Johann Caspar Bluntschli, *Das moderne v ölkerrecht der civilisirten staten* (Nördlingen: Beck, 1878), 215–216 (§ 365), which was first published in 1868. Blüntschli makes use of the older *Heimatlosigkeit.*

22 See, e.g., Ernest J. Schuster, "The Effect of Marriage on Nationality," in *Thirty-Second Conference of the International Law Association (Conference on Nationality and Naturalization)* (International Law Association, 1923), 9–44; James Brown Scott and Victor M. Maúrtua, *Observations on Nationality* (Oxford: Oxford University Press, 1930).

23 G. M. W. Jellinghaus and R. S. Fraser, "International Law Association," in *Report of the Conference of the International Law Association*, vol. 30 (International Law Association, 1921), 293.

24 See, e.g., Scott and Maúrtua, *Observations on Nationality.*

25 On the reintroduction of passport controls, see Torpey, *Invention of the Passport*. For an example of the problem of the postwar emphasis on documentation and border security as expressed in postwar literature, see Traven, *Death Ship*.

26 Alexander Porter Morse, *A Treatise on Citizenship* (Boston, MA: Little, Brown, 1881), 114.

27 Ibid.

28 Bluntschli, *Das moderne v ölkerrecht der civilisirten staten*, 215–216 (§ 365).

29 Lassa Oppenheim, *International Law: A Treatise* (London: Longmans, Green, 1905), 1:345 (§ 291).

30 Ludwig von Bar, *The Theory and Practice of Private International Law*, 2nd ed. (Edinburgh: William Green, 1892), 137–138 (§ 55).

31 Census of the Russian Empire 1897.

32 This problem was further compounded by the mass internal displacement of Russians that had occurred during the war, a topic covered in depth in Peter Gatrell, *A Whole Empire Walking: Refugees in Russia During World War I* (Bloomington: Indiana University Press, 2005).

33 Michael Robert Marrus, *The Unwanted* (Oxford: Oxford University Press, 1985), chap. 2.

34 LNA: CRR 2, 1–3.

35 Qtd. in Annual Digest of Public International Law Cases, 1933–1934, No. 115, 116.

36 LNA: CRR 2, 4.

37 Wolf's letters on the subject from the summer of 1921 can be found in the archives of the League and the ILO. In addition he penned letters to the International Emigration Commission and the Secretary General of the League himself. See, e.g., Wolf to the Secretary Drummond with Attached Memoranda, August 15, 1921, LNA: CRR 8, ILO: R 201/10; Wolf to Ullswater, President of the International Emigration Commission, July 28, 1921, ILO: R 201/10. For an excellent account of Lucien Wolf's activities, background, and activities during the war, see Mark Levene, *War, Jews, and the New Europe: The Diplomacy of Lucien Wolf, 1914–1919* (Oxford: Littman Library of Jewish Civilization, 2009).

38 LNA: CRR 3 (45/14387/14387). Emphasis in original. Acting upon the advice of the Central Committee of the Russian Red Cross, a conference was convened in Paris in August of 1921. The conference contained representatives from more than a dozen Russian "committees." Present were the Conference of Russian Ambassadors, the Representatives of the Russian Army, the Central Committee of the Russian Red Cross, the Committee of the Zemstvos and Villages, the Committee of the Russian Parliament, the Russian National Committee, the Union for the Liberation and Restoration of Russia, the Commercial and Industrial Union, the Committee of Banks, the Association of Universities, the Association of Men of Letters, the Association of Private Railways, and the Association of Attorneys.

39 Ibid.

40 Ibid.

41 Hannah Arendt, *The Origins of Totalitarianism* (New York: Meridian, 1962), 290–304.

42 LNA: CRR 13A, 2 (August 26, 1921).

43 Vera Brittain, *Testament of Youth* (London: Weidenfeld/Nicolson, 2009), 485. For "athletic frame," see Robert Cecil, "Nansen and the League of Nations," *Le Nord*, no. 3 (1938): 191.

44 Brittain, *Testament of Youth*, 485.

45 Note for the International Labor Office, October 28, 1921, ILO: 204/2/1.

46 Extract of Report of the Meeting of Private Organizations, November 4, 1921, at the League of Nations, ILO 204/2/1.

47 Report of the Judicial Section on the Meeting of Private Russian Organizations, November 4, 1921, ILO: R 204/2/1, LNA: C.C.R.R./Organisations Privées/7; Memorandum on the Question of Russian Refugees, Presented at the Conference, August 1921, LNA: C.R.R. 9.

48 Note sur la situations juridique des réfugiés Russes en tane eu'ouvriers, er sur la manière de leur assurer la jouissance d'un statut regulier, November 24, 1921, ILO: R 204/2/1; Russian Refugees, General Report on the Work Accomplished up to February 1922, by Dr. Fridtjof Nansen, high commissioner of the League, pp. 15–16. ILO: R 201/20/4; Conférence Gouvernementale relative aux pieces d'indentité et facilities de visa pour les Réfugiés Russes, (Geneve, 3 Juillet 1922). LNA: C.R.R. 26; ILO: R 204/2/1. "Deux solutions semblent possibles: (1) Les Gouvernements des

pays où se trouvent les réfugiés leur délivreraient eux-mêmes des certificats d'identité speciaux," à titre temporaire. (2) Le Haut-Commissaire, au nom de la Société des Nations, et d'accord avec les Gouvernements, délivrerait des certificats d'identité spéciaux. See also LN Doc.: C.130.M.77.1922). The ILO was one of the organizations whose leadership did not think it was necessary that the Certificate be dealt with by the individual governments but could instead be handled by the high commissioner. See Note sur la situation juridique des refugies Russes en tant qu'ouvriers, et sure la maniere de leur assurer la jouissance d'un statut regulier, ILO: R 204/2/1.

49 On the issue of the status of Jews in the early discussions of international passports, see Dzovinar Kévonian, "Les juristes juifs russes en France et l'action internationale dans les années vingt," *Archives Juifs* 34 (2001/2): 90.

50 Circular to the delegates of the High Commissariat…, LNA: 45/29389/1593, box R1729.

51 Dzovinar Kévonian, "André Mandelstam and the Internationalization of Human Rights (1869–1949)," in *Revisiting the Origins of Human Rights*, eds. Pamela Slotte and Miia Halme-Tuomisaari (Cambridge: Cambridge University Press, 2015), 242; Kévonian, "Les juristes juifs russes en France et l'action internationale dans les années vingt," 90.

52 See Ukrainian Self-Reliance League of Canada to League of Nations Consultative Commission of High Commissioners, April 20, 1930. See also Le Délégué du Haut-Commissariat p.l. Réfugiés à Varsovie à M. T. F. Johnson, Chef de la Section d. Réfugiés, April 9, 1930; Ukrainian National Association to Commissioner Consultative Pre de Haut Commissaire de La Societé Des Nations, April 23, 1930. LNA: 20B/17080/17080, box C1568.

53 Arrangement Concerning the Extension to Other Categories of Refugees of Certain Measures Taken in Favour of Russian and Armenian Refugees, June 30, 1928, 89 LNTS 65.

54 For Nansen's request, see Report by the High Commissioner, L.N. Pub. 1927. XIII.3, p. 13.

55 LNOJ 8 (1927), 1137–1138.

56 This observation adds further support to Jane McAdam's claim that persecution was an implicit part of the legal construction of the refugee even in the early twentieth century. Jane McAdam, "Rethinking the Origins of 'Persecution' in Refugee Law," *International Journal of Refugee Law* 25, no. 4 (2014): 667–692.

57 Commission speciale technique pour l'examen de la situation juridique des réfugiés russes et armeniens, A.V./P.V.9 1928, League of Nations, Ninth Ordinary Session of the Assembly, Fifth Committee, Provisional Minutes, Ninth Meeting (Public), September 19, 1928, p. 8, LNA: Box C1913; ILO: R 409/0/5.

58 Ibid.

59 Ibid.

60 Special Technical Commission for the Examination of the Juridical Situation of the Russian and Armenian Refugees (1928), LNA: R 409/0/5, box C1413.

61 Ibid.

62 Arendt, *Origins of Totalitarianism*, 392.
63 André N. Mandelstam, "La protection internationale des droits de l'homme," *Recueil des cours de l'Académie de Droit International de la Haye* 38 (1931): 27–38.
64 See, e.g., Ukrainian Self-Reliance League of Canada to League of Nations Consultative Commission of High Commissioners, April 20, 1930; Le Délégué du Haut-Commissariat p.l. Réfugiés à Varsovie à M. T. F. Johnson, Chef de la Section d. Réfugiés, April 9, 1930; Ukranian National Association to Commissioner Consultative Pre de Haut Commissaire de La Societe Des Nations, April 23, 1930; LNA: 20B/17080/17080, box C1568.
65 LNA: 19/28033/28033x, box R1282.
66 LNA: 19/28033/28033x, box R1282 (emphasis in original).
67 For an example of a later form response, see LNA: 20A/80167/80165, box C1548.
68 Mandelstam, "La protection internationale des droits de l'homme":37–38.
69 Egidio Reale, "Le problème des passeports," *Recueil des cours de l'Académie de Droit International de la Haye* 50 (1934): 148–149. See also Egidio Reale, "The Passport Question," *Foreign Affairs* (April 1931).
70 See Nicolas Politis, *The New Aspects of International Law* (Washington, DC: Carnegie Endowment for International Peace, 1928), 18–31.
71 Qtd. in Report by the High Commissioner of the League, LNOJ Special Supplement 69 (1928), 93.
72 Stefan Zweig, *The World of Yesterday*, trans. Anthea Bell (Lincoln: University of Nebraska Press, 2013), 436.
73 André Siegfried, *La Crise de l'Europe* (Paris: Calmann-Lévy, 1935), 39. Siegfried himself made ample use of the quote and the idea of a borderless world for specifically Europeans in many of his other works as well. See, e.g., André Siegfried, *L'âme des peuples* (Paris: Librairie Hachette, 1950), 19–20: "I could actually say '*civis Romanus sum*,' and all barriers were lowered." André Siegfried, "Les nationalismes asiatiques et l'Occident," *Revue française de science politique* 1, nos. 1–2 (1951): 11: "If the white man encountered an obstacle he had only to say: '*civis Romanus sum*.'" For a larger contextualization of Siegfried within the debate over the meaning and fate of Europe in the interwar world, see Yannick Muet, *Les géographes et l'Europe: L'idée européenne dans la pensée géopolitique française de 1919 à 1939* (Geneva: Europa, Institut européen de l'Université de Genève, 1996), 32. Sadly, while Siegfried yearned for a return to a borderless world, for *la race blanche*, he did not want the same for *les jaunes* and the second half of his *La crise de l'Europe* harmonizes well with the oeuvre of Lothrop Stoddard. Siegfried, *La Crise de l'Europe*.
74 For criticisms of the saccharine nostalgia of Zweig and others of his ilk, particularly in the context of the actual rampant anti-Semitism in end of the century Vienna, see Robert S. Witrich, "Stefan Zweig and the 'World of Yesterday'," in *Stefan Zweig Reconsidered: New Perspectives on his Literary and Biographical Writings*, ed. Mark H. Gelber (Tubingen: Max Niemeyer, 2007), 60–61; Robert S. Witrich, *Laboratory for World Destruction: Germans and Jews in Central Europe* (Lincoln: University of Nebraska Press, 2007), 283; Steven Beller, "The World of Yesterday Revisited: Nostalgia, Memory,

and the Jews of Fin-de-siècle Vienna," *Jewish Social Studies* 2, no. 2 (1996): 37–53.

75 For a fascinating example of this requirement in action, see *O'Brien* v. *Cunard S.S. Co.,* 154 Mass. 272 (1891), a case in which an Irish immigrant to the United States sued for battery after having to undergo a mandatory smallpox vaccination she'd rather not have had. She lost.

76 See Adam M. McKeown, *Melancholy Order: Asian Migration and the Globalization of Borders* (New York: Columbia University Press, 2011); Aristide R. Zolberg, "The Great Wall against China: Responses to the First Immigration Crisis, 1885–1925," in *How Many Exceptionalisms?: Explorations in Comparative Macroanalysis, Politics, History, and Social Change* (New York: Temple University Press, 2009), 225–249; For restrictions on non-Asian migration and challenges to the golden age of migration narratives, see Laurent Dornel, *La France hostile: Socio-histoire de la xénophobie (1870–1914)* (Paris: Hachette, 2004); David Feldman, "Was the Nineteenth Century a Golden Age for Immigrants? The Changing Articulation of National, Local and Voluntary Controls," in *Migration Control in the North Atlantic World: The Evolution of State Practices in Europe and the United States from the French Revolution to the Inter-War Period,* eds. Andreas Fahrmeir, Olivier Faron, and Patrick Weil (New York: Berghahn Books, 2005), 167–177; Torpey, *Invention of the Passport,* chap. 4.

77 Herman Melville, *Moby Dick* (Boston, MA: St. Botolph Society, 1892), 46.

78 Jules Verne, *Le tour du monde en quatre-vingts jours* (Paris: Pierre-Jules Hetzel, 1873), chap. 7. While Nellie Bly packed a passport "signed by James G. Blaine," its true purpose (that of providing access to protection) was emphasized by a friendly suggestion that a "revolver would be a good companion piece or the passport." Nellie Bly, *Around the World in Seventy-Two Days and Other Writings* (New York: Penguin, 2014), 149.

79 Qtd. in Vincent Chetail, "Sovereignty and Migration in the Doctrine of the Law of Nations: An Intellectual History of Hospitality from Vitoria to Vattel," *European Journal of International Law* 27, no. 4 (2016): 904.

80 Hugo Grotius, *The Freedom of the Seas or the Right Which Belongs to the Dutch to Take Part in the East Indian Trade,* ed. James Brown Scott, trans. Ralph Van Deman Magoffin (New York: Oxford University Press, 1916), 8.

81 See Chetail, "Sovereignty and Migration in the Doctrine of the Law of Nations" for an excellent summary of the thought of Vitoria, Grotius, Wolff, Pufendorf, and Vattel on the subject.

82 For example, the US Supreme Court, quoting Vattel, held "It is an accepted maxim of international law, that every sovereign nation has the power, as inherent in sovereignty, and essential to its self-preservation, to forbid the entrance of foreigners within its dominions, or to admit them only in such cases and upon such conditions as it may see fit to prescribe." *Ekiu* v. *U.S.,* 142 U.S. 651 (1892). See also McKeown, *Melancholy Order.*

83 Institute of International Law, Principes recommandeés par l'Institut, en vue d'un projet de convention en matieère d'émigration, art. 1 (1897).

84 Torpey, *Invention of the Passport,* 111–117.

85 John Maynard Keynes, *The Economic Consequences of the Peace* (New York: Harcourt/Brace/Howe, 1920), 11–12.

86 While researching this section, I became a bit of a fan of Bonn, so, please excuse this long and self-indulgent footnote. One of Bonn's more notable achievements (from the perspective of the present author) was spending what was undoubtedly a temperate autumn of 1914 teaching at the University of California (when there was only one campus that bore the name – Go Bears). He then made his way eastward, spending an undoubtedly less-temperate winter and spring at the formidable University of Wisconsin and then to the less public, but no less frigid, Cornell University. See Moritz Julius Bonn, *So macht man Geschichte? Bilanz eines Lebens* (Munich: List, 1953), 162–169; Moritz Julius Bonn, *Wandering Scholar* (New York: John Day, 1948), 172–178. While a visiting professor in America, Bonn became an astute observer of American higher education and identified what was then (although it is probably no longer applicable) the primary difference between German and American higher education, writing "[While a visiting professor at the University of California in the autumn of 1914,] I had to adapt myself to American university conditions. In Germany the university may be said to have existed for the benefit of the professor, who considered himself a kind of demigod. In the United States the scales were inverted. The university existed for the benefit of the students, for the glory of the trustees and the reminiscent happiness of the alumni." Ibid., 172. Bonn also had the less notable achievements (again, from the perspective of the present author) of serving as a member of the German delegation to the Paris Peace Conference and of preparing the German translation of John Maynard Keynes' *The Economic Consequences of the Peace*. See Gerald D. Feldman, *The Great Disorder: Politics, Economics, and Society in the German Inflation, 1914–1924* (Oxford: Oxford University Press, 1993), 310; Bonn, *Wandering Scholar*, 227. He also had the dubious honor of being expelled from his academic post by the Nazi government on the same day as Albert Einstein and receiving a comparable level of attention from the press. Patricia Clavin, "A 'Wandering Scholar' in Britain and the USA, 1933–1945: The Life and Work of Moritz Bonn," in *Refugees from the Third Reich in Britain*, ed. Anthony Grenville, Yearbook of the Research Centre for German and Austrian Exile Studies (New York: Editions Rodopi, 2003), 27. Needless to say, one of those two figures has since seen a considerable decline in public attention. Patricia Clavin seems to have been the only anglophone scholar to have recently written about him at length – hence, why I felt compelled to write this overlong footnote.

87 Moritz Julius Bonn, *The Crisis of European Democracy* (New Haven, CT: Yale University Press, 1925), 2–3. The ease with which Bonn was able to move is well illustrated in his delightful memoir, *Wandering Scholar*. See Bonn, *Wandering Scholar*.

88 Siegfried, *La Crise de l'Europe*, 39.

89 Zweig, *World of Yesterday*, 436–438.

90 Verne, *Le tour du monde en quatre-vingts jours*, chap. 7.

91 Patrick Leigh Fermor, *A Time of Gifts* (New York: New York Review Books, 1977), 111. In yet another example of the type of service one could expect from a consul, while in Munich, Fermor's backpack was stolen with his passport and money. He turned, as one would, to the trusty British consul

who provided him with a new passport, five pounds, and suggestions on where to find temporary employment.

92 Traven, *Death Ship*.
93 Ibid. 44.
94 Ibid., 41.
95 Zweig, *Collected Stories of Stefan Zweig*, 587.
96 Covenant of the League of Nations, art. 23(e).
97 *Handbook on the League of Nations*, 1920–1923, League of Nations 5, no. 4 (New York: World Peace Foundation, 1923), 287; Minutes of the Meetings of the Provisional Committee of Communications and Transit Held at Paris, October 15, 1920, LNA: 14/7612x/5097, box R1092.
98 Ibid.
99 See Adam Tooze, *Statistics and the German State, 1900–1945: The Making of Modern Economic Knowledge* (Cambridge: Cambridge University Press, 2001), 77; David M. Kennedy, *Over Here: The First World War and American Society* (Oxford: Oxford University Press, 2004), chap. 2; Axel R. Schäfer, "The Emergence of the Liberal Welfare State," in *American Progressives and German Social Reform, 1875–1920: Social Ethics, Moral Control, and the Regulatory State in a Transatlantic Context* (Stuttgart: Franz Steiner Verlag, 2000), 213–233.
100 Minutes of the Meetings of the Provisional Committee of Communications and Transit. . . .
101 Ibid.
102 League of Nations, Provisional Committee on Communications and Transit, Conference on Passports, Customs Formalities and Through Tickets, Resolution Adopted by the Conference, p. 3. LNA: 14/7730/5097, box R1092. Also produced as LN Doc. C.641.M.230.1925.VIII.
103 Other major NGOs supporting the abolition were the International Shipping Conference ("the state of affairs prevailing before the war should be restored as quickly as possible . . . the passport system should disappear.") and the Passport and Postal Reform Committee (10). League of Nations, Organisation for Communications, Passport Conference, LNA: C.P./P.V.1, pp. 9–10. Also produced as LN Doc. C.423M.156.1926.VIII.
104 League of Nations, Organisation for Communications, Passport Conference, LNA: C.P./P.V.1.
105 League of Nations, Organisation for Communications, Passport Conference, LNA: C.P./P.V.1, 21–22.
106 Ibid.
107 Ibid.
108 See, Minutes of the Meetings of the Provisional Committee of Communications and Transit. . . .
109 League of Nations, Advisory and Technical Committee for Communications and Transit, Passport Conference, Preparatory Documents, May 7, 1926, Annex, "I. Issue of Uniform Internationally-Recognised Passports to Persons Without Nationality," LNA: C.P./1.1926 (CCT/Passports/1).
110 League of Nations, Passport Conference, Final Act, LN Doc. C.320.M.119.1926.VIII, § 3.

111 Qtd. in League of Nations, Third General Conference on Communications and Transit, Geneva, August 23–September 2, 1927, Vol. III, Records and Texts Relating to Identity and Traveling Documents for Persons Without Nationality or of Doubtful Nationality, 44. LN Doc. C.558(b).M.200(b).1927.VIII; LNA: 14/61455/48711; See also Reale, "Le problème des passeports," 148.
112 League of Nations, Third General Conference on Communications and Transit, Geneva, August 23–September 2, 1927, Vol. III, Records and Texts Relating to Identity and Traveling Documents for Persons Without Nationality or of Doubtful Nationality. LN Doc. C.558(b).M.200(b).1927.VIII; LNA: 14/61455/48711.
113 Ibid., 9.
114 Ibid.
115 Ibid., 10.
116 Ibid., 11–12.
117 Ibid., 14–15.
118 Ibid., 11, 34, 36.
119 Ibid., 15–18.
120 Ibid.
121 Peter Pavel Remec, *The Position of the Individual in International Law According to Grotius and Vattel* (The Hague: Martinus Nijhoff, 1960), 243.
122 Ibid.
123 For a late example also, e.g., the writing of German jurist Franz von Liszt, who wrote "International law grants rights and obligations only to states themselves, not their nationals. A state stands between its nationals and the international community of states." Franz von Liszt, *Das Völkerrecht systematisch dargestellt* (Berlin: O. Häring, 1906), 40.
124 August Wilhelm Heffter, *Das Europäische Völkerrecht der Gegenwart auf den bisherigen Grundlagen* (Berlin: G. H. Schroeder, 1867), §§ 1–2.
125 Ibid.
126 See, e.g., Henry Wheaton, *Elements of International Law*, 8th, ed. Richard Henry Dana (Boston, MA: Little, Brown, 1866), pt. I, § 10; Politis, *New Aspects of International Law*, 19.
127 Again, the German jurist Franz von Liszt is a great illustration here. While he was adamant in 1906 that only states were subjects of international law, he conceded that "in the decrees of the 'International Commission' we have the first beginnings of an international law directly binding the citizens of the various states" before reiterating that it was "these shy beginnings" tended to confirm the more general rule. Liszt, *Das Völkerrecht systematisch dargestellt*.
128 See the excellent work here by Cécile Laborde: Cécile Laborde, "Pluralism, Syndicalism and Corporatism: Léon Duguit and the Crisis of the State (1900–1925)," *History of European Ideas* 22, no. 3 (1996): 227–244; Cécile Laborde, "The Concept of the State in French and British Political Thought," *Political Studies* 48 (2000): 540–557. For a brief overview of different theories on the subject, see Carl Aage Norgaard, *The Position of the Individual in International Law* (Copenhagen: Munksgaard, 1962), chaps. 4–5.

129 Qtd. in Georges Davy, *Le droit, l'idéalisme, et l'expérience* (Paris: Félix Alcan, 1922), 76.

130 Quincy Wright, "The Legal Nature of Treaties," *American Journal of International Law* 10 (1916): 717. See also Shinohara, *US International Lawyers in the Interwar Years: A Forgotten Crusade*, 27.

131 Georges Scelle, "Règles générales du droit de la paix," *Recueil des cours de l'Académie de Droit International de la Haye* 46 (1933): 343; See also Georges Scelle, *Précis de droit des gens: Principes et systematique* (Paris: Sirey, 1932), 1:35–38.

132 Politis, *New Aspects of International Law.*

133 See, e.g., Hans Kelsen, "Les rapports de système entre le droit interne et le Droit International Public," *Recueil des cours de l'Académie de Droit International de la Haye* 14 (1926): 280–283; Hersch Lauterpacht, *Private Law Sources and Analogies of International Law: With Special Reference to International Arbitration* (London: Longmans, Green, 1927), 74–79; Jean Spiropoulos, *L'Individu en droit international* (Paris: Librairie générale de droit et de jurisprudence, 1928); Hans Herz, "Le sujet de droit en droit international public," *Revue internationale de la théorie du droit* 10 (1936): 100–111; and see the survey of the literature made by Cezary Berezowski, "Les sujets non souverains du droit international," *Recueil des cours de l'Académie de Droit International de la Haye* 65 (1938): 5–87. See also Peters, *Beyond Human Rights: The Legal Status of the Individual in International Law*, 16–21.

134 *Legal Personality in International Law* (Cambridge: Cambridge University Press, 2010), chap. 10.

135 See, e.g., Berezowski, "Les sujets non souverains du droit international."

136 Edvard I. Hambro and Edgar Turlington, "Individuals before International Tribunals," *Proceedings of the American Society of International Law at Its Annual Meeting (1921–1969)* 35 (April 1941): 22.

137 See the response of Alwyn Freeman to Frederick Dunn in Frederick Sherwood Dunn and Alwyn V. Freeman, "The International Rights of Individuals," *Proceedings of the American Society of International Law at Its Annual Meeting (1921–1969)* 35 (April 1941): 14–22.

138 Edwin M. Borchard, "The Access of Individuals to International Courts," *American Journal of International Law* 24, no. 2 (April 1930): 359–365. Although as the Convention on the Settlement of Investment Disputes between States and Nationals of Other States seems to make clear, quite a few states were willing to do just that when it was tied to claims of economic efficiency.

139 Borchard, "Access of Individuals to International Courts" 362.

140 Ibid., 361: "This is often a matter of form only, that in practice the private individual is the essential prosecutor and beneficiary of the claim, and that his State . . . actually appears in most cases in a representative character only."

141 Ibid., 362–363.

142 Dunn and Freeman, "International Rights of Individuals" 20–21.

143 Dunn himself noted that law often had two competing functions, descriptive and normative. "One is a description of reality, and the other is a norm of conduct." Ibid.

144 References to the US Supreme Court in discussions of international courts abounded in the 1880s and 1890s. Even as far back as 1865, John Stewart Mill looked upon the US Supreme Court with awe and envy, noting, "The Supreme Court of the Federation dispenses *international law*, and is the first great example of what is now one of the most prominent wants of international society, a real international tribunal." John Stuart Mill, *The Collected Works of John Stuart Mill*, ed. John M. Robson, vol. 19 (Toronto: University of Toronto Press, 1977), 558, emphasis added.

145 See the Dutch and German proposals as well as the submission made by Henri La Fontaine on behalf of the Inter-Parliamentary Union: Permanent Court of International Justice and Advisory Committee of Jurists, *Documents Presented to the Committee Relating to Existing Plans for the Establishment of an International Court of Justice* (The Hague: Van Langenhuysen Brothers, 1920), 27–31, 127, 285, 335–337; Rapport au nom de la commission spéciale de l'Union Interparlementaire, Projet de convention relative à l'établissement d'une cour internationale de justice, June 1920, p. 2, LNA: 21/6018/859, box R1300.

146 Permanent Court of International Justice and Advisory Committee of Jurists, *Documents Presented to the Committee Relating to Existing Plans for the Establishment of an International Court of Justice*, 211.

147 Rapport au nom de la commission spéciale de l'Union Interparlementaire, Projet de convention relative à l'établissement d'une cour internationale de justice, June 1920, p. 2, LNA: 21/6018/859, box R1300.

148 Permanent Court of International Justice and Advisory Committee of Jurists, *Procès-Verbaux of the Proceedings of the Committee, June 16th–July 24th, 1920 with Annexes* (The Hague: Van Langenhuysen Brothers, 1920), 203–217.

149 Ibid., 204, 215–216.

150 Manley O. Hudson, *The Permanent Court of International Justice: 1920–1942* (New York: Macmillan, 1943), 187; Permanent Court of International Justice and Advisory Committee of Jurists, *Procès-Verbaux of the Proceedings of the Committee, June 16th–July 24th, 1920 with Annexes*, 216.

151 See *Mavrommatis Palestine Concessions* (*Greece* v. *Gr. Brit.*), 1924 P.C.IJ. (ser. A) No. 2, at 12; *Panevezys-Saldutiskis Railway* (*Est.* v. *Lith.*), 1938 PCIJ (ser. A/B) No. 76 (February 28). However, this was challenged with the proposed creation of a chamber for commercial disputes. See Chapter 5, *infra* Proposals were also put forward by the Institute of International Law in 1929 advocating for an expanded competency.

152 Edwin Borchard's proposed solution to the inefficiencies of diplomatic protection was to make use of Article 36 of the Statute of the Permanent Court of International Justice, which recognized the PCIJ's compulsory jurisdiction and set up a process for individuals to bring claims so long as they have the endorsement of their own state. Borchard, "The Access of Individuals to International Courts," 364. There were others who made similar proposals, e.g., Martin T. Manton, "Reorganization and Rehabiliation of Government

Bond Issues," *Proceedings of the American Society of International Law at Its Annual Meeting (1921–1969)* (1934): 146–155.

153 See, e.g., *Societé Commerciale de Belgique* (*Belg.* v. *Greece*), 1939 PCIJ (ser. A/B) No. 78 (June 15); *Losinger and Co.* (*Switz.* v. *Yugo.*), 1936 PCIJ (ser. A/B) No. 69 (Order of December 14); *Payment of Various Serbian Loans Issued in France* (*Fr.* v. *Yugo*), 1929 PCIJ (ser. A) No. 20 (July 12); *Payment in Gold of Brazilian Federal Loans Contracted in France* (Fr. Braz.), 1929 PCIJ (ser. A) No. 21 (July 12); See also Manley O. Hudson, *International Tribunals: Past and Future* (Washington, DC: Carnegie Endowment for International Peace, 1944), 190.

154 Publications of the Permanent Court of International Justice (1922–1946), Series E: Annual Reports, no. 1, Annual Report from 1922 to 1925, p. 153–156; Politis, *New Aspects of International Law*, 30.

155 See, e.g., the declarations issued by the American Society of International Law and the International Juridical Union. Both texts are available in: Annuaire de l'Institut de Droit International (1921): 208–210. The American Declaration also available in: Elihu Root, "The Declaration of the Rights and Duties of Nations Adopted by the American Institute of International Law," *American Journal of International Law* 10, no. 2 (1916): 211–221.

156 See, e.g., the American Society of International Law's Declaration of the Rights and Duties of Nations, article 4: "Every nation has the right to territory within defined boundaries...," article 3: "Every nation is in law and before law the equal of every other nation... " Ibid., 213; the International Juridical Union's Declaration of the Rights and Duties of States, article 2: "L'État est independant...," article 3: "Les états sont égaux devant le Droit." *Annnuaire de l'Institut de Droit International* (1921), 210.

157 *Annuarie de l'Institut de Droit International* (1921), 208: "Art. 6 – Les états ont des devoirs, au regard non seulement des autres Etats, mais des hommes; ils est des cas où le devoir, au regard des individus et des groups, de faire respecter leur vie, leur liberté, leurs croyances, prime celui de respecter la libterté des autres états."

158 Ibid., 218.

159 See "Déclaration des droits internationaux de l'Homme," *Annuaire de l'Insitut de Droit International* (1929), 538. For Mandelstam's earlier reports by the committee, see *Annuaire de l'Insitut de Droit International* (1925), 246–392; *Annuaire de l'Insitut de Droit International* (1928), 275–311; *Annuaire de l'Insitut de Droit International* (1929), 1:715–732, 2: 110–138. See also Mandelstam, "La protection internationale des droits de l'homme," 199–203. For an analysis of Mandelstam's ultimate role in the later Universal Declaration of Human Rights, see Helmut Philipp Aust, "From Diplomat to Academic Activist: André Mandelstam and the History of Human Rights," *European Journal of International Law* 25, no. 4 (November 2014): 1105–1121; Burgers, "The Road to San Francisco: The Revival of the Human Rights Idea in the Twentieth Century." See also Dzovinar Kévonian, "Exilés politiques et avènement du 'droit humain': La pensée juridique d'André Mandelstam," *Revue d'histoire de la Shoah*, nos. 177–178

(January 2001): 245–273; Kévonian, "André Mandelstam and the Internationalization of Human Rights (1869–1949)." For the resolution suggesting the desirability of recognizing individuals in certain cases, see *Annuaire de l'Insitut de Droit International* (1929), 311; Mandelstam, "La protection internationale des droits de l'homme," 203.

160 On the impact of the declaration in later years, see Burgers, "Road to San Francisco."

161 See Jean Eyma, *La cour de justice Centre-Américaine* (Paris: E. Sagot, 1928); Manley O. Hudson, "The Central American Court of Justice," *American Journal of International Law* 26, no. 4 (October 1932): 759–786.

162 Ibid.

163 Polish Convention concerning Upper Silesia of 15 May 1922, 9 LNTS 466.

164 *Steiner and Gross* v. *Polish State*, 4 AD 291 (1928).

165 For an example of this type of subsequent advocacy, see Georges Silvain François Charles Kaeckenbeeck, *The International Experiment of Upper Silesia: A Study in the Working of the Upper Silesian Settlement, 1922–1937* (Oxford: Oxford University Press, 1942).

166 See, e.g., Hersch Lauterpacht, "The Subjects of the Law of Nations," *Law Quarterly Review* (1947).

167 For Mandelstam as an intellectual pioneer of the Universal Declaration, see Burgers, "Road to San Francisco." For Mandelstam's advocacy of individual rights as an alternative to the minority regime, see Aust, "From Diplomat to Academic Activist." For a contemporary view of human rights as a response to the failure of minority rights, see Mark Mazower, "The Strange Triumph of Human Rights," *Historical Journal* 47, no. 2 (June 2004): 379–398. For an example of advocacy in favor of the generalization of the minority rights regime, see Howard B. Calderwood, "The Proposed Generalization of the Minorities Régime," *American Political Science Review* 28 (1934): 1088–1098.

168 Soboleff, *Nansen Passport*, 92.

169 Ibid.

170 Soboleff, *Nansen Passport: Round the World on a Motorcycle*, 94.

171 Ibid., 138–139.

172 Ibid., 139.

173 Ibid.

174 Ibid.

175 Ibid. He had previously been supported by Dunlop (switching brands was apparently easier in the days before exclusivity contracts). Ibid., 91.

176 Soboleff, *Nansen Passport*, 213.

177 Ibid., 216.

178 See Soboleff, *Nansen Passport: Round the World on a Motorcycle.*

179 Ibid., 235.

180 See Ibid., 238.

Chapter 5

1 *Fifth International Congress of Chambers of Commerce and Commercial and Industrial Associations: September and October, 1912* (Boston, MA: Boston Chamber of Commerce, 1912), 162.

2 V. V. Veeder, "International Arbitration: A Lesson Learnt from Anglo-US Mining Concessions in Soviet Russia (1920–1925)," in *International and Comparative Mineral Law and Policy: Trends and Prospects*, eds. Elizabeth Bastida, Thomas Walde, and Janeth Warden-Fernandez, International Energy and Resources Law and Policy Series (Kluwer, 2004), 118.

3 Short for Lenskoye Zolotopromyshlennoye Tovarishchestvo or Lena Goldmining Company. Terence E. Armstrong, *Russian Settlement in the North* (Cambridge: Cambridge University Press, 1965), 94. Lena Goldfields, Ltd. acquired its shares from the Lena Shares Company (Lenskoe Paevoe Tovarishchestvo), established in 1861 as the parent company of Lenzoto. Michael Melancon, *Lena Goldfields Massacre and the Crisis of the Late Tsarist State* (College Station, TX: Texas A & M University Press, 2006), 26.

4 V. V. Veeder, "The Lena Goldfields Arbitration: The Historical Roots of Three Ideas," *International and Comparative Law Quarterly* 47, no. 4 (October 1998): 757; Armstrong, *Russian Settlement in the North*, 94. In the 1840s, gold had been discovered in Siberia in the Lena watershed and a minor rush to Siberia ensued. The hostile climate and inaccessibility of Siberia, no doubt, was responsible for this Gold Rush being somewhat smaller than its more well-known contemporary in the beautiful and temperate foothills of the Sierra Nevada mountains in the Golden State. In the Lena watershed, nighttime summer temperatures often fall below freezing (to say nothing of the winter temperatures). At the height of summer, the mosquitos were apparently so bad that even the elk "withdrew into the swamps and immersed themselves to their necks to protect their bodies." Yet, despite the hostile climate, gold drew in enough prospectors to sift through surface sands in search of fortune so that by the 1860s the region had been all but stripped of the easily accessible gold on the surface. To draw out gold from beneath the surface would require a substantially greater investment than some shovels, picks, and pans, hence the creation of Lenzoto. Melancon, *Lena Goldfields Massacre and the Crisis of the Late Tsarist State*, 11–12, 14, 26.

5 Veeder, "Lena Goldfields Arbitration: The Historical Roots of Three Ideas":757.

6 Exact figures on the number of casualties are unavailable with reports varying from roughly 200–500. Melancon, *Lena Goldfields Massacre and the Crisis of the Late Tsarist State*, 102–103.

7 Ibid., 3.

8 Veeder, "International Arbitration," 99.

9 Gustav Cassel, "An International Monetary Conference," *Economist* (May 1919): 819. One of the first cases of conciliation that would come before the International Court of Arbitration set up by the International Chamber of Commerce (ICC) involved a dispute between a Dutch and English firm over just this issue. ICC, "Arbitration Report," *Record* 7 (June 1923): 2.

10 Charles Frist, "Protection and Free Trade in the Europe of To-day," in *Europe Year-Book*, eds. Michael Farbman, Ramsay Muir, and Hugh F. Spender (London: Europa, 1926), 126.

11 Joseph S. Davis, "World Currency and Banking: The First Brussels Financial Conference," *Review of Economics and Statistics* 2, no. 12 (December 1920): 356.

12 Frist, "Protection and Free Trade in the Europe of To-day," 155; London, "The Economic Situation in Europe," in *Europe Year-Book*, eds. Michael Farbman, Ramsay Muir, and Hugh F. Spender (Europa, 1926), 158.

13 See League of Nations, *The World Economic Conference, Geneva, May 1927, Final Report*, 29. See also League of Nations, *Final Report of the Trade Barriers Committee of the International Chamber of Commerce*, C.E.I. 5(1), League Pub. 1926.II.62.

14 Territorial sovereignty was indirectly guaranteed by Articles 10 and 16 of the Covenant. Covenant of the League of Nations, arts. 10, 16.

15 See Arendt, *The Origins of Totalitarianism.*

16 Douglass C. North, "Institutions," *Journal of Economic Perspectives* 5, no. 1 (January 1991): 30; See also Peter Mathias, "Risk, Credit, and Kinship in Early Modern Enterprise," in *The Early Modern Atlantic Economy*, eds. John H. McCusker and Kenneth Morgan (Cambridge: Cambridge University Press, 2001), 15–35; Francesca Trivellato, *The Familiarity of Strangers: The Sephardic Diaspora, Livorno, and Cross-Cultural Trade in the Early Modern Period* (New Haven, CT: Yale University Press, 2009).

17 Jacob M. Price and James D. Tracy, "Transaction Costs: A Note on Merchant Credit and the Organization of Private Trade," in *The Political Economy of Merchant Empires*, ed. James D. Tracy (Cambridge: Cambridge University Press, 1991), 279; Trivellato, *Familiarity of Strangers*.

18 See S. R. Epstein, *Freedom and Growth: The Rise of States and Markets in Europe, 1300–1750* (London: Routledge, 2000). On the role of institutions in facilitating global trade and economic growth, see North, "Institutions." However, the view that these trade associations enabled rather than hindered global trade has not been without criticism. See Sheilagh Ogilvie, *Institutions and European Trade: Merchant Guilds, 1000–1800* (Cambridge: Cambridge University Press, 2011).

19 Philipp Karl Ludwig Zorn, *Das Deutsche Reich und Die Internationale Schiedsgerichtsbarkeit* (Berlin: Walther Rothschild, 1911), 45–47. At the Congress of the Inter-Parliamentary Union in 1912, Zorn would himself propose the establishment of a court to decide on judicial rather than political questions (like the PCA did) and particularly to decide issues on matters of private international law between both states and individuals. Union interparlementaire, *Compte rendu de la XVIIe conférence, tenue a Genève du 18 au 20 septembre 1912* (Brussels: Misch and Thron, 1913), 210. See also Philipp Karl Ludwig Zorn, "La juridiction arbitrale dans la vie des peuples et dans le droit international," in *Compte rendu de la XVIIe conférence, tenue à Genève du 18 au 20 septembre 1912*, 14.

20 Although there had been dozens of Claims Commissions established in the previous century via treaty. As discussed in earlier chapters, these commissions were established by two states in order to allow their nationals to bring claims against the states assenting to the commission.

21 In Britain, for example, since the sovereign could do no wrong, any individual wishing to make a claim against the government had to revert to the legal fiction presented in the Petition of Right. This requirement to get the permission of the Crown to sue it in court lasted until 1947.

22 See John Fischer Williams and Charles de Visscher, *International Law and International Financial Obligations Arising from Contract* (Leiden: Brill, 1924), 11; For excerpts of Lord Palmerston's famous circular on the subject, see Jackson H. Ralston, *The Law and Procedure of International Tribunals*, revised ed. (Stanford, CA: Stanford University Press, 1926), 76.

23 On power-differences and legalist imperialism, see Benjamin Allen Coates, "Securing Hegemony through Law: Venezuela, the U.S. Asphalt Trust, and the Uses of International Law, 1904–1909," *Journal of American History* 102, no. 2 (September 2015): 380–405.

24 Williams and Visscher, *International Law and International Financial Obligations Arising from Contract*, 50–51; G. Hornsey, "Foreign Investment and International Law," *International Law Quarterly* 3, no. 4 (October 1950): 554–555 The United States was particularly good at obtaining compensation for expropriated oil and mineral resources. In only six non-Soviet cases did investors lose the value of their investments. See Noel Maurer, *The Empire Trap: The Rise and Fall of U.S. Intervention to Protect American Property Overseas, 1893–2013* (Princeton, NJ: Princeton University Press, 2013), 3. States did, indeed, acknowledge the hazard. But, as the British Foreign Secretary Edward Grey put it, "Such a large amount of British money had been invested in countries of doubtful honour, under the impression that the British government would prevent swindling," that it would be difficult to resist intervening. Qtd. in Martha Finnemore, *The Purpose of Intervention: Changing Beliefs About the Use of Force* (Ithaca, NY: Cornell University Press, 2003), 35.

25 See, e.g., Conrad Georg Friedrich Elias von Schmidt-Phiseldek, *Der Europäische Bund* (Copenhagen: Friderich Brummer, 1821), chap. 9; P. R. Marchand, *Nouveau projet de traité de paix perpétuelle* (Paris: J. Renouard, 1842), 327: P. R. Marchand, in Article 96 of his proposal for perpetual European peace, calls for a court with jurisdiction over disputes "3. Between citizens of different states; 4. Between a state or its citizens or subjects and foreign states, citizens, or subjects."

26 For an overview of the crisis, see Brian S. McBeth, *Gunboats, Corruption, and Claims: Foreign Intervention in Venezuela, 1899–1908* (Westport, CT: Greenwood Press, 2001).

27 The letter quickly became a hot topic of discussion within international law circles. See Luis M. Drago, "State Loans in Their Relation to International Policy," *American Journal of International Law* 1, no. 3 (July 1907): 692–726; Amos S. Hershey, "The Calvo and Drago Doctrines," *American Journal of International Law* 1, no. 1 (January 1907): 26–45; Henri-Alexis Moulin, *La doctrine de Drago* (Paris: A. Pedone, 1908). See also Luis M.

Drago and H. Edward Nettles, "The Drago Doctrine in International Law and Politics," *Hispanic American Historical Review* 8, no. 2 (May 1928): 204–223.

28 United States Department of State, *Foreign Relations of the United States, 1903* (Washington, DC: Government Printing Office, 1904), 1–2.

29 One criticism of the intervention in Venezuela explicitly compared it to the Don Pacifico affair and, with nostalgic approval, cited Cobdon's outraged response to Palmerston's armed intervention. "Don Pacifico – Venezuela: A Parallel," *The Manchester Guardian*, February 4, 1903, p. 10.

30 The Hague II: Limitation of Employment of Force for Recovery of Contract Debts (The Hague 1907 [II]), art. 1, October 18, 1907, 205 CTS 537. For a fantastic overview and argument about the negotiations and the origins of the convention, see Finnemore, *Purpose of Intervention: Changing Beliefs About the Use of Force*.

31 *Fifth International Congress of Chambers of Commerce and Commercial and Industrial Associations: September and October, 1912*, 159.

32 Ibid.

33 Edwin M. Borchard, "Contractural Claims in International Law," *Columbia Law Review* 13, no. 6 (June 1913): 458.

34 Borchard, "Contractural Claims in International Law":498.

35 Joseph Conrad, *Nostromo* (New York: Everyman's Library, 1992), 51–54.

36 Oona A. Hathaway et al., "War Manifestos," *University of Chicago Law Review* 85, no. 5 (September 2018): 1139–1226.

37 Débats parlementaires, Chambre des députés, Journal official de la République française, June 7, 1907, p. 1231.

38 Ibid.

39 Roosevelt to Jacob H. Hollander, July 3, 1905, in Elting E. Morison, ed., *Letters of Theodore Roosevelt* (Cambridge, MA: Harvard University Press, 1951), 4:1259. Qtd. in Cyrus Veeser, *A World Safe for Capitalism* (New York: Columbia University Press, 2002), 148; For extensive discussion of the controversy over the San Domingo Improvement Company, see Ibid. and Coates, "Securing Hegemony through Law":388.

40 Pittard, *La protection des nationaux à l'étranger*, 334; see, e.g., Pittard, *La protection des nationaux à l'étranger*, 333–339; Pradier-Fodéré, *Cours de droit diplomatique*, 533–548; Henry Bonfils also objected to the practice of intervention for the interests of investments, arguing, "Interventions in favor of nationals, creditors of a foreign state, besides striking at the right of independence, are dangerous in their consequences." Henry Bonfils, *Manuel de droit international public* (Paris: A. Rousseau, 1908), 163, 165–168.

41 See, e.g., Fritz Stern, *Gold and Iron: Bismarck, Bleichröder, and the Building of the German Empire* (New York: Vintage, 1979).

42 This was part of a broader critique of imperialism that was beginning to take shape at the turn of the century with figures like J. A. Hobson. See John Atkinson Hobson, *Imperialism: A Study* (London: J. Nisbet, 1902); John Atkinson Hobson, *Capitalism and Imperialism in South Africa* (New York: Tucker, 1900).

43 Evelyn Waugh, *Robbery Under Law: The Mexican Object-Lesson* (Mount Pleasant: Akadine Press, 1999).

44 Ibid., 84.
45 Waugh, *Robbery Under Law*, 80.
46 E.g., *The Fine Art of Squeezing* (New York: Standard Oil Company, 1940); *Diplomatic Protection* (New York: Standard Oil Company, 1939).
47 Ibid., 15.
48 The predilection for commercial arbitration and the creation of an international court to decide contract claims among German jurists may be the result of their peculiar federal structure and a long history in the Holy Roman Empire of multijurisdictional contract disputes. For a summary and bibliography of German proposals for an international court for commercial disputes between individuals and sovereign states, see Otto Fischer, *Die verfolgung vermögensrechtlicher ansprüche gegen ausländische staaten* (Leipzig: A. Deichert, 1912), 15–16.
49 Hans Wehberg, *Ein internationaler Gerichtshof für Privatklagen* (Berlin: Liebheit/Thiesen, 1911), 23; see also Martin Domke, *International Trade Arbitration: A Road to World-Wide Cooperation* (New York: American Arbitration Association, 1948), 66.
50 *Fifth International Congress of Chambers of Commerce and Commercial and Industrial Associations: September and October, 1912*, 159.
51 Ibid., 161.
52 Ibid., 161–162.
53 Ibid., 165.
54 The IPU was the first permanent international forum for political negotiations. It had been established in 1889 to bring together individual parliamentarians to discuss and advocate for the establishment of a permanent system of arbitration. Part of the broader peace movement, the IPU was instrumental in the eventual creation of the Permanent Court of Arbitration at the First Hague Peace Conference in 1899. See Ralph Uhlig, *Die Interparlamentarische Union 1889–1914: Friedenssicherungsbemühungen im Zeitalter des Imperialismus* (Stuttgart: F. Steiner Verlag Wiesbaden, 1988); James Douglas, *Parliaments across Frontiers: A Short History of the Inter-Parliamentary Union* (London: H.M. Stationary Office, 1976).
55 *Compte rendu de la XVIIe conférence, tenue à Genève du 18 au 20 septembre 1912*, 210.
56 Ibid.
57 See the proposal put forward by Philipp Karl Ludwig Zorn, "La jurisdiction arbitrale dans la vie des peuples et dans le droit international," in *Compte rendu de la XVIIe conférence, tenue a Genève du 18 au 20 septembre 1912*, 72–73. See also *Compte rendu de la XVIIe conférence, tenue a Genève du 18 au 20 septembre 1912*, 14.
58 See Resolution II, Article III of the 17th Conference of the Inter-Parliamentary Union. *Compte rendu de la XVIIe conférence, tenue a Genève du 18 au 20 septembre 1912*, 349.
59 Henri La Fontaine, *The Great Solution, Magnissima Charta: Essay on Evolutionary and Constructive Pacifism* (Boston: World Peace Foundation, 1916), 69.
60 Ibid. For more plans for such a court and for evidence of Fontaine's claim, see, e.g., Philipp Karl Ludwig Zorn, "Der Rechtsschutz der Staatsgläubiger

gegenüber fremden Staaten," *Bank-Archiv* 6, no. 9 (1907): 105–108; G. S. Freund, *Der Schutz der Gläubiger gegenüber auswärtigen Schuldnerstaaten, insbesondere bei auswärtigen Staatsanleihen* (Berlin: J. Guttentag, 1910); Fischer, *Die verfolgung vermögensrechtlicher ansprüche gegen ausländische staaten*, esp. 15–16; *Berliner Jahrbuch für Handel und Industrie*, vol. 1 (Berlin: Georg Reimer, 1913), 497–514; Borchard, "Contractural Claims in International Law," 498–499.

61 Qtd. in Ray Stannard Baker, *Woodrow Wilson and World Settlement* (Garden City, NY: Doubleday, 1923), 3:43.

62 Ibid., 415–428.

63 Covenant of the League of Nations, art. 23e.

64 These collections would later be published as The League of Nations Treaty Series (LNTS) in partial fulfillment of the Wilsonian commitment to "open diplomacy."

65 Charles Howard Ellis, *The Origin, Structure and Working of the League of Nations* (London: G. Allen/Unwin, 1928), 171–175.

66 For a comprehensive history of Drummond's role as secretary general, see *Office Without Power: Secretary General Sir Eric Drummon, 1919–1933* (Oxford: Oxford University Press, 1979).

67 See Michael N. Barnett and Martha Finnemore, "The Politics, Power, and Pathologies of International Organzations," *International Organization* 53, no. 4 (1999): 707–709.

68 See International Labor Organization, Constitution of the International Labor Organization preamble, April 1, 1919.

69 *International Trade Conference* (New York: Chamber of Commerce of the United States of America, 1919).

70 Ibid., 461–501. The International Congress of the Chambers of Congress had been established in 1904, and by 1912, the Permanent Committee in Brussels had affiliated itself with 480 commercial organizations in 50 sovereign states. To put it into perspective, there were only fifty-seven recognized sovereign states in 1912. *Fifth International Congress of Chambers of Commerce and Commercial and Industrial Associations: September and October, 1912*, 8, 117.

71 See George L. Ridgeway, *Merchants of Peace: The History of the International Chamber of Commerce* (Boston: Little, Brown, 1958).

72 See Dominic Kelly, "The International Chamber of Commerce," *New Political Economy* 10, no. 2 (2005): 261.

73 Patricia Clavin, *Securing the World Economy: The Reinvention of the League of Nations, 1920–1946* (Oxford: Oxford University Press, 2013), 16.

74 See Benny Carlson, "Who Was Most World-Famous – Cassel or Keynes? The Economist as Yardstick," *Journal of the History of Economic Thought* 31, no. 4 (2009): 519–530; Cassel, "An International Monetary Conference," 807; Clavin, *Securing the World Economy*, 16; Yann Decorzant, "Internationalism in the Economic and Financial Organisation of the League of Nations," in *Internationalism Reconfigured: Transnational Ideas and Movements between the World Wars*, ed. Daniel Laqua (London: I.B. Tauris, 2011), 118; "Powers to Confer on World Finance to Save Europe," *New York Times*, January 15, 1920.

75 Ibid., 119.
76 Ibid., 123–124.
77 Clavin, *Securing the World Economy*, 75.
78 Davis, "World Currency and Banking," 355.
79 Ibid., 21–22.
80 For some notes on the extent to which the British were able to push their own free trade agenda at the League, see Robert W. D. Boyce, *The Great Interwar Crisis and the Collapse of Globalization* (Basingstoke: Palgrave Macmillan, 2009), chap. 3. On the outsized role the British played in the League, see, e.g., Pedersen, *The Guardians: The League of Nations and the Crisis of Empire*.
81 Guillaume Sacriste and Antoine Vauchez, "The Force of International Law: Lawyers' Diplomacy on the International Scene in the 1920s," *Law and Social Inquiry* 32, no. 1 (January 2007): 88.
82 Kurt Wilk, "International Organization and the International Chamber of Commerce," *Political Science Quarterly* 55, no. 2 (June 1940): 233–234, 241.
83 Kelly, "International Chamber of Commerce," 261.
84 Qtd. in Ibid.
85 Ibid., 247.
86 Ibid., 246.
87 Arthur Balfour, "The International Chamber of Commerce," *Annals of the American Academy of Political and Social Science* 134 (November 1927): 125.
88 By 1953, the UN was taking the ICC's draft treaties as the base starting points for what would become the New York Convention on the Enforcement of Foreign Arbitral Awards. See, e.g., UN ECOSOC, Recognition and Enforcement of International Awards: Report of the Secretary-General, Annex I, p. 8, UN Doc. E/2822 (January 31, 1956).
89 Wilk, "International Organization and the International Chamber of Commerce," 240.
90 George L. Ridgeway, *Merchants of Peace: Twenty Years of Business Diplomacy through the International Chamber of Commerce, 1919–1938* (New York: Columbia University Press, 1938), 247.
91 Speech of Joost van Hamel to the International Chamber of Commerce, January 19, 1923, LNA: 10/25542/25542.
92 Paul R. Milgrom, Douglass C. North, and Barry R. Weingast, "The Role of Institutions in the Revival of Trade: The Law Merchant, Private Judges, and the Champagne Fairs," *Economics and Politics* 2, no. 1 (March 1990): 184; Emily Kadens, "The Myth of the Customary Law Merchant," *Texas Law Review* 90 (2012): 1202 n189.
93 See Bruce H. Mann, "The Formalization of Informal Law: Arbitration Before the American Revolution," *New York University Law Review* 59, no. 3 (June 1984): 443–481. See also, the incomparable Christian R. Burset, "Merchant Courts, Arbitration, and the Politics of Commercial Litigation in the Eighteenth-Century British Empire," *Law and History Review* 34, no. 3 (August 2016): 623 ("by the 1760s, arbitration had become both insufficiently coercive and too much like litigation."); Christian Russo Burset, "A Common Law? Legal Pluralism in the Eighteenth-Century British Empire"

(Dissertation, Yale University, 2018), 183 ("After the middle of the eighteenth century... debt transactions became increasingly impersonal and divorced from other business relationships.").

94 These jurisdictions are those of Britain, France, Spain, and Portugal. This leaves out the various American Indian jurisdictions, which are not relevant for this analysis.

95 Richard B. Lillich, "The Jay Treaty Commissions," *St. Johns Law Review* 37, no. 2 (May 1963): 260–283.

96 Two scholars have argued that the expansion of the use of commercial arbitration began as a result of the American Civil War, which disrupted the Atlantic cotton trade and created too many contract disputes for British courts to handle. See Bruce L. Benson, "The Spontaneous Evolution of Commercial Law," *Southern Economic Journal* 55, no. 3 (1989): 644–661; Clarence F. Birdseye, *Arbitration and Business Ethics* (New York: Appleton, 1926).

97 Lynden Macassey, "International Commercial Arbitration: Its Origin, Development and Importance," *Transactions of the Grotius Society* 24 (January 1938): 195.

98 Memorandum attached to MacKinnon to Schuster, March 12, 1922, UKNA: LCO 2/755.

99 Ibid.

100 U.S. Congress, *Arbitration of Interstate Commercial Disputes: Joint Hearings on S. 1005 and H.R. 646 Before the Sub-commission of the Commission on the Judiciary*, 68th Cong., 1st sess. (1924), Sudoc: Y4.J89/1:In8/6, CIS: S215–216.

101 U.S. Congress, *Arbitration of Interstate Commercial Disputes: Joint Hearings on S. 1005 and H.R. 646 Before the Sub-commission of the Commission on the Judiciary*, 68th Cong., 1st sess. (1924), 8.

102 American Arbitration Association, *International Year Book on Civil and Commercial Arbitration*, ed. Arthur Nussbaum (New York: Oxford University Press, 1928), 398.

103 See American Arbitration Association, *Year Book on Commercial Arbitration in the United States, 1927* (New York: Oxford University Press, 1927).

104 *Arbitration for Disputes in Trade between the United States and the Argentine Republic* (Chamber of Commerce of the United States of America, 1919), 16. The American-Argentinian arbitration committee handled more than two dozen cases in the first two months of its operation according to the *Report of the Second Pan American Conference: Pan American Commerce Past, Present and Future from the Pan American Viewpoint* (Washington: Pan American Union, 1919), 57. Similar agreements were also formed between the national Chamber of Commerce of the United States and the national chambers of commerce of Ecuador, Guatemala, Panama, and Uruguay. John Bassett Moore, "The Work of the International High Commission," *Advocate of Peace* 82, no. 2 (February 1920): 48. In 1933, the Seventh International Conference of American States encouraged that all of the American chambers of commerce "draw up and sign a Convention on commercial arbitration, identical to the convention of 1916 between the Bolsa

de Commercio of Buenos Aires and the United States Chamber of Commerce." *Resolutions of the Seventh International Conference of American States* (1933). For a theoretical discussion of this process, see North Milgrom and Weingast, "The Role of Institutions in the Revival of Trade":3.

105 Ibid.

106 Macassey, "International Commercial Arbitration," 194.

107 Roberto Pozzi, "Conciliation and Arbitration Between Merchants of Different Countries," in *Commercial Arbitration*, International Chamber of Commerce, First Congress, London (June 27 to July 1, 1921) 13 (Paris: International Chamber of Commerce, 1921), 6.

108 In England arbitral clauses had been invalid since the 1746 ruling *Kill* v. *Hollister*, 95 Eng. Rep. 532 (K.B. 1746) in which the court held, "agreement of the parties cannot oust this court."

109 U.S. Congress, *Arbitration of Interstate Commercial Disputes: Joint Hearings on S. 1005 and H.R. 646 Before the Sub-commission of the Commission on the Judiciary*, 68th Cong., 1st sess. (1924), 16.

110 UN, ECOSOC, Committee on the Enforcement of Arbitral Awards, Summary Record of the First Meeting, p. 5, UN Doc. E/AC.42/SR.1 (March 23, 1955).

111 W. G. McAdoo, "The International High Commission and Pan American Cooperation," *American Journal of International Law* 11, no. 4 (October 1917): 772–773, 780.

112 Union interparlementaire *Compte rendu de la XVIIe Conférence, tenue a Genève du 18 au 20 septembre 1912* (Brussels, 1913), 207–26.

113 See various correspondence related to the international arbitration protocol. UKNA: LCO 2/755.

114 Pozzi, "Conciliation and Arbitration Between Merchants of Different Countries," 7; *Fifth International Congress of Chambers of Commerce and Commercial and Industrial Associations: September and October, 1912*.

115 "Growth of Commercial Arbitration: Reducing Friction in Business," *Outlook* 100, February 3, 1912, 258.

116 Edward Manson, "The City of London Chamber of Arbitration," *Law Quarterly Review* 9 (1893): 86.

117 International Chamber of Commerce, Court of Arbitration, Rules (1922), p. 3.

118 *Fifth International Congress of Chambers of Commerce and Commercial and Industrial Associations: September and October, 1912*, 162.

119 Julius Henry Cohen, "The Law of Commercial Arbitration and the New York Statute," *Yale Law Journal* 31, no. 2 (December 1921): 150. See also, Amalia D. Kessler, "Arbitration and Americanization: The Paternalism of Progressive Procedural Reform," *Yale Law Journal* 124, no. 8 (2016): 2983–2991. For other contemporary summaries on the advantages of arbitration in France, see *Journal official de la Republique Française, debates parlementaires* 125 (December 9, 1925) 1691–1701; in England, see Samuel Rosenbaum, "Commercial Arbitration in England," *American Bar Association Journal* 3, no. 1 (January 1917): 21–27.

120 *Lochner* v. *New York*, 198 U.S. 45 (1906).

121 "Commercial Arbitration," *Economist*, November 1, 1884, 1323.

122 Mercator, "Arbitration in Commercial Cases," *Economist*, November 21, 1891, 1501.
123 For a modern meditation on this problem in the contemporary world, see Jerold S. Auerbach, *Justice Without Law* (New York: Oxford University Press, 1983).
124 U.S. Congress, *Arbitration of Interstate Commercial Disputes: Joint Hearings on S. 1005 and H.R. 646 Before the Sub-commission of the Commission on the Judiciary*, 68th Cong., 1st sess. (1924), 15.
125 For this quote and further examples of Pozzi's role as a major supporter of international arbitration, see Pozzi, "Conciliation and Arbitration Between Merchants of Different Countries," 11, 5–21.
126 Association, *International Year Book on Civil and Commercial Arbitration*, ix.
127 *Journal officiel de la Republique Française, debats parlementaires* 96 (July 10, 1925) 1430.
128 "Qu'on le respecte comme un homage à la liberté du citoyen; mais élever trop haut ses bienfaits [d'arbitrage], c'est préférer l'ombre de la justice à l'éclat dont elle brille sur le siège du magistrat." This phrase originated with Louis O. Bourbeau in his popular textbook. Louis O. Bourbeau and Pierre Boncenne, *Theorie du procédure civile* (Paris: Videzoq, 1847), 6:423. It was later included in Eugène Garsonnet and Charles Cézar-Bru, *Traité théorique et pratique de procédure civile et commerciale* (Paris: L. Larose/L. Tenin, 1912).
129 U.S. Congress, *Arbitration of Interstate Commercial Disputes: Joint Hearings on S. 1005 and H.R. 646 Before the Sub-commission of the Commission on the Judiciary*, 68th Cong., 1st sess. (1924), 15.
130 Qtd in. Etienne Clémentel, "A propos de la discussion de la clause compromissoire au groupe lyonnais de la Société de legislation comparée," *Bulletin de la Société de Législation Comparée* 53 (1923-1924): 213. Note that Clémentel had been, among other things, Georges Clemenceau's Secretary of Commerce and at the time he wrote a piece advocating for the recognition of commercial clauses.
131 Already by 1922, as one legal advisor noted, "The movement in favor of arbitration was growing daily, and the International Chamber of Commerce was doing most valuable work in this respect." Minutes of the Economic Committee, 4th Session, 2nd Meeting, Geneva, March 21, 1922, LNA: 66/1/1, box S127.
132 Rapport au nom de la commission spéciale de l'Union Interparlementaire, Projet de convention relative à l'établissement d'une cour internationale de justice, June 1920, p. 2, LNA: 21/6018/859, box R1300.
133 Proceedings of the Advisory Committee of Jurists, 205–206.
134 Ibid., 210, 211.
135 Ibid., 206. Several years later, Edwin Borchard would gripe about the PCIJ's lack of competence in this field, noting "There are today in the archives of probably every Foreign Office hundreds of pecuniary claims involving no political issues and entirely capable of submission to judicial settlement. Were there a serious will to give cases to the Court, these hundreds of claims could be at once placed on the docket. Under the present arrangement, the unfortunate fact is that these purely monetary claims are subjected to the vicissitudes of diplomacy, and the claimant is fortunate who

obtains satisfaction in his lifetime.... Were nations willing to have these purely legal and non-political cases determined by judicial methods, the Court would be overwhelmed with business." Edwin M. Borchard, "The Permanent Court of International Justice," *Proceedings of the Academy of Political Science in the City of New York* 10, no. 3 (July 1923): 137–138.

136 Hudson, *International Tribunals: Past and Future*, 187; Proceedings of the Advisory Committee of Jurists, 216.

137 For the PCIJ's reassertion of the Vattelian fiction see, *Panevezys-Saldutiskis Railway* (*Estonia* v. *Lithuania*), 1938 PCIJ (ser. A/B) No. 76 (February 28), ¶ 65 (holding, "In the opinion of the Court, the rule of international law on which the first Lithuanian objection is based is that in taking up the case of one of its nationals, by resorting to diplomatic action or international judicial proceedings on his behalf, a State is in reality asserting its own right, the right to ensure in the person of its nationals respect for the rules of international law. This right is necessarily limited to intervention on behalf of its own nationals because, in the absence of a special agreement, it is the bond of nationality between the State and the individual which alone confers upon the State the right of diplomatic protection, and it is as a part of the function of diplomatic protection that the right to take up a claim and to ensure respect for the rules of international law must be envisaged. Where the injury was done to the national of some other State, no claim to which such injury may give rise falls within the scope of the diplomatic protection which a State is entitled to afford nor can it give rise to a claim which that State is entitled to espouse."). For examples of states espousing claims of private interests before the PCIJ, see, e.g., *Societe Commerciale De Belgique* (*Belg.* v. *Greece*), 1939 PCIJ (ser. A/B) No. 78 (June 15); *Losinger and Co.* (*Switz.* v. *Yugo.*), 1936 PCIJ (ser. A/B) No. 69 (Order of December 14); *Payment of Various Serbian Loans Issued in France* (*Fr.* v. *Yugo.*), 1929 PCIJ (ser. A) No. 20 (12 July); *Payment in Gold of Brazilian Federal Loans Contracted in France* (*Fr.* v. *Braz.*), 1929 PCIJ (ser. A) No. 21 (12 July); See also Hudson, *International Tribunals: Past and Future*, 190. A way around this was proposed by Judge Martin T. Manton, who argued that individuals ought to be granted the right in statute to sue on behalf of the United States at the PCIJ. Martin T. Manton, "Reorganization and Rehabiliation of Government Bond Issues," *Proceedings of the American Society of International Law at Its Annual Meeting (1921–1969)* (1934): 146–155. Such a proposal would not have solved the nationality problem, however.

138 While success was not to be had with the PCIJ, there were proposals floated in the interwar period that the older Permanent Court of Arbitration (PCA) could be given new utility by becoming a court for commercial arbitration. See, e.g., Cecil B. Hurst, "Wanted! An International Court of Pie Powder," *British Yearbook of International Law* 6 (1925); Frances Kellor, "Idle Machinery at the Hague," *Arbitration Journal* (1937): 217–222. There was some movement in the Permanent Court of Arbitration during the interwar period. Under the terms of the 1907 Hague Convention on the Pacific Settlement of International Disputes, which modified and expanded upon its 1899 predecessor, the PCA could be used for "any special Board of

Arbitration," which was interpreted to mean any arbitral tribunal not constituted pursuant to the convention. The Hague Convention for the Pacific Settlement of International Disputes, art. 47 (1907), 1 Bevans 577. As interpreted, the PCA could hear cases involving states and individuals, so long as the state party agreed to the arrangement and agreed to be bound by the judgment. See, e.g., PCA: *Radio Corporation of America* v. *China*, case no. 1934-01 (1934). For reference to the interpretation of Article 47 as permitting the PCA to hear a dispute between a private individual and a state, see ICSID, *History of the ICSID Convention* (Washington, DC, 1968), 11–12. But such cases were rare (indeed, there was only one before 1939), owing to the fact that states had to agree after the disagreement had arisen to have their claim arbitrated. Individuals could not hail an unwilling state before the PCA. Ibid.

139 Czechoslovak London Legation to Eric Drummond, April 5, 1922, LNA: 10/20068/20068, box R376.

140 Frank Nixon to Eric Drummond, May 6, 1922, LNA: 10/20068/20068, box R376.

141 Resolution of July 21, 1922, LN Doc. C.512.M.287.1927.II; Eric Drummond to Vilim Popisil, September 12, 1922, LNA: 10/22222/20068, box R376; See also, Comments by Van Hamel, July 4, 1922, LNA: 10/21607/20068, box R376.

142 Edwin M. Borchard, *State Insolvancy and Foreign Bondholders*, vol. 1: General Principles (New Haven, CT: Yale University Press, 1951), 37.

143 Eric Drummond to Frank Nixon, April 23, 1922, LNA: 10/20068/20068, box R376.

144 For a broader discussion of League loans and politics, see Clavin, *Securing the World Economy: The Reinvention of the League of Nations, 1920–1946*. For an example, of how anti-communist politics could play into interwar economic policy, see Carole Fink, *The Genoa Conference: European diplomacy, 1921–1922* (Chapel Hill: University of North Carolina Press, 1984). For a discussion of the League Loans in the context of postwar reconstruction and development, see Margaret G. Myers, "The League Loans," *Political Science Quarterly* 60, no. 4 (December 1945): 492–526.

145 One in which there were several successes. When a dispute between bondholders and Bulgaria arose, the League Council appointed an arbitrator, the award went entirely against the Bulgarian government, and yet the government still complied with the terms of the arbitral award. Report of the Committee for the Study of International Loan Contracts, LN Doc. C.145.M.93.1939.II.A (II. Economic and Financial 1939 II.A.10.), p. 25.

146 LNOJ 6 (1925), 1363.

147 See Pedersen, *Guardians*, 235.

148 Nephew of Ralph.

149 Frank H. Nixon to Ronald Vaughan Williams, March 21, 1922, LNA: 10/19809/19809, box R373.

150 Ronald Vaughn Williams to Frank H. Nixon, March 22, 1922, LNA: 10/19809/19809, box R373.

151 He was not alone. By 1923, bilateral treaties had been signed by European states to deal with the proliferation of frontiers that had come with

the collapse of the European land empires. Many of these treaties established procedures for normalizing relations between legal systems. See, e.g., Czechoslovakia and Yugoslavia, Convention Concerning the Regulation of Legal Relations, March 17, 1923, 30 LNTS 219. Many more established tribunals for arbitrating disputes between nationals or provided for the recognition and enforcement of arbitral awards. See, e.g., Estonia and Latvia, Arbitration Convention between the Estonian and Latvian Governments, March 22, 1920, 2 LNTS 187; Belgium and the Netherlands, Convention concerning Territorial Jurisdiction, Bankruptcy and the Authority and Execution of Judgments, Arbitral Awards, and Notarial Acts, with Additional Protocol, March 18, 1925, 93 LNTS 431; See also the list of Conventions cited in Macassey, "International Commercial Arbitration: Its Origin, Development and Importance," 193–194. Amidst these bilateral agreements, local and national chambers of commerce were active in establishing many more immediate interwar arbitral agreements. Ibid., 194. But, like their predecessors in the prewar world, these programs were ad hoc and limited in application insofar as many were still confined to specific industries, see, e.g., The International Wool-Textile Arbitration Agreement of 1926 discussed in the Committee on Industry and Trade, *Survey of Textile Industries, Cotton Wool Artificial Silk* (London: HMSO, 1928), 182; Ibid.

152 Schuster to MacKinnon, March 8, 1922, UKNA: LCO 2/755.

153 "The Conference at Genoa," *Advocate of Peace through Justice* 84, no. 5 (May 1922): 182–189; Fink, *Genoa Conference*, 6.

154 Schuster to MacKinnon, March 8, 1922, UKNA: LCO 2/755. Amusingly, in his response MacKinnon, when quoting portions of Schuster's letter, replaces the phrase "semi-civilised" with "certain foreign states." MacKinnon to Schuster, March 12, 1922, UKNA: LCO 2/755.

155 In the correspondence Schuster notes, "They state that they are much pressed by traders (by which they mean the Associated Chamber of Commerce) to consent to such an arrangement." Schuster to Mackinnon, March 8, 1922, UKNA: LCO 2/755.

156 Qtd. in The Work of the Provisional Economic and Financial Committee; Report by M. Hanotaux and Resolutions Adopted by the Council, on September 16th, 1922 (C. 657. 1922. II.), LNA: 10/23714/19961, box R375.

157 Cohen, "Law of Commercial Arbitration and the New York Statute," 152.

158 Robert J. Bennett, *Local Business Voice: The History of Chambers of Commerce in Britain, Ireland, and Revolutionary America, 1760–2011* (Oxford: Oxford University Press, 2011), 251, 319.

159 Statement by H. Llewelyn Smith to the Economic Committee, "Recognition of Arbitration Clauses in Commercial Contracts," March 21, 1922. LNA: 10/19961/19961, box R375.

160 See, e.g., Jacob Robinson et al., *Were the Minorities Treaties a Failure* (New York: Institute of Jewish Affairs of the American Jewish Congress/the World Jewish Congress, 1943).

161 Roger Davidson, "Smith, Sir Hubert Llewellyn (1864–1945), Civil Servant and Social Investigator," Oxford Dictionary of National Biography.

162 Malkin to Schuster, February 28, 1923, UKNA: LCO 2/755.

163 Provisional Economic and Financial Committee, Report to the Council on the Session of the Committee held at Geneva, September 1922 (A.73.1922): 16. LNA: 10/26303/19961, box R376.
164 For the text of the treaty and a list of ratifications deposited with both the League and the United Nations see: United Nations, Register of Texts of Conventions and Other Instruments Concerning International Trade Law, vol. 2 (New York: United Nations Publication, 1973), 8. By 1931, twenty-seven totally independent countries had ratified the treaty along with seven additional 'countries' within the British Empire.
165 UN, Protocol on Arbitration Clauses, Multilateral Treaties Deposited with The Secretary General.
166 Ernest Gustav Lorenzen, "Commercial Arbitration: Enforcement of Foreign Awards," *Yale Law Journal* 45, no. 1 (November 1935): 67.
167 Protocol on Arbitration Clauses, September 24, 1923, LNTS, vol. XXVII, p. 158, No. 678 (1924).
168 Malkin to Schuster (February 28, 1923) UKNA: LCO 2/755; Drafting Committee to Llewelyn Smith (April 11, 1923) UKNA: LCO 2/755.
169 Arthur Nussbaum, "Treaties on Commercial Arbitration: A Test of International Private-Law Legislation," *Harvard Law Review* 56, no. 2 (October 1942): 235.
170 Ibid.
171 Giorgio Balladore Pallieri, "L'arbitrage privé dans les rapports internationaux," *Recueil des cours de l'Académie de Droit International de la Haye* 51 (1935): 382–385.
172 Ibid.
173 René David, *Rapport sur l'arbitrage conventionnel en droit privé* (Rome: L'Universale, 1932), 9. Even advocates for arbitration in Great Britain balked at overly strong enforcement mechanisms, with judicial authorities being the most reluctant to cede their powers. In addition to concerns over other European states, traditional concerns with the enforcement of decisions rendered in non-European states remained. See Chitty to Schuster (July 26, 1926). UKNA: LCO 2/1038: "It seems to me altogether wrong that our Courts should be compelled whether they like it or not to enforce an award made in, say, one of the States of South America in favour of a native against an Englishman who has no notice of such proceedings . . . [or because] . . . the arbitrator may have been corrupt or an interested party or he may have wholly misconducted the proceedings according to our notions of natural justice."
174 Van Hamel to Nixon (August 31, 1922) LNA: 10/20038/20038 box R376.
175 Lorenzen, "Commercial Arbitration: Enforcement of Foreign Awards," 66. While he was exceedingly pessimistic, he did shower the Pan-American Union with praise for its creation in 1933 at the Seventh International Conference of American States at Montevideo for creating the Inter-American Commercial Arbitration Commission. The Commission represented an alternative to the methods pursued by the ICC and other organizations and was more firmly grounded in the interests of the states involved.
176 David, *Rapport sur l'arbitrage conventionnel en droit privé*, 9.

177 Nussbaum, "Treaties on Commercial Arbitration: A Test of International Private-Law Legislation," 237–239. For a nice piece reflecting Nussbaum's role in commercial arbitration, see Martin Domke, "Arthur Nussbaum: The Pioneer of International Commercial Arbitration," *Columbia Law Review* 57, no. 1 (January 1957): 8–10.
178 Heinrich Kronstein, "Business Arbitration: Instrument of Private Government," *Yale Law Journal* 54, no. 1 (December 1944): 38. To be fair, Kronstein was a strong critic of corporate influence in the law. So strong, in fact, that he believed that his habilitation was rejected for being too critical. Heinrich Kronstein, *Briefe an einen jungen Deutschen* (Munich: Beck, 1967), 119–125.
179 Report of the Committee for the Study of International Loan Contracts, LN Doc. 1939.II.A.10. / C.145.M.93.1939.II.A., p. 5.
180 Ibid., 21.
181 Ibid., 24.
182 Ibid., 24–25.
183 Ibid., 25.
184 Ibid., 26.
185 League of Nations, Special Joint Committee on Private Foreign Investment, Conditions of Private Foreign Investment (Princeton, 1946).
186 Veeder, "International Arbitration," 118.
187 Ibid.
188 For a detailed summary of the agreement, see Veeder, "Lena Goldfields Arbitration":758.
189 Ibid., 759.
190 Veeder, "The Lena Goldfields Arbitration: The Historical Roots of Three Ideas," 762.
191 Ibid.
192 Ibid.
193 Ibid., 762–763.
194 Indeed, the detailed press accounts are still the source of much of the day-to-day activities and arguments and for a while was the primary source of the English version of the award, as much of the documentation had been lost in the war. Arthur Nussbaum, "Arbitration Between Lena Goldfields, Ltd. and the Soviet Government," *Cornell Law Review* 36, no. 1 (1950): 31–53; Veeder, "Lena Goldfields Arbitration," 748 no. 1, 754–755.
195 Nussbaum, "Arbitration Between Lena Goldfields, Ltd. and the Soviet Government," 52. The economic power of that sum less the interest in 2015 would be 5.31 billion GBP. See Lawrence H. Officer and Samuel H. Williamson, "Five Ways to Compute the Relative Value of a U.K. Pound Amount, 1270 to Present," Measuring Worth, 2016. Andrea Ernst, however, has placed the value of the award at the far more staggering 889 billion GBP. It is unclear whether she factored the interest into the calculation. Andrea Ernst, "Lena Goldfields Arbitration," in *Max Planck Encyclopedia of Public International Law* (2007). Veeder, probably the preeminent expert on the case, placed the value of the award in 1998 GBP at around 350 million GBP. Veeder, "Lena Goldfields Arbitration," 748.

196 Scholars have made numerous claims over which dispute might have the title of being the "first" modern investor-state arbitration. Timothy G. Nelson, "'History Ain't Changed': Why Investor-State Arbitration will Survive the 'New Revolution'," in *The Backlash against Investment Arbitration*, eds. Michael Waibel and et al. Asha Kaushal (Kluwer: Kluwer Law International, 2010), 555–556. And there were certainly some examples of investor-state disputes that were settled by arbitration prior to that here. See, e.g., Ibid., 555-556; Veeder, "Lena Goldfields Arbitration," 750.

197 *Fifth International Congress of Chambers of Commerce and Commercial and Industrial Associations: September and October, 1912*, 162.

Part III

1 Ibid., 23.

2 Ibid., 24.

3 Ibid., 29.

4 LNOJ Special Supplement 194 (1946), 30.

5 UN Charter, art. 13; See also UN, General Assembly resolution 1/94, Progressive Development of International Law and its Codification (December 11, 1946).

6 Clyde Eagleton, "International Law and the Charter of the United Nations," *American Journal of International Law* 39, no. 4 (October 1945): 752.

7 See Stephen Wertheim, "The League That Wasn't: American Designs for a Legalist-Sanctionist League of Nations and the Intellectual Origins of International Organization, 1914–1920," *Diplomatic History* 35, no. 5 (November 2011): 797–836.

8 UN Charter, art. 2.

9 See, e.g., Manley O. Hudson, "Integrity of International Instruments," *American Journal of International Law* 42, no. 1 (January 1948): 105–108; Hans Kelsen, *The Law of the United Nations: A Critical Analysis of Its Fundamental Problems* (New York: Frederick A. Praeger, 1964 [1950]), 41.

10 UN Charter, art. 2.

11 Statute of the International Court of Justice, arts. 36–38.

12 See Mark Lewis, *The Birth of the New Justice: The Internationalization of Crime and Punishment, 1919-1950* (Oxford: Oxford University Press, 2014); Arieh J. Kochavi, *Prelude to Nuremberg: Allied War Crimes Policy and the Question of Punishment* (Chapel Hill: University of North Carolina Press, 1998).

13 Rome Statute on the International Criminal Court, July 17, 1998, 2187 UNTS 90. For a general history of international criminal justice, particularly following 1945, see Gary Jonathan Bass, *Stay the Hand of Vengeance: The Politics of War Crimes Tribunals* (Princeton, NJ: Princeton University Press, 2002).

Chapter 6

1 Eduard Benes, "The Organization of Postwar Europe," *Foreign Affairs* 20, no. 2 (January 1942): 239.

2 For background on the case, see Erwin Loewenfeld, "Nationality and the Right of Protection in International Public Law," *Transactions of the Grotius Society* 42 (1956): 5–6. For the best contemporary piece on the case, see Robert D. Sloane, "Breaking the Genuine Link: The Contemporary International Legal Regulation of Nationality," *Harvard Law Review* 50, no. 1 (2009): 2–60. For more detailed information on Nottebohm unrelated to the case itself, but rather to his detention in the United States, see Cindy G. Buys, "Nottebohm's Nightmare: Have We Exorcised the Ghosts of WWII Detention Programs or Do They Still Haunt Guantanamo," *Chicago-Kent Journal of International and Comparative Law* 11 (2011): 1–76.

3 Or, rather, a foreigner from a *powerful* state.

4 The opinion set off a flurry of writing. See, e.g., Erwin Loewenfeld, "Der Fall Nottebohm," *Archiv des Völkerrechts* 5 (1956): 387–410; Jack H. Glazer, "Affaire Nottebohm – A Critique," *Georgetown Law Journal* 44 (1955–1956): 313–323; J. Mervyn Jones, "The Nottebohm Case," *International and Comparative Law Quarterly* 5 (1956): 230–246. For criticisms, see, e.g., Georg Dahm, *Völkerrecht* (Stuttgart: Kohlhammer, 1958), 1:446 n. 1; 1:447 n. 6; 458; 459 n. 13; Alfred Verdross, *Völkerrecht* (Vienna: Springer-Verlag, 1959), 237 n. 3; The decision itself inspired an entire book (according to the book's unattributed blurb: "Inspired by a critical analysis of the 'Nottebohm Judgment' of the International Court of Justice (1955), the author has approached the problem from a different angle." H. F. van Panhuys, *The Role of Nationality in International Law: An Outline* (Leiden: A. W. Sythoff, 1959). For a brief assessment of the coverage of the decision, see Josef L. Kunz, "The Nottebohm Judgment," *American Journal of International Law* 54, no. 3 (July 1960): 537–539. See also Paul Weis, *Nationality and Statelessness in International Law*, 2nd ed. (Germantown, MD: Sijthoff/Noordhoff, 1979), 178–179. For a fairly comprehensive bibliography of writing on the case, see Weis, *Nationality and Statelessness in International Law*, 2nd ed., 318–321.

5 Nottebohm had experienced World War I as an enemy alien in Guatemala and, no doubt, wanted to try to mitigate any complications that might arise for him or his business on account of his German nationality. Buys, "Nottebohm's Nightmare":3–4. As for the timeline: Mr. Nottebohm applied on October 9; he was naturalized by a "Supreme Resolution of the Reigning Prince" on October 13; he received a certificate of naturalization acknowledging that fact on October 20. See L. F. E. Goldie, "The Critical Date," *International and Comparative Law Quarterly* 12 (October 1963): 1269.

6 Kunz, "Nottebohm Judgment":536.

7 See Weis, *Nationality and Statelessness in International Law*, 177.

8 This is entirely an assumption made for dramatic effect – call it a metaphor. Mr. Nottebohm may very well have kept his passport as a keepsake, but, by the terms of the German Nationality Law of 1913, naturalization in Liechtenstein automatically deprived Mr. Nottebohm of his nationality. The point

is, Mr. Nottebohm was no longer a German national when he returned to Guatemala and was no longer permitted to hold a German passport. So by becoming a Liechtensteiner, Mr. Nottebohm rendered his passport useless. On the German Nationality provision, see Goldie, "Critical Date":1269.

9 Real or juridicial.

10 In July 2016, the high temperature was 100°F with a maximum humidity of 100 percent and a "feels like" temperature of 109°C.

11 The low temperature on January 1, 1946, while our protagonist was still interned, was 2 degrees Fahrenheit. Temperatures as low as −41 have been reported in January.

12 On the U.S. policy of interning German nationals from Latin America, see Max Paul Friedman, *Nazis and Good Neighbors: The United States Campaign against the Germans of Latin America in World War II* (Cambridge: Cambridge University Press, 2003).

13 Kunz, "Nottebohm Judgment," 536.

14 Ibid.

15 Counter-Memorial submitted by the Government of Guatemala, April 20, 1954, pp. 188–197.

16 Nottebohm Case (second phase), Judgment of April 6, 1955: ICJ Reports 1955, p. 11.

17 Counter-Memorial submitted by the Government of Guatemala, April 20, 1954, p. 214.

18 Ibid., 242.

19 Nottebohm Case (second phase), Judgment of April 6, 1955: ICJ Reports 1955, p. 11.

20 Rejoinder submitted by the Government of Guatemala, November 2, 1954, p. 516.

21 Convention on Certain Questions Relating to the Conflict of Nationality Law chap. I, art. 1, 1930, 179 LNTS 89 (the convention never entered into force).

22 See, e.g., "The Harvard Research on International Law: Nationality," 26.

23 Nottebohm Case (second phase), Judgment of April 6, 1955: ICJ Reports 1955, p. 28.

24 Ibid., p. 26, emphasis added.

25 See Sloane, "Breaking the Genuine Link":3.

26 Nottebohm Case (second phase), Judgment of April 6, 1955: ICJ Reports 1955, p. 23.

27 See "Claims of Dual Nationals in the Modern Era: The Iran–United States Claims Tribunal," *Michigan Law Review* 83, no. 3 (December 1984): 600.

28 See, e.g., UN, First report on diplomatic protection, by Mr. John R. Dugard, Special Rapporteur, UN Doc. A/CN.4/506 and Add. 1, art. 5, contained in YBILC 2000, vol. 2, part 1, UN Doc. A/CN.4/SER.A/2000/Add.1 (Part 1), pp. 226–230; Report of the International Law Commission on the work of its fifty-fourth session (April 29–June 7 and July 22–August 16, 2002) UN Doc. A/57/10, contained in YBILC 2002, vol. 2, part 2, UN Doc. A/CN.4/SER.A/2002/Add.1 (Part 2), pp. 69–70; Sloane, "Breaking the Genuine Link."

29 Benes, "Organization of Postwar Europe":239.

30 Matthew Frank, *Making Minorities History: Population Transfer in Twentieth-Century Europe* (Oxford: Oxford University Press, 2017), 231–232.
31 Benes, "Organization of Postwar Europe," 239.
32 W. P. Crozier, *Off the Record: Political Interviews, 1933–1943*, ed. A. J. P. Taylor (London: Hutchinson, 1973), 356; Also qtd. in Frank, *Making Minorities History*, 233.
33 Ibid., 238; See also the fantastic Laura Robson, *States of Separation: Transfer, Partition, and the Making of the Modern Middle East* (Berkeley: University of California Press, 2017).
34 R. M. Douglas, *Orderly and Humane: The Expulsion of the Germans after the Second World War* (New Haven, CT: Yale University Press, 2013).
35 Timothy Snyder, *The Reconstruction of Nations: Poland, Ukraine, Lithuania, Belarus, 1569–1999* (New Haven, CT: Yale University Press, 2003), 187–201.
36 See, e.g., Douglas, *Orderly and Humane*; Bohdan S. Kordan, "Making Borders Stick: Population Transfer and Resettlement in the Trans-Curzon Territories, 1944–1949," *International Migration Review* 31, no. 3, 704–720; Philipp Ther and Ana Siljak, eds., *Redrawing Nations: Ethnic Cleansing in East-Central Europe, 1944–1948* (Lanham, MD: Rowman & Littlefield, 2001).
37 Qtd. in Mazower, "The Strange Triumph of Human Rights."
38 Sloane, "Breaking the Genuine Link," 16.
39 Richard W. Flournoy, "Nationality Convention, Protocols and Recommendations Adopted by the First Conference on the Codification of International Law," *American Journal of International Law* 24, no. 3 (July 1930): 467–485.
40 See Karen Knop, "Relational Nationality: On Gender and Nationality in International Law," in *Citizenship Today: Global Perspectives and Practices*, eds. T. Alexander Aleinikoff and Douglas Klusmeyer (Washington, DC: Carnegie Endowment for International Peace, 2001), 89–126.
41 John R. Dugard, Special Rapporteur, First Report on Diplomatic Protection, UN Doc. A/CN.4/506 ¶¶ 95–96 and Add. 1.
42 See Mazower, "Strange Triumph of Human Rights."
43 Glenda Sluga, "René Cassin: Les droits de l'homme and the Universality of Human Rights, 1945–1966," in *Human Rights in the Twentieth Century*, ed. Stefan-Ludwig Hoffmann (Cambridge: Cambridge University Press, 2011), 110–111.
44 See Mazower, "Strange Triumph of Human Rights."
45 See James C. Hathaway, "The Evolution of Refugee Status in International Law: 1920–1950," *International and Comparative Law Quarterly* 33, no. 2 (April 1984): 350.
46 See Ibid., 370–380.
47 Convention Relating to the Status of Refugees art. 1, 189 UNTS 150.
48 The pre-war arrangements were incorporated by reference and, at least initially, the Convention was limited to those displaced as a result of events occurring before 1951. Ibid.
49 Ibid.
50 Ibid.

51 Ibid.
52 UN Doc. A/CN.4/13 and Corr. 1-3.
53 First Report on International Responsibility, UN Doc. A/CN.4/96, p. 194. See also Francisco V. Garcia-Amador, "State Responsibility: Some New Problems," *Recueil des cours de l'Académie de Droit International de la Haye* 94 (1958): 421.
54 Philip C. Jessup, "Responsibility of States for Injuries to Individuals," *Columbia Law Review* 46, no. 6 (November 1946): 904.
55 Robin C. A. White, "Expropriation of the Libyan Oil Concessions Two Conflicting International Arbitrations," *International and Comparative Law Quarterly* 30 (January 1981): 3.
56 28 U.S.C. § 1350.
57 See, e.g., *Kiobel* v. *Royal Dutch Petroleum Co.*, 569 U.S. 108 (2013).
58 "Introduction to ECOSOC Consultative Status," UN, ECOSOC. See Dominic Kelly, "The International Chamber of Commerce," *New Political Economy* 10, no. 2 (2005): 259–271.
59 UN ECOSOC, Recognition and Enforcement of International Awards: Report of the Secretary-General, Annex I, p. 8, UN Doc. E/2822 (January 31, 1956).
60 UN ECOSOC, Enforcement of Arbitral Awards: Statement Submitted by the International Chamber of Commerce, a non-governmental organization having consultative status in category A, E/C.2/373 (October 28, 1953), 7–8.
61 The work of the committees all took the ICC draft as their point of departure.
62 UN ECOSOC, Enforcement of Arbitral Awards: Statement Submitted by the International Chamber of Commerce, a non-governmental organization having consultative status in category A, UN Doc. E/C.2/373 (October 28, 1953), 12.
63 UN, ECOSOC, Report of the Committee on the Enforcement of International Arbitral Awards, ¶ 20, UN Doc. E/2704 (March 28, 1955); Paolo Contini, "International Commercial Arbitration: The United Nations Convention on the Recognition and Enforcement of Foreign Arbitral Awards," *American Journal of Comparative Law* 8, no. 3 (July 1959): 292.
64 UN Convention on the Recognition and Enforcement of Foreign Arbitral Awards ("New York Convention"), art. 1, June 10, 1958, 330 UNTS 38; UN, ECOSOC, Report of the Committee on the Enforcement of International Arbitral Awards, ¶ 23.
65 New York Convention, art. I.1.
66 The implementing legislation for this treaty did, however, vary. The United Kingdom implementing legislation, for example, applied to any agreement providing for arbitration, irrespective of the nationality of the parties. English Arbitration Act of 1975, ¶ 4. The United States implementing legislation, however, did not apply to an agreement for arbitration made by two US citizens. An Act to Implement the Convention on the Recognition and Enforcement of Arbitral Awards, 84 Stat. 692 (July 31, 1970) § 202. But the

latter method of implementing the treaty is rare and, in general, nationality has been banished from the primary international instrument governing arbitration.

67 UN, ECOSOC, ICC, Statement explaining the difference between the 1927 Geneva Convention and the ICC Draft Convention, and giving a bibliography on the subject, pp. 2–3, UN Doc. E/C.2/373/Add. 1.

68 New York Convention, art. III.

69 Eugene F. Mooney, *Foreign Seizures: Sabbatino and the Act of State Doctrine* (Lexington: University of Kentucky Press, 1967), 3–4.

70 See Isi Foighel, *Nationalization: A Study in the Protection of Alien Property in International Law* (London: Stevens, 1957).

71 In the United States, this manifested in the articulation and elaboration of the "Act of State Doctrine," which forbade courts from questioning the acts of foreign governments (including property expropriations) done in the territory of that government. See, e.g., *Banco Nacional de Cuba* v. *Sabbatino,* 376 U.S. 398 (1964).

72 See, e.g., ICC, *Fair Treatment for Foreign Investments: International Code*, ICC Brochure no. 129 (1949).

73 See, e.g., Jacob Viner, "Conflicts of Principle in Drafting a Trade Charter," *Foreign Affairs* 25, no. 4 (July 1947): 626–628. See also Quinn Slobodian, *Globalists: The End of Empire and the Birth of Neoliberalism* (Cambridge, MA: Harvard University Press, 2018), chap. 4.

74 For an overview, see A. A. Fatouros, "An International Code to Protect Private Investment–Proposals and Perspectives," *The University of Toronto Law Journal* 14, no. 1 (1961): 77–102.

75 United Nations Conference on Trade and Employment, Final Act and Related Documents (1948), art. 12.

76 A silly affair put together by Stanford Research Institute and Time-Life International that brought together some 600 business and government officials from more than 60 countries.

77 "The Capitalist Challenge: The Capitalist Magna Carta," *Time*, October 28, 1957.

78 Ibid.; see also Slobodian, *Globalists*, 136.

79 Two years after his speech, Germany and Pakistan signed the first modern bilateral investment treaty.

80 This was, in part, pursuant to a resolution adopted by the UN General Assembly in 1954 which encouraged states and organizations to study ways to encourage foreign capital investment in lesser developed countries. See General Assembly resolution 9/824, *International flow of private capital for the economic development of underdeveloped countries*, A/RES/9/824 (December 11, 1954).

81 ICSID, *History of the ICSID Convention*, 2:1, https://catalog.loc.gov/vwebv/search? searchArg=Convention+on+the+Settlement+of+Investment+Disputes+between+States+and+Nationals+of+Other+States.+1968 &searchCode=GKEY%5E*&searchType=0&recCount=25.

82 See, e.g., the complaints of Max Apt: "But above all no obligation exists for the home State to interfere [on behalf of an investor]; on the contrary it is left to the judgment of the State, if it wishes to intervene, and it generally

finds reasons to refuse to put the diplomatic apparatus into motion." *Fifth International Congress of Chambers of Commerce and Commercial and Industrial Associations: September and October, 1912*, 159.

83 ICSID, *History of the ICSID Convention*, 2:1.

84 Ibid., 2:2.

85 Ibid., 2:3–4.

86 See, e.g., the comments of Mr. Krishna Moorthi, Mr. Rajan, and others in Ibid., 2:15, 182, 477.

87 See, e.g., Ibid., 105, 182, 383, 417, 452, 471, 477, 481.

88 Ibid., 182.

89 Ibid., 383.

90 Ibid., 471.

91 Ibid., 417.

92 Convention on the Settlement of Investment Disputes Between States and Nationals of Other States (Washington Convention), art. 1, 575 UNTS 159 (1965).

93 Kenneth J. Vandevelde, "The Bilateral Investment Treaty Program of the United States," *Cornell International Law Journal* 21, no. 2 (1988): 201; Zachary Elkins, Andrew T. Guzman, and Beth Simmons, "Competing for Capital: The Diffusion of Bilateral Investment Treaties, 1960–2000," *University of Illinois Law Review* (2008): 265; See also Andrew T. Guzman, "Why LDCs Sign Treaties That Hurt Them: Explaining the Popularity of Bilateral Investment Treaties," *Virginia Journal of International Law* 38 (1997): 639–688.

94 See Niall Ferguson et al., eds., *The Shock of the Global: The 1970s in Perspective* (Cambridge, MA: Harvard University Press, 2011).

95 "International Chamber of Commerce: New Rules of Conciliation and Arbitration," *International Legal Materials* 28, no. 1 (January 1989): 233.

96 Convention on the Recognition and Enforcement of Foreign Judgments in Civil and Commercial Matters, The Hague, February 1, 1971, 1144 UNTS 249.

97 Ahmadou Sadio Diallo (*Republic of Guinea* v. *Democratic Republic of the Congo*), Preliminary Objections, Judgment, ICJ Reports 2007, p. 582.

98 Ibid., ¶ 88.

99 Natalino Ronzitti, *Rescuing Nationals Abroad through Military Coercion and Intervention on Grounds of Humanity* (Dordecht: Martinus Nijhoff, 1985), 24.

100 Mercator, "Arbitration in Commercial Cases," *Economist*, November 21, 1891, 1501.

101 See, e.g., the so-called lex constructionis, a "private 'law' developed by the major engineering companies in the world to establish a common mode of dealing with the strengthening of environmental standards in a growing number of countries." Saskia Sassen, "Neither Global Nor National: Novel Assemblages of Territory, Authority and Rights," *Ethics and Global Politics* 1, nos. 1-2 (2008): 62, citing Gunther Teubner, ed., *Global Law without a State* (Brookfield, VT: Dartmouth Publishing, 1996).

102 George L. Ridgeway, *Merchants of Peace: Twenty Years of Business Diplomacy through the International Chamber of Commerce, 1919–1938* (New York: Columbia University Press, 1938), 246.
103 Jan Paulsson, "Arbitration in Three Dimensions," *International and Comparative Law Quarterly* 60 (April 2011): 292. See also Jan Paulsson et al., *International Commercial Arbitration: Cases, Materials, and Notes on the Resolution of International Business Disputes*, 2nd ed., University Casebook Series (St. Paul, MN: Foundation Press, 2015).
104 See Susan Strange, *The Retreat of the State* (Cambridge: Cambridge University Press, 1996).
105 United States and Venezuela Claims Committee, *Claim of Albino Abbiatti* v. *The Republic of Venezuela,* no. 34, p. 84.
106 In a humorous example of the reach of corporate power in the popular imagination, in Peter Sellers' classic 1964 film, *Dr. Strangelove,* the fictional Colonel "Bat" Guano warns Group Captain Lionel Mandrake as he was taking money from a vending machine, "If you don't get the President of the United States on that phone, you know what's gonna happen to you? . . . You're gonna have to answer to the Coca-Cola company."
107 Lord Goldsmith, QC, "The Privatisation of Law: Has a World Court finally been created by modern international arbitration?" (lecture, Barnard's Inn Hall, London, June 27, 2013).
108 Emmanuel Gaillard, for example, argues that international arbitration is now an autonomous legal order. See Emmanuel Gaillard, *Aspects Philosophiques de Droit de l'Arbitrage International* (Leiden: Martinus Nijhoff, 2008). There are detractors to this view. See Paulsson, "Arbitration in Three Dimensions," 301–306. However, Paulsson would not dispute that the regime has become pluralistic and more globally enforceable, just that it still requires and interacts with the law of individual states and is thus not "autonomous." See Ibid., 300.
109 John Dugard, "Diplomatic Protection and Human Rights: The Draft Articles of the International Law Commission," *Australian Yearbook of International Law* 24 ((2005)): 75–91.
110 As John Dugard noted, "While the European Convention on Human Rights may offer real remedies to millions of Europeans, it is difficult to argue that the American Convention on Human Rights, or the African Charter on Human and Peoples' Rights, have achieved the same degree of success." Ibid.
111 Marco Duranti, *The Conservative Human Rights Revolution: European Identity, Transnational Politics, and the Origins of the European Convention* (Oxford: Oxford University Press, 2017). For more on Human Rights as grounded in conservative European politics, see Samuel Moyn, *Christian Human Rights* (Philadelphia: University of Pennsylvania Press, 2015).
112 Duranti, *Conservative Human Rights Revolution*, 326–331.
113 Duranti, *The Conservative Human Rights Revolution: European Identity, Transnational Politics, and the Origins of the European Convention*, 340–342.
114 *Oao Neftyanaya Koompaniya Yukos* v. *Russia* (just satisfaction), no. 14902/04.

115 However, in addition to filing a claim in the European Court of Human Rights, the savvy (and well-paid) lawyers for the majority-shareholders of Yukos also brought a complaint before the Permanent Court of Arbitration (PCA) under the Energy Charter Treaty, which contained investment dispute provisions. The PCA found for the shareholders of Yukos in the amount of 50 billion USD. Again, Russia has refused to pay. But under the terms of the New York Convention the claimants are having governments around the world seize Russian assets to turn them over to the awardees. Neil Buckley and Katherin Hille, "Yukos Shareholders Face Battle to Claim 50bn," *Financial Times*, July 28, 2014; Neil Buckley and Courtney Weaver, "France and Belgium Freeze Russian State Assets over Yukos Case," *Financial Times*, June 18, 2015.

116 *Fifth International Congress of Chambers of Commerce and Commercial and Industrial Associations: September and October, 1912*, 162.

117 Wilhelm Röpke, "Economic Order and International Law," *Recueil des cours de l'Académie de Droit International de la Haye* 86 (1954): 237.

118 For economic evidence of the idea of the "exceptional" state, which thrived between roughly 1914 and 1970, see Thomas Piketty, *Capital in the Twenty-First Century* (Cambridge, MA: Harvard University Press, 2013). Thanks to Erica Lee and Danny Kelly for this insight.

119 UN, First report on diplomatic protection, by Mr. John R. Dugard, Special Rapporteur, UN Doc. A/CN.4/506 and Add. 1, art. 5, contained in YBILC 2000, vol. 2, part 1, UN Doc. A/CN.4/SER.A/2000/Add.1 (Part 1), pp. 226–230.

120 Report of the International Law Commission on the work of its fifty-fourth session (April 29–June and July 22–August 16, 2002) UN Doc. A/57/10, contained in YBILC 2002, vol. 2, part 2, UN Doc. A/CN.4/SER.A/2002/Add.1 (Part 2), pp. 69–70:

the Commission took the view that there were certain factors that limited Nottebohm to the facts of the case in question, particularly the fact that the ties between Mr. Nottebohm and Liechtenstein (the Applicant State) were "extremely tenuous" compared with the close ties between Mr. Nottebohm and Guatemala (the Respondent State) for a period of over 34 years, which led the ICJ to repeatedly assert that Liechtenstein was "not entitled to extend its protection to Nottebohm vis-à-vis Guatemala." This suggests that the Court did not intend to expound a general rule applicable to all states but only a relative rule according to which a state in Liechtenstein's position was required to show a genuine link between itself and Mr. Nottebohm in order to be permitted to claim on his behalf against Guatemala, with whom he had extremely close ties. Moreover, the Commission was mindful of the fact that if the genuine link requirement proposed by Nottebohm was strictly applied it would exclude millions of persons from the benefit of diplomatic protection, as in today's world of economic globalization and migration there are millions of persons who have drifted away from their State of nationality and made their lives in States whose nationality they never acquire, or who have acquired nationality by birth of descent from States with which they have a tenuous connection.

121 See, e.g., ICSID, *History of the ICSID Convention*, 2:67, 256–257, 284, 324.
122 Aron Broches, "The Convention on the Settlement of Investment Disputes between States and Nationals of Other States," *Recueil des cours de l'Académie de Droit International de la Haye* 136 (1972): 358; ICSID, *History of the ICSID Convention*, 394: In this connection he recalled the decision of the International Court of Justice in the Nottebohm Case which had dealt with effective nationality as opposed to a nationality of convenience."
123 Broches, "The Convention on the Settlement of Investment Disputes between States and Nationals of Other States," 356.
124 See, e.g., ICSID, *History of the ICSID Convention*, 394, 396, 401–402: "The complex problem of the nationality of such bodies corporate as limited companies has baffled many leading authorities in international law."
125 Convention Relating to the Status of Refugees, art. 1, 189 UNTS 150.
126 Peter J. Spiro, *At Home in Two Countries: The Past and Future of Dual Citizenship* (New York: New York University Press, 2016), chap. 2.
127 Spiro, *At Home in Two Countries: The Past and Future of Dual Citizenship*, introduction.
128 See Patrick Weil, "From Conditional to Secured and Sovereign: The New Strategic Link between the Citizen and the Nation-State in a Globalized World," *Journal of International Constitutional Law* 9, nos. 3–4 (2011): 625–626; Patrick Weil, *The Sovereign Citizen Denaturalization and the Origins of the American Republic* (Philadelphia: University of Pennsylvania Press, 2012); Spiro, *At Home in Two Countries*, chaps. 2–3.
129 Convention on Certain Questions relating to the Conflict of Nationality Laws, April 12, 1930, 179 LNTS 89.
130 T. Alexander Aleinikoff, "Plural Nationality: Facing the Future in a Migratory World," in *Citizenship Today: Global Perspectives and Practices*, eds. T. Alexander Aleinikoff and Douglas Klusmeyer (Washington, DC: Carnegie Endowment for International Peace, 2001), 63–88.
131 Weil, "From Conditional to Secured and Sovereign":629.
132 Spiro, *At Home in Two Countries*, chap. 6. For a 1996 survey on the permissibility of dual nationality in domestic law that found more than sixty states that permitted their nationals to retain their naturalization upon a foreign naturalization, see Eugene Goldstein and Victoria Piazza, "Naturalization, Dual Citizenship and Retention of Foreign Citizenship: A Survey," *Interpretive Releases* 73, no. 45 (April 1996): 517.
133 The biggest improvement came with the 1957 Convention on the Nationality of Married Women, which required the marriage not change the nationality of the husband nor automatically affect the nationality of the wife. UN General Assembly, Convention on the Nationality of Married Women, January 29, 1957, 309 UNTS 65. See Knop, "Relational Nationality;" Weil, "From Conditional to Secured and Sovereign," 629.
134 Knop, "Relational Nationality;"
135 Aleinikoff, "Plural Nationality," 63.
136 Council of Europe, European Convention on Nationality, arts. 4–6, November 6, 1997, ETS 166.
137 Ronzitti, *Rescuing Nationals Abroad through Military Coercion and Intervention on Grounds of Humanity*, 24.

Conclusion

1 E. P. Thompson, *Whigs and Hunters: The Origin of the Black Act* (New York: Pantheon Books, 1975), 21.
2 Thompson, *Whigs and Hunters*, 266.
3 Ibid., 269.
4 Ibid., 266.
5 Ibid., 269.
6 See Duranti, *The Conservative Human Rights Revolution: European Identity, Transnational Politics, and the Origins of the European Convention.*
7 UNCTAD, IIA Issues Note, no. 2 (June 2016).
8 See, e.g., *CMS Gas Transmission Co.* v. *Republic of Argentina*, No. ARB/01/8 (ICSID 2007); *Desert Line Projects LLC* v. *Republic of Yemen*, No. ARB/05/17 (ICSID 2008); *Victor Pey Casado* v. *Republic of Chile*, No. ARB/98/2 (ICSID 2008); *ADC Affiliate Ltd.* v. *Republic of Hungary*, No. ARB/03/16, Award (ICSID 2006); *Occidental Petroleum* v. *Ecuador*, LCIA Case No. UN 3467 (2004).
9 Work that culminated with the 1985 publication of Richard Epstein, *Takings: Private Property and the Power of Eminent Domain* (Cambridge, MA: Harvard University Press, 1985). On Epstein's influence, see James W. Ely, "Impact of Richard A. Epstein," *William and Mary Law Review* 15, no. 2 (2006): 421–428.
10 See North American Free Trade Agreement, U.S.-Can.-Mex., art. 1101–1120, December 17, 1992, 32 I.L.M. 289 (1993).
11 Ibid.
12 José E. Alvarez, "Critical Theory and the North American Free Trade Agreement's Chapter Eleven," *The University of Miami Inter-American Law Review* 28, no. 2 (1996/1997): 6–8.
13 José E. Alvarez, "The Public International Law Regime Governing International Investment," *Recueil des cours de l'Académie de Droit International de la Haye* 344 (2011): 298–300.
14 *BG Grp., PLC* v. *Republic of Argentina*, 134 S. Ct. 1198 (2014).
15 Ibid. at 1204.
16 Ibid. 1204–1205.
17 Ibid. at 1205.
18 Ibid.
19 Ibid. at 1206.
20 Ibid. at 1213.
21 Ibid. at 1216.
22 Ibid.
23 Charles H. Brower, "Investor-State Disputes Under Nafta: The Empire Strikes Back," *Columbia Journal of Transnational Law* 40 (2002): 43–88; Carlos G. Garcia, "All the Other Dirty Little Secrets: Investment Treaties, Latin America, and the Necessary Evil of Investor-State Arbitration," *Florida Journal of International Law* 16 (2004): 301–370. See also, e.g., Jonathan Weisman, Trans-Pacific Partnership Seen as Door for Foreign Suits Against U.S.," *New York Times* (March 25, 2015); See also Joseph

E. Stiglitz, *The Euro: How a Common Currency Threatens the Future of Europe* (New York: W. W. Norton, 2016), xiv.

24 For some of the more scandalous abuses, see Chris Hamby's *excellent* and lengthy series of investigative articles. Chris Hamby, "Secrets of a Global Super Court," *BuzzFeed* (2016), `www.buzzfeed.com/globalsupercourt`. See also Haley Sweetland Edwards, *Shadow Courts: The Tribunals the Rule Global Trade* (New York: Columbia Global Reports, 2017).

25 Dinah Deckstein, Simone Salden, and Michaela Schießl, "Protests Threaten Trans-Atlantic Trade Deal," *Der Spiegel*, May 6, 2016.

26 Paul Ames, "ISDS: The most toxic acronym in Europe," *Politico*, September 17, 2016.

27 Todd Tucker, "The TPP has a provision many will love to hate: ISDS. What is it, and why does it matter?," *The Washington Post*, October 6, 2015.

28 Jan Paulsson, "Arbitration in Three Dimensions," *International and Comparative Law Quarterly* 60 (April 2011): 310. Other proponents of alternative dispute resolution and arbitration have also linked the system to justice, arguing that the excessive formality of courts and the lack of judicial resources makes it difficult for the average person the access them. This was, indeed, one of the arguments made by American supporters of Arbitration in the 1920s. See Hiro N. Aragaki, "Constructions of Arbitration's Informalism: Autonomy, Efficience, and Justice," *Journal of Dispute Resolution*, no. 1 (2016): 147–155.

29 Wendy Brown, *Walled States, Waning Sovereignty* (New York: Zone Books, 2010), 22; See also, e.g., Saskia Sassen, *Losing Control? Sovereignty in an Age of Globalization* (New York: Columbia University Press, 1996); Susan Strange, *The Retreat of the State* (Cambridge: Cambridge University Press, 1996); Saskia Sassen, *Territory, Authority, Rights: From Medieval to Global Assemblages* (Princeton, NJ: Princeton University Press, 2006).

30 Brown, *Walled States, Waning Sovereignty*, 24.

31 Moria Paz, "Between the Kingdom and the Desert Sun: Human Rights, Immigration, and Border Walls," *Berkeley Journal of International Law* 34, no. 1 (2016): 1–43.

32 See, e.g., Samuel Huntington, *Who Are We?* (New York: Simon/Schuster, 2005).

33 See Atossa Araxia Abrahamian, *The Cosmopolites: The Coming of the Global Citizen* (New York: Columbia Global Reports, 2016).

34 The instrumentalization of nationality is, likewise, decried outside the human realm. The use of flags of convenience – the registering of ships in a country other than that of the ships' owners, usually in Panama, Malta, Liberia, to reduce operating costs, avoid taxes, discourage litigation, and skirt regulations – has become a controversial and much decried practice. Rodney Carlisle, *Sovereignty for Sale: The Origin and Evolution of the Panamanian and Liberian Flags of Convenience* (Annapolis, MD: Naval Institute Press, 1981). For an example of press coverage, see James Brooke, "Landlocked Mongolia's Seafaring Tradition," *New York Times*, July 2, 2004. For a legal application of the "genuine link" principle to the issue, see Ariella D'Andrea, *The "Genuine Link" Concept in Responsible Fisheries: Legal Aspects and Recent Developments* (FAO Legal Papers Online, November 2006).

35 Spiro, *At Home in Two Countries: The Past and Future of Dual Citizenship*, chap. 8.
36 Noah Pickus, *True Faith and Allegiance: Immigration and American Civic Nationalism* (Princeton, NJ: Princeton University Press, 2005), 181–182.
37 Laurie A. Brand, *Citizens Abroad: Emigration and the State in the Middle East and North Africa* (Cambridge: Cambridge University Press, 2005).
38 See, e.g., John Dugard, "Diplomatic Protection and Human Rights: The Draft Articles of the International Law Commission," *Australian Yearbook of International Law* 24 ((2005)): 75–91; Politis, *The New Aspects of International Law*.

Index